THE ARMIES OF
QUEEN ANNE

THE ARMIES OF
QUEEN ANNE

BY

MAJOR R. E. SCOULLER

Royal Signals, p.s.c.

OXFORD
AT THE CLARENDON PRESS
1966

Oxford University Press, Ely House, London W. 1

GLASGOW NEW YORK TORONTO MELBOURNE WELLINGTON
CAPE TOWN SALISBURY IBADAN NAIROBI LUSAKA ADDIS ABABA
BOMBAY CALCUTTA MADRAS KARACHI LAHORE DACCA
KUALA LUMPUR HONG KONG

PRINTED IN GREAT BRITAIN
AT THE UNIVERSITY PRESS, OXFORD
BY VIVIAN RIDLER
PRINTER TO THE UNIVERSITY

FOREWORD

THIS volume deals with the organization and administration of Queen Anne's armies. I have deliberately omitted, as belonging more properly to the field of tactics, a detailed study of the regimental organization of cavalry or infantry, of drill in barracks and battle, and of armament. Dress and music I have left untouched as specialist subjects, of which the former is already adequately covered in various works, and the latter has been touched on by Sir John Fortescue in *The Last Post* and by Dr. Henry Farmer in various articles.

ACKNOWLEDGEMENTS

I HAVE to acknowledge with gratitude the unstinted assistance from Anthony G. Hepburn, Esq., Head Librarian, Mitchell Library, Glasgow, and from my father in checking numerous references from which I was separated by many miles. To my father also go thanks for assistance in checking proofs and the correction of solecisms attributable either to an inadequate education or subsequent neglect. The errors and offences which still remain are in references not put to the question and in passages where good advice has been rejected. I am also mindful of the invaluable advice and encouragement given by the late John Dunlop, Esq., former Head Librarian, Mitchell Library, while this study was still in its very early stages.

CONTENTS

INTRODUCTORY

QUEEN Anne's armies were not only among the most outstandingly and brilliantly successful British armies in history: they were unique in that they did not start off their career with a series of defeats. In the main theatre they won every battle; the politicians lost the last.

What had been done for the country at sea in Cromwell's day was done in this reign on land. Previously, the reputation of British soldiers as individuals or in small free-lance contingents had been good, but, as a country with a 'military potential', Britain had been of little account. In this short reign, under a woman who was certainly no Elizabeth—in, one might say, four years of this reign—all this was changed. The continent of Europe, long under the shadow of 'the inordinate power of France', was brought suddenly to realize it had, set beside it, a nation whose military strength had to be heeded; and the soldiers of Britain themselves acquired that 'self-assured, unaffected disdain' of other troops which has carried them through many dark days since.

The layman, even, perhaps, the political student, has inevitably been so dazzled by the lights of Blenheim, Ramillies, and Oudenarde (while remaining slightly unperceptive of the *ne plus ultra* lines or Bouchain) that he has been blind to the shades of the background. There is practically nothing extant on how the troops were got into battle; how they were fed on their way there, how their ammunition reached them, how they were paid, how they were cared for when wounded, how discipline was imposed to fit them for battle: on all these problems, which bulk so large in any commander's planning and execution, little has been written. The foundations of the 'famous victories' were, nevertheless, laid in swift movement, skilful management of long lines of communication, and good husbanding of men—all factors dependent on organization and administration before the battle, which is as much a test of them as it is of the men snapping their firelocks or pushing their pikes.

The study of any particular war or period of British military history tends to be less productive than might reasonably be expected. This is largely due to our inability as a nation to remember any war's lessons beyond the first post-war election. Each conflict remains—to greater or lesser purpose—equally instructive. In each the tendency is, except in technical matters, not to learn, but to have to apply the same lessons in the same weary sequence. In tactics we may, as alleged, begin by trying to fight the previous war—but at least it is the previous war, and not the manœuvres in preparation for it.

In administration and organization the cycle is probably longer. The evils of an inefficient or non-existent medical service, which even a Florence Nightingale could not finally cure— as those who saw the barge-loads of miserable humanity come down river in Mesopotamia in 1916 will testify—can be paralleled in William III's Irish campaign to almost the last detail; the interference with and hamstringing of commanders by timid or Napoleon-minded politicians who drove Sir John Moore and Wellington to desperation were, if anything, less immanent in Marlborough's time, although rising to a more disastrous crescendo; rationing and feeding were in exactly the same state in 1815 and 1714—only to be achieved by superhuman and 'irregular' efforts on the part of selfless and single-minded men on the spot: as for divided control and blanketing of military decisiveness and drive by dilution of the army and creation of a coterie of Civil Service supporting organizations, there are those who contend that today we are headed for the same troubles as beset Crimea.

Marlborough had the great advantage that for a considerable period of his campaigning he had a sympathetic Government fairly firmly behind him. His recommendations and suggestions were often acted upon, and his importunities for inconvenient luxuries like money or stores were often successful.[1] He was, however, much too busy, and too intent on pursuing the immediate aim to risk urging on his Government any long-term schemes of reform whose advocacy, or even acceptance, might

[1] It does not come within the scope of this book, but in assessing Marlborough's captainship (if anyone may be so presumptuous), it is necessary to remember that this transient advantage was fully outweighed by his incredible and heart-breaking difficulties with obstructive and timid allies.

have hazarded the near future. He bent himself, and strained the existing machinery until it worked. Shrewd observer as he was, he no doubt realized that the only reform which could hold any lasting interest for the politicians was one which, once the war was over, would produce an army of as few men as possible, and, preferably, make a profit for the State.

The administrative machinery was, if not quite like the Icelandic snakes, absolutely incapable, to present-day eyes, of functioning at all. It was inefficient, corrupt, cumbersome, and yet tenuous. It endured for centuries, to be sure; but how, only the corpses of Dettingen, the backwoods of North America, the cold Spanish sierras, and the plains of India or of Inkerman could tell. The distinctive feature is that, in Anne's time, in Flanders at least, it undoubtedly worked. That it did so is due, above all, to two men—John Churchill, Duke of Marlborough, and Sidney, Earl Godolphin, Lord Treasurer of the Council for eight years of Anne's reign.

I tried, at first, to keep this book from being the story of Marlborough's army—but that is impossible. His work and his personality are woven into the pattern of the Queen's army in every square. Despite the several theatres in which, at one time or another, battles were fought, the story of Anne Stuart's army is the story of John Churchill's army.

There is little here of Godolphin's part, but it is quite impossible to say how far, without him, Marlborough could have gone. He was the tireless, brilliant, and loyal (three attributes not frequently found in one politician—of Stuart times, at least) provider of Marlborough's men, money, and arms; his 'manager' of politicians; the guardian of his interests in the Council; his sure confidant; and good and sympathetic friend. It is improbable that Sidney Godolphin, who 'generally did more than he promised', ever heard a shot fired, but the British army owes him a large debt for the brilliant start he helped to give it on its career.

In a study of the structure, these two architects stand head and shoulders, in the foreground, above all else; but those for whom they worked, the officers and men of the brigades, the regiments, and the squadrons are, if anything, more unforgettable. In a cold survey of the armies of the period, there is plenty to strike, even to appal, the student—the diversity of control;

the futile meddling of men who knew nothing of the business of fighting; the corruption and inefficiency in every sphere; the penalties inflicted on the honest, painstaking, or efficient; the rewards for the dishonest, the dilettantes, and the inefficient; the irresponsibility of politicians in high places who cast patient officers and humble soldiers indiscriminately on far strands without arms, food, medicine, or even orders; the miracle of the transformation of the sweepings of the country, recruited haphazard and by barely concealed press, into an army unsurpassed then or since; the intractability of pettifogging allies; and the resilience of a well-tried enemy. Above, far above it all, however, shines with a glow as of a lighted tower the sheer endurance, patient loyalty, and capacity for infinite suffering of the officers and men who stood in the files and in the squares.

The troops were ill fed, when they fed at all; they were massacred in sea-transports; wounded, they were—not as lucky as Corporal Trim with his Beguine to look after him—mangled by surgeons more akin to carpenters than doctors; they marched without shoes and with their clothes in rags; they were cut off almost as effectively as if dead from those who are sickly referred to today as their nearest and dearest.

For all that they were entitled to a pay incredible in its parsimony, but seldom, in any case, received. They were thrown incontinently on to the streets without thanks, or gratitude, or money when disabled. Or, when danger had passed, they were looked on as criminals with the additional disadvantage that they were not safely behind bars. Yet, when their loyalty was tried, they performed feats of skill-at-arms, of marching, and of sheer straightforward courage not to be equalled. Any officer who today called on his men for a fraction of the devotion to duty which Corporal Trim's successors took as a daily matter of course would have a mutiny on his hands in a quarter of an hour: and probably be relieved of his command by due process of question in the House.

That toughness and that single-hearted loyal devotion have today been replaced by intricate organization and elaborate administration with a corresponding and welcome diminution of avoidable suffering. These are, however, for all their cumbersomeness, delicate mechanisms. In the event of failure they have not the reserves to draw on which the loyal toughness and patient devotion of Anne's well-trained men provided ready to hand.

The problem—or the lesson, for the military student—is to make an army in which all four are present. By the time this is so, humanity will, perhaps, have reached such a stage of perfection that armies will be unnecessary.

I

GOVERNMENT AND CONTROL
OF THE ARMY

THERE are two aspects of a nation's military organization. There is, on the one hand, the control of the military machine by the State, and the methods by which the politicians' wills are imposed upon the soldiers. There is, on the other, the army machine itself: the formations, the staffs, arms, and services. The method by which the State controls the army, although not intimately connected with military internal organization, undoubtedly sets the standard and pattern for the army. Examination of this mechanism must precede, especially when dealing with a period of flux like the early eighteenth century, consideration of the army itself.

The problem of integration of the army into the national framework, its effective control, and the co-ordination of political and military strategy projected themselves sharply in Queen Anne's reign. Solutions were found, either directly, or by the more British method of procrastination and evasion. There was no universal perception of a distinction between civil and military power. Thus, the boundaries between statesmanship and military strategy, politics and discipline, or, for that matter, politicians and generals, were not at all obvious to either politicians or soldiers. The Commander-in-Chief participated in meetings of the Privy Council: the officer of state answering for the army to the Commons was technically a clerk to the Commander-in-Chief: and bodies such as the Board of General Officers were as much links between 'Cabinet' and army as integral parts of army organization. Command and organization of the army today have much that is similar to those of Queen Anne's forces. The methods of direction from the top, or 'War Cabinet' level, have little. It would possibly be unfair to say that the generals and soldiers of those days functioned in spite of the politicians. It is undoubtedly the case that the organization

B

which the politicians and servants of state suffered to grow up and spread haphazard brought little to officers and soldiers but worry, inter-departmental wrangles, cumbersome delays, and exasperation. If little had been achieved by Anne's soldiers, one could well have said it was miraculous that they did anything: in fact, wonders were accomplished. To deal adequately with the failures of bureaucracy, the conflicts of authority, abuse of position, peculation, disorder, breaches of faith, and defiance of authority which marked the age would take more than one large volume. However adept her officers were in strategy or tactics, they were learners in administration. Her government servants were either novices in a rapidly expanded segment of public activity, or too few to cope with the numerous unfamiliar problems. There was thus scope for mismanagement, and ample latitude—with some aptitude—for corruption.

It was a time of change and adaptation in the constitution, not only so far as the government of the army or its place in the state was concerned. That would have been burden enough to bear in time of war. The entire machinery of state executive power was itself in process of transformation. The Cabinet system, with its concomitant of collective responsibility, and, in fact, if not in theory, party rule, did not establish itself firmly until George I's time. Throughout Anne's reign, nevertheless, those who believed in a government of good men of all parties, responsible each to the Queen, and working broadly within the framework of the Privy Council, rather than adopting new forms, were being steadily outmoded, and, indeed, out-manœuvred. In addition, therefore, to the constraint of anti-militarist tradition among the politicians, the army found itself even when accepted as a regrettable, if temporary, necessity, caught up in a constitutional wrangle. There were no firmly ordained 'channels of correspondence', and there were few matters in which determined men could not go behind a superior's back. There was no one, except the Queen herself, who could not be by-passed or intrigued against in some matter for which he held responsibility. Even in theory, the army was controlled by two masters—the Northern and Southern Secretaries of State. Its government depended on its location, since this decided in which Secretary's governance its sphere of operations lay. Thus could it happen, for instance, that, on a movement of troops, one Secretary would be concerned with their concentration and dispatch, and the other with their reception and deployment. There was no co-ordinating minister, and each Secretary answered to Parliament for his particular share—determined by geography—of the army. Neither was simply a titular head. The evidence to the contrary lies in the mass of correspondence in the letter books, the signatures on warrants and commissions, the instructions issued to commanders-in-chief, and the problems referred by the Secretary at War or the Board of General Officers.

The position is accurately summed up by Clode:

In treating of the prerogative of the Crown in the government, command, and disposition of the army, the office of primary importance is that of the Secretary of State. From the time of the establishment of a Standing Army that Minister had been held responsible for three essentials: firstly the number of the military forces to be maintained, secondly the appointment of officers duly qualified, and thirdly the employment of the army.

These responsibilities, he goes on, were secured, first by the post-Restoration warrant of 1 January 1669, secondly the countersign of the Royal Sign Manual upon every commission for which Parliament held the Secretary of State responsible, and thirdly the constitutional rule that every command of the Crown required authentication by a Secretary of State.[1] A vigorous secretary intervened extensively in the campaigning, normally after reference to the commanders-in-chief, but occasionally without any consultation. In 1703, for instance, while Marlborough's power and influence were as great as ever, Nottingham could take from him without discussion 2,000 men for service in the Peninsula. It was again, while Secretary of State, that Henry St. John, towards the end of the war, inspired —for it could hardly be dignified with the word organized—Jack Hill's Canadian filibuster.

---

[1] *The Military Forces of the Crown; their Administration and Government*, Charles M. Clode (London, 1869), vol. ii, p. 316. (*Clode*.)

The procedure followed with references in all chapters has been to give, on first occurrence, name or title of book or document, followed by author or other identification. In the case of Public Record Office documents, the identifying letters and figures in the Record Office catalogue are shown, followed, where appropriate, by pages. Finally, in italics is shown the short title used in future references. Full details of publishers, dates, etc., are given in the bibliography which also repeats, in appropriate cases, the short titles.

No matter how vigorous the Secretary of State, however, he had always to take account of, and in most cases give way to, the Lord Treasurer. In a time of financial stringency when £11,000,000 had to be raised for war by a country whose ambassadors were often years in arrears of pay, the man who provided the cash obviously had a large influence. When, for a large part of the reign, he was a close friend of the Commander-in-Chief, in high favour with the Queen, and an honest but shrewd man of unquestioned brilliance, his influence was bound to be predominant. He had the last word in so many things—contracts, establishments, pay, the apportionment of the trickle of cash as it came in from taxes—that it was inevitable that 'my Lord Treasurer's' views should be taken on almost anything of importance. Godolphin's patient forbearance on behalf of his country, leading to a long tenure of office, and his close friendship with Marlborough, which engaged them both in matters beyond their sphere, gave him a standing which remained with the office even when he himself had gone.

The Secretaries of State and the Lord Treasurer were the ministers of Cabinet rank, as it would be termed today, who gave orders to the Commander-in-Chief. At one time, the Lord President of the Council, as what might be designated the Sovereign's Chief Executive Officer, had made a bid for direction. This, however, depended on the office-holder's personality, and seldom did he show himself as vigorous as Danby who in 1691 had provoked Marlborough to complain to William of his interference on the grounds that he was 'very ignorant of what is fit for an officer, both as to recruits, and everything as to a soldier'. When Marlborough issued orders, he complained, the Lord President did as he thought fit, and 'enters into the business of tents, arms, and off-reckonings . . . so that . . . business is never done'.[1]

As the Lord President's authority declined, that of the Secretary at War increased, and it may well be claimed that confirmation and acceptance of his position in the chain of army government was the leading constitutional development of the reign. As is the way with important constitutional changes, there was no formulated alteration, but, for all that, his role and

---

[1] *Marlborough and the Rise of the British Army*, C. T. Atkinson (London, 1921), p. 127. (*Atkinson*.)

standing increased markedly. The office of Secretary at War is dealt with later in the chapter, and only an outline of his position will be given here. Technically he was secretary to the Commander-in-Chief. So strong was tradition that, in spite of his extensive field of activities, and the mass of orders and correspondence which he originated on routine matters, it was near the end of the reign before he took up a strong position *vis-à-vis* the Commander-in-Chief in counselling Queen or Cabinet. As the influence of Marlborough declined, the Secretary at War, while his function changed, tended to become the official link between the Cabinet, or the Queen, and the army, even when the orders were, in the first instance, communicated to him by the Lord Treasurer or Secretary of State. He was early considered to have particular responsibilities in the field of finance: Clode indeed claims that these were his primary duties—as is supported in degree by his joint presentation with the Paymaster-General of estimates from 1702 onwards. The position was, in fact, eventually to arise where he claimed, in money matters, to be under the immediate direction of the Treasury, and therefore supreme over the Commander-in-Chief, but that was some time ahead.

An office which might have created further confusion but for the good sense of the holder and his friendship with Marlborough was that of 'generalissimo of all Her Majesty's Land Forces', held by H.R.H. The Prince Consort.[1] In the event, he communicated practically all of his instructions through either the Secretary at War, or, when it was a matter requiring the attention of the Board of General Officers, through the Judge-Advocate-General. The Prince, nevertheless, constituted, by virtue of his appointment, yet another court of appeal to which points could be referred by anyone wishing either to overturn or delay a decision.

The Board of General Officers, formally constituted in this reign as a semi-disciplinary body to check abuses in recruiting, was an organization with potentialities for the exercise of considerable power. It underwent, however, a change of function to become the authority on what today would be Military Secretary or Adjutant-General matters (officers' promotion, seniority, etc.), and on disputes regarding pay, and the administration of

---

[1] *English Army Lists and Commission Registers*, Charles Dalton (London, 1892–1904), vol. v, p. 15. (*Dalton*.)

widows' pensions. It did, indeed, usurp the Commander-in-Chief's functions in some minor administrative matters, but, even when backed most strongly by the political intriguers, it never rose to have the influence and control at Cabinet level to which it might well have aspired.

Finally, the Queen, as factual and titular head of the State, commanded the army, and did, in practice, give a personal decision on many matters, particularly when the cloud was spreading over Marlborough. It is most important not to overlook this personal control by the Sovereign. It was not simply a question of the role of a constitutional monarch in a state where occupation of the throne entailed more than ceremonial or symbolic functions. The army has always been peculiarly the royal instrument—so much so that, even two hundred years after Anne, Palmerston was to claim Secretary at War's authority over the Commander-in-Chief, because, he maintained, commanders-in-chief, when of non-royal blood, were, by constitutional precedent or convention, merely 'captains-general' and not 'generalissimos'. Even the bitterest of the army's opponents did not wish to infringe the royal prerogative in the matter of its government and control. It was, in fact, precisely because they could not envisage it as other than an instrument of the royal, as opposed to the people's will, that they opposed and harassed it. Comparatively early in history, the Sovereign had delegated power over the navy to the Board of Admiralty, from whom the naval officer holds his commission. The army officer's commission, on the other hand, is issued by the Sovereign 'and the language of the document implies that the holder enjoys his Sovereign's especial confidence, for which reason the Sovereign directs all of the officer's subordinates to yield him due obedience'.[1] Similarly, the army estimate was submitted to Parliament under the Sovereign's signature, and Parliament's control over it ceased once the vote had been passed. This independence, paradoxically enough, exposed the army to irritating interference. The Commons, feeling always over them the threat of this anonymous tyranny, which might one day produce another Colonel Pryde, attempted to resolve their frustration and helplessness by interfering extensively in the only field open to them, that of finance.

[1] *The Last Post*, J. W. Fortescue (Edinburgh, 1934), p. 221. (*Last Post.*)

Obviously, even in Stuart times, if a war was to be won, these competing agencies had to have some arbiter before whom problems could be officially threshed out before formal presentation to the Sovereign. This appears to have been provided by a concatenation (one hardly dares call it a system) of Committees of the Privy Council. For domestic army matters there was undoubtedly a body known as the Lords of the Committee for the Affairs of the Army, to which there are numerous references in the Proceedings of the Board of General Officers, and with which the Board in fact on occasion joined their names in the issue of orders.[1] This conception of a Committee, however, was not quite ours as can be gathered from the authoritative statement in the official collection of the Acts of the Privy Council:

Evidence of the existence of temporary or special committees is not convincing. . . . Reference (of a case) to a committee, whether under a general or a specific title did not imply the attendance of any particular persons.[2]

A committee, in short, was not a committee appointed from the Council, but a committee consisting of the Council. In effect, of course, as for example happens today in lawsuits before the House of Lords, or the Judicial Committee of the Privy Council, the members attending such a committee tended to be those particularly interested or concerned, who acted with the tacit consent of their fellows; with them would sit one or other of the Secretaries of State and probably the Lord Treasurer. The precise field of activity of the Committee for the Affairs of the Army is no more easy to define than that of the army's other masters. It did not have exclusive jurisdiction, for it was also the practice to appoint special committees to deal with all matters concerning specific theatres or expeditions—for example, the Secretary at War's office transmits the orders of one such committee (concerning the Portuguese expedition) on 9 September 1703 about medicines.[3] It would be again, through such a committee, or through the Board of Trade and Plantations, that the captain of the St. John's garrison in 1702 laid before the Privy Council complaints about his agent.[4] It has been suggested

[1] Board of General Officers: Proceedings, Public Record Office. (*PGO WO 71.*)
[2] *Acts of the Privy Council of England: Colonial Series*, vol. ii, 1680–1720. (*APC Col.*)
[3] Secretary at War: Out Letters, Public Record Office, WO 4. (*War Letters, WO 2–4.*)
[4] *APC Col*, p. 399, 26 Mar. 1702.

further, that there was also, in the far inner circles, what amounted to a high-powered 'War Cabinet'. On this hypothesis there was, for the greater part of the reign, a 'Secret Committee' which dealt almost exclusively with high-level strategy. On it were Nottingham, Secretary of State, Godolphin, Lord Treasurer, the Lord Lieutenant of Ireland, four naval commissioners, and Blathywayt, the Secretary at War, besides Marlborough who attended when in England. Nottingham is believed to have acted as secretary until George Clarke added the duty to those of Joint Secretary to the Admiralty, Deputy Secretary at War, Secretary to the Prince Consort, and Judge-Advocate-General. Hedges, as a Secretary of State, joined the committee at the same time as Clarke. It alone was charged with the co-ordination of the war in theatres other than the Netherlands, where the task was no doubt viewed as devolved on Marlborough. Later in the reign, a still more highly powered 'inner committee' is thought to have come into existence consisting of Godolphin, Rochester, Nottingham, Rooke, and Marlborough to deal with very secret future plans. This committee must indeed have been exceedingly powerful because it is reputed to have by-passed even the Admiralty in the issue of instructions to commanders.[1] Whatever its powers, and however secret its decisions, it represented yet another source of orders and counter orders for sorely tried commanders.

The Treasury, of course, diligent in supervision of spending, although a trifle hesitant in the provision of money, snuffled like a suspicious watchdog in most corners. It was only in the previous reign that two overseas expeditions had carried, in addition to their naval and military commanders, a Commissary-General from the Treasury, who, for the sake of economy, was in control of money, stores, and provisions, besides being Muster-Master, and Judge-Advocate-General. As he was in charge of the ammunition he could put considerable pressure on the military commander, and, as a Treasury representative, kept a close eye on its share of the prize-money 'not omitting', it is recorded, 'to deduct a considerable commission for his own services'.[2] There is no record of a case in Anne's reign in which a Treasury

---

[1] 'Queen Anne's Defence Committee', Julian S. Corbett in the *Monthly Review*, 1904 (London). (*Monthly Review*.)

[2] *Last Post*, pp. 226–7.

representative held such a power of veto as control of the ammunition, but commanders in the field were certainly in the
situation of being dependent on a number of bodies over which
they had no control, and upon which they could not even bring
much pressure. There was the Board of Ordnance, a high-
powered piece of state machinery, the Commissariat, the Commissioners of Transports and Victualling, the Paymaster and his
muster-masters, and the host of civilian contractors and sutlers.
Marlborough could influence the Board of Ordnance because
he was Master-General, but this was fortuitous. As an organ of
State, and not of the army, the Board frequently bridled at
orders from other than the Lord Treasurer to whom they could
appeal from Secretary of State's instructions when Marlborough
was overseas.

The Commissariat, a civilian organization, technically under
the Treasury, was responsible for the supply, or deficiency, of
provisions and fuel. In sea transport, the Commissioners of
Transport and Victualling took a hand. Their responsibility for
victualling extended only to the navy and to soldiers at sea, and
they took their orders normally from the Admiralty, although
Dartmouth as Secretary of State did at times exercise a tenuous
control. While the organization of sea transport appears, perhaps through lack of opportunity, to have been not as corrupt
as that of victualling, the commissioners and their local agents
at sea ports were hopelessly overwhelmed with work, and responsible for the deaths of very many British soldiers.

The Paymaster-General was hampered chiefly by being frequently and for long periods without his stock-in-trade. Political
prejudice pinned on one Paymaster-General a responsibility
which, had it been brought home in other departments, would
have led to wholesale impeachments. Examination of documents
in recent years shows that the Commons resolution of 7 December 1702, 'that it appears to the House that the Paymaster-
General of the Army hath misapplied several sums of the public
money',[1] was activated by political spite rather than financial knowledge or solicitude for the 'poor soldiers'. Coming
on Ranelagh after twenty years' service and the handling of
£21,000,000, its naked injustice probably prevented its having
any deterrent effect on his subordinates.

[1] *Journals of the House of Commons*, vol. xiv. (*Journals Commons.*)

THE SECRETARY AT WAR

The outstanding development in organization and direction during the reign was the alteration in status of the Secretary at War. This placed the army firmly under civilian and parliamentary control—and thereby secured its future. Any criticisms of the principle of a standing army which had previously had any semblance of validity now lost their substance. Like other revolutionary or permanently beneficial acts of the reign—such as the Treaty of Union or that of Utrecht itself—the change did not take place with any consciousness of high endeavour, nor indeed with the purpose in view which was finally achieved. Parliament had not really previously considered the question of controlling the army, the very mention of whose name—except when danger threatened or battle was nigh—had produced reactions akin to those evident, until comparatively recently, on the mention of conscription. 'Whereas', the M.P.s repeated their creed yearly in the Mutiny Act, 'the raising or keeping a standing army . . . is unlawful.' Prohibition of armed land forces was the aim. Control had not been considered. In the eyes of the faithful Commons, and in those of the country at large, the army was an instrument either of royal oppression or of the tyranny of generals, as in the days of Cromwell, still in many men's memories. By the end of the reign, however, the politicians had in the House of Commons, almost by accident, one of themselves who answered for this dangerous, but, at times, regrettably necessary body. The process by which they achieved this is a fascinating example of the flexibility of British constitutional growth. Strictly speaking, the Secretary at War exercised the royal prerogative over the land forces. Appearing in the House on their behalf, he gave Parliament, however, a means of communication with the army, and the reins by which they might guide it. This vital constitutional development has received little attention except from Fortescue, who, however, tended to see only the evil effects of civilian 'meddling', and not the long term benefits for both the army and the nation at large.

The first step towards the change was not made by the politicians. It was taken, in a sense casually, by the Commander-in-Chief as a matter of convenience for himself while stationed overseas. The consolidation of the change was, for all its long-term beneficial effects, only part of the factious anti-Marlborough intrigue of the latter part of the reign. When the reign began, the Secretary at War was a clerk to the Commander-in-Chief. By the time the Treaty of Peace had been signed at Utrecht, he held an office 'through which were exercised the Royal Prerogative of the command, government, and disposition of the Army. . . . The post possessed peculiar facilities for the exercise of political patronage, and . . . was allowed to control . . . all matters bearing on Army finance, the relations of the Army to the civil community, and indeed its government generally.'[1] Thus, although not the lineal ancestor of the Secretary of State for War, the Secretary at War was the first hesitant, but quite effective, attempt to create an Army Office.

The origins of the post can be traced on both the royalist and commonwealth sides. While in exile, Charles II appointed in 1657 a military secretary, Sir Edward Nicholls, who carried out duties concerning the civilian secretaries on the general's staff. When Charles continued a post similar to Nicholls's after the Restoration, under the title of 'Secretary to the Forces', he appointed Sir W. Clarke, who had served in the same capacity during the Commonwealth.[2] His commission 'in military terms' allowed himself and clerks a salary of 10s. per day. Locke, who was appointed his successor on 5 June 1666, had his appointment given in the same form as for a military officer—'to follow such orders as he should from time to time receive from the King, or the General of the Forces for the time being, according to the discipline of war'.[3] He indeed saw its first rise in status, for in 1669 the pay was raised to £1 per day, in addition to the fees paid by officers.[4] At the same time his office establishment remained insignificant—as can be seen from the specimen bill of costs for nine months of 1673,[5] which totalled only £14. 9s.

---

[1] *The War Office*, J. Hampden Gordon (London, 1935), p. 38. (*Hampden Gordon.*)

[2] Clode, i, p. 71: appointment dated 28 Jan. 1661.

[3] Clode, i, pp. 71–72.

[4] £5 for the Secretary plus £1 for his clerks was the fee for a captain over a considerable period. *Samuel Pepys: The Saviour of the Navy*, Arthur Bryant (Cambridge, 1938), p. 160.

[5] Disbursements of the office from 25 Mar. to 10 Dec. 1673 totalled £14. 9s. They included seven 'best penknifes', and one 'penknife blad fitted in a haft'; 1,300 'large Dutch quills'; '1 Dousin of ye largest pencells'; four 'Duble bottles of inke'; one bag of sand; one hone; and half a pound of 'best vermillion'. The pen knives were 2s. 0d. apiece, the blade 1s. 1d. The ink was 2s. 8d. per 'duble bottle', and the sand

Locke's duties were concerned with the 'detail of the business arising from the maintenance of a standing army', and his status was that of a clerk in the Treasury or the Secretary of State's office.[1] The distinction between the civil and financial business of the army, and its purely military activities, appears to have been appreciated, but there was no question of the Secretary at War being responsible for either. 'No military establishment or alterations thereof', stated Charles II's warrant of 1666, 'shall be presented for Our Signature without having been previously approved by Our Lord High Treasurer, and one of Our Secretaries of State, to whom We have referred the care and consideration thereof.'[2] The Secretary at War was not a Secretary of State. This was reiterated in the warrant signed by Arlington on 21 January 1669:

> Our Will and Pleasure is that the Establishment of our Troops of Guards, Regiments, and Garrisons, as now signed by Us, with all other Officers and other Charges therein mentioned, be continued, and that nothing be offered to Us for Our Signature for alteration thereof but what shall be first approved by Our Commissioners of Our Treasury for the time being, and one of Our two principal Secretaries of State to whom We have referred the care and consideration thereof.[3]

Locke, nevertheless, signed documents 'By His Majesty's Command' although to begin with he did not sign warrants.

The appointment of Monmouth as Commander-in-Chief eight years after the death of Monk was the occasion to make a change. Monk, because of his standing with the army, and his services at the Restoration, held powers and privileges not since granted. The Sign Manual Warrant issued on 27 September 1676 redefined duties. In it, there is clear evidence to support the theory that one of the aims in enhancing the Secretary at War's appointment was to create an officer wholly subordinate to the King or the General without parliamentary responsibility. The Secretary was given 'the cognizance and care of the appointment, the removal of quarters, the relief of any of our established troops or corps, and the sending of all convoys need-

---

1s. The hone was comparatively expensive at 3s. 6d., while the vermilion cost no less than 4s. 0d. Clode, i, pp. 472–3.

[1] Clode, i, p. 72.   [2] Clode, ii, p. 690.   [3] Clode, i, p. 472.

ful for the service', as well as 'authority to quarter the troops in inns'. Further,

Whereas we continue to issue from Ourself some kinds of Warrants and Military Orders which did belong to the office of Our late General, and which he was wont to dispatch and sign, We being desirous to distinguish such Warrants and Orders from other affairs of Our Crown, passing our Signet and Sign Manual, have thought fit, and it is Our will and pleasure, that all such kinds of Warrants and Orders as formerly issued from George Duke of Albemarle, Our late General deceased (in regard of that office, and which we continue to issue from Ourself) shall pass Our Sign Manual only, and shall be countersigned by the Secretary to Our Forces, as by Our Command.

From that date onwards, Palmerston reported after research in 1811, there is no instance of any warrant or order signed by the King being countersigned by any military officer.[1] A civilian thus replaced a military officer, and it is difficult to see the strength of Clode's claim that his duties were 'purely civil duties'. In a very few years, indeed, we find the Secretary issuing an order forbidding officers and soldiers to carry a dagger or bayonet at any time other than when on duty, on pain of punishment by court martial—not what one would normally term a 'civil duty'.[2]

On 18 August 1683, during Monmouth's term as Commander-in-Chief, William Blathwayt was appointed to succeed Locke.[3] Although his commission bound him to obey the commands of the Captain-General, he undoubtedly communicated and transacted business with the King direct. In the following reign, he went with James to Salisbury in 1688, and was even then extensively engaged on regulating army affairs 'as well with regard to discipline as finance . . . down to the conclusion of the reign. He issued orders of almost every description for paying, mustering, quartering, marching, raising, and disbanding troops, and also upon various points of discipline, such as the attendance, duty, and comparative rank of officers and regiments.'[4] Blathwayt, who continued to retain his post after the Revolution, was a notable bureaucrat of the period—he held at one

[1] Clode, i, p. 72; ii, p. 690–1.
[2] Clode, ii, pp. 597–8: order of 4 Mar. 1687.
[3] Clode, ii, p. 691; Dalton, v, p. 155.
[4] Clode, ii, pp. 691–2: Palmerston's memo of 16 Aug. 1811.

time or another, and sometimes simultaneously, six 'civil service' posts, the most noteworthy of which was probably the Presidency of the Board of Plantations. He went to Flanders with King William in 1692, and acted then, and in subsequent campaigns, as military secretary. It has been suggested that William's reason for taking Blathywayt with him was his irritation at the crippling division of army responsibility between the two Secretaries of State.[1] There probably never has been anyone who could say what went on in William III's mind. Irritated as he might be, however, at the cumbersome machinery of army control—and it was certainly not the least of the irritations from which he suffered—it does not follow that that was why he took Blathywayt with him. If the Secretary at War was to act under the Captain-General as his secretary, then the logical place for him to be was with his general. His original title—certainly used in one instance at least as late as 1704[2]—was, after all, Secretary *to* and not *of* the Forces. There would appear to be more basis for the complementary conjecture that the Ministers of State became themselves irritated at the status acquired by Blathywayt,[3] for his activities seem to have gone beyond those of a military secretary—bordered on those of a Defence Secretary. In Flanders he issued in the King's name, and by his command, orders and regulations of every kind to the army, signed proclamations, passes to individuals, and protections to towns and villages, and gave orders even to the naval force forming part of the expedition.[4] It is, however, reasonable to conclude that all of those actions did not stem from his appointment as Secretary to the Forces. He was not only a military secretary to the King as Commander-in-Chief, but was acting as a Secretary of State because there was no minister accompanying William.[5] In Article 48 of the 1673 Articles of War, he had been referred to as 'the Secretary' and in 6 & 7 William and Mary, c. 8, stat. 5, as 'Secretary of the Commander-in-Chief'.[6] He must, at any

---

[1] Hampden Gordon, pp. 37–38.   [2] *Journals Commons*, xiv, 10 Jan. 1704.
[3] Hampden Gordon, p. 38.   [4] Clode, ii, p. 692.
[5] It could only be as a Minister that he countersigned the grant of the Alford Peerage in 1698, and the King's assent to the Archbishop of Canterbury's nomination for the see of Bangor. Clode, ii, p. 255.
[6] There is, in fact, some doubt as to who was intended by the reference in the 1695 Act. It prohibits payments for commissions 'other than the usual fee to the Secretary of State or the Secretary of the Commander-in-Chief signing such Com-

rate, have been a valuable servant to William, for, while his pay was originally fixed at £1 a day at home, and £3 a day in the field,[1] he was, in 1695, granted £1,000 for horses, carriages, and other necessaries, in addition to a salary of £2,242.[2]

While Blathywayt was absent, the Judge-Advocate-General was appointed, with a temporary commission, to act as Secretary at War at home. He was required 'to follow such orders and instructions as you may receive from Us, the General of our Forces, or the Commander-in-Chief of Our said Forces'. In practice, this temporary secretary appears to have been no more subordinate to the Commander-in-Chief than Blathywayt. He repeatedly signified the pleasure of the Queen Regent, the Lords Justices, and even of the King. He issued a proclamation for pardoning deserters, granted leave to officers, issued a circular to the army by the King's command about levy money, signed orders for apprehending deserters and enlisting debtors, and an order from the Lords Justices to the Duke of Schomberg, the Commander-in-Chief, directing him to reprimand certain officers for neglecting to keep their regiments up to strength.[3] The indications are that Blathywayt exercised his powers, not because of the status of his office, but because of his access to and close contact with the King. The fact that his 'substitute' in England exercised similar powers, even over the Commander-in-Chief, does not necessarily invalidate this contention. As the

missions'. 'Secretaries to the Commander-in-Chief' in addition to the Secretary to the Forces are shown in the Establishment lists for 1689. While there is no doubt that fees for commissions went to the Secretary at War, there is equally no doubt that secretaries to Commanders-in-Chief collected fees. Walton supports the indication thus given that the Secretary to the Forces was not intended by the phrase 'Secretary of the Commander-in-Chief'. He adds that, although prior to Blathywayt, military warrants and orders were countersigned by the Commander-in-Chief, or a Chief Secretary of State, there was scarcely a document of authority signed after 1683 by anyone but the Secretary at War. *History of the British Standing Army 1690–1700*, Clifford Walton (London, 1894), pp. 769–70. (*Walton*.) The first objection to this view is that it seems unlikely that an Act of Parliament at that early date would designate a subordinate official, such as the Secretary at War then was, a Secretary of State. The second is that the Secretary of State undoubtedly signed military documents of importance after 1683, including, in fact, countersignature of those in question—officers' commissions. Nevertheless, if the 'Secretaries to the Commander-in-Chief', additional to the Secretary to the Forces, were drawing fees for signatures on commissions, there can be no doubt whatever that the latter would do so also.   [1] Clode, ii, p. 255.

  [2] Treasury Papers, 1/52/18, 5 Mar. 1695, Public Record Office. (*Treas.*)

  [3] Clode, ii, pp. 692–3.

Commander-in-Chief was only 'acting' in the absence of the King, he would have to be guided by a government officer, to whom he would tend to leave much with which he himself would probably have been concerned had he been a 'fully fledged' Commander-in-Chief. On the King's return to England, Blathywayt continued to act as before. He called for states and returns of effectives, granted leaves, ordered officers to their posts, pardoned deserters, disposed of prisoners, ordered colonels to account with their regiments, directed embarkations, and ordered the raising and disbanding of regiments. He issued orders to the 1695 expedition to the Straits of Gibraltar, and, later in the same year, issued, by the King's order, a general code of regulations for dress and arming of the Foot, and regulated in many cases the seniority and promotion of officers.[1]

On Anne's accession, Blathywayt's commission was renewed, almost automatically, but this time '*for*' all the land forces 'raised in England, Wales, or Berwick-on-Tweed', but still 'to observe and follow such orders and directions as you shall from time to time receive from Us or the General of the Land Forces'.[2] He continued to pour out a stream of orders, principally in the Queen's name, but also in the Prince Consort's, and in Marlborough's for the provision of guards and escorts, the grant of leave, recruiting, the provision of reliefs, shipping, quartering, clothing, and the preparation of medicines.[3] He even dabbled in minor operations at Tilbury in the same year when he ordered all movements of troops and action to counter the mutiny.[4] This was as far as his operational jurisdiction was to stretch for some years, for even his powerful successor was to find, five years later when Jacobite invasion threatened, that serious danger brought about the intervention of the Secretary of State.

In 1702 Blathywayt and the Paymaster-General presented the estimates to the House 'by order'—an indication that, so far as he was recognized by Parliament at all, he was looked upon as being primarily concerned with finance. His official status for some years was to be that of a financial and ministerial agent of subordinate importance. He was referred to as such, so

[1] Clode, ii, p. 693.
[2] State Papers Military 44/30, Public Record Office. (*SP Mil.*)
[3] War Letters WO 4. Secretary at War: Out Letters—Marching Orders: Public Record Office. (*Marching Orders WO 5.*)
[4] Marching Orders WO 5/11, 11 and 15 Dec.

far as finance was concerned, in the 1704 Mutiny Act where army agents were directed to follow, in matters of small importance, the directions of the 'Secretary at War, Royal Sign Manual, or the Treasury'. He was referred to in a similar way as far as recruiting and desertion were concerned in the 1704, 1705, and 1708 Recruiting Acts.

Although he had no jurisdiction over the Board of Ordnance, his influence was such that it was with him that the Secretary of State took up a complaint on 27 May 1702 from the Governor of Guernsey about the poor quality and armament of the garrison, so that, the Secretary wrote, 'you may take proper steps for recruiting and arming the said regiment'.[1] The Board had, in the previous month, asked him to issue orders for shipping and provisions for 230 officers and men and 24 horses to go with the train to Holland.[2] It was left to Blathywayt himself, in May, to write in reply to an inquiry about shipping for officers, gunners, matrosses, and carters for the train, and for its victualling that 'all matters of this kind relating to the train are intirely in the disposition of the officers of the Ordnance'.[3] Ordnance dug in their toes in the following year by refusing his claim to issue arms other than on the orders of the Crown with the countersignature or letter of a Secretary of State.[4] It was this which produced his letter of clarification that stated that when it was necessary to supply arms, he notified the officers of Ordnance 'whereupon a warrant has been procured from the Secretary of State'.[5] He had, nevertheless, himself on 15 April 1702, signed an order, on behalf of the Queen, that Sir Henry Bellasyse's regiment was to be issued with 'all fire arms and no pikes'.[6] In February 1703, on Marlborough's instructions, he asked for the General Officers to take action in a case involving an officer's wife, and in December of that year refused, in his

---

[1] *Calendar of State Papers (Domestic Series) of the Reign of Queen Anne*, vol. i, p. 90. (*Dom. Cal.*)

[2] Ordnance Entry Book of Warrants and Orders in Council WO 55, Public Record Office, 342/163. (*Ord. Warrants WO 55.*)

[3] Dom. Cal. 1, p. 90.

[4] Clode, ii, p. 260.

[5] War Letters WO 4/27, 24 Mar. 1703.

[6] Secretary at War: Entry Books of Warrants and Precedents WO 26/11, Public Record Office. (*Entry Books WO 26.*) The Board was still in a position twelve years later to point out that the charge of fortifications was entrusted by the Crown to them and not to the Secretary at War. Clode, ii, p. 260.

own name, to provide guards requested by the Commissioners for Sick and Wounded Seamen.[1]

While Blathywayt was driving his busy quill at home, his duties as Commander-in-Chief's secretary fell to Adam de Cardonnel who accompanied Marlborough on all his campaigns, and who was, in fact, 'groomed' by the Duke for the appointment of Secretary at War. On 8 May 1702, Cardonnel actually signed a letter on Blathywayt's behalf,[2] and was in due course to consider himself hard done by when he was not given the actual appointment. His close contact with Marlborough serves to demonstrate the hiving off of the purely secretarial duties to the Commander-in-Chief, which was complementary to the extension of the Secretary at War's powers. Up till now the Secretary had been essentially a 'King's (or Queen's) man' who implemented the royal prerogative when not simply signing for the general. Although Blathywayt sat in Parliament, it was as placeman, rather than a politician risen to office. His widespread exercise of powers was the result of his close contact with William and his long tenure of office rather than of any constitutional status. On 20 April 1704 the post went to Henry St. John, the first political nominee. Under him its authority and influence, although not, perhaps, its range, were immeasurably increased. Blathywayt had moved from Commander-in-Chief's secretary to the equivalent of a combination of senior civil servant and junior assistant Secretary of State. Now the post rose to minor Cabinet rank. St. John worked directly under the Lord Treasurer in such things as the preparation of warrants, but had frequently direct access to the Queen. While he still referred many important matters to the Secretaries of State for a decision, he exercised considerable initiative, and in many matters his opinion ranked equally with theirs. He firmly established the convention of speaking for the Government in the House on military matters, and was the Cabinet's 'director' of army affairs. With the increasing complications of establishments, movements, garrisons, and recruiting, it became impossible for any other department to attempt either to supervise or question actions of the Secretary's office. St. John had scarcely the application necessary for a task such as it was at that time. His eyes

[1] War Letters 4/27, 15 Feb. 1703; 7 Dec. 1703.
[2] Entry Books WO 26/11.

were so fixed on bigger prizes that it is doubtful if he realized the power he held in his hands. In later days, he must at times have looked ruefully back at the opportunities he had had to forward his own intrigues in the post he had looked upon as no more than a stepping-stone. The office required a diligent pains-taking organizer not afraid of a large amount of drudging hard work. Expeditions such as his presence at an embarkation, alongside the Lieutenant-General of Ordnance, were more in St. John's line. The almost gleeful chuckle in his letter can be heard to this day. Erle, he wrote, acted as 'commissary, agent, and everything else'. His claim that all went swimmingly except for the Pay Office's part of the work can certainly be accepted as probable so far as the final part of the statement is concerned.[1] It is to be hoped that the Pay Office did their duty a little more competently later in the year when he was granted extra pay of £1,000 with £455 for his clerks.[2] St. John himself expressly ab-jured the Judge-Advocate-General from his control, but there was not much else he deliberately excluded.[3] Among his many activities are listed notification to the Transport Board of a list of forces for transportation to Holland with the Queen's orders for embarkation, presentation to the Queen of matters of his office, issuing orders by her command about marching, quarter-ing, mustering, pardoning, recruiting, embarking, and hiring of transports. He directed officers to join corps, detailed escorts for treasure, ordered Invalides to do duty at Kensington in the absence of the Guards, superseded officers for absence without leave, called on the Governor of Guernsey to explain his conduct in discharging prisoners, ordered a commanding officer to pro-hibit Mass, signified the Queen's pleasure to the Ordnance for delivery of stores, and countersigned the Queen's warrant order-ing all commissions to be entered in his office, and yet another prohibiting the sale of commissions.[4] Intrusive as he might be on the authority of others, he was jealous of his own, and repri-manded the commanding officer of one unit for writing about the misconduct of officers to the Prince Consort, nominal Generalissimo, instead of to St. John himself.[5]

[1] SP Mil. 41/3, 25 July 1706.
[2] Clode, ii, p. 255, footnote 4.
[3] *A History of the British Army*, vol. i, J. W. Fortescue (London, 1899), p. 584. (*Fort.*)
[4] Clode, ii, p. 694.   [5] Ibid., p. 260, footnote 5.

In the Cabinet reshuffle of 1708, Walpole succeeded St. John (commission dated 25 February), and continued the tradition of a political chief. Walpole, in fact, quite frequently took the chair in committee of the House when military matters were being discussed. On 29 June 1709 he requested the Secretary of State to order absentee officers to their posts, and make examples of those who 'neglect their duty'. The Secretary of State, after consultation with the Queen, wrote back that Walpole himself should issue orders 'so that in case of disobedience they may be immediately broke': which was a long way for a general's amanuensis to have come.[1] He gathered firmly into his hands control of the army estimates. These were submitted under the Sovereign's signature to Parliament, whose control over the detail ceased once the vote had been passed. Yet, the House had now someone to whom they could at least put their queries on the army, and he was well on the way to becoming the 'channel of reference on all questions between the civil and military part of the community . . . and . . . the constitutional check interposed for regulating their intercourse'.[2] The day was yet distant, but it could be foreseen, when one of the country's greatest captains was to remark with approval, 'The Commander-in-Chief cannot . . . move a corporal's guard from London to Windsor without going to the civil department for authority'.[3]

With the army so firmly under their control, the politicians could now afford to put a 'light weight' in office, and on 28 September 1710 Walpole was succeeded by Grenville as part of the anti-Marlborough campaign.[4] For the first time, the Duke was not consulted about this appointment of a man technically his clerk. Previously he had accepted a 'political' secretary either as part of an involved bargaining process, or as a means of strengthening the 'army' point of view in government circles. Now times had so changed that he could only write to Walpole, 'As it so nearly concerns me, I was in hopes that I might have been written to about it first. However, I begin now to think nothing strange after all that has passed. . . .'[5] On the very day the

---

[1] Sp Mil. 41/3/184, 193.

[2] Clode, ii, p. 688; Memorandum of Principal Duties of Secretary at War in 'Army and Navy Promotion 1833' (précis of).

[3] Clode, i, p. 219.　　　　　　　　　　　　　　　[4] Dalton, vi, p. 155.

[5] *Marlborough's Letters and Despatches*, vols. i–v, Sir G. Murray (London, 1845), dispatch of 20 Oct.1710 at v, p. 192. (*Murray.*)

appointment was made, Cardonnel, not knowing the change had taken place, wrote that he had already kissed Her Majesty's hand for it, and pointed out that it 'does in some measure depend' upon the Duke.[1] Grenville, later Lord Lansdowne, industrious, pleasant, weak, and dilettante, was succeeded by Wyndham on 28 June 1712. He was still paid from the army estimates.[2] Wyndham made way in his turn on 21 August 1713 for Gwynn whose most notable success was in having his allowances raised to £1,000 for his clerks plus £200 for rent.[3] Wyndham had to meet resistances to further accretion of powers when he 'conveyed Her Majesty's pleasure' to the Admiralty that a regiment for the Leewards be taken in the West Indies convoy which was also to bring one back to the kingdom. To this, their Lordships replied that, in the past when they had directed convoys, it had been customary 'for Her Majesty's Pleasure to be signified by a Principal Secretary of State'.[4]

The reduction of forces at the armistice, followed by the Hanoverian Succession which brought about the return of Marlborough, caused the office to lose some of its lustre. The precedents had, however, been established, and the machinery set up for the fitting of the army into its place in the British constitution. So rapid and haphazard was the growth of the office that, during Anne's reign, even in the term of office of an administrator like Walpole, the branch was the most disorganized of an incredibly inefficient governmental machine. There was no firm allocation of duties; at times the multifarious commissioners of this or that would accept orders, at others they would insist on receiving them direct from a Secretary of State, or the Lord Treasurer; bodies like the Admiralty were never sure of the status of the office, and made the most of their uncertainty; there were no channels of correspondence—the Secretary issued orders to generals and to ensigns in charge of detachments quite indiscriminately; financial powers were quite vague; and officers of any rank were always prepared to argue with the Secretary's decisions if they had not been sought in an endeavour to overturn someone else's. There were, in such

[1] SP Mil. 41/3.
[2] *Journals Commons*, xvii, 29 Feb. 1712: Estimates for Guards, Garrisons, and Independent Companies.
[3] Clode, ii, p. 255, footnote 4.
[4] SP Mil. 41/4.

a state of affairs, three really bad things which could happen—
first to have as Secretary a volatile genius (like St. John) or a
well-meaning wallflower (like Grenville); secondly to make the
office the shuttlecock of quite unscrupulous politicians interested
in it only as a piece of patronage or a weapon with which to
spite their enemies; and thirdly, above all, to have a major war
to wage. The result of all this was that subordinate officials were
flung into jail for debt after spending their lives, savings, and
property in their country's service; overworked clerks like
Samuel Lynn 'puzzled their brains to pieces' (it was on similar
service their naval predecessor Pepys destroyed his eyes); while
troops who raised their country's name to a height never exceeded perished miserably in insanitary transports, in bedlams
of hospitals, or in garrisons with neither barracks nor fire. Yet
had there been a firm man in charge, or even an enthusiastically
efficient one with skilfully framed plans and the time to put
them into operation, there would undoubtedly have been a
clash with either the army or Parliament. Such was the temper
of the time that anything but shilly-shallying 'make-do' and
the type of unidealistic compromise that brought about the
other great constitutional stroke of the reign—the Union of the
Parliaments—would have torn a fissure in the nation's constitutional covering which might never have been repaired. Had
there been anything but 'muddle through', the development of
the constitutional convention of parliamentary control of the
army through an officer appointed with a commission 'in military terms' by virtue of the Sovereign's prerogative would have
been stultified—with results undoubtedly more crippling for
army and nation than those, serious though they were, which
actually occurred.

FINANCE

Develop as it might, the office of the Secretary at War,
responsible for the army's financial estimates, was at the mercy
of the Treasury. The Treasury in its turn was at the mercy of
forces far beyond the control of it or any of the statesmen of the
day. Part of almost every section of this book touches on financial mismanagement, chicanery, or shortcomings. A large part
of the sufferings and difficulties of the reign had their origins
in financial troubles. Tale after harrowing tale can be told of

apparently callous neglect of faithful servants who spent their lives and their fortunes in their country's service, and were left not only unrewarded, but unfed; but it is necessary to keep all this in perspective and in the context of time and custom. Although Parliament considered—as indeed most Parliaments have considered—the armed forces an evil, probably necessary at times, which should always be kept short of, and in time of peace without, money, the divergence between its treatment, in time of national peril at least, and that of other servants of the country was not as great as appears at first glance. Similarly, although there was undoubtedly widespread corruption, inefficiency, and defalcation, this is not the whole story. It is true that Samuel Pepys had shown, a generation earlier, how far money could be made to go with clean administration and efficient supervision, but he had not had to cope with a ten years' war, and it was, after all, in his time that the Dutch burned the English fleet in the River Thames. A much larger part of the Stuarts' financial troubles than is normally appreciated arose because the men who were responsible for the contents of the national purse were in the grip of economic forces which they not only did not understand (for can we say that they are particularly obviously understood today?) but of whose very effects they were only vaguely conscious. Since Elizabeth's reign, there had been a steady devaluation of money, speeded up in William's and Anne's time. Consequently, the bewildered and angry members of Parliament found themselves year after year called upon to vote larger and larger sums for seemingly insatiable appetites. This is partly, in fact, the truth of much of the widely alleged 'extravagance' and 'dissipation' of some of the later Stuarts. These increasing sums had to be raised by antiquated machinery which did not include any efficient means of estimating or collecting. This was particularly grievous in days when 'appropriation of supplies' was a literally correct term. Each item of expenditure was ordered to be charged on a specific tax, with the result that if the tax did not come up to expectations, then the proposed beneficiaries of the expenditure as often as not went short. The total cost of all the armed services for the whole of William III's reign was £47,000,000, of which £20,000,000 was for the army.[1] The appropriation of

---

[1] *Journals Commons*, xiv, 3 Nov. 1704.

supply for the year 1711 showed £13,000,000 as war expenditure, of which nearly £7,000,000 was current. William's last peacetime budget catered for a total expenditure of £3,000,000. The army alone cost nearly £1,000,000 more than that in 1709, and the State's debts rose during Anne's reign from £16,000,000 to £54,000,000.[1]

In modern days, with airy talk of inflation and bankrupt governments, debt repudiation, and so on, we have become accustomed to our own forms of financial crises. It is difficult fully to appreciate that, without a funded National Debt, or a Treasury Bill market, a government's financial difficulties meant that frequently it had literally no money in the till, and was in the same state as an ordinary citizen unable to pay his bills. Non-payment of State debts was probably more often due to non-existence of money than to mismanagement by officials. By Queen Anne's time government penury was no new experience. In 1690, Sir Stephen Fox had announced to Parliament that there was not another day's subsistence in the Treasury. Nor was this condition by any means peculiar to the army. The Secretary to the Lord Lieutenant of Ireland wrote in 1703 that they had in hand in Ireland approximately £100, 'so that we are very pleased we are in perfect quiet—for if the Government should upon any sudden emergency need anything extraordinary, I don't know where it could be had'.[2] The position did not quickly improve, and three years later he wrote that 'this last week (there) was but £8 remaining' in the Treasury.[3] Estimates of the tax yields were so unreliable as to be almost arbitrary. The Paymaster, for instance, told the House of Commons in 1697 that taxes appropriated to bring in £3,500,000 to him had, in fact, yielded only £2,000,000—an error of over 40 per cent.[4] In 1703 the Ordnance Department was voted £70,973 (to meet its estimate of £104,478),[5] but received only £60,000. In the following year, it received £91,728 after being voted £118,362 to cover an estimate of £176,169.[6] The members of

[1] Clode, i, p. 124.   [2] Dom. Cal., ii, p. 103.
[3] Ibid., p. 112.   [4] Fort, p. 284.
    [5] Estimates were normally thus cut by Parliament. That of 1705 for Land Ordnance, for example, was reduced to £120,000 when voted from a bid of £173,980. Journals Commons, xv, 15 Nov. 1705.
    [6] Board of Ordnance: Out Letters, Public Record Office. WO 46/6; letter of 9 Jan. 1705. (Ord. Letters WO 46.)

the Board no doubt agreed with Ranelagh when, some years later, he declared: 'You know that fayre words will neither pay clerkes, nor goe to markett, and that whilst the grass is growing the horse may starve.'[1]

The reign started with heavy arrears. In 1697, the Paymaster-General had told the House that arrears of pay since 1692 amounted to £120,000 and arrears of subsistence to another £1,000,000, plus £100,000 due to regiments on transfer to the English from the Irish establishment.[2] The Commissioners Examining Debts due to the Army in 1702 reported a total outstanding of nearly £1,000,000, including £94,000 for transport in the years 1693–7, and on which there was due interest alone of nearly £32,000.[3] The Paymaster had his work cut out if he was to observe closely the provision of the 1703 Mutiny Act which ordered him to give an account every four months of debts due to regiments. In 1711 those carried over from the previous reign still totalled almost £400,000, plus £43,000 for William's Dutch troops, even after over £69,000 had been whittled off on one specious plea or another.[4] The appropriation of supplies for that year showed a war expenditure of nearly £13,000,000 without any provision for ordnance, bread waggons, or forage money—say £100,000 for the army alone. Outstanding debts in the £13,000,000 amounted to just over £6,000,000, and £100,000 was a grant to Nevis and St. Christopher Islands for losses during the French invasion of 1705. A further £2,000,000 was naval expenditure, so that the current army cost was probably about 4½ millions, although from the varying figures given in different sources for a straightforward demand like guards and garrisons, it is apparent that no one was perfectly sure to within half a million what anything was costing.[5] For 1712—when the war had petered out—the estimates were just under £4,000,000, with no allowance for extraordinaries, bread waggons, or forage money, and without allowing for ordnance.[6]

---

[1] *Calendar of State Papers* (*Treasury Series*) *of the Reign of Queen Anne* (*1702–1714*), vol. iv, p. 291, 13 July 1711. (*Treas. Cal.*) [2] Fort, p. 384.
[3] *Dom. Cal.*, i, pp. 317–19. [4] Treas. 137/22.
[5] Flanders, including artillery, augmentation, Saxons, and Palatines, cost nearly £1,300,000. When the war in the Peninsula was at its height, that theatre had accounted for nearly 50 per cent. of the total.
[6] Treas. 1/157.

In such conditions flexibility and drive were required. Flexibility in voting supplies was exceedingly difficult to achieve. There was no such thing as a supplementary estimate. As a result, the Treasury, to avoid incurring debts which it might find Parliament unwilling to honour, had, with the army's help, to make, for each set of estimates, an inspired guess for the heading 'contingencies', which could cover such things as transport ships, waggons, extraordinary charges for provisions, or additional bread and forage costs. An example of a 'contingency' or 'extraordinary' which was not allowed for was provided by Francis Robinson, a Provost Marshal, who, in the two years 1695–7, advanced £52 to prevent the French prisoners in his care from starving to death. He was still trying to get his money in 1703 from those sticklers for procedure, the Commissioners for Accounts, who claimed, with the force of tradition on their side, that they could not possibly deal with contingencies.[1] The Queen herself had on more than one occasion to meet contingencies out of her Privy Purse in order to honour undertakings for which Parliament would not pay.[2] The companies of Invalides raised for garrison duties owed a lot of their troubles to the difficulty of paying for contingencies. Four companies ordered to Portsmouth in June 1711, for example, appear never to have got further than 'the Brentfords' for want of money, although the scheme had been under discussion for at least a year. The last coherent record I have seen concerning the incident was a minute from the Treasury on a Secretary at War's letter 'to know if there be any fund for these augmentations'.[3] Commanders on the spot could not, of course, afford such leisurely measures, and, as often as not, their pockets were the victims of official procrastination. The trouble-dogged and seeking Peterborough had to reject Archduke Charles's bold Aragon project in mid-1706 because of lack of troops and money, and he was later to claim 'I never had the money to make magazines in Valencia'.[4] Initiative in raising money locally was not always commended. On 14 January 1707 the Cabinet reproved him for 'taking up of great sums of money at a most extraordinary

[1] *Journals Commons*, xiv, 14 Feb. 1704.
[2] Murray, i, p. 241.
[3] *Treas. Cal.*, iv, pp. 297, 356–7, 519.
[4] *Historical Manuscripts Commission: House of Lords Papers*, New Series, vols. vi–vii. Vol. vii, pp. 470, 473. (*H.M.C.H. of L.*)

price'. No doubt on its advice, the Queen ordered that the bills be not accepted, and Peterborough was left to be content with the news that 'provision was otherwise made for supplying the army with money'—a procedure so uncharacteristic as to be unlikely. It was even eventually alleged that Peterborough, who, with all his faults, was probably financially clean, had failed to hand over £50,000 to the Deputy Paymaster abroad. In his reply, he showed that not only had he taken with him and spent in the Queen's service £30,000, but had committed his entire estate. He concluded with the familiar plea that the service would ruin him.[1]

Every department and many servants were perpetually and heartbreakingly in debt. The Office of Ordnance started the war with a cash balance of £110,865. In three years this dropped to £36,642, of which £20,000 was earmarked for the following year. By 1710 they were £122,000 in debt, and the artificers two years in arrears; they were due £37,000 for themselves and their equipment.[2] The Commissioners of Transports were nearly £500,000 in debt in 1709, and the Commissioners for the Sick and Wounded who, in July 1702, had received six months' salary in six and a half years, were by the following year £40,000 in debt.[3] Nineteen shipowner contractors were two and a quarter years in arrears in October 1708, and had last received anything on account in November of the previous year.[4] Among contractors, the Medina family, to whom Marlborough's victories owed much, suffered badly as their protector's influence declined. In 1708 Moses, pleading for nearly £15,000 'due long since' and without which it was 'almost impossible to subsist', was ordered £5,000.[5] His brother Solomon, pleading in 1712, claimed that creditors were prosecuting him with all possible violence while others 'tear my poor wife to pieces'. He had lost, he said, £80,000 and did not dare to show his face in London.[6] The government debt to him a little previous to this, when he and Moses had had to sell or pawn 'all . . . in the world', was £60,000, for £20,000 of which he was vainly begging.[7] James Milner, another merchant or financier, remarked almost casually

---

[1] Ibid., pp. 371, 398, 404.
[2] Ord. Letters WO 46/6; *Treas. Cal.*, iv, pp. 160, 191, 193.
[3] *Journals Commons*, xvi, 2 Feb. 1709; *Treas. Cal.*, iii, pp. 198, 279.
[4] Treas. 1/111.   [5] *Treas. Cal.*, iv, p. 22.
[6] Ibid., pp. 438, 446.   [7] Ibid., p. 386.

at the commencement of a memorial that he had £74,290 due from the Government. Officers of two marine regiments were a trifle more forceful when they pointed out in 1706 that they were due over £7,000. They asked whether they would be paid their arrears by the Lord Treasurer, or must they 'go to Parliament'. Unmoved, Godolphin had this minuted: 'When there is money applicable to their use, my Lord will consider them.'[1] Employing tact to meet a similar difficulty in that year, Marlborough advised the Marquis de Langey that, since the Queen was 'finding it so difficult to raise money for the war', he dared not raise the question of a pension at the moment.[2] A few years later, he was to write to St. John that he had had to give the regiments 600 pistoles 'to keep the men together and save them from starvation'.[3]

The Treasury sought to gain some breathing space towards the end of the war by ordering that all debts on contracts before July 1711 be paid in South Sea stock.[4] Unpopular as this was, it is doubtful if the stock was any less value than the universally detested tallies. These were in fact I O Us issued by the Treasury. The measure of expectation of payment can be gauged from their perpetual discount of at least 30 per cent. This was no new development. In 1697 the Paymaster-General's accounts laid before the House disclosed a holding of £80,000 in tallies which no one would cash.[5] In 1708 the Office of Ordnance had on hand £66,000 in tallies and £24,000 in cash. In the following year the tallies were at a discount of 30 per cent.[6] Their suspicious 'artificers' (i.e. contractors and manufacturers) 'insisted' on being paid in ready money. The Government continued to give tallies until the balance in the Board's hands was £20,000 cash and £124,000 tallies.[7] In 1711 the discount had risen to 35 per cent. Many considered themselves lucky to get even tallies.[8] Marlborough himself pointed out to Raby, Ambassador to Prussia: 'I assure ye neither myself nor any of the ministers have any other payment, and we take it as a favour my Lord Treasurer will provide so well for us under the scarcity we are

[1] *Treas. Cal.*, p. 406.   [2] Murray, ii, p. 447.
[2] Murray, v, p. 471.   [4] *Treas. Cal.*, iv, p. 318.
[5] Fort., p. 385.
[6] *Journals Commons*, xvi, 11 Dec. 1708; *Treas. Cal.*, iv, p. 160.
[7] *Journals Commons*, xvi, 21 Nov. 1709.
[8] *Treas. Cal.*, iv, p. 306.

in for money.'[1] (Already, in the first year of the war, a procedure with recent echoes was adopted by which the General Officers in the Low Countries deferred drawing pay while abroad in order to save foreign exchange.)[2]

So the catalogue could continue. Like so much else, all that could be said for the financial machine was that it worked: but this ever-growing burden on the country gentlemen of England was no small contribution towards the revulsion which brought the war to a close in shameful betrayal.

THE PAYMASTER-GENERAL

The chief difficulty under which the Paymaster-General laboured was that he was frequently and for long periods without his stock-in-trade. His office displayed, nevertheless, no lack of initiative in diverting what it did receive away from the pockets of the army's officers and soldiers. Since the Standing Army, save for the small force of Guards, had been, in Charles's and James's reigns, unrecognized by Parliament the appointment was difficult to regularize. Charles had paid for the army from his privy purse and from Louis XIV's subsidies, while James had diverted money voted for the militia. Thus again Parliament found, largely due to its own unwavering hostility to the army, that it was without control over a vital part of the organization, which would have given it considerable power of direction. One result was that when it did bestir itself, and assailed Ranelagh (part of the superficial confusion of whose accounts was due to the mixture of military expenditure and privy purse), it struck blindly.[3] It refused, firm in its knowledge that something was wrong, to study evidence contrary to its prejudices, and very successfully blackened for upwards of 250 years the name of a Paymaster who is now seen to have dealt straightforwardly with a complicated problem. At the appointment of Sir Stephen Fox in May 1679, the pay of the office had been fixed at £400 per year with house. Much greater than that, however, had been the income from his commission of 1s. in the £ of army pay in return for advances on his private credit to pay the regiments weekly. For sums not reimbursed to him by

---

[1] Murray, iv, p. 675.   [2] *Treas. Cal.*, ii, p. 117.
[3] *Journals Commons*, xiv, 30 Nov. 1702.

the Treasury at the end of each four months, he had been
granted interest at 8 per cent. per annum. His lawful profits
have been estimated at over £10,000 a year, a most lavish sum
at that period.[1] It is to his credit that a very large part of what
he made was returned to the army in his donations towards the
foundation of Chelsea Hospital. By warrant of 16 March 1684,
it was laid down that the Paymaster-General need no longer
advance funds, but was to draw by imprest from the Treasury.
The deduction of 1s. in the £, however, continued, but Sir
Stephen received only fourpence of this. Out of it he had to meet
exchequer fees. The remaining eightpence was allocated to
Chelsea 'or towards the payment of the establishment of the
forces'—that is to say that the army had deductions made from
its pay in order to pay it, which seems almost to rival twentieth-
century economics. The pay of the Secretary at War was one
item which (by a warrant in 1690 giving Blathwayt £1,000
per year) was met from these eightpences.[2] This was the situation when Lord Ranelagh, who remained in office till early in
Anne's reign, succeeded Sir Stephen.

In issuing pay for the troops, the Paymaster-General's traditional duty was, once the strengths on the muster rolls forwarded
by the muster-masters had been passed by the Commissary-
General of the Musters, to issue the money in bulk to the regiments.[3] In the course of the Commons inquiry into his accounts,
Ranelagh claimed, however, that, irrespective of action by the
Commissary-General of the Musters, the actual warrants for
paying the forces were prepared by the Secretary at War, and
the Paymaster had to issue money according to these warrants
'notwithstanding defects in, or want of muster rolls'.[4] This was
an indication of the growing pretensions of the Secretary at
War, rather than a guide to the status of the Paymaster-General
who had never claimed to be more than a subordinate official.
The House did not view with favour at that time the Secretary
at War's issue of these warrants, which, on Ranelagh's evidence,
superseded establishments or muster rolls. The Commons, in
fact, made, at the commencement of the reign, little distinction
between the status of the two offices. In 1702 the army estimates

---

[1] *History of the British Standing Army, 1660–1700*, Clifford Walton (London, 1894),
pp. 640–1. (*Walton.*)   [2] Ibid., p. 641.
[3] Ibid.   [4] *Journals Commons*, xiv, 31 Nov. 1702.

were presented jointly 'by order' and later 'by address'.[1] These 'estimates' were not, of course, the moneys thought of today as 'army estimates'. The Ordnance Board and the Victualling and Transport Commissioners each submitted their own estimates separately. The Paymaster was concerned with figures for pay and associated items such as bread waggons and forage allowance. At this time he probably issued the money direct to colonels' agents or to the colonels. In some theatres, however, there were paymasters who were also muster-masters. Throughout the war, too, there were, dotted throughout Europe, deputy paymasters (of whom Sweet at Amsterdam was probably the best known), but their duties were more akin to agents of the Treasury than deputies of the Paymaster-General. Provision of pay for the troops was only one part of their duties. They produced the money for rations, horses, equipment, and any other local payments which might be required. They seem, in general, to have been paid a commission on moneys passing through their hands, although they may have received fixed salaries as well. Sweet had one per cent. on all money issued for the Medinas, Marlborough's bread contractors. There were also in the field with the troops Deputy Paymasters at 12s. 6d. per day, who were more properly part of the army and were exclusively concerned with pay.[2] In garrisons in England there were Commissaries or Commissioners of Pay. Their quality may be judged from the letter of the Paymaster for the Marines, who wrote to the Lord Treasurer on 3 November 1703 that the Commissioner at Portsmouth was 'a poor superannuated man that was rolled about in a wheel barrow, fitter much to be amongst the invalides than to be a commissary'.[3] On the other hand, Whitefield, the Paymaster for the Marines, was to write in January 1704 that, until a particular commissary was appointed for the marines, with deputies at Plymouth, Portsmouth, and Deal, muster rolls would never be returned in due time.[4]

The earliest employment of Anne's first House of Commons was to attack such faithful officials of William's as it could grip. One of the earliest and most severely hit of the victims was Ranelagh. The Committee of Public Accounts fastened its teeth in him, and

[1] Clode, ii, p. 259.
[2] *Journals Commons*, xvii, 20 Feb. 1712.
[3] *Treas. Cal.*, ii, p. 207.   [4] Ibid., p. 227.

produced allegations of irregular book-keeping, falsification of accounts, embezzlements, and fraud.[1] There was indeed confusion, due partly to the House voting moneys without naming sources, and its absurd over-estimation of receipts, but Ranelagh had at least brought a limited amount of pay out of the chaos. After two days' examination of the documents, the House voted on 7 December 1702 that 'the Paymaster General of the Army hath misapplied several sums of the publick money'. It passed a composite resolution—that all moneys issued to the Paymaster-General ought to be applied for the use of the army and forces only; and that all 'Privy Seals or Warrants to the Auditors of the Imprest' to pass accounts without proper vouchers to make any allowances other than according to the law were 'illegal and void'.[2] Ranelagh suffered as a result of a battle fought over and round him. Any 'misapplication' was due to the mixture of privy purse with army funds. He had indicated that it was the practice to make payments on receipt of warrants from the Secretary at War, irrespective of what the muster-masters might say.[3] Part of his offence in the eyes of the House was undoubtedly the handing over of pay for William's Dutch regiments in bulk—for the Orange king knew better than to let any of the English agents or subordinate officials get their hands on it. The House continued its pursuit and voted on 1 November 1703 that Ranelagh had been 'guilty of a high Crime and Misdemeanour in misapplying several sums of the public money . . . and for his said offences be expelled the House'.[4] This was severe enough punishment, but the high Tories were determined to see him in fetters if possible. At this point, however, the Government intervened, and such influence was brought to bear in the Lords that, even although the Commons called on 6 March 1704 for an 'immediate and effectual prosecution'[5] of the late Paymaster, the subject gradually faded from public view and Ranelagh himself was eventually re-employed.

[1] Some of his entries no doubt invited query, e.g.: 'Paid to several persons for especial services and for sundry disbursements for especial services to the Forces £27,150-16s-3d: Paid to several persons for contingencies of divers natures £50,929-17s-3¼.' *Journals Commons*, xiv, 11 Nov. 1702.

[2] Ibid., 7 Dec. 1702.

[3] Blathwayt's escape, despite Ranelagh's direct implication of him in the matter of warrants, is tribute to his widespread influence and his importance in the detailed administration of the army.

[4] *Journals Commons*, xiv, 1 Nov. 1703.   [5] Ibid., 6 Mar. 1704.

When Ranelagh was dismissed, two Paymasters-General were appointed, one for the home troops, and one for those abroad. This was followed by establishment under the Great Seal on 10 May 1703 of the Office of Comptroller of Army Accounts—with a salaries bill of £1,500 to be carried on the army estimates. On 26 June Godolphin issued the two Comptrollers—Sir Joseph Tredenham and William Duncombe—with their instructions. They were, roughly, to act as roving auditors of all army accounts, from those kept by the Paymaster down to regimental accounts and muster rolls, as well as watching over issues of arms, provisions, tents, and the quality of clothing. Fuller details are given in Appendix B. Obviously if they were to carry out their duties whole-heartedly or efficiently they were quite inadequate in numbers and resources. They presented periodic reports, however, and may have restrained some of the wilder abuses. The pattern was, at any rate, followed in 1708 when a special appointment was made of Commissioners for Inspecting the Army Abroad. In spite of their title, their activities seem to have been concerned solely with the troops in Spain, Portugal, and Italy. Their instructions recapitulated that, as a result of 'great abuses in mustering and the management of public money, stores, and provisions in several parts beyond the seas', the House of Commons had asked by an address on 7 June for a body to inquire into the number and quality of troops in British pay in Spain and Portugal, and also to investigate the accounts of the agent victuallers and commissaries of stores 'in those parts'.

We, thinking it incumbent on Us to prevent all frauds and other evill practices prejudicial to our service [went on the charter], as likewise for the satisfaction of Our faithfull subjects who have so freely spent their blood and treasure in this just and necessary war . . . as We repose especial confidence in your ability, integrity, and diligence, We empower you to enquire into all abuses where you have just reason to suspect any are committed of what nature or kind soever that may be for the good of our service to detect, especially relating to publick accounts or false musters.[1]

The commissioners corresponded directly with the Lord Treasurer and the Secretary of State. They detected a certain number of false musters (even seeing through a favourite stratagem

---

[1] State Papers (Foreign), 109/1, Public Record Office. (*SP For.*)

of the Prussians by which a man mustered first as a grenadier, and then as a private of the line), and reported some of the fraudulent practices and mismanagements in connexion with stores and hospitals, as well as being involved in at least one interesting battle of prestige with the navy. Asking Admiral Jennings at Barcelona to visit them, they were informed, no doubt with perfect accuracy, that they could find him on board before noon any day.

We must [pompounded the Inspectors in reply], desire to be excused removing Our Office on board. . . . Our Commission arises from an address of the House of Commons and is under the broad Seal of England.

I must agree with you [was the unexpected opening to the answer], that your Office stands mighty well already; and since you do not think it convenient to let me have a copy of that part of your Instructions relating to Naval Affairs, which prevents my giving the necessary directions to the respective officers . . . I shall content myself with observing to you that I have the Queen's Commission too under the Broad Seal.[1]

After which no one could grudge the Admiral such perquisites as might fall unbidden into his lap under, no doubt, the Broad Seal of England.

There were separate paymasters for the trains (who dealt direct with the Board of Ordnance and were not responsible to the Paymaster-General), and the marines. The appointment of a Paymaster of the Queen's Marines was a sequel to the sufferings of the previous reign when, according to a petition by five colonels, the regiments were 'in a deplorable condition . . . multitudes of them having starved'.[2] Since it was an order that troops must be mustered by sub-units no smaller than companies, and since it was infrequent that a marine company was on shore complete, it was only logical that the consequent contradiction should be resolved by refraining from issuing any pay for marines. As a result, however, there was on 1 May 1702 the petition by the colonels asking that 'Mr. Whitefeild' be appointed Paymaster of Marines,[3] and the formal sanctioning of the office on 10 May.[4] Whitefeild or Whitefield was appointed

[1] *SP For 109/1.*
[3] Ibid., p. 11.
[2] *Treas. Cal.*, iii, pp. 19–20.
[4] *Dom. Cal.*, i. p. 484.

on 16 May,[1] and Rules and Instructions for the Better Government of Our Marine Regiments were issued by the Secretary at War on 1 July 1702.[2] The post of Muster-Master-General of Marines was probably created about the same time, although the first appointment to it that I have traced was Samuel Lynn from the Secretary at War's office in 1709.[3] The Rules and Instructions laid down that subsistence and clearings for marines should be treated as for land forces, including the same deductions for clothing and one day's pay per year for Chelsea. While at sea they were to have the same provisions as seamen 'without any Deductions or Defalcations' and were to receive 'short allowance money as the Seamen do'. The important provision was that at musters for parties ashore the Muster-Master was to pass as present all officers and soldiers shown by voucher to be at sea. The officers commanding marine regiments at sea were to make a return of their men every two months to the Commissary-General at the Navy Office, and, as a further protection against fraud, parties afloat were to muster not less than one officer and fifteen men. The money for the pay was to be drawn from the Treasurer of the Navy. The Paymaster and his staff's salaries were to come from a deduction of 6d. in the £ from all moneys handled—an indication of how desperately they wished the appointment was the offer of marine officers also to make a subscription towards the salary bill. Presumably the Paymaster was of some help. In the circumstances of the time, any service probably found that a Paymaster, while providing adequately for himself, was probably as good a defender of their interests as any.

THE BOARD OF ORDNANCE

The Board of Ordnance was not part of the army. It was a department of State which controlled an army quite separate from the cavalry and infantry in almost everything except command in the field. Their blue coats instead of red, their different system of pay and rations, and the absence of purchase and sale of commissions were among the more obvious differences from the troops of the line. Study of the Ordnance Department is to

[1] *Audit Office Enrolments*, xv, p. 429, quoted at *Treas. Cal.*, iii, p. 20.
[2] Entry Books WO 26/11.
[3] Dalton, vi, p. 200.

a great extent study of the nation at war. Small but significant reminders of its once widespread dominion remain with us in such titles as Ordnance Factory and reference to guns as ordnance, heavy or light.

That department of State charged, from the earliest times, with the care of Crown fortresses and armaments, is said to have taken its name from an ancient ordinance to regulate the bore, size, and bulk of artillery.[1] It was under Charles II, however, that the Ordnance Department achieved its dominating position. By his reorganization it was given the duty of providing armament for all the ships and forts, and was bound to obey equally the Lord High Admiral or the Lord Treasurer.[2] It was only later that the army, increasing in numbers and political importance, came to control the Ordnance.[3]

The Master-General of the Ordnance and his Principal Officers, to whom was thus entrusted 'a vast amount of Public Treasure', were consequently persons of high political importance, subordinate only to the Treasury and the Auditors of Imprest for Accounting, and to the Secretary of State for issue of military equipment.[4] The Master-General was one of the few officers of State empowered to spend money on unforeseen services which had not been considered and for which funds had not been specifically granted by Parliament—for the obvious reason that if, for example, an overseas siege-work were destroyed, then there must exist an authority for immediate repair.[5] So far as the army was concerned, the Board was responsible for all material of war, the artillery, engineers, manufacture of arms, barracks in Britain, and its own transport. Its influence in the army was predominant, and on the war effort and conduct of the nation considerable. The Master-General was responsible for commissioning his own officers, who were not allowed to buy or sell their commissions. His responsibilities

[1] Clode, i, p. 8. The first appointment of a Master of Our Works, Engines, Cannon, and other kinds of Ordnance for War recorded is 1414. *A History of the Army Ordnance Services*, A. Forbes (London, 1929), vol. i, p. 7. (*Forbes.*)

[2] Clode claims that 'the presence of a Naval officer in the councils of the department gave an assurance to the Royal Navy that its requirements would not be considered a matter of secondary importance'. I have seen no evidence in the records of a naval officer as such being 'high in the councils of the department'. Dartmouth was simultaneously Lord High Admiral and M.G.O., but this was coincidental and not *ex officio*. Clode, i, p. 75.   [3] Clode, ii, p. 204.

[4] Ibid., pp. 204–5.   [5] Clode, ii, p. 188.

ranged from candles for Chelsea, and firing the guns at the Tower on State occasions, to care of the fortifications at New York, and supply of salad oil to Jamaica. This chapter will deal exclusively with the higher organization which coped with these tasks. Details of execution will be dealt with separately later.

Marlborough was appointed Master-General of the Ordnance on 30 June 1702. One of his first acts was to restore the organization introduced by James, Duke of York, in execution of Charles II's warrant of 1683 which had fallen into desuetude for want, no doubt, of adequate supervision, and of an army to be catered for.[1] Under James's Order of 25 July 1683 the 'government of our Office of Ordnance under Our Master General thereof' was committed to the Five Principal Officers of Ordnance:

The Lieutenant-General.
The Surveyor-General.
The Clerk of the Ordnance.
The Keeper of Stores.
The Clerk of the Deliveries.[2]

The review of estimates and demands for money was to be carried out 'By Order of the Master of Ordnance with the advice and concurrence of Our Principall Officers or Major Part thereof', but there is no doubt that the members of the Board recognized that 'major parts' are not a very effective way to run an army, and each officer was given extensive discretion in his own sphere.

The Lieutenant-General was the Master-General's deputy and carried a large part of the responsibility for the actual running of the office. During Anne's wars when Marlborough was campaigning in the field, the post was even more akin to that of the functioning Master-General than in other times. Apart from his overall responsibility as the Master's deputy, he was particularly responsible for the artillery, the Board's transport commitments, and the estimates and 'vetting' of contracts. In ensuring that the artillery trains were always ready, he had to direct and oversee the Master Gunner, Fire Master, gunners, and fire workers, 'and frequently to require an account of the Master Gunner and Fire Master of . . . all gunners, fire

---

[1] Ord. Warrants WO 55/342/291.　　　　　　　　　[2] Ibid. 55/536.

workers, practitioners, and scholars of their proficiencies'. In the absence of the Master-General he was also to give orders in writing for 'shooting-off of Great Ordnance at Our Tower of London' on State occasions.[1] It was in connexion with this duty that, during the reign, one of the significant assertions of the Master-General's status occurred. In July 1708, the Board wrote to Boyle, one of the Secretaries of State, that they had been informed that 'on the recent Flanders victory' (Oudenarde) he had ordered the Lieutenant-Governor of the Tower to fire the guns. Since, it was pointed out, this entrenched upon the right of the Master-General, they desired that in future he would signify his commands to the Master-General, or in his absence, to the Principal Officers.[2]

Just as the Lieutenant-General was responsible for the artillery as well as a specific branch of what we today look upon as ordnance services—the obtaining of stores and preparation of estimates—so the other lieutenant-general, the Surveyor-General, had a special responsibility for the engineers, including works, and was also charged with the custody and care of the stores, the supervision of labour, and the passing of bills. Although, strictly speaking, any of the Board's Principal Officers might be naval, military, or civilian, the Surveyor was the only one of the leading three who at this period was, in fact, frequently a civilian. James Moore, one of the founders of the Royal Society, had been Surveyor in Pepys's time, and Christopher Wren has left us a token of the office's standing in national affairs by his signature as Surveyor-General to the proclamation of George I.

The Clerk of the Ordnance was, by and large, responsible for records—of patents, grants of warrants, estimates, letters, commissions, survey certificates, debentures, ledgers, quarter books, and (no doubt a large task) the quarterly state of debts. His tasks may seem, to present-day minds, very much clerical for so highly placed an officer. Judging by the fees to which he was entitled, however, they cannot have been unprofitable. In those days, quill driving was not necessarily a task unbecoming a gentleman, but it was a task with which only limited numbers,

---

[1] Ord. Warrants WO 55/536.

[2] Manuscript Calendar of State Papers (Domestic) of the Reign of Queen Anne (1702–14), Public Record Office, p. 477. (*Anne Cal.*)

even of gentlemen, could cope. After all, Secretaries of State wrote many letters with their own hands, and Marlborough's apologies for writing by Cardonnel's hand, even over his own signature, are frequent. The 'only fees' to which the Clerk was entitled were:

Entry of patent, commission, or warrant constituting any officer or minister upon the quarter books	£2–0–0
Entry of warrants or significations for admission of under ministers, clerk, artificer, or tradesman	£1–0–0
Entry of commission for gunner, warrant for labourer or workman in the Office of Ordnance or the Armoury	£0–10–0

He should have had little difficulty in making ends meet with these and his salary of £500 per annum.[1] Remembering the perquisites collected by even the outstandingly conscientious Pepys at the Navy Office, we may presume a liberal interpretation of 'only fees'.

The Storekeeper and the Clerk of Deliveries carried out the tasks which their names imply. The storekeepers at least were frequently of military rank.[2]

These five Principal Officers were to stay in or near the Tower, and were ordered to meet at least every Tuesday and Thursday 'about eight o'clock in the morning' to transact 'committee' business. They comprised the Board of Ordnance, one of the hardest-worked bodies of the war. It was undoubtedly in effect in continuous session. All members did not, of course, attend every meeting. The Surveyor-General seems to have been invariably present, and frequently he is minuted as being the only one present, although the Lieutenant-General, under his charter, was supposed to keep the minutes. I feel that the minutes were probably, in fact, kept by the secretary or chief clerk to the Master-General. He was definitely a Master-General's clerk and not a clerk of the office, but his specific duties were to act as a link between the M.G.O. and the Lieutenant-General, or the Board. At a time like the war which kept Marlborough overseas for more than half the year, his liaison officer with the Board would be the secretary, or chief clerk. The secretary

---

[1] Ord. Warrants WO 55/536.

[2] Ibid. Board of Ordnance: Journals of Proceedings, WO 47/22. (*Ord. Minutes WO 47.*)

was authorized to attend all meetings but presumably only as an observer, as his presence is not minuted.[1]

Next below the Principal Officers came the Treasurer of Ordnance, of whom the originator of the Instructions was sufficiently suspicious to demand security on his appointment. He was to 'take no poundage, fee, gratuity, or reward directly or indirectly'; was to pay out all money and—surely one of the most difficult jobs in all England—to get money from the Lord Treasurer.[2]

Then came the Under Ministers, who 'either attend the Officers as their clerks, or the Office, (such) as the Deputy Keeper of the Armoury, Keeper of the Small Gunne Office, Storekeepers, Engineers, Master Gunner, Master Firemaster, Proof Masters, Waggon Master, Clerk of the Cheque, Purveyor, Messenger, Labourers, Gunners etc.'. Their duties were assigned by the Principal Officers, who in accordance with the charter, issued general instructions 'for the Common Dutys of the Storekeeper, Master of the Brass Foundery,[3] Clerk of the Survey, and Clerk of the Cheque, and to the Office of Ordnance at Woolwich'.[4]

The Master Gunner was the first assistant to the Lieutenant-General and was responsible for the artillery. Under him came the Firemaster, also known as Chief Firemaster and Fire-watcher, below whom came the Comptroller of Fireworks and his staff, as well as the artillery trains. For transportation of the trains there were the Waggon-Master for Land Transport, and the Purveyor for Sea. There was also a Purveyor for Land Transport, who, in a memorandum urging increased pay which was presented about the middle of the reign, is classified with the clerks. In the same document, however, the Purveyor for Sea Service also appears as a clerk, although in the Instructions of 1683 the Sea Purveyor appears among the Under Ministers, along with the Waggon-Master and the Clerk of the Cheque. The Waggon-Master received a salary of £100, but the Purveyors had only £60—recommended to be raised to £90 in the document referred to. This was the same rate as the Lieutenant-General's and other senior clerks, and £20 less than, for example,

---

[1] Ord. Minutes WO 47/22.   [2] Ord. Warrants 55/536.
[3] Included among the duties of the Clerk of the Brass Foundry was that of estimating the amount of 'loam, hair, cow and horse dung' consumed at Woolwich brass foundry within the previous quarter. Ibid.   [4] Ibid.

the storekeeper at Plymouth. On the engineering side, the Surveyor-General had under him the Principal or Chief Engineer, who was responsible for fortifications in Britain.[1] He, in turn, had under him the Second and Third Engineers of Great Britain. On the Surveyor's 'general duties' side he had his staff of storekeepers and, with the troops in the field, commissaries to take care of his stores supervision.

The senior officers of the Ordnance Department were very well paid. The M.G.O.'s salary of £1,500 was a considerable sum when we remember the value of money at the time. The Lieutenant-General's was £800, and the Surveyor's £500. These almost lavish sums may have permitted strict application of the rule that they were not to take any 'poundage, fee, gratuity, or reward, directly or indirectly . . . by reason of any bill, debenture, contract, or bargains of payment', and that no Principal Officer was to sell a clerk's place.[2] There were, nevertheless, sinecures, such as the post of Master Workman of Her Majesty's Stores and Fortifications which was declared by the Board on 22 May to carry no duties, or that of Assistant to the Surveyor of the Ordnance, created by William at a salary of £250 a year, with no apparent functions. The latter was abolished on 3 July 1702.[3] For some time, too, the Surveyor was also designated Assistant to the Lieutenant-General of Ordnance, which meant a salary of £400, plus £300 with, so far as can be seen, no additional work. The Board in 1709 attempted to have the balance of £200 restored to Brydges who was at that time Surveyor on a salary of £500, but I have been unable to trace whether they succeeded.[4] Even in those pre-income-tax days, too, there was the ticklish question of travelling expenses. James's warrant of 4 February 1686 specifically prescribed that these would not be allowed automatically for absences over ten days. Periods exceeding this limit, it was laid down, were to be considered as special cases by the Board.[5] The remainder of the salaries paid are unremarkable—the gunners were a trifle wealthier, or less

[1] *Journals Commons*, xiv, 15 Nov. 1704 call him Chief Engineer: the normal title seems to have been Principal Engineer. [2] Ord. Warrants WO 55/536.
[3] Ord. Warrants WO 55/392/235; Ord. Letters WO 46/6. Marlborough on at least one occasion expressed his reluctance to fill engineers' posts 'which would be pensions' at fortresses. Ord. Letters WO 46/6, 28 May 1708.
[4] Letter of 29 Nov. 1709.
[5] Ord. Warrants WO 55/789. Specimen expense figures from the warrant book:

poor, than the rest of the army, while the engineers, as befitted those versed in the arts and mysteries of fortifications, and the niceties of local labour, were almost handsomely rewarded. Pay for artillery officers and men ranged from £150 per year to 1s. per day (or 10d. per day if we include the Keeper of the Small Guns at the Tower), and engineers from £300 to 10s. per day, or 1s. 6d. if we count miners who were the only other ranks of the engineers in those days.[1] Men of the department had also the privilege of full rations on board ship.[2]

On 15 November 1704 the total cost of salaries was stated to be £22,260 for a staff of 311, excluding labourers, but including the clerks, the Yeoman of Tents and Toyls, an astronomical observer, and the Keeper of the Water Engines at the Tower. It included overseas installations in the plantations and watchmen at 1s. per night, but not trains with expeditions. In this estimate, the Lieutenant-General got £300 for his house, and in 1712 £500 for fire and candle. Total payments for similar housing allowances were £1,135.[3]

The Board was responsible for the issue of its own commissions, signed by the Master-General, but certain appointments were governed by royal warrant. Marlborough himself was appointed under the Great Seal, signed by Nottingham as Secretary of State on behalf of Her Majesty and granting to the Master 'all Fees, profitts, privileges, and advantages thereunto belonging'. Seals were issued at the same time for Brydges as 'Master Surveyor of Our Ordnance, Ammunition, and Habilments of Warr' (that is, Surveyor-General).[4] In the filling of these senior appointments, of course, the Department itself obviously had considerable say, and we find Marlborough conveying Her Majesty's Pleasure to the Secretary of State for preparation of warrants in similar cases.[5]

Until the Union, Scotland had her own M.G.O. at a salary of £300, but on 15 February 1709 all Ordnance officers in that

storekeeper 10s.; clerk of cheque and survey 5s.; extraordinary clerks 2s. 6d. This was issued for expenses incurred when boarding homecoming ships to check stores. Ord. Warrants WO 55/536.

[1] *Journals Commons*, xiv, 15 Nov. 1701.   [2] *Forbes*, p. 111.

[3] *Journals Commons*, xiv, 15 Nov. 1701; xiv, 15 Nov. 1704.

[4] *SP Mil* 44/170, 20 June 1702.

[5] e.g. Talbot-Edwards to succeed Holcraft Blood as Second Engineer of Great Britain on 17 Feb. 1710. SP Mil. 41/3116.

country were, by the Queen's command, brought under the Master-General.[1]

The Board had cognate responsibilities to the navy, and on its procurement side was in many ways akin to our own late Ministry of Supply. Since the Revolution the department had, for practical purposes, been dividing into two distinct branches,[2] the military under the M.G.O. and the Lieutenant-General, and the civil branch to administer the military and to act as custodians of public treasure in lands and stores, and as contractors or manufacturers to supply the navy and army with their munitions and equipment.[3] The war emphasized the separation which was to lead early in the next reign to the formation of the Artillery and the Engineers, and stressed by this separation the fact that the Master-General and his Principal Officers, as custodians of the public treasure (i.e. in their 'civilian' capacity), were accountable to Parliament, and that their subordinate officers were under the Board itself, and not under the generals with whom they worked. More than one hundred years later, the Duke of Wellington himself was to stress that in matters of Ordnance expenditure a commander-in-chief was powerless without the authority of the M.G.O. who was directly answerable to Parliament.[4]

When, therefore, we condemn the Ordnance's numerous failures in so many branches of organization and supply, we must also bear in mind the magnitude of its responsibilities and its multifarious roles, and set against these its perpetual shortage of money and comparatively minute staff. At Blenheim, for example, there was a total of five officers and eleven men of Ordnance as we understand it, that is exclusive of artillery and engineers. Further, although the department was never really equipped to supply more than one theatre at a time, the Board did, by and large, produce at approximately the proper time and place, arms, shot, and shell: which is, fairly recent experience would suggest, not a task automatically performed by some supernatural agency.

[1] *Treas. Cal.*, iv, p. 497; Ord. Letters WO 46/6.
[2] See the return in the *Journals Commons*, xiv, p. 420, 15 Nov. 1704.
[3] Clode, ii, p. 205 et seq.
[4] Clode, ii, p. 406. An interesting sequel to the Ordnance Department's independent status was that until 1855 men of the Ordnance Corps were not included in those detailed in the preamble to the Mutiny Act. Clode, i, p. 86.

THE BOARD OF GENERAL OFFICERS

Just as the Secretary of State for War could, if he wished, have traced a shadowy ancestor in the Secretary at War, so yesterday's Army Council might have been able to discern dimly amid the growth at the top of their family tree that remarkable body, the Board of General Officers. There are several features which make it remarkable, but it fits neatly into the paradoxical picture of contemporary army government. The Commander-in-Chief was not only without doubt the most brilliant general England had ever had, but was also one of the strongest personalities who had ever stood at the head of her armies. Yet, in this period, his secretary became controller of the army. The considerable field of army affairs governed by the Ordnance Department, of which the same forceful Commander-in-Chief was Master-General, fell under the control of the Board of Ordnance. Of the remaining army organization and administration, a very large proportion came in turn to be carried out by the Board of General Officers.

Even although a committee may have commended itself to Stuart parliamentarians as one of the more inefficient ways of running an army, it is still strange to find created in an age whose fear of dictatorship was the accepted motive over a large field of political conduct, a body which could only too easily have been converted into a junta or 'military Cabinet'. As it turned out, the Board became so entangled in matters of clothing, petitions for arrears of pay, questions of seniority, claims by one officer against another, and widows' pensions, that it had hardly the opportunity, even had it had the desire, to interfere in higher politics. In the latter stages of the war, an endeavour was made to use the Board against Marlborough. Although it had, however, no option but to act in matters normally the prerogative of the Captain-General (such as the seniority of officers) when these were directly referred to it, there is no evidence that it spontaneously took active sides in the quarrel. Since it consisted of all available senior officers it was, of course, exceedingly difficult to alter its composition without large scale 'purging' for which the temper of the times was not sufficiently warm. Its character could not be radically and at the same time unobtrusively changed. At the time of its reconstitution and reinvigorating in 1711, there was some emphasis on its composition being of 'serving' senior officers, which may have been an attempt to break the grip of the 'old guard' of Marlborough's supporters, but there is no firm evidence on this. The officer in connexion with whom the clause had to be specifically invoked, Lieutenant-General Hamilton, was not, as far as I am aware, outstandingly engaged at any time in the Marlborough controversies; his subsequent Jacobite sympathies would tend to make him, if anything, of the Tory faction.

The Board is generally accepted as dating from the warrant on 9 February 1706, with its first meeting on 20 February 1706, but there is in existence a warrant of 1 February 1705, signed by Harley, Secretary of State, constituting a predecessor which seems fully qualified to rank as the first Board.[1]

Whereas [runs the warrant], We have received Information of Great Abuses and Disorders that have been committed by Severall Officers and Soldiers of Our Army as well as of Disputes that have happened between officer and officer, and more especially of the ill-practices of some officers Employed in Recruiting Our Forces pursuant to the Recruiting Act and the Act for Discharge of Insolvent Debtors contrary to the true intent and meaning of the Said Acts and to the great prejudice of Our Service; for the more speedy redressing and preventing whereof and for the due punishment of offenders we have thought fit to constitute and appoint and we do hereby constitute and appoint a Councill of the General Officers of Our Army or a General Court Martiall to meet of Munday next the Fifth instant. . . .[2]

Marlborough's brother, Charles Churchill, Lieutenant-General of Foot, was appointed President of the 'said Councill or Court Martiall', which was to consist of 'the Genl Officers of Our Army or Such of them as can be conveniently summon'd to attend the same'. Thirteen, it was laid down, were to constitute a quorum. It is worth noting that this document, and the one signed by St. John, quoted below, are entered in the Court Martial Warrant Books, which shows very clearly the first

[1] As early as 1703, *ad hoc* boards sat to carry out investigations and tender advice to the Commander-in-Chief at his request—perhaps the predecessors of today's ubiquitous Board of Inquiry. See, for example, War Letters WO 4/2: letter of 15 Feb. 1703.
[2] Register of Court Martial Warrants, WO 30/18. (*CM Warrants WO 30*.)

intention of the creation of this body. It was to meet the civilian criticisms about army recruiting (false enlistment of debtors, releasing pressed men for bribes, and so on) and to ensure the army had its own house in order before further measures for recruiting were put into effect. Harley's warrant was followed by one signed by St. John on 3 February—the executive officer putting into effect what had been ordered and laid down by the Secretary of State. It[1] had the same preamble and ordered and appointed 'the Genl Officers of Our Forces to meet together and to receive, hear, and Examin all Information and complaints that shall be brought before them of the Misbehaviour of any officer or soldier . . . or any Abuses committed by them'. It was to consist of the Lieutenant-General of Foot, the lieutenant-generals, major-generals, and brigadiers of the army and was to meet as required. Any six plus the Lieutenant-General of Foot, or the senior lieutenant-general, were to constitute a quorum. As well as being authorized to impose punishments itself, it was given power to order cases before a court martial.[2]

The predecessor to the Board had thus a fairly closely defined field of investigation. I have not been able to trace any records of its proceedings, but there is considerable evidence to show that it functioned. In the following year, under the warrant of 9 February 1706, and assembly notice of 18 February 1706 (for the first meeting on 20 February), the *ad hoc* body was transformed into a permanent council, and the terms of reference were slightly widened.

We have . . . thought fit and accordingly do hereby order and appoint the General Officers of Our Forces to meet together and to receive, hear, and examine all Information and Complaints that shall be brought before them of the Misbehaviour of any Officer or Soldier in our Service; or any other Abuses or Irregularities that are or shall be committed as aforesaid; which meeting is to consist of such of the General Officers as can be conveniently summoned.

Sitting as often as the service required, with a quorum of three, the Board's functions were 'Redressing and Preventing as much as possible the great Abuses and Disorders that are

---

[1] The first is endorsed in the margin 'For holding a genll Court Marshal at the Horse Guards of Genll Officers'; the second 'For a meeting of the genll officers'.
[2] CM Warrants WO 30/18.

frequently committed by Officers and Soldiers . . . and more especially the ill practices of some Officers Employed and other Irregularities committed, in Recruiting Our Forces'.[1]

Most unfortunately two pages of the minutes of the first meeting are missing from an otherwise excellently kept minute book (by the Judge-Advocate-General who was secretary to the Board). It is, therefore, not possible to discover for certain what action was recommended or decided on the general terms of reference. Most of the part of the sitting of which a record is extant was taken up in investigating muster rolls to confirm that men stated by the civil authorities to have been enlisted were actually in the service. There were ten officers present at this first meeting—Lieutenant-Generals Steuart, the Earls of Portmore and Orkney, Major-Generals Withers, Sidcomb, Hamilton, Compton, Lords Montjoy and John Hay, and Brigadier Meredyth. Safeguarding the dignity of their office from the start, the generals minuted concerning two officers who had appeared before them in a dispute over an account that one 'expressed himself very unbecomingly and not with that Respect and Deference which is due to the Board', and the other 'in his Answers (had) not observed that Decorum which he ought'. They were both ordered to be severely reprimanded by the Judge-Advocate-General. The generals themselves appear to have been lacking in deference and respect on 5 March 1706, for the scheduled meeting had to be abandoned for lack of a quorum. Six turned up on 8 March 1706—Major-Generals Gustavus Hamilton, Sidcomb, Lord Montjoy, the Earl of Essex, Lord John Hay, and Brigadier Meredyth. Illegal imprisonment and soldiers detained unduly in the Savoy without trial exercised the minds of the generals in the following year. A series of orders was passed with provisions such as that which laid down that an officer claiming a soldier lying untried beyond a specified time might have him. On 17 June 1708 they decided to have a report at every meeting from the Provost Marshal of all soldiers confined for any offence whatever, and once again emphasized the need for speedy trials. The reports submitted by the Provost Marshal are not entered in the book, so that it is not possible to tell how numbers fluctuated, if at all, after this.

In 1708 occurred the move which probably more than any

[1] PGO WO 71/1.

other ensured that the Board would not become a military junta. Clothing was the cause of some of the greatest discontents in the army, and one of the best tilled fields of corruption. It is not clear with whom the suggestion originated, but at the end of 1707 Marlborough certainly supported a plan that the Board should look thoroughly into the whole question, and should be responsible in future for passing all patterns of clothing. On 19 January 1708 St. John wrote to the Treasury to say that Her Majesty had signed an order for several general officers to meet to regulate and inspect the clothing according to the Duke's proposals.[1] He asked the Lord Treasurer where they were to meet, and from where the clerks were to be provided. Godolphin frugally decided that the staff of the General Officers' Board could cope with this work, and, whether it had been intended all along to utilize existing machinery, this decision certainly clinched the matter. For a considerable number of years this inspection of clothing with its concomitant disputes with tailors and agents took up the bulk of the generals' time. Even although they appointed special subcommittees approximately every quarter, this task, on top of their studies of petitions, and adjudications in financial disputes, took them quite away from the semblance of high policy they had discussed when they had ventured into the field of recruitment. Even as glorified clothiers, however, they still retained a sound conception of the honour of an officer, as Viscount Charlemont's son, who had insulted Captain Crespigny, found when referred to the Board. On 5 May 1708 they recommended to the Prince Consort that the least Charlemont could do 'to repair so great an Injury and Affront to a Gentleman's Honour is, in the ... Guard Chamber, during the Sitting of the Board, on his knees, to ask pardon of Captain Crespigny, who is at the same time to have a Cane in his Hand, with Liberty to use it, as he please'.[2]

Over the next two or three years the Board went downhill somewhat, and the generals themselves seem not infrequently to have considered 'this troublesome service', as it was described by Craggs, the Secretary at War, in 1717, rather futile, for meetings had more than once to be abandoned for want of a quorum. During this period, however, it had a specially paid

---

[1] Treas. 1/105/17.
[2] PGO WO 71/1.

secretary—Gregory King at 16s. 5¼d. per day.[1] On 22 March 1711 it was rejuvenated under another warrant. This time there was to be a Board of General Officers not under the rank of major-general which was entitled to appoint a subcommittee of three or more brigadiers, to act as directed by the Board. The superior Board, consisting of major-generals and upwards actually in the service or having commands (not quite the same in theory, but I doubt if there were many generals no longer in the service but still holding regiments[2]), was to refer problems with which it felt unable to deal to the Committee of the Privy Council (for Army Affairs) and the General Officers of the Privy Council. This warrant was signed by Grenville (Secretary at War) on Her Majesty's behalf, and at the first meeting on 27 March 1711, there were present Lieutenant-Generals Erle, Echlyn, Fannington, the Marquis de Montandre, Sankie, Earl Barrymore, Major-Generals Baines, Rooke, Satton, and Wroth.[3] The subcommittee or 'inferior board' was appointed to consist of Brigadiers Wade, Bor, and Hubbald. It held its first meeting on 29 March 1711, and was fully engaged on the considerable number of routine complaints by commanding officers against other regiments alleged to have stolen their recruits. By this time the business before the Boards was of the level of individual cases of recruiting abuses, disputes about brevets, pay wrangles, petitions by widows for debts due by brother officers to their late husbands, and even one representation by a member of the Invalides that his captain had treated him harshly. Occasionally they reviewed the proceedings of courts martial overseas, and they invariably accepted the reports of their subcommittee on clothing. In mid-1711 they and the Lords of Committee of Council were making joint recommendations about the effective date of respiting dead, discharged, or deserting men.[4] A considerable amount of the drudgery was taken over by the brigadiers, but their reports were by no means automatically accepted. The last meeting of the brigadiers of which I have found a separate record was on 6 June 1711, but the generals were still selecting brigadiers for their tour of duty on at least

---

[1] Secretary at War: Establishments 24/55, 30 Sept. 1710. (*Ests. WO 24.*)

[2] There were, of course, some cases like Lord Raby, Ambassador to Prussia, and Colonel of the Royal Dragoons.

[3] PGO WO 71/2.   [4] *Treas. Cal.*, iv, p. 290.

24 December 1711, and there is a reference to the inferior board in the minute of 19 June 1714, so that the brigadiers may have kept their minutes elsewhere in a record which has been destroyed.

With the finish of the war, accompanied by large-scale disbandment, the Board was overwhelmed with complaints, petitions, and representations, as can be judged from the frequency of their meetings. They held five in March 1712; in July 1712 they had fourteen. At this time they were also dealing with the seniority of regiments, which called for a series of decisions obviously productive of endless bickerings—stopped sharply by an acid reprimand from the Queen. The Board themselves were irritated to similar action on the subject of pay, but the tradition of arguing with orders and pleading tearfully was too strong to be broken thus easily. It was during the term of sittings of this board that Lieutenant-General Hamilton was ordered to withdraw from the meetings. At the session of 2 May 1712 he was requested to leave 'having sat two or three Board days last'. The Board was 'reminded', according to the minutes, of Her Majesty's orders forbidding non-serving generals to sit—a reminder whose inspiration is not traceable. Hamilton had actually been present on the two previous Board days, for which the minutes refer to him as major-general, although he was, in fact, appointed lieutenant-general on 1 January 1709.[1] It is not clear why Hamilton was judged to be non-serving—it may have been either because he was recuperating from the severe wounds suffered at Malplaquet, or because he was considered to be on the Dutch establishment.

So far as can be judged, re-emphasis of the restriction to serving officers was the only reason for the reconstitution of the Board by warrant of 3 May 1714. Under this, it was to consist of major-generals 'as do actually now continue their commands

---

[1] PGO WO 71/2; SP Mil. 44/173/241. Hamilton's career is noteworthy as a representative Scots case. With the Scots Brigade in Holland before the Revolution; Captain in Wauchope's Foot on 11 Mar. 1688; Colonel on Scots Establishment, Flanders, 1694; Brigadier-General in the Dutch service, 1704; Major-General in the British Army, 1 Jan. 1707, and Lieutenant-General 1 Jan. 1709; severely wounded at Malplaquet where he commanded four battalions of infantry as a Dutch Major-General; Lieutenant-General in the Dutch service at the time of disbandment of his regiment in 1714; 1715 chief military adviser to the Earl of Mar in the Jacobite rebellion; executed and his property confiscated. Dalton, vi, p. 302.

in Our Service and Receive pay in the Standing Corps'—an appreciably narrower definition than the previous. This warrant also provided for an inferior Board of Brigadiers to sit twice a week.[1] There is little remarkable in its proceedings from then until the end of the reign, except when it dealt on 1 June 1714 with a case of false musters. Reference was made then to the fact that part of the reason for its existence was to obviate proceedings on such offences, which were, strictly speaking, offences against 'civil' as distinct from 'military' law. It seems indeed to have replaced the ordinary processes of law to a certain extent where protection of civilians wrongly enlisted was concerned. Formerly, pressed men and others who claimed to have been recruited against their will appealed to the Queen's Bench, but on 4 February 1712 even M.P.s were bringing before the Board complaints about a recruit who had been levied—and having them rejected. When, on the other hand, it was considering the case of Colonel Leigh's regimental accounts in 1714, Captain Douglas refused to await their decision. Not only did he arrest the regimental paymaster and agent, but 'declaring . . . in open contempt of (the Board's) authority . . . that he would prosecute without more ado the Agent and Paymaster He is for the same suspended from his half pay'.[2] The Board was most heavily engaged at this time in administering the various widows' funds—granting pensions, investigating claims, and producing suggestions to attempt to keep the consolidated fund solvent. This was, of course, an exceedingly heavy labour of which the extant minutes—bare records of decisions without even a 'count' of the innumerable petitions which must have been received—can only give an indication.

In spite of the talent assembled and the status of its members, the Board turned out to be a body which did no more than take off the shoulders of the people involved in the operational side of the war a number of irritating pay, clothing, charitable, and seniority troubles—but even in these matters no one who was dissatisfied felt himself bound to accept its decisions. Its influence lasted longest in dealing with clothing.

---

[1] PGO 71/3.   [2] Ibid.

II

INTERNAL ARMY ORGANIZATION

EVEN military histories of Anne's reign have been largely confined to battles and the 'operational' side of the war. The army's ambiguous position in the State and the empirical machinery of its control and government have consequently passed largely unexamined and unremarked, while the unformulated nature of internal army organization and staffs has, in turn, been over-emphasized. It has been widely stated, and accepted, that the armies were merely a collection of regiments, without divisions or corps, with no real staffs as we know them today, and that such organization as existed in the larger forces was simply the putting together of improvised brigades for specific campaigns. This is over-simplification. The true position is more adequately indicated by Atkinson:

> A rough organisation did exist in the normal distribution of an army into two wings and two lines, the infantry and cavalry of each wing forming separate commands roughly corresponding to corps, while the two lines were usually formed of quite separate brigades, and may be said to have corresponded to divisions. Troops were usually definitely allotted to wings and lines as contemporary Orders of Battle show, but it is clear that this arrangement had no connection with administration. Brigades seem to have been more or less regularly constituted, consisting of from eight to twelve squadrons in the horse and three to five battalions in the foot. The British contingent usually formed two brigades of horse and foot, but occasionally foreign battalions and squadrons are found brigaded with British units.[1]

Owing to the strong 'personal property' nature of regimental commands—a characteristic encouraged by Marlborough himself to keep the army as inexpensive, and therefore as inoffensive, as possible to Parliament—a large-scale, firm, administrative organization and plan was unlikely, and, in fact, unnecessary.

[1] Atkinson, p. 8, footnote.

The centrifugal tendency which these proprietary interests induced, however, probably entailed little more relative lack of co-operation and co-ordination in the field than did the division of modern forces into three services in the earlier stages of the 1939–45 war. A hundred years later, to be sure, Castlereagh was to say that, prior to 1792, the British Army assembled under the same general 'had no more uniformity of movements, of discipline and appearance in its various regiments than one composed of the troops of different sovereign states', but he was considerably more familiar with the conference table than the battlefield, or even the parade ground.[1]

There were not, indeed, the firm corps or divisions of today: but there were not the numbers involved. The total number of *British* deployed in Flanders at any one time was on an average little over one strong present-day division plus one brigade. There were not the exceedingly large staffs of today; but there was undoubtedly more in the way of staffs than is generally conceded. The difference between the staffs of Anne's time and those of today is adequately accounted for by the complexity of arms, the difference in numbers, distance, and mobility, the development of facilities for long-distance communication, and the increased standards of comfort provided for the troops. To say that brigades were simply created for specific campaigns does not really take us very far. So were the bulk of those which took part in recent modern wars. Changes both in establishment and composition were probably, in fact, much greater between 1939 and 1945 than in the eleven years 1702–13. Rowe's, Macartney's, or Meredyth's brigades had quite as much corporate spirit, continuity, and cohesion as, say, the 8th or 14th Armies of the recent war—comparable forces in relation to the total numbers of troops deployed. In the field there was, in broad outline, rather what would be expected in forces of their size and mobility—a grouping in brigades, tightly controlled by the general personally, with assistance on the administrative side from a well-picked staff, and with no more devolution below the Force Headquarters level than in a force of the same size today. There were two notable differences. First, owing to the lack of an intercommunications system, staff officers issued the general's orders by word of mouth on the

[1] Clode, ii, p. 355.

battlefield, and personally carried out detailed tasks—for example, Cadogan, the Quartermaster-General, marked out bivouac areas and frequently led reconnoitring parties. Secondly, the 'General Staff' as we know it today was practically non-existent. That was because of the much greater personal control the general himself kept over the minute-to-minute direction of the battle. The company and platoon commander of today seldom run to a 'G' staff, but always need an administrative staff—and good, unobtrusive administrative staff work was one of Marlborough's outstanding successes.

THE CAPTAIN-GENERAL OR COMMANDER-IN-CHIEF

The supreme commander of the army was the Sovereign. When for any reason the Sovereign did not command in person, a general officer was selected. The principal staff officer was the Adjutant-General. He was not necessarily of high rank; the warrants of 1711, for example, show him as a Brevet Colonel.[1]

The first Commander-in-Chief to be designated as such was George Monk, described as 'Captain General and Commander-in-Chief of all Forces' in his commission of appointment dated 3 August 1660.[2] Constitutional authorities later attempted to emphasize the difference between a Captain-General and a Commander-in-Chief on the basis that the Captain-General was in command of all forces when the Sovereign himself did not command, and commanders-in-chief were deputed for territories (even within the U.K.) distant from headquarters.[3] The assertion remains unsupported by any officially formulated statement of difference in function or power, and it is probably safe to say that a Captain-General was always Commander-in-Chief, but a commander-in-chief (e.g. of an overseas theatre) was not, of course, necessarily Captain-General.

Monk was given authority to raise, arm, muster, apportion, quarter, and pay the army, fix the establishment, issue officers' commissions, promulgate Articles of War, disperse and pardon rebels, and sign warrants for expenditure of money or stores—a much greater accretion of power than any Commander-in-Chief

---

[1] Clode, ii, p. 256. Nor was his partner, the Quartermaster-General (first appointed for England in 1704).

[2] Walton, p. 616.   [3] Clode, ii, pp. 256, 257, 690, 694, 695.

has, by virtue of his office, had since.[1] On Monk's death the appointment lapsed until 1678, when Monmouth was designated, but with more restricted powers, although titled Captain-General.[2] James II, first appointed on Monmouth's disgrace in 1679, followed the example set by Charles II, and acted as his own Commander-in-Chief, when he, in turn, came to the throne. Like most other tasks which he undertook, he fulfilled this one enthusiastically, and even supervised personally the drilling of the army.[3] William III in his turn held the office himself, but in his absence from England in 1690 he appointed Churchill Lieutenant-General of all the forces in England. The future Marlborough's title was not quite accurate as he also commanded the English contingent in Holland where he was reputed to have made the British troops the best in Waldeck's army.[4] Whether he would have been able, in face of William's fractious Parliament, to rescue the army as a whole from its appalling state we cannot tell, since, shortly afterwards, he fell into disgrace, and remained out of office until, on the outbreak of the War of the Spanish Succession, he was appointed General of all the Land Forces in the Kingdom.

Although Anne on her accession appointed the Prince Consort Lord High Admiral and Generalissimo of all Her Land Forces, she vested real control in Marlborough by appointing him Captain-General. The limitations which had been imposed since Monk's days can be gauged from the wording of the commission of 14 March 1702. He was to be Captain-General 'for the commanding, regulating, and keeping in Discipline our Troops and Land Forces':[5]

He is authorised [the commission ran] to exercise the troops, cause them to be weaponed, have musters taken as often as he thinks

[1] Walton, pp. 779–82.

[2] He was sometimes referred to as the Lord-General, a Commonwealth title which had been frequently applied to Monk.

[3] James later wrote in his autobiography that, when he heard of Monk's impending death, he 'advised His Majesty not to make anybody General in his room, for that it was too great a power and trust, as matters stood, to be put in any one body's hand not excepting even himself (i.e. James) . . . and that in time of peace there was no need of one'. Walton, p. 617.

[4] This was no mean feat, since, on his arrival, the English contingent was described as consisting of ill-paid officers, ill-conducted colonels, and sickly, listless, undisciplined, and disorderly men. Fort., p. 338.

[5] Secretary at War: Registers WO 25/3207. (*Registers WO 25*.)

fit, divide the Army into parties, regiments etc., as he thinks fit, resist invasion and repress rebellion, to fight with, kill, etc., and, at his discretion, to pardon all enemies and rebels, to hold military or martial courts at his discretion in pursuance of the Act of King William III and to exercise and execute martial law accordingly.[1]

He thus had no longer the power to raise forces, nor to control money or stores. The expenditure of money Marlborough did, in fact, influence through Godolphin, and allocation of stores he directed by virtue of his office of Master-General of the Ordnance. In this way, he could overcome the difficulty by which the Commander-in-Chief was instructed to 'cause' the troops 'to be weaponed', although their arms were issued by the Board of Ordnance on a warrant signed by a Secretary of State.[2] The authority to hold 'military or martial courts at his discretion' was neither as wide nor as particular as it might seem. The holding of courts martial in the kingdom was restricted by the Mutiny Acts and Common Law. On the other hand, every commander-in-chief had powers, under the Articles of War, to hold courts in his overseas theatre. This power was claimed (despite Parliament's gratuitous 'granting' of it in 1713)[3] under Common Law, and given to commanders under the Great Seal.[4]

Marlborough received £10 per day basic pay as Commander of the English Forces,[5] but had, of course, various perquisites such as £1,500 equipage money (compare £3,000 for a commander-in-chief in Portugal and £5,000 for Ormonde when he went to Flanders),[6] apart from his pay as Allied Commander-in-Chief from the Dutch, and as Ambassador.[7] The continental tradition—not observed in its entirety—was to have, in addition to this, or partly out of it, 'a sumptuous table, sumpter horses, waggons, even mistresses, actors, poets, painters, and historians'.[8] Peterborough's baggage in Spain included 17 wag-

---

[1] *Dom. Cal.*, i, p. 6.   [2] Clode, ii, p. 325.
[3] Cap. 4: 'The Queen may continue Articles of War beyond the seas, except in Ireland, as in time of war.'
[4] SP Mil. 41/4: opinion of Attorney-General, 21 Jan. 1712.
[5] *Journals Commons*, xiv, 19 Nov. 1703.   [6] *Treas. Cal.*, iv, pp. 368-9.
[7] The commander-in-chief of the expedition on Ormonde's early Peninsular campaign received only £2 per day. Ormonde himself no doubt recouped any losses from the further £600 allowed for 'extraordinary charges' when he succeeded Marlborough. Ibid., p. 641. Argyll in Spain had £20,000 per annum.
[8] *Marlborough: His Life and Times*, W. S. Churchill (London, 1938), vol. i, p. 472. (*Churchill.*)

gons, over 50 mules, and several valuable horses—a total value of approximately £8,000, or perhaps £80,000 at 1965 prices. The more frugal Marlborough, in spite of his 'pilgrim bottles, silver vessels, coach with six horses' and a special staff of servants with stewards and controllers, all paid for by him, curtailed the traditional equipage considerably.[1] His allowance on appointment as General of Infantry, Commander-in-Chief of all the English Forces in the United Provinces, and Ambassador Extraordinary and Plenipotentiary included, however, says Edwards: 5,893 oz. of white plate; 1,066 oz. gilt plate from the Jewel House; £1,500 for his equipage; £100 per week for his 'ordinary entertainment' plus whatever he thought necessary for secret service. The last item must be treated with reserve in view of the later disputes over the use of the famous bread perquisite.[2] By present day standards he did not live austerely, but he confined his entertaining as a rule to his small staff of Cadogan, Cardonnel, and Hare. He himself shared a considerable part of his troops' hardships. This may have been due as much to his well-known prudence in money matters as to any idea of 'living hard' to encourage the troops. The latter conception would probably have rung strange to most officers (and soldiers) of Marlborough's day.

The English Government did not interfere with Marlborough's strategy in Flanders. Other overseas commands received, and frequently requested, fairly close instructions. Even Peterborough, for example, frequently wrote home for advice—which he seldom took. As the war wore on, however, Marlborough felt the pin-pricks of obstructionism, particularly in the field of promotion. He felt that he himself was not in as secure a position as a general waging a considerable war ought to be, and that his post was in danger of becoming a political bargaining counter. Committing the first political blunder of his career, he proposed, in order to keep the army above politics, that he be appointed Captain-General for life. This suggestion could never, of course, be countenanced in Britain, particularly in an England which still shuddered slightly at the mention of

---

[1] *Life of the Duke of Marlborough*, J. W. Fortescue (London, 1932), p. 34. (*Fort. Marl.*)

[2] *A Short Life of Marlborough*, H. J. and E. A. Edwards (London, 1926), p. 103 (quoting Wolseley). (*Edwards.*)

the name Cromwell. He was firmly rebuffed, and the lesson rubbed in by his dismissal, just over a year later.

Ormonde, his successor, was commissioned on 1 January 1712 as Commander-in-Chief of all the British Forces in the Netherlands (the Allies refused him as an over-all commander-in-chief) and Commander-in-Chief of 'all and singular our Land Forces employed or to be employed in this part of our Kingdom of Great Britain called England'.[1] On 26 February 1712, he was further commissioned as Captain-General of all the British forces at home and abroad.[2] On 18 June of that year, Rivers was appointed to be Commander-in-Chief in Britain during Ormonde's absence abroad.[3]

On the accession of George I, Marlborough returned to his high office, but his tenure was largely nominal, and it was not until the Duke of York's appointment over a century later that the Commander-in-Chief again played any considerable part in the life of the country.

STAFF OFFICERS

An officer not subordinate to the Captain-General was the Judge-Advocate-General. He was appointed to ensure the execution of the powers of the Crown under the Mutiny Act, but later the convention was to be established that he gave up office with each change of the administration, so that it was hard to term it a strictly judicial office.[4] In origin it dated back considerably before the standing army, and was originally filled by a lawyer. There was normally one Judge-Advocate-General for England, one for Ireland, and a Deputy in the Channel Islands.[5] In the warrant of 20 April 1709 he is described as Advocate-General and Judge-Martial, which would seem to combine effectively the conceptions of an officer taking up and laying down office with change of governments, and at the same time

---

[1] Dalton, vi, p. 18; SP Mil. 41/4. He was at the same time given Marlborough's colonelcy in the 1st Foot Guards. Dalton, vi, p. 50.   [2] Ibid.

[3] Ibid. So the commission is worded, but on 11 June 1712, Webb, of the famous Lille convoy, was appointed Commander-in-Chief of all forces in England. This is a particularly curious appointment as it appears in Dalton's Register under 'non-regimental commissions' (vi, p. 193), but not under 'general officers' commissions' (vi, pp. 17–18). Such commissions are normally entered in both. On appointment, Webb was appointed Lieutenant-General, and it is possible the commission signifies a distinction between England and Great Britain.

[4] Clode, ii, p. 359.   [5] Walton, p. 552.

having restricted judicial functions.[1] His subordinates in the various theatres were known as Deputy Judge-Advocates-General, or Judge-Advocates.[2] These officers, while representing the legal powers of the Crown and acting as the commanders' legal advisers or experts, carried out over a wide field many of those duties concerning discipline which we envisage as falling to 'A' Branch. It was their task to prepare the Articles of War (the disciplinary code for troops), and to organize courts martial as required. It was their duty to investigate cases, and bring to trial suspected offenders, but the actual prosecution before the court had passed by this time to the appropriate town majors or unit adjutants or quartermasters.[3] The Judge-Advocates' independence of the commanders-in-chief with whom they were serving makes more understandable the superficially curious arrangement by which they were frequently also Commissaries of Musters, for these, too, were officers whose responsibilities and loyalties were envisaged as lying to a superior authority outside the theatre in which they were serving.

Originally, the Commissariat had been responsible for the moving, feeding, and foraging of the army, and for the raising, maintaining, and issuing of all supplies of money, provisions, transport, or (in the field only) munitions. Its chief, the High Treasurer, had under him Commissaries-General who governed the provost-, carriage-, pay-, and muster-masters, the commissaries, contractors for victuals and clothing, and the captain of the pioneers. He also consulted with the Master of the Ordnance on the issue of powder and the provision of munitions. After the Restoration, the High Treasurer's powers fell away considerably, and by Anne's time he had no control over ordnance or pay. The other services split up into a number of independent departments, with no acknowledged co-ordinating chief, although on active service the Commissary-General might be held vaguely responsible for them. In Charles I's and the parliamentary armies, Commissary-General had been not merely a titular rank, but an officer in actual command. The Commissary-General of Horse, for example, appears to have stood in the same regard to the cavalry as the Major-General of Foot stood

---

[1] SP Mil. 44/173/89.
[2] *Treas. Cal.*, iii, p. 396; Ests. WO 24–75.
[3] Walton, p. 551.

to the infantry. It seems unlikely, however, that the Commissaries-General of the Musters or of Victualling (added later)
ever held command, although they were undoubtedly given
their due precedence as staff officers. After the Restoration,
potentially lucrative military appointments tended, by sale and
by their presentation to courtiers as rewards, to fall into civilian
hands. One of those which was thus transferred was that of
Commissary-General. While, however, the holder thus lost military command, he still retained his precedence in military
courts and council.[1] By Anne's time, the Commissary-General
of the Musters, or Muster-Master-General, had, as an independent officer, the duty of passing the muster rolls which showed
the officers and men of regiments for whom the Paymaster was
to issue pay. The rolls were checked on the spot, at musters, by
his muster-masters, or commissaries of the musters[2] who had
military status and were subject to military law. Through these
muster-masters the Commissary-General of the Musters was
responsible for seeing the ranks were kept up to establishment,
equipment kept in good order, leave periods not exceeded, and
so on. The muster-masters also administered the oath of allegiance, and read any royal proclamations the soldiers had to
hear.[3] While the Commissary of the Musters, or Muster-Master,
was appointed as a Treasury watchdog, he nevertheless appears,
at least when not combining his duties with those of Judge-
Advocate, to have been for some purposes 'under command' of
the general with whom he was serving. Fortescue, for example,
states that, as an integral part of the Headquarters staff, there
were added to his duties in 1664 those of Scoutmaster, or head
of the Intelligence. I have been unable to find any conclusive
evidence concerning their performance of these duties during
the war. It seems unlikely that Marlborough at least, with his
highly developed appreciation of the value of intelligence,
would delegate responsibility for it to any of the breed. It seems
probable that, at times, partly no doubt due to the old tradition

[1] Walton, pp. 631–5.

[2] The pamphleteer M. P. Hutcheson, writing at the time, classified the Commissary of the Musters as a 'warrant officer' by which he appears to have meant
an officer over the normal establishment authorized by, presumably, a royal
warrant. The latter interpretation is in accordance with the conception of his
responsibility lying not to the theatre commander, but to an 'outside authority'.

[3] Walton, pp. 642–3.

of commissariat responsibility, the Muster-Master was given other administrative duties.

The Paymaster-General, whose responsibility it was to issue money in gross to the regiments, and whose office has been dealt with separately, ranked immediately above the Commissary-General of the Musters.

With the exception of the Office of Ordnance, the Paymaster, and the somewhat tenuous control by the Judge-Advocate-General, there was little in the way of direction or organization of the various theatres from Britain. Each expedition had its own commander-in-chief, who, partly because Marlborough, the Captain-General, was committed in one theatre, and partly because of the rudimentary ideas of control and 'channels of correspondence', had direct access to the Lord Treasurer, the Secretaries of State, the Board of Ordnance, the Board of General Officers, the Secretary at War, the Privy Council, or indeed to the Sovereign herself. Although given little in the way of money, supplies, or even men, these commanders received considerable powers of organization, discipline, and promotion —Peterborough's warrant of 3 March 1705, when he set out on the Spanish expedition, authorized him to publish 'such rules and ordinances as he thought fit', to punish infractions by death, and, later, to make awards to deserving persons.[1] Each commander-in-chief had under him his general officers[2] to whom he

[1] *H.M.C.H. of L.*, vii, pp. 361–2.
[2] The following list of general officers at Malplaquet is given as an example:

Generals 1; staff lieutenant-generals 7; major-generals 3 (plus Macartney as a volunteer—cashiered early in 1709 for 'disgraceful conduct', but allowed to sell his regiment, and was present at Malplaquet as an unpaid volunteer—certainly one of the highest ranking in history [Dalton, vi, p. 302]); brigadier-generals 7; adjutant-generals 1.

Included in the staff were the following:

Aides-de-camp 8; secretary to the Captain-General 1; quartermaster-general 1; deputy quartermaster-general 1; deputy judge-advocate 1; waggon-master-general 1; physician-general 1; surgeon-general 1; provost marshal-general 1; chaplain-general 1; brigade-majors 5.

It is not possible to be dogmatic on the allocation of general officers to 'global' as distinct from theatre command. While Marlborough, for example, does appear at times on the Flanders establishment, that of 1712, for instance, appears to debit him and his three aides-de-camp, secretary, chaplain, physician, and surgeon to Guards and Garrisons. In these estimates there were a Physician and a Surgeon 'to the Forces', as well as Marlborough's personal attendants, and besides Cadogan as Quartermaster-General there are two Adjutants-General—presumably one for each wing. The Secretary at War appears under Guards, Garrisons, and Independent

delegated certain of his powers. The titles 'general' and 'major-general' are abbreviations of colonel-general and sergeant-major-general. Lieutenant-general (first introduced in British formations in 1673) is self-explanatory. All staff officers, other than subordinates such as aides-de-camp or other assistants, but including such as the Provost Master-General and Commissary-General, appeared in the estimates as 'general officers of the army'.[1]

The Adjutant-General bore to his general commanding the same relation as an adjutant bore to his colonel—the title 'adjutant' means simply assistant. He relieved him of 'the more laborious details of his duties and (provided) the medium of contact with the troops on any matter of discipline generally or of tactical movement'.[2] The office is classed by Clode[3] as of 'great antiquity', and is probably the next oldest post after Scoutmaster-General, but its first appearance in the Standing Army was in 1673, and even then it disappeared until shortly after 1680.[4]

A theatre commander's principal staff officer was his Quarter-master-General, an office first instituted in 1689, before when most of his duties were divided between the Scoutmaster-General and the Provost Master-General. Any such definition, however, is as misleading as the title itself is to modern ears. Cadogan, for example, when we allow for the closer personal control of the battle exercised by the commander himself in those days, was certainly more approximate to a Chief of Staff than a Quartermaster-General as we know it. The Quarter-master-General inherited, in some fields, the tasks of the High Marshal, and, so far as construction of the camp was concerned, went into considerable detail. Cadogan, however, also under-took many intelligence tasks, and, on occasion, independent command. On the battlefield he acted alongside Marlborough.

The forces in the field were normally organized in wings, each with its General of Infantry and General of Cavalry, normally lieutenant-generals in rank, and appearing in the estab-

Companies. Erle was Lieutenant-General in South Britain, and Leven Lieutenant-General in North Britain. *Journals Commons*, xvii, 29 Feb. 1712.

[1] Walton, p. 618.   [2] Ibid., p. 623.

[3] Clode, ii, p. 341.

[4] Walton, p. 621.

lishments as 'general officers of the army'.[1] Each of these had a major-general to assist him, while the Commander-in-Chief had his own staff of aides-de-camps and six to ten general officers without command. The figure for general officers on the staff varied with the expedition and depended to a certain extent on the pressure which the commander-in-chief in question could bring to bear, and the co-operation he received from the Treasury. In the 1711 campaign, for example, there was no General of Horse. He was reappointed for the 1712 campaign, but, when the war finished in that year, Parliament refused to ratify any such appointments of general officers to the staff.[2] Marlborough's headquarters staff consisted of his aides-de-camp, his Quarter-master-General, Provost Marshal, Chaplain-General, Physician-General, Surgeon-General, and Waggon-Master-General. His artillery and engineer advisers were in the train.[3] There is no specific mention of Ordnance Officers other than those in the train. As it was the custom for other large-scale expeditions to have an Ordnance Staff Officer,[4] the appointment may have been omitted because either of the proximity of the Board in England, or Marlborough's own post of Master-General. A commander's aides-de-camp had a function to fulfil on the battlefield in addition to those normally associated with the post today. They were his liaison officers to carry his orders to subordinate generals and brigadiers. They were not his only liaison officers—for example, Cadogan was thus employed at Ramillies as one of the eight required to draw Orkney off from his cross-river attack—but they were his first and normal.

The Waggon-Master-General was an important member of the staff. The successor to Elizabeth's Carriage-Master, he controlled vehicles and animals on the march, and no load could move without his orders. Any which strayed without his permission were liable to the penalty of plundering on the spot, even if, in theory at least, they belonged to the Commander-in-

---

[1] As was the case with many appointments, these officers in Flanders were frequently designated as though they were part of a General Headquarters with 'global' command.

[2] Treas. 1/154: Secretary at War, 19 Feb. 1712; SP Mil. 41/4: Establishment of 5 Apr. 1712; *Treas. Cal.*, iv, p. 518: Board of General Officers' Minute reference Stair's letter of 22 Oct. 1713.

[3] Dalton's figures for Malplaquet at vi, pp. 299–300.

[4] e.g. Lieutenant-General of Ordnance in Portugal. *Dom. Cal.*, ii, pp. 396–8.

Chief. As the chief of the transport train, it was his duty to attend the commander-in-chief or general of division (or the officer deputed by the commander) every morning and evening in order to receive instructions and consult with him on the movements of the following day. He had two lieutenants or deputies, and under them there were waggon-masters with each regiment. Sometimes these waggon-masters were officers attached to the regiments, and sometimes sergeants or corporals of the regiments, specially detailed for this duty. Once so detailed they were subject exclusively to the Waggon-Master-General and owned no other authority, just as, so long as the regiment was on the march, its baggage and munitions were exclusively at the disposal of the Waggon-Master and his staff.[1] It is recorded that on William's Irish campaign of 1690, the Waggon-Master-General was for the first time instructed to take his orders daily through the Quartermaster- General instead of direct from the Commander-in-Chief.[2] The procedure which was followed in Anne's time appears to have depended on the theatre, the commander, and the circumstances of the case.

The Provost Marshal, apart from his disciplinary duties of custody of prisoners, carried out the more detailed tasks of Elizabeth's High Marshal, but did not, of course, have the status of the High Marshal. He controlled the execution of justice, the internal construction and organization of camps, and the operation of the order of march. He also had to supervise the foraging parties, a duty carried out in Tudor times by the Forage-Master.[3] There was a Provost Marshal-General in Britain in charge of the Marshalsea and Savoy prisons, where he seems also to have had occasional responsibilities in connexion with the custody of recruits, but he had no powers over the provost marshals abroad.

Each expedition included also its surgeons, apothecaries, and physicians on the staff. The Surgeon and Apothecary-General on the British Establishment do not appear to have exercised any technical or professional control over their colleagues abroad, although they performed certain minor (but perhaps profitable) functions such as inspecting medicines destined for overseas.

[1] Walton, pp. 700–1.   [2] Ibid., p. 704.
[3] *Elizabeth's Army*, C. G. Cruickshank (London, 1946), p. 37. (*Cruickshank.*)

I have nowhere seen an appointment to Scoutmaster-General during Anne's reign, and it may be that the office was dropped in 1689 on the creation of that of Quartermaster-General. It dated back to at least 1518, for there is in existence a document of that date giving his duties of intelligence and reconnaissance. Included in his reconnaissance duties was the allocation of quarters.[1]

A post which in Britain did continue in existence—with no apparent justification, for there were no duties attached—was that of Drum-Major-General. It was held by one man (on behalf of another of the same name) from 1689 till 1705. Whether confusion over this led to the belief that stern measures would be required to move him one cannot say, but he was, at any rate, murdered in 1706.[2]

The subsidiary staff officers in the field included a floating population of commissaries—in addition to the frequent Commissary-General—of War, of Provisions, of Transports, or for the Exchange of Prisoners of War.[3] Some were military, some civilian, and they had to cope with a considerable diversity of tasks. Captain Jacques Frances, Baron de Bette, for example, appointed in 1706 as Commissary of Troops in English and the States' Pay in Italy, was responsible for 'subsistence, pay, deliveries of bread, forage, and other necessaries, and the inspection of hospitals'. In the event of any 'malversation, neglect, or other cause of complaint', he was to report to the Generals and Commissaries of War. He was in addition to report to Marlborough 'from time to time' in his spare moments, no doubt.[4] He should have been able to exchange an interesting tale with one of Cadogan's assistants, Captain Richard King, who was a captain of infantry, assistant-quartermaster-general, and ordnance stores officer, besides serving at intervals with the artillery batteries.[5] Originally a captain in the Royal Scots Fusiliers, but a gunner by training, he drew £100 a year as a skilled engineer, and was attached to Cadogan as Assistant Quartermaster-General. At the siege of Menin, he brought forward the victuals,

[1] Walton, pp. 621, 624. [2] Dalton, v, pp. 155, 160.
[3] The Train had its own commissaries—from whom descended the appointment of the same name in the Royal Army Ordnance Corps.
[4] Murray, ii, p. 5.
[5] *Historical and Military Essays*, J. W. Fortescue (London, 1928), pp. 177–8. (*Fort. Hist.*)

and, with great difficulty, the guns and ammunition. Thereafter he did duty in the trenches as an engineer, and then in the batteries as a gunner. Finally, while serving with his regiment of foot, he snatched a moment to write to an acquaintance: 'I have very little time to myself.' Few will doubt that he earned his promotion to colonel in 1710.[1]

At Brigade level, the Brigade-Major occupied the post corresponding to Adjutant-General at a higher level, or Adjutant in a unit. In the regiments of horse and battalions of foot, there were present in command lieutenant-colonels, and over the companies and troops there were captains. The appointment of major was firmly established. Originally the title had been sergeant-major, with the duties a combination of those carried out by the second-in-command, adjutant, and sergeant-major of today. He was the medium of communication from commander to unit. He received and distributed into their proper channels all orders, detailed parties and guards, visited and inspected these, drilled and exercised the regiment, and was responsible for order on the march, and for ensuring that the men were allocated their quarters or properly tented.[2] The office of aide-major, or adjutant, had been created in 1661, and on him had devolved much of the detail of the major's duties, just as since then much has in turn passed to the sergeant-major.[3]

Already, too, the retentive breed of lieutenant-quartermaster had made its appearance. Until at most thirty years before the war, the quartermaster had been a warrant-officer unless he also held in his own personal right a combatant commission. The only exceptions were in the Life and Horse Guards where he ranked as a junior captain. Even in those days, however, 'the office must have been a highly respectable one . . . and a fairly remunerative one, to judge by the style of men seeking it, often officers on full or half pay'.[4] His duties were the distribution of quarters or billets, the receipt and distribution of regimental supplies and stores, including arms and clothing, and frequently the duties of Provost Marshal within the unit. He was no longer responsible for the receipt of pay from the colonel's clerk nor for its distribution.[5]

---

[1] *Fort. Hist.*, pp. 188–9, 190; Dalton, v, footnote 2, p. 8.
[2] Walton, p. 408.   [3] Walton, pp. 15, 408.
[4] Walton, p. 412.   [5] Walton, p. 413.

In static garrisons there was the post of Town Major, corresponding to a Brigade Major in the field. Since England was a country of garrisons rather than mobile forces, it is a considerably older title than that of Brigade Major, or indeed of Adjutant. In very large garrisons he might have a Town Aide Major to assist him, and this was also the title given to the officer occupying the corresponding post in a small station.[1]

MILITARY SECRETARY'S BRANCH

Queen Anne's armies had no staff officer corresponding to the present-day Military Secretary, whose office dates only from 1795.[2] The old-style Secretary at War, and Cardonnel, Secretary to the Commander-in-Chief, could conceivably be described as military secretaries, but they were essentially secretaries in the civilian sense. The role of the Commander-in-Chief's secretary, in particular, approximated to that of the Personal or Military Assistant of today. Of the present-day functions of the Military Secretary, military honours and awards (except for bounties) did not then exist, and senior promotions were handled for the most part by the commander in person.

Largely because of the system of purchase and the conception of regiments as personal property, commanding officers had, either in peace or war, a control over promotion within their regiments which they possess today only in wartime, and subject, even then, to limitations. There were conventions concerning seniority, but within these limits the colonels had a wide discretion which they utilized to the full. Promotion was, of course, theoretically the Queen's prerogative. For the higher ranks she reserved the right of at least formal assent. The extent to which her influence (or that of her political advisers) was made felt depended on the Commander-in-Chief's relations with her and the Cabinet.

There has always been a strong personal tie between the army and the Sovereign, by, or on behalf of, whom every commission has customarily been signed. 'The language of that document', one historian points out, 'implies that the holder enjoys his Sovereign's especial confidence, for which reason the Sovereign directs all of the officer's subordinates to yield him due obedi-

[1] Walton, p. 627.　　　　　　　　　　　[2] Clode, ii, p. 342.

ence.' This is in contrast to the navy where the Sovereign's powers have been delegated. A naval officer holds his commission from the Board of Admiralty which directs him to obey its commands 'as you will answer the contrary at your peril'. This does not so much 'imply confidence in the bearer as convey a threat from the authority which confers the powers'.[1] Originally the colonel of a regiment forwarded his recommendations for promotion to the Secretary at War who passed them to the Sovereign. From an overseas force they would be passed through the commander-in-chief of the theatre, who sent them straight to the Sovereign. William is stated to have refused to deal with any recommendations which did not come to him through a general.[2] Commissions (usually prepared in later years by the Secretary at War) were normally issued (in the Queen's name) by one of the Secretaries of State. The records show commissions signed by the Queen, the Lord Lieutenant of Ireland, or commanders-in-chief in the field, and countersigned by the Secretary to the Cabinet, the Secretary to the Lord Lieutenant, the Secretary at War (in William's time only), Adam de Cardonnel, and other staff officers to the commander-in-chief.[3] Commanders overseas generally had the power to grant commissions. Peterborough's warrant of 31 March 1705 is only one random example, which seems to have been followed almost always in the special case of the West Indies.[4]

None of the above applied to the Ordnance Department, who remained exclusively responsible for their own commissions, which were issued by the Master-General. They were signed by him or by the Lieutenant-General, and countersigned by three other members of the Board. Ordnance commissions could be neither bought nor sold, and promotion went by seniority.[5] Indications are that the engineer and ordnance officers at least found other means of recouping themselves. A remarkable exception is the evidence of a case of purchase during the Protectorate. In 1660 Elias Palmer, the Surveyor of Ordnance, petitioned to be continued in his office because he had paid (in 1656) £750 more for his commission than he had yet received in pay, which was a year in arrears.[6]

[1] *Last Post*, pp. 20–21.   [2] Walton, p. 447.
[3] Registers WO 25/8.   [4] H.M.C.H. of L., vii, p. 361.
[5] Forbes, p. 110.   [6] Walton, p. 449, footnote 1172.

In the cavalry and infantry an officer purchased his cornet's or ensign's commission (or, in time of war, raised a regiment if he had the means), and thereafter bought his way up the scale, unless a senior was killed. He might then expect to be promoted free of charge, subject to such exceptions as the Flanders scheme under which the purchase price was paid into the widows' fund.[1] If an officer did not have the means to buy his next step, he normally remained unpromoted. There was a fairly generally recognized scale of charges (with variations between regiments), but this was indicative rather than mandatory. The author of the *Recruiting Essay* commented: '... the real cause of complaint is, to see almost all vacancies (except such as happen in battel) filled by the Almighty Power of Gold, and too often with those that never saw a Company drawn up, but as he past over the Parade to take out the Commission.'[2] This was undoubtedly due in part to the conduct implied by his further remarks: 'I believe several commanders of Regiments despise a gratuity for any commission (above an ensign's especially) with the same scorn and contempt, as the most nice and virtuous lady would a sordid bribe of gold, that should be offerred to corrupt her chastity.' The same author, however, set a limit to his criticisms: 'Whatever the Personal Folies and Extravagancies of some . . . have been, yet, I never could learn that any of 'em were ever so much as accused of betraying their Trust, either in the late or present War; and wish the same could be said of all the officers of the Fleet.'

Even if the officers were guilty of no betrayal in the field, and the actual buying and selling of commissions was not a corrupt practice, the opportunities for bribery laid the system open to criticism. That certain decencies were expected to be observed may be deduced from an official advertisement published in the *London Gazette* of 19 October 1711:

---

[1] An interesting example of promotion from the ranks which did not entail purchase was that of the 'thirty able and experienced serjeants . . . whose experience in military affairs have inclined Us to employ them in our Service on the foot of Ensign's Pay'. They were sent on the 1711 North American expedition as lieutenants—perhaps because it was not a very popular campaign with others. SP Mil. 41/3; Granville, 15 Feb. 1711; Ests. WO 24/75, 12 Jan. 1711 and 24/75/29. They would have commended themselves to Mother Ross, who declared: 'I think it more becoming the character of a soldier to gain a commission by his bravery than to purchase one with money.'

[2] *The Recruiting Essay*. By A Lover of His Country and the Army (London, 1707). (*Recruiting Essay*.)

Whereas a scandalous advertisement has been twice published in the 'Post Boy', 'That whoever has a mind to treat about the purchasing commissions in the Army, either in our regiments or others, might apply themselves to Mr. Pyne, at his coffee-house under Scotland Yard Gate, near Whitehall, and they should be further informed about it,' which being directly contrary to Her Majesty's express will and pleasure, some time since declared and signified, as well at home as to all her Generals abroad, against the sale of commissions upon any account whatsoever; it is thought fit to give this public notice to prevent any abuses or impositions that might happen therefrom; and whoever shall discover to Her Majesty's Secretary at War at his office in Whitehall the authors of the said advertisement, shall have due protection and encouragement.[1]

Prohibitions against sale were, in fact, almost hardy annuals. The Mutiny Act of 1695 contained a clause compelling officers to take an oath before their commission could be registered that they had not paid anyone for it.[2] The custom was, if not of recent growth, of recent revival. There were those who remembered, or were at least aware, that Cromwell's not unsuccessful officers owed nothing to the 'Almighty Power of Gold'. Although it was nigh to high treason to suggest that anything done by Oliver was right, the example could not be erased. The industrious producer of the *Recruiting Essay* had this to say of the officers of Almanza: '. . . if their conduct was not every way answerable to their courage, I don't see to what cause it may be so justly attributed as the buying and selling commissions', and later discoursed on officers who 'cannot relieve a guard without raising the merry glee of spectators'.

On the other hand, the mark of the Protectorate beast was the professional army, apropos of which a much later constitutional authority's comment was:

The pay of the officer cannot be looked upon—having regard to the purchase of his commission—in any other light than as 'honorarium', clearly indicating the policy of employing men of independent means—not mere professional officers—in the military service of the Crown. 'It is the promotion by purchase', wrote the Duke of Wellington, 'which brings into the Service men of fortune and character—men who have some connection with the interests and fortunes of the country, besides the commissions which they hold

[1] Clode, ii, p. 608.
[2] 7 & 8 Wm. III, cap. 93, quoted at Walton, p. 453.

from His Majesty. It is this circumstance which exempts the British Army from the character of being a "mercenary army" . . . three fourths of the whole number receive but little for their service besides the honour of serving the King'.[1]

Fortescue commented with slightly less pomposity that the system:

. . . was economical, for an officer's pay little exceeded the interest on the price of his commission; it was secure, for every officer was practically bound over to good behaviour in the price of his commission which was forfeited if he were cashiered; and it was convenient, for it assured a steady flow of promotion. But the most weighty point is that it made colonels not only commanders, but proprietors of their regiments, captains not only commanders but proprietors of their companies. Each regiment was, in fact, a little independent and self-contained possession. The colonel was supreme. Its financial, physical, and moral requirements were entrusted to three of his servants, namely the agent, the surgeon, and the chaplain. The military law which he meted out had as yet no statutory sanction.[2]

It was not a risk-free venture even considered exclusively from the point of view of finance. Desertion, for instance, might completely ruin an officer engaged on recruiting. Levy money was payable only on first raising or drafting, so that, in the event of desertion, the officer had to pay from his own pocket.

Whatever the failings or the wider issues involved (Marlborough himself favoured the system of purchase as a means of protecting the army from Parliament), there were too many vested interests to permit a speedy change to be seriously considered. The Government itself had one of the heavier stakes in the form of deductions from sale price for the Paymaster, and 12d. in the £ from either party for Chelsea Hospital. The prohibition to the Secretary of State not to issue a commission until the Paymaster had certified that his deduction had been made was renewed in the Royal Warrant of 1 April 1712, twenty-eight years after its first publication, and a year after being re-emphasized in the Regulations for the Better Government of the Forces.[3] Straightforward purchase may appear, in fact, a

---

[1] Clode, i, p. 106. [2] *Last Post*, pp. 13–19.
[3] SP Mil. 44/69; Dalton, v, p. 379. Purchasers (or other recipients) of commissions had not finished paying at this stage. Secretaries normally had their own fees in addition—e.g. Cardonnel, for each commission passed by Marlborough,

more wholesome transaction than the scramble which took place for a killed man's place. Blackader tells of the chicanery and canvassing that took place before a dead commanding officer was cold on the battlefield. It was not only a question of qualified men having to outmanœuvre their rivals, but: 'They do not think a man deserves any post in the army, who either gives himself any rest or any other about him, general or other, till he gets what he is seeking.' He commented, when in expectation of Cranstoun's post: 'I commit all to God. I know promotion comes not from the east or the west. I leave myself in thy hands, O Lord, to dispose of me as thou seest fit.' He was, nevertheless, on the spot, rendering the Lord a little assistance by putting in his claim the day after he had 'viewed the dead' of Malplaquet. Four years earlier, when awaiting his promotion to major (consequent on his Brigadier's death) he had consoled himself: 'I must confess I am grown weary of living in the tents of wickedness, in a place of so much profanity as an army is....'[1]

There were occasions when a commander might interfere even in regimental matters. A striking example of such concerned the Scots Brigade (where there was no purchase of promotion)[2] in 1703. Although the Brigade was in the Dutch service,[3] Cardonnel wrote to Brigadier Lauder[4] on 26 July:

My Lord Duke of Marlborough having been informed that you have recommended a stranger to be major to your regiment preferably to several other officers who are much his seniors and have deserved encouragement for their good service; and his Grace being sensible of the Queen's intention to preserve the six regiments entire in the Scotch nation, and how much concerned her Majesty would be that any foreigner should be preferred in these regiments to the prejudice of her own subjects; his Grace, in friendship to you, commands me to acquaint you therewith before any representation be made in England which might occasion her Majesty's commands to

had £6. 7s. 6d. from colonels, lieutenant-colonels, majors, and captains; £5. 7s. 6d. from lieutenants; £3. 7s. 6d. from a cornet of horse; and £2. 7s. 6d. from cornets of dragoons or ensigns. *Journals Commons*, xvii, 19 Feb. 1712.

[1] *The Life and Diary of Lieutenant Colonel John Blackader*, Andrew Crichton (Edinburgh, 1824), from Busse, 7 Nov. 1705, p. 267. (*Blackader*.)

[2] *Papers Illustrating the History of the Scots Brigade*, James Ferguson (Edinburgh, 1899), vol. i, pp. xxiv–xxv. (*Scots Brigade*.)

[3] The general officers of the staff, however, also held commissions from Queen Anne. Dalton, vi, p. 298.

[4] The only regiment in the Brigade which was 'diluted' to any great extent by the admission of non-Scots.

his Grace to make application to the States in her name for prevention thereof.[1]

Which shows a solicitude for the susceptibilities of the Scotch nation not, it is often alleged, present in these later enlightened days.

In an intriguing case which called down the intervention of the Board of General Officers, a sub-brigadier in the Horse Guards was found to have been previously sentenced to death for horse-stealing. Being ruled 'so infamous' that he could not be allowed to remain in the regiment, he was given £350 for his troop.[2] Other cases of interference were when the commanding general stepped in to force the sale of commissions of persistent absentees. In this, Marlborough struck on occasion at Ordnance officers, who, although not allowed to sell their Ordnance places, frequently also held infantry companies. The Board of Ordnance itself fought hard in 1711 to prevent the allocation of a company of gunners to Colonel Pendlebury, as other field officers, they considered, would follow suit, and thus discourage junior officers.[3]

Higher promotion was never completely sheltered from the winds of politics, but Marlborough showed no tendency, from his earliest years, to political favouritism. He had, as Commander-in-Chief, a fairly free run for some time. His dispatches up till about 1708 contain lists of general officers to be promoted and officers to be commissioned, with the covering letters in the tone of almost a routine matter and giving details of dates both for ranks and pay and allowances. In that year there is the first whisper of a change when, in a letter to Walpole, he 'hopes His Royal Highness will approve dating all commissions 1st May to avoid disputes'. After the Jack Hill fracas, with the Queen and the Captain-General in open disagreement, political influence was paramount. Harley's friends were given leave to absent themselves when they wished without permission from the Commander-in-Chief, Argyll was favoured with an independent command, and Orrery (who had openly alleged that Marlborough was using his power 'only to create a faction') was promoted in place of one of the three generals cashiered for an ambiguous toast. In 1710 the Government created, in effect, a

[1] Murray, i, p. 151.　　　　　　　　　　　　　[2] PGO WO 71/1.
[3] Ord. Letters WO 46/6.

military secretary's committee when they set up a special board under Ormonde (later to be Marlborough's successor) to deal with all questions of promotion. Among its first acts was to dismiss all the Commander-in-Chief's brigadiers, but it would not move as fast as desired by Harley, who wished all general officers to hold annual tenures, and no one but the Queen to dispose of regiments.[1] Harley's inertness, on the other hand, has been advanced as the cause of the failure of the scheme of 1713 by which Ormonde wished to compel Hanoverian officers to sell out. A plausible reason for setting up the board, whose real purpose was to cripple Marlborough's power, was to try to clear up the considerable confusion and ill-feeling over brevets. Although promotion to what we would term substantive rank was, in the last resort, the Queen's prerogative, local or 'brevet' rank was at the discretion of theatre commanders. Once an officer obtained brevet rank, however, he used it to claim seniority over others who, perhaps, served in a theatre where the commander was not so liberal with his brevets. The answer, apart from the prohibition of brevets, which was ordered without avail several times, was a central over-all authority on promotions. The slighting of Marlborough by setting up his own juniors as a board over him was, in part, another consequence of having the nominal Commander-in-Chief campaigning in one of the theatres.

The number of brevets granted up to 1 January 1707, exclusive of the marine regiments, was 214, made up as follows:

By Marlborough	129
In England	58
In Spain	27[2]

Marlborough, who, like many commanders, frequently preferred to get himself given an unpleasant order rather than impose it apparently on his own initiative, wrote in the following year to Walpole to have the Queen give orders against the further issue of brevets. He mentioned specifically about that time the undesirability of giving a *lieutenant-colonel's* brevet to *captain* the Lord Tarpichen, or the grant of a second major's brevet in the Coldstream Guards 'as it will only tend to create new

---

[1] *Cambridge Modern History* (Cambridge, 1908), vol. v, p. 470. (*Cambridge.*)
[2] Dalton, v, pp. 165–7; vi, p. 199.

disputes'. In the second case, his further comment showed the confusion into which ranks had fallen. 'Besides *Colonel* Hollins having a commission of *brigadier*', he wrote, 'does nowise exempt him from his duty of *major*, there are older *captains* in the first regiment to whom it would be a prejudice when they come to roll together.' Brevets were prohibited 'on any account or pretext whatsoever' under a Royal Order of 12 July 1708,[1] and again under the Regulations for the Better Government of the Forces dated 1 May 1711, but, for all that, 246 were granted between 1707 and 1714. Marlborough signed four, Spain and Portugal produced thirty-nine; and there were a few in Ireland, the West Indies, and the North American Colonies. The largest number, remarkably enough, was at home.[2]

The order of 12 July 1708 had laid down that officers of twenty-two regiments were to do duty in their regiments in the rank for which they were receiving pay 'notwithstanding any brevet granted for superior posts or ranks' because 'the granting brevets to officers for rank in particular regiments hath proved highly prejudicial to our service in regard the same hath very much suffered for want of officers to do Duty in their respective Regiments according to the Posts for which they are Commissioned and Receive Pay'.[3] The Board of General Officers made heavy weather of a cognate case involving Brevet Major Douglas of Livesay's regiment. Major Douglas refused to march at the head of his company or to do duty as a captain, and was put under arrest by the major of the regiment. The Board ruled that he ought not to do duty as a captain, and that the major had not the power to put him in arrest for refusing to march as such, but that, nevertheless, the brevet major ought to have obeyed orders.[4] Apart from the complication of brevets, it was the custom of the service that the infantry officers should take precedence by their regiments, but cavalry officers by their date of commission, with the proviso that an officer was always bound to obey the governor of a garrison. In garrison, brigadiers of infantry took precedence over brigadiers of horse, but in the field the position was reversed. The Guards were specially

---

[1] SP Mil. 41/3/37. PGO WO 71/1. [2] Dalton, vi, pp. 176-9.

[3] Entry Books WO 26/13. Commanding officers retained their regiments while prisoners, but brevet promotions in their place were banned. SP Mil. 41/3/10; Walpole, 20 July 1708.

[4] PGO WO 71/1.

provided for. Captains of Foot Guards were given the right of command as lieutenant-colonels by William, and lieutenants of the 1st and 2nd Foot Guards were given the rank of captains.[1]

Difficulties were also encountered over ranks granted by foreign governments. Marlborough, for instance, on 24 June 1706, wrote to Hedges that he had no objection to Stanhope being commissioned a major-general by the King of Spain, but 'in justice to officers here, it should not be of force when the army returns home'. Such instances, he continued, were frequent, and he instanced Fagel who 'is contented to roll and do duty as' a lieutenant-general 'although commissioned as a Field Marshal by the King of Portugal'.[2] It was, no doubt, as a sequel to this that Hedges wrote to Peterborough on 23 July 1706: 'The Queen wishes (you) to know that no commission whatever given to any of Her Majesty's subjects by any other Prince can alter the ranks she has given them by her commission.'[3]

The Regulations for the Better Government of the Forces, despite the comprehensive title, were really a strenuous paper attempt to deal with the subject of officers' ranks.[4]

Whereas [the preamble declared], many irregularities and abuses have been introduced into our Armys to the great prejudice of our service and Discouragement of such as are Employed therein, For remedy thereof, and preventing as much as possible the like for the future and for the keeping better order and Discipline amongst our forces we have taken the same into our Royal consideration, and have thought fit hereby to establish and declare the following Rules and Orders.

The kind of 'irregularity' of which they were no doubt thinking was the case of Lieutenant Samuel Breton in 1708. He was allowed the pay of a lieutenant and all the servants in his troop from the Horse Guards, and a quartermaster was appointed to do his duties. The quartermaster was in turn replaced by a corporal, while both continued to draw their old rates of pay. In 1709, again, when Colonel Joseph Johnson resigned his commission to Marlborough's brother, Charles Churchill, he was

---

[1] Walton, pp. 444–6.
[2] Murray, ii, p. 629. [3] SP Mil. 41/3.
[4] With the exception of the significant paragraph which ordered that the Horse, Dragoon, and Grenadier Guards were to be natural born subjects, and that private gentlemen in them were 'to take oaths and tests forthwith'.

given his company for life. On his death, it was to be sold for his heirs, and the first other company to fall vacant was to go to Churchill.[1]

Under the Regulations for the Better Government, all promotions to brigadier were suspended, and no general officer or brigadier who sold his commission was to be an officer again. Clause 4 re-emphasized against brevets the order of 1708 'which has been lost'. The Board of General Officers was confirmed as the 'Court of General Officers' for which the Judge-Advocate was to summon 'only those . . . who are fit to redress grievances'. No officer was to sell his commision without the Queen's permission unless he had served twenty years, or was disabled, and the provision for 12*d*. in the £ for Chelsea from buyer and seller was repeated. Even at this stage in his career, Marlborough was able to recommend successfully certain amendments to the last clause. He asked that it apply only to commissions above captain as, if subalterns had 'run so far behind' that they could not continue in the service because, for instance, of misfortunes with recruits, the debt would fall on the regiment if the officers were not allowed to sell. Other officers left 'great families behind in starving condition'. A further instance where the rule would operate unfavourably was where a colonel wished to give a vacancy to an officer not of his own regiment. In such a case, the officers of the regiment 'might be easily satisfied with a small acknowledgement'—presumably a 'slice' of the purchase price —'and the service benefit'. Under the proposed rules the delay involved in waiting for the Sign Manual would be so great that the service would suffer.[2]

Another clause dealt with the commissioning of children, an abuse which threatened to become serious, but was, by some strange chance, stamped out. The custom is said to have started in the time of Charles II, a monarch reputed to know of a considerable number of children for whom provision was required. During William's reign, however, there were only four recorded cases, including that of William Theresa Douglas, daughter of Lieutenant-Colonel John Douglas of General Hamilton's regiment. She was a godchild of the King, who gave her his name, and ordered her the pay of a captain and a company. When the regiment was disbanded in 1714, she went on

[1] Entry Books WO 26/13.　　　　　　　　[2] Murray, v, p. 412.

half pay, and in 1717 was struck off altogether. Her father was killed in suppressing the 1715 rebellion, and William Theresa petitioned in 1718 for her 'future subsistence'. The minuted reply was: 'My Lords cannot advise anything against the rules in the Act of Parliament.'[1] In 1705 it was ruled that no one of age insufficient to serve should be admitted to a regiment except the children of officers who had been slain or suffered 'extreamly in the service'. Of those at that time qualified, there were never to be more than two in one regiment, and they were to be exchanged for officers of home regiments when their own was ordered overseas.[2] Fortescue quotes, nevertheless, a case of an officer on service in Flanders at the age of 12, and in 1708 Marlborough wrote to the Prince Consort on behalf of Lord Portmore's son, as Portmore had done good service for many years.[3] Two years earlier, the Duke had written that he had received repeated orders from the Queen against the custom. His objection to a grant in 1707 shows a nice distinction, as he commented that it ought not to be given as the proposed officer was 'not over five'. The Regulations for the Better Government ordered that no commission was to be granted in future to anyone under 16. Every colonel applying for a commission was to sign a declaration that the nominee was at least that age, and children already holding commissions were to serve as soon as they reached the age of 16, or to be cashiered. In 1711, however, Grenville wrote to the Paymaster concerning a child, Fitton Minshull, ensign in Stanwix's regiment, who had been granted his commission to support his mother and family. He was given furlough until further orders, and the Paymaster instructed to pay over to the agent, for the ensign's mother, his subsistence.[4] The custom probably died as much because of the end of the war, when the need for provision for dependants became less, as because of any orders or regulations against it.

It remains to comment briefly on a number of ranks peculiar to the Life Guards and other of the Sovereign's personal forces. A corporal of the Life Guards was commissioned as 'eldest

[1] Dalton, iv, p. xii.
[2] Entry Books WO 26/14.
[3] Fort., p. 577; Murray, iv, p. 200.
[4] Report of Commissioners Naval and Military Enquiry, p. 32, quoted at Clode, ii, p. 610.

lieutenant of Horse' or brigadier. A lance-corporal, who commanded as an officer, but held no commission, was known as a sub-brigadier.[1] A guidon held rank one grade below a cornet and took his title—of French derivation—from the pennant he bore. Others of French derivation were the Exons in the Yeomen of the Guard—otherwise exempts, sub-officers who were reserves to the captain and lieutenant. In their commissions, they were styled corporals, took it in turn to command the guard, and were exempt ordinary military duties. Captains of the Life Guards ranked as eldest colonels of horse, lieutenants as eldest majors, cornets as eldest captains, and guidons as youngest captains.[2] The Esquires of the Gentlemen of Arms ranked with captains of the army, and the Captain of the Gentlemen of Arms immediately after the Captain of the Horse Guards in waiting, and before the Captain of the Yeomen of the Guard.[3]

---

[1] Walton, pp. 416–17.　　[2] Ibid., p. 443.　　[3] Clode, i, p. 359.

III

ESTABLISHMENTS AND STRENGTHS

'I AM sure I may puzzle my brains to pieces, and not be able to make out such an account. . . . All that you can collect . . . can only be upon the best information you can get, and not from anything of your knowledge or mine.' So wrote Mr. Samuel Lynn of the Secretary at War's office on 17 December 1710, while trying to trace his troops at the behest of an angry House of Commons.[1] Although today we have information on which Mr. Lynn could not at the time lay hands, figures of strengths and establishments remain nevertheless, in many cases only estimates, and are compounded, to a greater or lesser degree, of deduction and guess-work. The forces which fought for British money were of four types:

(a) 'Subject troops', i.e. subjects of the Queen;
(b) foreign troops under commanders of their own nationality, but on establishments and at rates of pay laid down (after negotiation) in estimates formally voted by the British Parliament;
(c) foreign subsidized troops, some of whose cost was met by a lump sum paid to their monarchs;
(d) refugees, deserters, renegade prisoners, &c., under either British officers, or officers of their own nationality—on establishments and rates of pay laid down by the British.

We are here concerned with 'subject troops' only. These were voted yearly by Parliament under the following heads:

(i) Guards and Garrisons;
(ii) 'The 40,000' for Flanders;
(iii) 'The augmentation' for Flanders;
(iv) Portugal and Spain;
(v) The Ordnance vote.

[1] SP Mil. 41/3.

'SUBJECT TROOPS'

Guards and Garrisons

Strictly speaking, the only troops allowed in the country in time of peace, were those deemed necessary for attendance upon the Sovereign to guard the palace 'in an extraordinary manner from "intrusion" '. These had been allowed by continuous sanction of Parliament since the Restoration.[1] In addition, however, it was a tradition or convention, considerably older than any part of the army, that all fortified places in the country should have small forces 'indissolubly attached to them, rather to keep the buildings in order than to provide for their defence'.[2] These were the 'garrisons' of the 'guards and garrisons', and the description will be seen to have had originally rather a special connotation, akin in some ways to what we might call 'station staff' rather than 'garrison'.

'The 40,000'

On the outbreak of war, Parliament voted 40,000 men to fight alongside the Dutch in Flanders. Only 18,000 of these were to be 'subject troops', and the remainder were hired from continental princes, chiefly German.

'The Augmentation'

At the same session as Parliament voted the 40,000, it pledged itself to support any further steps the Government might take to assist the Dutch. The English ministers contracted for an additional 20,000 troops, of which the Dutch were to pay half. Three thousand of the English Government's share were 'subject troops'.

Portugal and Spain

The Peninsula represented for a time a larger establishment than Flanders, and was a much heavier drain on manpower. There was little complication in the establishment, which had fewer foreign components than the Flanders force, but there were considerable payments of subsidies to Portugal, and to the Pretender, Archduke Charles.

[1] Clode, i, pp. 363–4. [2] Fort., p. 57.

G

The Ordnance Vote

Ordnance was a peacetime as well as a war commitment, and a considerable part of the responsibility for garrisons was the Board's. It is, in fact, difficult to say precisely how many of the staffs of fortified places appeared as 'guards and garrisons' on the army estimates proper, and how many on the Ordnance vote. In time of war, the Board had also to provide the theatres' Ordnance 'trains'—artillery, engineers (both carrying a considerable proportion of civilians), and a small stores component. The Ordnance Vote was submitted separately from the army estimates and was not handled by the Secretary at War—but there may have been some overlapping in accounting for garrisons.

18,638 British troops were voted in the 1701 estimates. These were almost doubled in the following year (31,254), had climbed to nearly 50,000 in 1706, and reached their peak of just short of 75,000 in 1711. Thereafter they were steadily reduced, but some 5,000 more were authorized at the end of the reign than in 1701. The biggest reduction was in the course of 1713, when establishments were cut from 47,430 to 23,486.

FLANDERS was consistently voted 22,000 men, with an extra 4,000 odd in 1710–11. Beginning with 8,015 in 1704, the PENINSULA had climbed by 1707 to nearly 29,000. It fluctuated between this figure and 25,000 until 1710. By 1713, just over 7,000 men were voted. At the end of the reign, 4,033 were still being approved for GIBRALTAR and MINORCA.

The remainder of the forces authorized were:

(a) troops in the United Kingdom—approximately 8,000 until the Union, and thereafter 15,000–16,000. The 'post war' reductions brought them down to just under 8,000;

(b) troops in the PLANTATIONS and WEST INDIES—approximately 2,000;

(c) in the later years a special DUNKIRK garrison of 4,000–8,000.

These were never, of course, the numbers of men in the field. They represented what the Commons approved, and were the maximum commanders could hope for. Regiments were always below strength. Frequently they were desperately so. This was due to an inefficient recruiting system, inadequate transport, and to the appalling mortality through sickness in the Peninsula, in the West Indies, and on the troopships. Mr. Lynn's confession, quoted at the beginning of the chapter, was evoked by the most discussed 'establishment scandal' of the time—ALMANZA. Of 29,000 voted for the 1707 campaign in Spain and Portugal only 8,000 were present at the battle. This was not, however, a phenomenal, although perhaps exceptional, state of affairs. In this chapter are considered only the authorized, and not the actual, strengths.

The United Kingdom

There were, in the Kingdom, in fact, three separate armies, under central control only by virtue of the Sovereign's prerogative. Until the Union of the Parliaments, there were the English, Scottish, and Irish establishments. Each was chargeable to the revenue of the country concerned, and each had its little idiosyncrasies of pay and conditions of service, officers' seniority, forage allowances, and other meticulae which could cause trouble, correspondence, or jobbery on the transfer of a regiment from one to the other. Regiments, on going overseas, normally came on to the English establishment (with the one exception of the Scots Brigade in Flanders which was a special case). The other two countries then normally replaced the regiments taken away by further recruitment, or were occasionally given a regiment returning from overseas.[1] The figures here considered are, until the Union, those of the English establishment only, and thereafter those of the combined English and Scottish establishments.

'*Guards and garrisons*' were the only troops authorized in Britain in time of peace. Estimates approved by the Commons during the war described the troops as the 'Guards, Garrisons, and Land Forces in England, Jersey, and Guernsey, the Plantations, and for the Sea Service'.

At the Restoration it had been Charles II's original intention to keep only one regiment of Foot Guards plus one regiment of

[1] Examples at *Dom. Cal.*, i, p. 592. Ests. WO 24/37 dated 10 Apr. 1704.

Life Guards (1st and 2nd Troops). Both of those consisted largely of Royalist *émigrés*, some of whom, such as the Foot Guards, had been on active service. The 5th Monarchy men's rising in 1661, however, showed the retention insufficient—or injudicious. Disbandment orders for the one remaining undispersed Parliamentary regiment—Monk's Coldstreamers—were revoked.[1] Similarly, the Earl of Oxford's Horse (later the Blues) was raised to strengthen the cavalry. It consisted largely of re-enlisted New Model men, but, unlike Monk's regiment, it was not itself a survival from the New Model. Nevertheless, the Tangier Horse (ancestors of the Royal Dragoons), bore, when raised a very little later, a distinctly Royalist flavour which made them, in a sense, a counterweight, aided by the Queen's Regiment of Foot.[2] The Corps of Gentlemen at Arms (constituted by Henry VIII in 1509), and the Yeomen of the Guard (by Henry VII in 1485), although attendants on the Sovereign, were not part of 'guards and garrisons'. They were both under the Lord Chamberlain and paid from the Civil List. Two hundred years later it was, in fact, to be ruled that they were not persons 'serving in any of Her Majesty's forces' and were, therefore, liable for militia service.[3] Similarly, the Chelsea Invalides, although the estimates were prepared by the Secretary at War, and although they took over garrisons to a total of 1,194 at one stage of the war, were not treated as part of 'guards and garrisons'.

The Guards

The GUARDS proper consisted of:

(*a*) *The Household Cavalry*

Three to four troops of Horse Guards (The Life Guards) with one to two troops of Horse Grenadier Guards attached.

(*b*) *The Royal Regiment of Horse Guards*
The Blues.

(*c*) *The Foot Guards*
(i) The 1st (later Grenadier) Guards;

---

[1] Fort., p. 56. Monk's troop of Life Guards was also reprieved: it has not survived.
[2] Fort., pp. 291–2.   [3] Clode, ii, pp. 359, 360, 363.

(ii) The 2nd (Monk's Coldstreamers) Guards;
(iii) The 3rd (Scots) Guards (from 1707).

Since the only troops allowed in the Kingdom were 'guards and garrisons', these guards regiments were accompanied on the estimate by other troops of the line. Thus, even in 1701, 390 men in the Plantations, and 71 in the West Indies, as well as 7,816 in regiments in Britain, appeared as 'guards and garrisons' —quite apart from the 'static garrisons' of forts and those 'guarding the palace from intrusion'. The term also covered an entry of miscellaneous troops dubbed 'for sea service', at one time 10,000 in number. An important body carried on the Guards and Garrisons establishment was that of H.Q. staff officers not debitable to any particular theatre. Not only officers such as the Captain-General, Adjutant-General, or Quarter-master-General were included, but also the Secretary to the Forces himself, the Paymaster-General, Commissary-General of the Musters, and his Deputy Commissaries, the Judge-Advocate-General, and his Deputy Judge-Advocates, and medical general officers. The Provost Master-General was also authorized, along with his three other ranks, as well as the Comptroller of Army Accounts, and clerks and messengers for all of these. Ceremonial appointments such as the St. James's Park Gunners, the Surveyor of the Guard, and the Drum-Major-General, were also borne on this list. Lists of these are given in the notes to the table of establishments in Appendix C. These 'miscellaneous' appointments totalled about fifty at their peak, but less than half were military, of whom about a third was ceremonial. In the case of the general officers, too, their appearance did not signify additional numbers, but was the authority for their pay. Since many of them were already carried on regimental establishments, I have endeavoured, in counting numbers, to eliminate such duplications, but it is difficult to be certain in some cases whether there was, in fact, duplication—the Provost Master-General, for instance.

Garrisons

As England was 'a country of garrisons rather than mobile forces',[1] among the oldest appointments—coeval with those associated with the Sovereign's Escort—were those connected

[1] Walton, p. 627.

with garrisons. The Board of Ordnance had, from the earliest times, been charged with the care of Crown fortresses,[1] but until 1667 execution and supervision was left almost exclusively in the hands of the local Governors. In that year, however, responsibility was placed more firmly on the Board, who were authorized to call to account all governors and commissioners holding fortress appointments. Attached to the fortifications were small bodies of men, as much caretakers as soldiers. These numbered from five or six upwards, of whom one would be a turnkey or porter, and most of the remainder gunners, who could only with hesitation be classified as 'soldiers'. Gunners and master gunners were, in general, appointed to particular places for life, and were not normally subject to military discipline— in 1783 they were still counted on the Ordnance's warrant as part of the 'civil' establishment. The number and pay of each appointment was fixed by the Secretary at War's office, but, apart from the men supplied by the Ordnance, the troops, except in time of emergency, were invalide or independent companies unfitted by age or disability for other service. In 1700 the Tower of London garrison numbered 57, and in the Channel and Scilly Isles there were 27. Others in the country ranged from 66, including the Governor, on the Isle of Wight, to 3 at North Yarmouth, and stretched from Berwick-on-Tweed, 10, to Plymouth, 23; and from Carlisle, 6, to Gravesend and Tilbury, 16. The Tower, for which a specimen establishment is given at Appendix D, included in its numbers a gentleman porter, a water-pumper, and a clock-keeper and bell-ringer.[2] These strengths remained substantially unaltered until the Union. Scotland, being a more turbulent country, had 336 in garrisons in 1707 when her establishment was absorbed. This was more than much larger and more heavily populated England, but rose, nevertheless, to 642 on the new establishment. The garrisons were concentrated at Edinburgh, 143, changed to 236; Stirling, 118, changed to 231; Blackness, 28, changed to 57; Dunbarton, 57, changed to 114; and Fort William, 4, porters not included. The totals undoubtedly included men who would more readily in England have been looked upon as infantry detachments stationed in those places, rather than as 'garrisons' in the accepted sense of the times. The stations mentioned did, however, on

[1] Clode, i, p. 8.   [2] Ests. WO 24/23, 25 Apr. 1700.

occasion have a further specific allocation of regular troops—
Fort William consistently housed one or two independent companies.[1] The difference in interpretation is, in fact, indicated by
the Commons Journal entry which puts the numbers in those
fortresses under the heading 'NORTH BRITAIN—Garrisons, etc.'[2]
Once the war was over, and the memory of the 1708 insurrection
had passed, the Scottish garrisons were heavily curtailed—no
doubt someone in the Secretary at War's office could not see
why Stirling should have more than North Yarmouth. According to the warrants, the total in 1714 was 182—which no doubt
gave much consolation to the Jacobites in the following year.[3]
The Commons estimates for the same year—presented before
the issue of the warrant—showed 232 in garrisons in Scotland,
plus 98 in independent companies. The difference was probably
due to confusion in the definition of the term 'garrison' and to
cutting down numbers after the money had been voted in order
to provide men elsewhere.[4] From 1712 onwards the estimates
ceased to differentiate, except in the case of independent
companies, between troops of the line stationed in England
and Scotland, i.e. their location became a question of military
security and operations and not of constitutional policy.

In 1708 there was formally constituted, in the Peninsula
estimates, a Gibraltar 'garrison'—or what would today be
termed a garrison staff. It comprised a governor, a commissary,
town-major, town-adjutant, deputy judge-advocate, chaplain,
surgeon-major and two mates, turnkey, postmaster and secretary to the commander-in-chief, signalman, and provost.[5] It
can be seen that not all of these were officers or men of the army.
They were in addition to any troops stationed there, and it is
probable that most of them who were of military status already
counted against regimental establishments. Gibraltar's garrison
staff remained authorized at approximately this strength until
the end of the reign, and was joined in the estimates by Dunkirk, at about the same strength, in 1711.[6] Minorca was authorized a slightly stronger staff, 18, in 1712, and, across the
Atlantic, Annapolis Royal and Placentia had seven apiece

[1] *Journals Commons*, xv, 28 Nov. 1707; Entry Books WO 26/14, 30 July 1712.
[2] *Journals Commons*, xv, 28 Nov. 1707.   [3] Ests. WO 24/70, 29 Apr. 1714.
[4] *Journals Commons*, xvii, 31 Mar. 1714.   [5] Ests. WO 24/45, 1708.
[6] Ests. WO 24/75 dated Dec. 1711 effective from June 1711.

from 1712 and 1713 respectively.[1] The seven in Annapolis Royal and Placentia were in addition to four independent companies shared between the two places on the 'Plantations' section of the Guards and Garrisons estimate.[2] On 27 May 1713 the estimate laid before the House for troops in the West Indies, Plantations, Minorca, Gibraltar, and Dunkirk for the last six months of 1713 totalled 11,225 against 18,682 up till then.[3] Neither of these figures as analysed in the warrants appears to have included the garrison staffs. On the day after the estimate was laid before them, the House ordered the Secretary to present to them an estimate of 8,000 men to be allowed for guards and garrisons in Great Britain, Jersey, Guernsey, and the Scillies.[4] Already the Mutiny Act of 1712 had stipulated that troops on the 'home establishment' were to be limited to 8,000 for a 'Guard to Her Majesty's person and the safety of this Kingdom', but they had only stipulated overseas strengths as 'a certain number of troops for the defence of Her Majesty's Dominions beyond the seas'.[5] In the second six months of 1713, the total number of troops of the line in the U.K. was 8,000, but there were also 636 in garrisons and general staff officers. For 1714 the grand total was just under 8,000. The net result was that the Flanders excess— 3,678 in 1714—had to be dealt with by retrospective sanction,[6] while Dunkirk, Gibraltar, and Minorca were dealt with as coming (temporarily or otherwise) under 'Her Majesty's Dominions beyond the Seas'. The West Indies, Annapolis Royal, and Placentia were by implication accepted as a projection abroad of the old-fashioned guards and garrisons. It all took place in great confusion and very casually, but was not at all insignificant: not since the raising of units for service in Tangiers had such an extra force in time of peace been sanctioned.

Flanders

The main theatre of war was Flanders. It was in Flanders that it was decided just as it concerned, despite its immediate occa-

---

[1] Ests. WO 24/75 dated 30 July 1712 and 6 Apr. 1713.

[2] Entry Books WO 26/14, 10 Apr. 1713; Ests. WO 24/75 dated 30 July 1712; 24/72 dated 26 May 1714; *Journals Commons*, xvii, dated 18 Apr. 1713. 27 May 1713, and 31 Mar. 1714.

[3] *Journals Commons*, xvii, 27 May 1713. Clode, i, p. 260, gives 11,125 for no apparent reason. *Journals Commons*, xvii, 6 Apr. 1713.   [4] Clode, i, p. 360.

[5] 12 Annae, cap. 13.   [6] *Journals Commons*, xvii, 31 Mar. 1714.

sion and title, the strategic disposition of a large part of Flanders. The vital part of the peace treaty round which there was any room for manœuvre in negotiations was Flanders. It was in the Flanders theatre that Anne's troops made their country's name. It was in Flanders that John Churchill of England took the field as Commander-in-Chief of the Allied forces. Yet only in two years of the war was Flanders allotted the majority of the English troops. English 'subject troops' were never in a majority in the theatre. They seldom reached 25,000 men. The threat of war in 1701 brought a treaty commitment of 10,000 men. There were barely 7,000 troops in the country, plus 3,000 marines, retained by a subterfuge. The Commons could frequently be put off their anti-militarist scent by a whiff of tarpaulin. The call was met by the dispatch of twelve battalions from Ireland (the Irish establishment at that time was 12,000). They were replaced by 10,000 English recruits. Parliament sought to expiate its past by voting 40,000 men, but of these only 18,000 were 'subject troops'. The remainder were hired, but on British establishments. Parliament further pledged itself to support any other steps taken by the Government to fulfil its international obligations. As a result, the country contracted for a further 20,000, of whom just over 3,000 were subject troops. The Dutch shared half the cost of this supplement, which was known throughout the war as the Flanders augmentation. It was a continual source of financial trouble. Although it was, in the terms of the Commons 'pledge', authorized, there was no source from which it could be paid for the first year, since Supplementary Estimates were at that time unknown. All of Godolphin's procrastination and jugglery were required to meet the difficulty, and there was, for almost the entire duration of the war, a persistent and despairing correspondence concerning money for pay, waggons, bread, and other 'extraordinaries'. For a number of years Flanders, which as a theatre covered all of continental Europe except the Peninsula, also had 4,000 troops who were formally voted on the Peninsula establishment. The English component of the 40,000 was approximately 3,300 horse and dragoons, and 15,000 foot. The augmentation was exclusively foot.

Reduction in strength started in 1713, but there were still, at the end of the year, 3,678 troops (entirely foot) in Flanders proper (Dunkirk was by then presented separately). These were not sanctioned in the estimates, but retrospective approval was subsequently given. The general officers in Flanders are of interest chiefly for the way in which a number of those designated as 'overall' commanders were carried on the establishment of this particular theatre. The command was first of all designated for a lieutenant-general. Marlborough was in due course appointed Captain-General (first described as Commander-in-Chief). He was also, by agreement with the Dutch, Allied Commander-in-Chief, but his control was limited by the supervision of the Dutch Deputies. He had, in addition, very extensive diplomatic functions. His command as Captain-General of the British troops was not delegated. He had under him his 'General(s) of Horse' and 'General(s) of Foot'. His General of Foot for many years was his brother Charles. In 1701 the posts were not specifically so described, but he had a lieutenant-general and a major-general under him. The appointment of 'General of Foot' (normally held by a lieutenant-general) was created later, to be joined in due course by that of 'General of Horse'. These cavalry and infantry commanders were supported by 'Lieutenant Generals of Horse' and 'Lieutenant Generals of Foot' (three in number, rising later to five), major-generals (two in 1704, rising to six in 1712), and brigadier-generals (five in 1704; eight in 1712). For staff officers he had a Quartermaster-General, Deputy Quartermaster-Generals (at first designated Assistant Quartermaster-Generals), a Waggon-Master-General, and Assistant Waggon-Master-Generals. There was a Provost Master-General with his two to four other ranks, a Surgeon-General, a Deputy Judge-Advocate, and a Deputy Paymaster-General. At lower levels, there were Brigade Majors (two in 1701; eight in 1712). This, except for aides-de-camp,[1] probably exhausted the military appointments, but a few clerks, a commander-in-chief's secretary, chaplain, physician, and surgeon were debited to 'general officers'. Parliament was careful in its scrutiny of estimates for general officers. The money under this head was voted separately from the main theatre estimates along, as a rule, with contingencies, baggage, and forage money. In late 1712 the Commons rejected outright one such estimate,

---

[1] One scale was six for a commander-in-chief; three for a general; two for a lieutenant-general; one for a major-general. It is difficult to establish any rule.

although they had sanctioned an identical one in February of the same year.[1]

The Peninsula

In Spain and Portugal British generalship was seen at its most undistinguished, and administration at its most impotent. Although at one time over 34,000 subject troops were voted for the Peninsula, it is very doubtful if more than 15,000 were ever present, sick or well, in the theatre at once. Wastage in troopships and through sickness in the theatre worked such havoc with paper establishments that even a disaster like Almanza came almost to be of the same order as the other losses. It was the Peninsula which set Mr. Lynn to 'puzzle his brains to pieces' in an endeavour to explain the slip which had lost 21,000 men out of 29,000 betwixt the cup of the House of Commons Journals and the lip of the generals' command in the field.

The shuffling and expedients to which the authorities were reduced in order to provide cohesive forces (consolidation of weak regiments to form stronger, or heavy drafting between one regiment and another, for example) made it steadily less possible for the Secretary at War's office to keep in touch with the situation. Grenville claimed in 1710 to have 12,175 British troops in Portugal alone: later in the year it was shown that there were, in fact, 9,791 in the entire Peninsula. The Commons had voted 25,367.[2] All the tortuous arithmetic of the Secretary at War's office did not succeed, until there were troops left only in Gibraltar and Minorca, in transferring from the Peninsula establishment five regiments which actually served throughout in Flanders. Bald statements of figures of votes, as the notes to the table in Appendix C show, mean very little. Mr. Lynn himself, still investigating Almanza in 1711, confessed 'there has been so great a jumble in regiments shifting and exchanging establishments . . . that I am not able to trace it regularly'. His final contribution, as accurate no doubt as any other, was 'a printed account of the matter which I remember was cooked up at the Treasury'.[3]

[1] *Journals Commons*, xiii, 12 May 1701; xiv, 19 Nov. 1703; xvii, 20 Feb. 1712; Ests. WO 24/24 dated from 1 June 1701; SP Mil. 41/4, 5 Apr. 1712. *Treas. Cal.*, iv, p. 518: minute to Earl of Stair's letter of 22 Oct. 1713.
[2] Treas. 1/131/3: letter to Dartmouth dated 29 Nov. 1710.
[3] SP Mil. 41/3 dated 17 Dec. 1710 and 26 Jan. 1711.

In 1703, 8,015 foot were voted for Portugal; in 1706 there were 10,210 horse and foot, and a further 5,004 for the expedition to Catalonia. The grand total in the following year was over 28,000. The voted strengths fluctuated between this and 26,000 until 1711. In 1712 there were barely 20,000, and thereafter the reduction was the swiftest of any theatre. By the end of 1713 the Peninsula was clear of British troops except for a voted strength of just over 4,000 for Gibraltar and Minorca.

The Ordnance Vote

The Ordnance Vote was not really part of the army estimates, but it involved a number of people who would now be considered part of the army. The 'base' part of the organization had a steady establishment of about 330 which probably changed very little in peace or in war.[1] This covered stores staff (all arsenal stores), foundry and firemaster's staff, and a large proportion of the 'caretaking staff' of gunners, engineers, and miners which has already been dealt with, for convenience, under garrisons. It is probable that the Board was responsible for the gunners and engineers in fortresses, but that the numbers appeared, nevertheless, for totalling in the Secretary at War's establishment books. It is not, in fact, easy to say how many of the garrison staffs were militarized in the sense of being subject to the Mutiny Act. Of the Board's staff outside the trains, and excluding garrisons, there were probably less than twenty militarized posts, and perhaps less than twelve. If garrisons are included, the division becomes quite arbitrary. Even the Board at times were not themselves quite sure. There was also a certain number of technical and 'caretaking' posts abroad, such as engineers of garrisons, which fluctuated according to the military situation.

The major new commitment brought by war was the provision of 'trains' for expeditions. These consisted of artillery, engineers, and a small stores detachment, chiefly required for the artillery and engineers themselves. The strength of the train depended on its role—but those in Flanders and the Peninsula averaged very roughly about 600,[2] of whom certainly 5 per cent.,

[1] *Journals Commons*, 15 Nov. 1704.

[2] An interesting comparison with present-day tendencies is obtainable from a post-1945 army establishment which showed artillery, engineers, and ordnance slightly exceeding the infantry in strength, and six times the strength of the armour.

and perhaps more than 50 per cent. were civilians—the artillery drivers, some of the gunners, and many of the engineer craftsmen. Many of the officers on the establishment were also carried on the strengths of regiments.

Medical

It was only with reluctance that a medical organization was recognized as part of the war, and it is only with difficulty that it can be identified. The 'chirurgeons' of regiments were looked upon more as part of the troops' 'welfare' (a physical counterpart to the chaplain's spiritual task) than as men who might fit into some wider plan. The Physician- and Apothecary-General exercised a vague supervision over the provision of medicines (for which the troops paid), but any central organization or arrangement in a campaign area was purely *ad hoc*, and had to be staffed from within the existing theatre establishment. Additional costs thus incurred were met by a further levy on the troops. Later it became not unusual for a portion of such cost to be met from 'contingencies' or 'extraordinaries of war'. Spain, with a hostile population, scarce accommodation, and conditions causing much sickness, first made the need for some central organization in the theatre inescapable. Some meagre provision of hospitals was eventually made, with intendants and other staff formally approved by the Treasury and the House.[1] A portion of the cost was met by estimate duly submitted, a portion from poundage, and the remainder from the same sources as before. Similar hospital staffs were later to be established at Dunkirk and Nieuport. It is doubtful how many of the staffs were military, and our figures will not be far wrong if we ignore them completely.[2]

REGIMENTAL ORGANIZATION AND STRENGTHS

Mr. Lynn, when he penned his complaint about the 'jumble of regiments' which nonplussed even his desk-trained mind,

[1] There had been such hospitals in existence once before, in 1690, with provision for hospital governor, master-surgeon, and others—but the Commons insisted on their early disbandment, and were reluctant, even when memories did stir again, to restore them.

[2] Ests. WO 24/25 dated 10 Oct. 1712 and 24/75 dated 30 June 1714; Treas. 1/153 dated 10 Oct. 1712.

indicated that there would probably be variations not only in the actual strengths of units, but considerable fluctuations in the theoretical organizations and strengths. A considerable amount of variation from theatre to theatre would not, in fact, be of itself a sign of disorganization or confusion. It might well display adaptability, and a flexible attitude to varying circumstances. Regiments, after all, which landed in Normandy in 1944 differed very considerably in numbers and fire-power from their opposite numbers at the same time besieged in Imphal. When variations within a theatre itself, however, become widespread, the disadvantages soon outtop the advantages. Even the commanders of Anne's time, used to improvisation and adaptations, felt that there was a limit. Galway himself complained from Spain in 1707 about the 'multiplicity of establishments'. Sunderland, the Secretary of State, reassured him that 'this year they are put upon one establishment'.[1] His assurance must, one feels, have been based, like Mr. Lynn's, on the best information he could get: so good and rare, in fact, that not a trace of it remains with us today.

Practically everything that can be written about regimental organization or strengths is subject to caveat or reservation of some kind. Few general statements are not liable to qualification in the case of some particular unit or some particular year. The following, therefore, is merely an attempt to present not the 'average' position, for in circumstances and cases so disparate, such is not really possible, but rather a representative selection.

In general, the horse and dragoons were organized in regiments subdivided into squadrons and troops. The foot were in regiments or battalions, subdivided into companies. With the exception of the First Foot Guards and the Royal Scots, infantry regiments contained only one battalion. The two titles, therefore, tend to be interchangeable.

The basic sub-unit of horse and dragoons was the troop. Organization of the troops into squadrons was uncertain, and far from uniform or universal. It is possible that grouping in squadrons was either administrative or purely a battle or march drill, for the ranks and numbers in horse troops correspond to those of companies in the foot. Any appointments as squadron

[1] *H.M.C.H. of L.*, vii, p. 387, 14 Feb. 1707.

commander must have been supernumerary, for they do not appear on the establishments.

Horse and Dragoon Guards

The Horse Guards require special consideration. In these units, traditional ranks remained which had disappeared from the other units of the army, and appointments in them carried ranks elevated in status, and sometimes in name. The senior units of the army were in the Household Cavalry, organized in troops of Horse Guards, known as the Life Guards, and attached troops of Horse Grenadier Guards. The troops were not organized into regiments and approximated to cavalry squadron strength, i.e. 156. There were three at the beginning of the reign, and four at the end. The Horse Grenadier Guard troops were a trifle smaller—140—and they increased from one in number to two. They were sometimes designated the Horse Grenadiers of the Life Guards.[1]

Next came the Royal Regiment of Horse Guards (The Blues), organized on the conventional lines of a horse regiment with nine troops.[2] They carried the title 'guards' at that time really only because of the special circumstances of their raising, mentioned at the beginning of the chapter. A further six regiments (of six to nine troops) were known as Dragoon Guards, but there was no functional reason for such a title.[3] It has been argued that, when the dragoons became cavalry, there was a precedence dispute between them and the original regiments of horse which still claimed seniority to mere mounted infantry. The Queen's Dragoons (Royal Dragoons, or Tangier Horse) were, however, senior to any horse except the Life Guards and the Blues. The original horse regiments, therefore, became Dragoon Guards, and the Queen's Dragoons took first place as cavalry of the line, after the Guards.[4]

Horse and Dragoons

The unit in the horse was the regiment, composed of troops, which could be grouped in threes in squadrons. The immediate

---

[1] Walton, p. 419; Dalton, vi, pp. 1–4; Fort., p. 388: which gives strengths of an earlier period.   [2] Dalton, vi, pp. 25–26, 40.

[3] Ests. WO 24/23 from 25 Apr. 1700; Dalton, vi, pp. 1–14.

[4] *Colonel of Dragoons*, Phillip Woodruff (London, 1951). (*Woodruff.*)

post-Restoration regiments had been nine troops strong,[1] but the great disbandments after William's wars reduced most of those which remained to six troops.[2] There is difficulty in finding any conclusive evidence that, even during the war, any of these ever reattained nine-troop strength. The dragoons, being mounted, were also in troops, but these were grouped in companies, without any specific company establishment. There were three troops per company in the early post-Restoration period, when the horse were nine per regiment. The cuts which reduced the horse to six probably brought the dragoons down to eight—the general reduction seems to have been about two-thirds.[3] Over the period 1707–14, there were eleven regiments of horse (including Hussars), and eighteen of dragoons, for whom there was much demand in Spain.

Foot Guards

The Foot Guards were, in a sense, comparable with the Royal Horse Guards. Although originally, and indeed primarily, a royal bodyguard, they did considerable overseas service. Their role as bodyguard was not, however, allowed to become purely nominal. In 1711 the Secretary at War issued an order 'as Her Majesty has commanded me to signify' that a field officer of the Foot Guards was to be always in waiting on the Queen 'in like manner as she is attended by an officer of the Horse Guards'. A repetition of this order some days later said that the field officer was to do duty 'as was formerly practised in the reign of Charles II for the better preservation of good order and discipline near her royal person'.[4]

Prior to the Union, the Guards were in two regiments—the 1st, and the 2nd, or Coldstreamers. After 1707 they included a 3rd Regiment, the Scots Guards.[5] The 1st Guards were organized in two battalions, and the Coldstreamers in one. All three regiments may have had two battalions each at some period of the war.[6] In 1700 the 1st Guards had twenty-eight companies,

---

[1] Walton, p. 419.   [2] Fort., p. 388.
[3] Dalton, vi, pp. 25–26, 40; SP Mil. 41/3/27 dated 19 Dec. 1710; Ests. WO 24/41, 1705, Portugal.
[4] Clode, i, p. 364: orders dated 9 Aug. and 15 Aug. 1711.
[5] They were formally given the title '3rd' in 1713.
[6] Fort., p. 555, footnote 2, and p. 556.

and the Coldstreamers fourteen. The two had been down to a joint total of fourteen companies in 1698.[1] There were very large numbers overseas during the war—in 1710 at least thirty-one companies. There was a plan on foot at one time to form a composite Guards Brigade in operations, but it never came to fruition.[2] Two of the regiments had battalions in Spain, and both were represented at Oudenarde.[3] At the close of the war, the Coldstreamers and the Scots Guards reverted to one battalion each.[4]

Foot

The foot regiments, commanded by colonels, consisted each, except the Royal Scots, of one battalion, divided into a headquarters and ten to twelve companies. One of the companies in each regiment, including the Foot Guards, was a grenadier company. At the peak of the war there were seventy-two regiments of foot, equivalent to seventy-three battalions.[5]

NUMBERS AND RANKS

In general, regiments of horse, dragoons, or foot were commanded by colonels, with one lieutenant-colonel and one major under them. The 1st Guards, with their customary two battalions, had two majors, but this reinforcement does not seem to have extended to either the other guards regiments or to the Royal Scots. The Life Guards were commanded by an officer nominally of the rank of captain, but in fact a hybrid 'captain and colonel'. This was also the case in the Horse Grenadier Guards.[6] They remained fairly constant in authorized strength

---

[1] Fort., p. 388.   [2] SP Mil. 41/3/27 dated Dec. 1710.

[3] Fort., p. 492, footnote 2; Dalton, vi, pp. 155, 160, 318; Ests. WO 24/41.

[4] Entry Book WO 26/14, 12 May 1713. Although of a strength justifying two battalions, Guards regiments, other than the 1st, cannot be conclusively claimed to have been formally so organized. Fortescue says their strength was such that they 'may be reckoned practically two battalions apiece'. Fort., p. 555, footnote 2. He also says that at one stage of the war they definitely had each a battalion at home to feed the one overseas. Ibid., p. 556. Only for the 1st Guards have I seen an establishment with two majors to indicate formal separation into two fully fledged battalions, although all had more than one adjutant—but the Royal Scots with two battalions were also without a second major.

[5] Dalton, vi, pp. 1–14.

[6] The titling of these officers can lead the unwary to conclude that captains in the regiments had majors serving under them. For fuller consideration of these ranks see the section in Chapter II, Military Secretary's Branch.

at 150 to 180 per troop. The Regiment of Royal Horse Guards, on the other hand, approximated to a normal horse regiment, and the Dragoon Guards were indistinguishable from ordinary dragoon regiments. Apart from their total strengths, the regiments of Foot Guards were similar in organization to the other regiments of foot. In general, therefore, references in the following to horse or dragoons may be taken to include the Royal Horse Guards and Dragoon Guards. Similarly the Foot Guards are included in references to foot regiments.

Horse and Dragoons

There was little difference between the headquarters of horse and dragoon regiments. Both had a colonel, a lieutenant-colonel, a major, an adjutant, a chaplain, and a surgeon. It is not possible to state firmly how often the colonel was present. If we count the number of horse, dragoon, and foot regiments, at their peak, as 108, and the number of general officers (in the broadest sense, down to brigadier-generals) and staff officers of the rank of colonel and upwards, who would have to be provided from these sources, it can be seen that the colonels actually present with their regiments would certainly be a minority. Horse regiment headquarters had a kettle-drummer, not so fortunate as his counterpart in the train where there was a pair of kettle-drums 'handsomely mounted on a travelling carriage with a seat for the drummer'.[1] It seems probable that on active service dragoon regiments were authorized a gunsmith. In the establishment on which the figures for 1702 in Appendix D are based[2] a gunsmith is shown. That from which the figures on reversion to peacetime strengths are drawn[3] shows none. His presence in some regiments is confirmed by at least one set of subsistence rates for Spain (in 1708), and also by an establishment for the Low Countries.[4] The authorization of a servant for him, and his rate of pay (4s. per day), indicate what we might call warrant officer status. His servant had 1s. per day. The gunsmith does not appear for dragoon regiments on the guards and garrisons establishments, and it seems reasonable that dragoons

---

[1] Walton, p. 464.   [2] Ests. WO 24/46 dated 1 June 1702.
[3] Entry Books WO 26/14 from 12 and 13 May 1713.
[4] Ests. WO 24/47 and 24/46.

should be specially authorized one on active service, where the wear and tear on their weapons in particular might be expected to be more severe. His status as a soldier, of course, may have been as doubtful as that of the chaplain or surgeon even, although he was, like them, carried on the regimental establishment.[1]

Troop and company strengths varied from about thirty-eight dragoons/troopers in peace to approximately fifty-four in war.[2] (In 1672 dragoons had been eighty to a company).[3] Appropriately enough, as an original compound of cavalry and infantry, the dragoons, although organized in companies, designated the subalterns in these companies cornets. The horse regiments did not have sergeants—the tradition remains today in the Household Cavalry with their corporals of horse—but the dragoons had two when of fifty-four dragoon strength, and one when of thirty-eight. There were the same number of corporals in either horse or dragoons—two per company on the lower scale, and three on the higher. The horse had trumpeters in their troops, one on the lower scale, two on the higher, but the dragoons followed the infantry model in having both side drums and hautbois—one on the lower scale, two on the higher.[4]

Foot

The headquarters of foot regiments remained fairly stable with a colonel, lieutenant-colonel, major, adjutant, chaplain, surgeon, surgeon's mate, and quartermaster. In addition, many regiments had a drum-major. It has been claimed that all were so authorized from 1700 onwards,[5] but it will be seen from the establishment for the West Indies 1704–7 quoted in Appendix D that it at least took some time for the ruling to become

---

[1] This is borne out by the unusually high proportion of his pay issued, according to one establishment, as 'subsistence'—4s. for him and his servant, which suggests little regimental provision of uniform and equipment. Ests. WO 24/41 dated 30 Apr. 1705.

[2] These dragoons/troopers included one or two 'widows' men', but not normally servants, whom it became the custom to allow for separately, and at the same time to stipulate 'no servants to be allowed the officers on the musters'. (Widows' men were fictitious soldiers for whom pay was drawn, normally to provide pensions for widows of deceased members of the regiment.)

[3] Walton, p. 422.

[4] Entry Book WO 26/14, 17 Oct. 1712 and 12 and 13 May 1713. Ests. WO 24/26 dated 1 June 1702 and 24/41 for 1705.

[5] Walton, p. 465.

applicable overseas. Establishments for Portugal for as late as 1705 do not show the appointment. It seems to have established itself during the reign on the grounds of the duties devolving on the drum-major in connexion with regimental provost.[1]

There was a higher scale for the Guards and the Royal Scots in order to meet their two battalion strength. The 1st Guards had two majors, three adjutants, two quartermasters, and two surgeons' mates. The other Guards regiments and the Royal Scots had two adjutants, two quartermasters, and two mates. All the Guards had a Deputy Marshal. The Guards had also a 'solicitor', first noted in 1678. His was a military appointment, but his duties are not clear. One authority claims that he performed the duties of agent,[2] but the latter post was specifically authorized in addition in the 1st and 3rd Guards. Walton suggests that he was a regimental baggage-master.[3]

The Royal Scots had a 'piper to the colonel's company'— presumably the only bagpiper in the army. There had been fifers in regiments previously, but, as their pay was the responsibility of the captains, they disappeared in hard times. Sir James Turner remarked in 1671, 'with us any captain may keep a piper in his company, and maintain him too, for no pay is allowed him, perhaps just as much as he deserveth'.[4] This is in agreement with the claim that, until 1824, the majority of bandsmen were not attested; excluding the Royal Scots' piper, the only musicians[5] provided for on establishment were drummers, trumpeters, and hautbois.[6] The Royal Fusiliers, for some exceptional reason, were the only foot regiment with a gunsmith, although this had been universal in Scotland in Monk's time.

---

[1] It is said that this association, which involved responsibility for the infliction of corporal punishment, came about because originally the drums were ordered to beat when men were running the gauntlet, in order to drown their cries. Walton, pp. 562–3.

[2] *Journal of the Society for Army Historical Research*, vol. xxxv, no. 141 (March 1957), p. 46, and no. 142 (June 1957), p. 92 (London). (*JSAHR.*)

[3] Walton, p. 441.

[4] Ibid, p. 464.

[5] The post-1944 change in title from 'bandsmen' to 'musicians' was not an onset of mealy-mouthedness in the army, but merely a reversion to a traditional name.

[6] *Armies and Armament: An Historical Survey of the Weapons of the British Army*, Charles Ffoulkes (London, 1945), p. 112. (*AA.*)

In each of a battalion's ten to twelve companies there were allowed a captain, and two other officers. In the foot companies these were one lieutenant and one ensign, but the grenadier companies had two lieutenants and no ensign. Three of the captains of companies were the colonel, lieutenant-colonel, and major. The adjutant frequently held one also, so that the actual command—but not, of course, the pay—of at least a quarter of them fell to the lieutenant. There were approximately sixty privates per company in war, and forty in peace. The Guards were at one time seventy per company, but later reverted, with the others, to forty. There were two sergeants per company (in the large Guards companies, three), two or three corporals according to strength, and one or two drummers. At their peak strength, the Guards companies had also three hautbois. The privates frequently included widows' men, and sometimes servants, although the tendency was to prohibit specifically the counting of servants against the establishment for privates.

There were a few miscellaneous appointments in regiments— of the nature of 'local ranks' with no status in establishments. The gentleman of arms was a storekeeper for the regimental arms and ammunition, and probably carried out also some gunsmith's duties. A gentleman of a company was a soldier on probation and acted as a file leader.[1]

Independent Companies

These were exactly what might be expected—units for tasks which were too small for a regiment, and unsuitable for a company detached from its parent unit. They were used principally in the Plantations, and, later, for garrison duty in Scotland. The strengths were determined entirely by their tasks, and ranged from 40 to 100 privates. They were commanded by a captain, with two or three lieutenants—it appears to have been unusual for them to have had ensigns. They had the appropriate proportion of N.C.O.s and drummers.

Others

The Corps of Gentlemen of Arms, and the Yeomen of the Guard were not, properly speaking, part of the military

---

[1] Walton, pp. 415–16.

establishment, but there is an indication of their strengths in Appendix C.

RECRUITING AND REINFORCEMENTS

> Our 'prentice Tom may now refuse,
> To wipe his scoundrel master's shoes,
> For now he's free to sing and play,
> Over the Hills and far away.

Chorus
> Over the Hills and over the main,
> To Flanders, Portugal, or Spain;
> The Queen commands, and we obey,
> Over the Hills and far away.

> We shall lead more happy lives,
> By getting rid of Brats and Wives,
> That scold and bawl both night and day,
> Over the Hills and far away.

> Courage boys 'tis one to ten,
> But we return all gentlemen,
> While conquering colours we display,
> Over the Hills and far away.
>   *The Recruiting Officer*[1]

Expansion of an army organized on a 'property' basis was, in theory, simple. Either companies were added to existing skeleton regiments, or 'gentlemen of position or known soldiers' were authorized to raise their own regiments. Keeping the regiments up to strength subsequently was the colonels' responsibility. Any lack of diligence in this respect would be visited on himself in a falling off in off-reckonings. It turned out in practice to be easier to raise new units than to reinforce those already existing, and the Government, failing to make a long-term budget of mobilizable resources, authorized an army of a size which the recruiting system proved unable to sustain. The system was bound to encounter difficulties when large numbers were engaged in hard fighting in nearby theatres such as Flanders. It was nearly impossible for places further afield, such as Spain and the West Indies. It was, in its time, indeed, to help to lose

---

[1] *The Recruiting Officer*, George Farquhar. (*Recruiting Officer*.)

the American Colonies. A regiment in a sickly theatre with, between it and home, a grievous journey which killed off or incapacitated anything up to a third of the recruits, had an intolerable burden, both financially, and as a fighting unit. Marlborough made, in this connexion, one of his few attempts to interfere as a 'global' commander-in-chief. 'The war in Catalonia', he wrote, 'must be carried on by troops from Italy, and not by the Queen's subjects, by which you may save money, and the service be better done.'[1] He was to repeat in the same year—before the Almanza post mortem made the problem, though not the solution, obvious—'. . . the war in Spain ought to be carried on by subsidies, which may get foreign troops: for Her Majesty's subjects can never come in time, nor indeed be kept in order in that country for want of troops.'[2]

To keep their regiments reinforced, the colonels abroad sent home, each winter, a small party of officers, sergeants, and drummers, who toured the country for recruits.

If any Gentlemen, Soldiers, or others have a mind to serve Her Majesty and pull down the French King [proclaimed Sergeant Kite on his expeditions], if any prentices have severe masters, any children have undutiful parents: if any servants have too little Wages, or any Husband too much wife [then their future was made]. . . . I don't beat up for common soldiers, but only for Granadeers . . . he that has the good fortune to be born six foot high was born to be a great man.[3]

It was a fortunate consequence of the natural order of the times that, in the season when units were compelled to go into winter quarters because of the weather, and could thus most easily spare recruiting parties, men were available at home because of lack of work on the land. The 'hard weather' in England bulked as large in Marlborough's calculations, because of its beneficial effects on enlistments, as did that in Flanders which determined the dates for winter quarters. Recruiting was not normally an unpopular task. Blackader tells us why:

[1] *The Wars of Marlborough 1702–1709*, F. Taylor (Oxford, 1921), vol. i, p. 16: letter to Godolphin, 4 July 1707. (*Taylor.*)
[2] Ibid.: letter to Godolphin, 1 Aug. 1707.
[3] *Recruiting Officer.*

This vexing trade of recruiting depresses my mind. I am the unfittest for it of any man in the army, and have the least talent that way. Sobriety itself is here a bar to success. I see the greatest rakes are the best recruiters. I cannot ramble, and rave, and drink, and tell stories, and wheedle, and insinuate, if my life were lying at stake.

I saw all this before I came home, and could have avoided coming: but it was the hopes of enjoying the blessings of the gospel that brought me to Scotland, more than recruiting: although I do not deny that I had an eye to that also.[1]

The recruiting parties, having gathered up their men, took them to specified ports for transport overseas, either on the packet-boats (this practice, although frowned upon, was never stopped, simply because there was insufficient other transport), on chartered vessels under the orders of the Commissioners of Transports, or even on men-of-war. Getting the recruits to the ships was not an easy task. A large proportion of the men was pressed, a number had enlisted while drunk, others were no doubt nauseated by their first contact with military life, and many were interested only in the levy money payable to them on enlistment. Stringent measures were necessary to safeguard these charges who could represent an investment of at least £2 per head (levy money), apart from clothing. Forty shillings was a large sum for an unskilled workman of Queen Anne's day, and one can well believe the M.P. pamphleteer Hutcheson's claim that to pay it was an inducement as much to desertion as to recruitment. (Cromwell, he said, had made it a 'breaking' offence for officers to pay out more than 1s.: thus may the regicide have started the 'King's shilling' on its career.) To prevent their escape, recruits in London, for example, were lodged in the Savoy, defined by Hutcheson as a 'prison kept by the Provost Marshal or Military Hangman' primarily for mutineers, deserters, and other offenders who were sent there at times without design of other punishment—for committal to the Savoy was punishment enough in itself.[2] The fate of the recruit in Steele's 'The Funeral, or Grief a la Mode', on the other hand, was to be whipped from constable to constable, 'the courtesy of England to all that want in red coats'.

---

[1] Blackader, p. 62.
[2] *Recruiting Essay.*

Officers [wrote Hutcheson], conduct recruits as prisoners, sometimes marching them pinioned or handcuffed, or with the buttons of their breeches cut off . . . and lastly (to) secure them in that Epitome of Hell, the Savoy, more dreadful to the newly listed Soldier than all the Dangers and Hardships of the War; where, if they lye long before the officer has an opportunity to ship them, what with the close confinement, nauseous stinks, etc. [they fell chronically ill.][1]

From which it would appear almost as though the Provost Marshal had not been informed of the revolutionary announcement of a previous reign that 'to encourage a better type of man to enlist . . . recruits would be well looked after'.[2]

Even Sergeant Kite could not bring himself to speak well of the Savoy:

Hunger and ambition, the Fears of Starving, and the Hopes of a Truncheon led me along to a Gentleman with a fair Tongue, and fair periwig who loaded me with promises; but 'gad it was the lightest load that ever I felt in my life. He promised to advance me, and indeed he did so—to a garret in the Savoy. I asked him why he put me in prison: he call'd me Lying Dog, and said I was in Garrison; and indeed 'tis a Garrison that may hold out till Doomsday before I should desire to take it again.

Nottingham's inquiry of Blathywayt on 20 February 1703 seems even apologetic. He asked if it were true as the 'Committee of the Council are informed that recruits brought up to the Savoy are ill cared for, and have to lie upon boards? Inform yourself and send me an account to lay before the Queen at the Cabinet Council tomorrow evening.'[3]

If recruits survived the terrors of the Savoy, they were spared any period of further training to fit them for service. Regimented straight away, they were shipped on service to practise their drill in the face of the enemy,[4] who may, indeed, have seemed an inoffensive adversary after Kite:

I was born and bred a gipsy, and bred among that crew till I was ten years of age; there I learned canting and lying. I was bought from my mother, Cleopatra, by a certain nobleman for three pistoles, who, liking my beauty, made me his page; there I learned impudence and pimping. I was turned off for wearing my lord's linen and

---

[1] Ibid.
[2] Cruickshank.
[3] *Dom. Cal.*, ii, p. 599.
[4] Walton, p. 506.

drinking my lady's ratafia, and then became bailiff's follower; there I learned bullying and swearing. I at last got into the army, and there I learned wenching and drinking; so that if your lordship care to cast up the whole sum, viz, canting, lying, impudence, bullying, swearing, drinking, and a halbert, you will find the sum total amounting to a recruiting sergeant.

The Legal Framework

Even before the actual outbreak of war, when the army was less than 8,000 strong, Parliament imposed a recruiting commitment of a further 13,000 men. One of the first measures to meet the new requirement was an Act to release insolvent debtors from prison if they would serve, or secure someone to serve, for the duration of the war.[1] A hastily drafted measure, it was, according to at least one contemporary opinion, unsuccessful, due to 'many doubts and various scruples',[2] and had to be revised the following session.[3] It nevertheless remained, throughout the war, one of the more popular vehicles of chicanery and corruption. Despite the provision in the amending Act that debtors discharged in order to enlist must proceed overseas within two months, large numbers managed to find themselves on leave, or enlisted (with due payment of levy money) several times over. Even though the debt itself was not extinguished by enlistment, accommodating commanding officers could find themselves suitably rewarded from the pay of soldiers whose drafting abroad was unaccountably delayed. The possibility of being suddenly impressed for overseas no doubt redirected the men's hearts to generosity if at any time they might feel a sense of grievance. The same Act also provided for the only form of conscription to be operated for the army during the war—the only form, indeed, to be imposed for the Standing Army prior to the First World War. It was declared lawful for the Justices of the Peace to 'raise and levy' able-bodied men with no lawful calling, employment, or visible means for their maintenance and livelihood. The recruit was to be given 20s. levy money, and the constable responsible for him 10s. The Articles of War were to be read to him, and, on payment of the levy money, or on its 'tender and refusal', he was to be 'deemed a listed soldier'.

---

[1] Annae 1, cap. 19.
[2] *Several Queries Relating to An Act of Parliament etc.*, By A Gentleman in the Country (London, 1704). (*Several Queries.*) [3] Annae 2 and 3, cap. 10.

Levying of rogues and vagabonds was not a new provision in English law, but obviously what constituted 'lawful calling or employment . . . or visible means for . . . maintenance and livelihood' allowed some discretion to magistrates. It was for this reason that Thomas Appletree declared in his cups that he'd be no Emperor, but a J.P. because 'since this Pressing Act they are greater than any Emperor under the sun'. The view taken by the J.P.s may be guessed from the scene later in *The Recruiting Officer*, where a miner is impressed because, working underground, he has no *visible* means of livelihood. As a precaution against undue abuses, the Act provided that no J.P. who was a military officer other than in the militia (which even the most extreme politicians would, presumably, have been unable to dub 'militaristic') was to operate the Act. No voters were to be conscribed—perhaps because they were deemed to have already sufficient access to liquor: 'recruiting and elections', remarked Captain Plume, 'are rare friends to the Excise'. A further provision of the Act permitted the release to the forces of capital offenders. This proved so popular with officers—for the enlistments represented no expensive touring and no levy money—that a roster had to be kept of the regiments wishing to take these recruits.[1] The enthusiasm was not entirely one-sided. Later in the reign, the prisoners in Newgate themselves petitioned the Queen to be allowed to enlist. Those not so enthusiastic might, nevertheless, be taken, like the three 'guilty of several notorious crimes but . . . convicted of Dear Stealing only' who were ordered by St. John to be 'secured in Northampton Gaol' till Marlborough could dispatch an officer to collect them.[2] Between July 1701 and April 1702, thirty-two of thirty-three men convicted at the Old Bailey were recorded as having been allowed to join one or other service.[3]

These measures were inadequate, and in 1704 the Queen, in her speech from the throne, had to make special mention of the recruiting problem. The House of Commons set up a committee, and, as a result of its report, passed the notable resolution of 7 January 1704:

---

[1] Secretary's Common Letter Book, 22 May 1704.
[2] SP Mil. 41/3; Letter Book 135 quoted at Clode, ii, pp. 585–6.
[3] Narcissus Luttrel quoted by Godfrey Davies, p. 151, *JSAHR.*, vol. xviii, no. 116 (London, 1950).

That a Power be given for one year to levy men in the respective counties of the Kingdom for increase of the marine companies, and for recruiting the land forces.[1]

A Bill was accordingly brought in, but when it came to detailed discussion the House shied. The clause which had originally allocated parishes a quota (to be laid down separately) was amended to read 'such able-bodied men' as were without lawful calling or visible means of subsistence—back, in short, to the original position.[2] The new Recruiting Act, in fact (Annae 3 and 4, cap. 10), recoiled even further, and supplied the early equivalent of a reserved occupation, for harvest workers were exempted from impressment between June and September. It was stated that, due to the press and men absconding because of it, the previous harvest had been brought in only with great difficulty, and the few men remaining had extorted extravagant prices for their labour. Until 1705 it was the custom at the commencement of the recruiting season to send each year a circular from the Privy Council to the J.P.s drawing their attention to the provisions for impressment of unemployed men. In that year this was considered insufficient and additional legal powers were given to the Justices to issue orders to constables to carry out searches for such men.[3] That the constables were not always completely co-operative is indicated by at least one case where they actually recovered some men from a recruiting party by force.[4] In the same year as these new instructions were issued, the Queen charged the General Officers of the Army to put their heads together. They were to constitute a 'councill or Court Martiall' to examine 'great Abuses . . . Disorders . . . and more especially ill-practices . . . in Recruiting our Forces'.[5] In the following year, this Council was transformed into the Board of General Officers, with instructions to 'redress and prevent' these 'Abuses . . . Disorders . . . and . . . ill-practices'.[6]

The only innovation sanctioned by Parliament in 1706 was

---

[1] *Journals Commons*, xiv.

[2] Ibid., 7 Mar. 1704. A certain measure of conscription of other than unemployed was imposed by stretching the Royal Prerogative in 1705, when, under Warrant, fifes, drums, and hautbois were impressed. This, however, had a precedent in Charles's reign in, e.g. 1667 and 1676: in 1680 pressing of a surgeon and mate for Tangier had been sanctioned. Walton, pp. 485–6.

[3] Annae 4 and 5, cap 21.

[4] *Dom. Cal.*, i, p. 574.

[5] CM Warrants WO 30/18.

[6] PGO 71/1.

the discharge of men erroneously enlisted—provided they repaid their levy money, and any other expenses involved, not
exceeding 20s.[1] It was about this time that the indefatigable
Hutcheson became so impressed with the difficulties that he
produced his essay on 'The Most Effective Way to Recruit the
Army'. Among his ideas was one that the number of footmen
permissible be regulated, or even that their height be limited,
as he considered that many soldierly types were thus mis-em-
ployed. In connexion with height, he attacked the army limitation of 5 feet 6 inches, because ''tis Service not Show that must
do our Business'. The proposal to recruit servants was not
entirely new. A Mr. J. Berger had in 1704 written from Amsterdam to the Secretary of State to suggest that every nobleman
with two or more lackeys should put one in the army. He had,
he stated, particularly noticed when in England the large number of men so employed and wished they had '20 or 30 thousand
in Her Majesty's Pay'.[2] Hutcheson suggested that the 20,000
might be obtained by calling up bailiffs who, he reckoned,
numbered that in London alone. These suggestions Parliament
did not adopt, but in the session 1706–7, coincident with the
drive to clear up abuses, it made some attempt to increase numbers. The Recruiting Act of 1707—Annae 6, cap. 45—showed,
if not an awareness that the existing system was insufficient, at
least an appreciation that more men had somehow to be got
into the army. The Government was ahead of the spirit of the
House. It proposed a compulsory levy on parishes and counties
of 16,000 men. The Commons rejected this part of the Bill by
185 votes to 177—the first defeat suffered by any Ministry in
Queen Anne's reign, and a symptom, discernible in retrospect,
of a slight hardening of opinion against the war.

It is not known how Hutcheson voted in the fateful division,
but his opinions on the enforcement of the existing laws seem to
have been strong enough. He discloses one of the areas of 'privilege' which did so much to weaken any efforts to 'infringe'
vested rights. A potential source of men, he wrote, was the number of 'artificers in manufactures carried on under disadvantage
due to the war, and reduced to great necessities'. Yet, not one in
one hundred would serve in the army, although they could not

[1] Annae 6, cap. 17.
[2] State Papers (Domestic Entry Book) Public Record Office (SPO) 34/4.

get bread at home without the help of the parish 'and though there is an Act of Parliament to force such idle Drones, yet their being Free of Corporat Towns tyes the Hands of the Magistrate who has not power to force them to what is so much for their own interest. For whose (advantage) is it more than the men of Sudbury, Colchester, Taunton, etc. to Fight For an Honourable Peace Abroad who are starving at Home for the want of it. But', and this may have explained why he himself renounced such a privilege, 'they tell you (and with too much truth too) that, as bad as their trade is, 'tis better than the pay of a Foot Soldier.' At any rate, the 1707 Act when finally passed tightened up the provisions for impressment of the unemployed. A central assembly of magistrates was ordered for each district on 18 March to organize a concerted 'drive' to round up those men not lawfully employed. This was to be followed by similar periodic assemblies. Anyone hindering or obstructing the execution of the Act was to be fined £5 (the money to go to the parish) with the option of one month's imprisonment. Constables showing 'neglect or default' in the execution of warrants issued were to be fined £5, 'to be levied by distress and sale of the offender's goods'. Half of this was to go to the informer, and half to the poor of the parish, excluding, presumably, the poor compulsorily enlisted. To encourage the more enthusiastic constables, their share of levy money was raised to 20s. Simultaneously, the money to volunteers enlisting before 1 May 1708 was to be raised to £5, and for those joining between 30 April 1708 and 1 March 1709 it was to revert to 40s. Those reading the Act carefully could guess from its tone that this time-limit was bluff, as there was no indication that the system of annual review was to be abandoned—and so it turned out when the 1708 Bill was passed into law.

Before then, however, there occurred the incident which really set the House of Commons by the ears. With what has been gauged to be deliberate maladroitness, St. John revealed in the course of a 'post mortem' on Almanza that, out of 29,395 English forces voted for Spain and Portugal, only 8,660 had been present at the battle. His figures on 12 January 1708 showed 800 horse and dragoons (10 regiments) and 5,600 foot (16 battalions). Elsewhere in the Peninsula there were 2 regiments of horse and dragoons, and 6 battalions of foot. He gave the strength of the horse as 80 per unit, against an establishment of 150, and the foot as 350 (his own total shows an average of just over 344) against an establishment of 500. The 14 Dutch battalions at Almanza totalled, he said, only 3,640 (just over 227 each), owing to non-arrival of reinforcements.[1] While the establishment figures in the original Votes had, it is true, to be regarded with reserve—they included, for example, officers' servants (who were not given in the 'present' figures) and did not allow for prisoners—the Government's case concealed other unpalatable truths, such as the losses in transit, although these were later to be blamed by St. John for the deficiencies. These losses 'during . . . long continuance on board ship' amounted to 300 in the most severe case, and about 250 in the remainder. That was in battalions of which the strongest was 876, and the average 807.[2] Before the Secretary produced the details which the Commons forthwith demanded, the members did realize that, whatever was at fault, men had to be provided, and the early part of 1708 shows evidence of some vigour in the approach to the problem. The first sign was an order by the House on 21 January that regiments broken in Spain be re-raised from impressment of men with no visible means of subsistence.[3] St. John's first supplementary report was presented on 3 February 1708, and is no doubt the one confessedly 'cooked up' at the Treasury. The troops in Spain and Portugal were, on paper, 28,634, but from this fell to be deducted immediately 8,550—made up of such items as a regiment counted twice, six entirely engaged on recruiting, and one taken prisoner. The remaining 19,084[4] were pulled down for various reasons to 15,585, from which there were other deductions of 3,964 due to losses in transit and prisoners, bringing the total finally to 11,621, of which 10,820 were accounted for. This remaining deficiency of 801, on St. John's own reckoning, took no account of a reinforcement of one battalion of guards—600—but the Secretary claimed that his failure to include them was outweighed by 'the great number of soldiers in hospital'. As the men inexorably 'melted' away

[1] *Journals Commons*, xv, 11 Jan. 1708.
[2] Ibid., 23 Feb. 1708.
[3] Ibid., xv.
[4] The figure should, in fact, be a trifle smaller. From other figures I have excluded a French regiment included on the English strength, but separate details are not available for this item.

for one reason or another, St. John presumably thought he was presenting a plausible case, to which he added the further consideration, that owing to the shortage of time between Parliament's Vote and the battle there had not even been time to enlist all the authorized men. The House of Commons was now really huffed. Rather than attempt to mend matters for the future by, for example, seeing to improved troopships, which would have saved some of the 4,000 reinforcement casualties, the members reiterated the figures in their previous resolution, and voted that out of 29,935 'English forces' (one regiment was, as noted above, in fact, French) provided, only 8,660 were in Spain and Portugal at the time of the battle of Almanza; Her Majesty was requested to lay before the House an account of how 'it came to pass'.[1] A second reply could not, of course, improve on that already given. The facts would remain unpalatable, and the remedy continue to require hard thought and work rather than oratory. Her Majesty pointed out that the Peninsula had, with the West Indies, been particularly favoured by drafting to fill up regiments in spite of the fact that this 'had been found ruinous to the Service'.[2] Eventually on 24 February 1708, the House resolved that the deficiency of English troops in Spain and Portugal at the time of Almanza had been chiefly occasioned 'by the want of timely and effectual Recruits being sent thither'.[3]

Lack of recruits for any theatre was emphasized in the figures laid before the House on 31 March 1708. Towards a requirement of 18,657, only 868 had so far been recruited—37 volunteers and 831 pressed men. (Fuller details are given at Appendix F.) The inevitable resolution which followed sagely noted that there appeared to be a 'great Deficiency in the Number of Recruits', and asked for a proclamation to be issued to the Justices of the Peace to impose strictly the impressment clauses of the Recruiting Acts. Although the evidence was that the real trouble was lack of men coming or being brought forward, the House asked that Her Majesty should show her particular displeasure to officers dismissing men or refusing to enlist them for a bribe or 'any other Pretence' or who should 'otherwise neglect or be wanting in their Duty upon this occasion'.[4]

[1] *Journals Commons*, xv, 3 Feb. 1708.   [2] Ibid., 18 Feb. 1708.
[3] Ibid.   [4] Ibid., 31 Mar. 1708.

Not to be outdone in vigorous words, the Government recast the entire Recruiting Act to which it even gave a new preamble declaring that it was 'to bring the present war to a speedy and happy conclusion'.[1] Faced with the House's rejection of conscription 'lest it prejudice chances at the election' (Marlborough in a letter to the Elector of Hanover[2]), the Government had to find some other plan. This was the first known provision in British military history for short-service volunteers.[3] In view of later quibblings over the interpretation of the Act, it is worth noting that the wording laid down quite specifically that 'every person who shall enter himself as a Volunteer, or be listed upon this Act' might demand his discharge in three years' time 'anything herein contained to the contrary notwithstanding'. In an endeavour to infuse more energy into conscription of the unemployed, the Commissioners of the Land Tax were made joint commissioners for recruiting with the Justices of the Peace. As in the previous year, there was to be a general assembly for a concerted 'drive' on an appointed day, and areas were to be subdivided to ensure closer attention. Voluntary recruits were to receive £5, while the officers of a town or parish raising men were to get 20s. per man, plus 6d. a day subsistence until he was taken away by his regiment. The man's pay was to commence from the day of enlistment, not, as previously, from the date actually taken into his regiment. A further reward of £3 per man was to be paid to the local churchwardens or Overseers of the Poor. The provisions regarding discharge were, in response to the House's resolution, tightened up, and the fine on defaulting constables was increased to £10, to be raised by distress. One gets the impression of some eminently practical man having a hand in this vigorously worded and businesslike act. It included provision for 5s. per recruit as pay for clerks to the Commissioners—no inconsiderable concession in days when staffs had normally to be paid by 'skimming' money allotted in bulk. All the rewards paid out by the

---

[1] Annae 7, cap. 2.

[2] Murray, iii, p. 665: dispatch of 23 Jan. 1708.

[3] The provision for enlistment for Tangier in 1679 had laid down a three-year tour, and the men to be 'well paid in the meantime', but it does not appear to have been intended that this was to be the entire obligation of service. Walton, p. 486. A Scots Act of 1696 for a compulsory levy of 1,000 men stipulated only three years' service.

Commissioners were to be charged to the regiments, which goes some way to explaining the generous scale voted by Parliament. The minimum height of recruits was set at 5 feet 5 inches (no limitation was previously laid down in the Act, but one was evidently applied—see Hutcheson's comments above), and Her Majesty was authorized to suspend the Act as soon as sufficient men should have been raised.[1] The drastic proposal that the Secretary at War should keep an 'alphabetical book of all enlisted persons' was too revolutionary, and was rejected.[2] One unexpected consequence of this Act was a claim by Coventry magistrates that, since all enlistment was now governed by Act of Parliament, officers were no longer entitled to recruit volunteers. The claim was rejected by the Secretary at War, whose ruling was confirmed by the legal authorities.[3]

During this year (between 12 March 1708 and 21 June 1709), there were at least eighteen pardons on enlistment from Newgate—specifically mentioned in Walpole's note of 20 August 1709,[4] but prisoners continued to petition for greater facilities for joining. Those in the Fleet asked on 21 December 1708 to be allowed to serve or to find a fit substitute, and were followed on 4 February and 9 February 1709 by those in Marshalsea, Wood Street, and Poultney Compters.[5] This source, of course, could not make a significant contribution, and at the winter season of 1708 there were 14,865 recruits required. In December it was reported that the Justices had handed over 1,750. Middlesex topped the list with 257, followed by Gloucestershire with 105. Berkshire produced 1 and Hereford 3. The bounty money figures show that the number of volunteers had increased to 257. The biggest drafts were to Mark Ker's and Bowles's regiments (125 and 114 respectively), while Tyrawly and Sabine got one apiece.[6] The winter of 1709 showed considerable improvement at 1,087 volunteers and 5,825 pressed men.[7] This left the field force deficiencies on 17 March 1710 at 4,253, made up as follows:

---

[1] It was so suspended on 9 June 1709, reimposed on 8 Nov. 1709, and finally revoked in 1713.
[2] *Journals Commons*, xv, 2 Feb. 1708.
[3] Entry Books WO 26/13.
[4] SP Mil. 41/3. [5] *Journals Commons*, xvi.
[6] Ibid., 11 Dec. 1708.
[7] Ibid., 13 Feb. 1710.

Great Britain	1,947
Flanders	962
Spain	700
Portugal	644[1]

By the end of 1711, however, it was calculated by Grenville that 5,000 men were required for the following year in Flanders —that is the force was about 75 per cent. of establishment. It is not surprising that Sergeant Kite was considered to have put up an outstanding performance by recruiting five men in one week, even if they were 'the strong man of Kent, the King of the Gypsies, a Scotch pedlar, a Scoundrel Attorney, and a Welsh parson'. He had indeed to let the attorney go—on the instructions of his captain who would not have men who could write since it meant they would draw up petitions. Shortage of seamen—a constant problem throughout the war[2]—aggravated the difficulties, and special provision was inserted in the 1710 Recruiting Act that commissioners should examine all recruits to make sure they were not sailors. That the commissioners were particularly diligent (or uncorrupt?) at their task is suggested by the General Officers' consideration of several cases where seamen had been handed over by the Commissioners to the land service. The generals made the best of it for their own service with the consoling reflection that the men had been at sea 'only a year or two'.[3]

The inevitable full-scale breakdown of the system took place in the Peninsula. By August 1711 efforts to keep the forces up to strength by reinforcement had been virtually abandoned. On 31 August instructions were issued that the weakest regiments should be disbanded, the troops transferred to the strongest, and the officers sent home. If the regiments of deserters from the enemy could not be kept up to strength by deserters, then they too were to be broken up, and the men distributed among the other regiments.[4] By then the authorities were already procras-

---

[1] Ibid., 17 Mar. 1710.

[2] The shortage of seamen, blamed at the time on the excessive wages paid in the merchant service (surely the only time in history?), engaged the attention of Defoe, who at one time submitted an elaborate scheme for a State Sea Service which would supply men for both Royal Navy and merchant service. A special Act was passed in 1705 'For the Encouragement and Increase of Seamen, and for the Better and Speedier manning of Her Majesty's Fleet'. Annae 4 and 5, cap. 19.

[3] SP Mil. 41/3.   [4] SP Mil. 41/4: minute from Cockpit, 31 Aug. 1711.

tinating over the release of the first 'three year men' enlisted under the 1708 Act. On 27 February 1711 Grenville, now Secretary at War, had first raised the point when two men in Portsmouth refused to take their pay after expiry of their service. This, being presumably not covered by No. 14 of the Articles of War—'if any number of soldiers shall presume to assemble and take counsel amongst themselves for the demanding of their Pay . . . (they) shall be punished with death'—the question was referred to the Attorney-General and the men to the guardroom. The Attorney-General replied that they would have to be released. Exhibiting a somewhat squeamish conscience, he went on to say that it was considered 'not proper' to put a clause in the next bill to extend their service by a further two years.[1] The opinion does not seem to have been accepted as conclusive guidance for the future. Indeed, with shortages of men such that the Lords of Committee in Council and the General Officers combined to recommend that 'in case any man die, desert, or be discharged', he should be allowed to remain on the rolls for the next two musters, to provide money for recruits, the Government was unlikely to surrender any more men than it could possibly help.[2] In January 1713 the Norfolk Commissioners for the Act, feeling, no doubt, some moral responsibility, petitioned on behalf of five short-service men of the area who, they said, on asking for their discharge were 'beat and threatened with further ill-usage'.[3] On 13 May 1712 the Attorney-General, in a further opinion, had stated that the Act applied, in fact, only to men enlisted at specific assemblies of the Commissioners. Even this seems to have been scant comfort in some quarters. A Flanders commanding officer wrote that, if the Act were applied, he would lose at least sixty of his best men. 'There is not a regiment of Foot of Her Majesty's Subject Troops in Flanders', he went on, 'but will lose at least as many.' As for the Attorney-General's ruling, it would take in most of the volunteers.[4] By the time they were eventually discharged, the men cannot have been out of the service very long before their comrades impressed or enlisted in the normal manner. The provision for three years' service, however, made its appearance

in the 1712 Mutiny Act,[1] the shortest period of voluntary peace-
time service for untrained soldiers in the British Army until
nearly 250 years later.

Regimental Finances: Levy Money

When new regiments were raised, a fixed sum was allowed for
each recruit, but there was certainly no guarantee, and probably no intention that this entire sum was for the men enlisted,
even if all colonels were not expected to model themselves on
Falstaff who, in his time, 'misused the King's Press (and) . . . got
in exchange of 150 soldiers, 300 and odd pounds'. The Government paid this levy money only on first raising. That for replacements for deserters, men killed or 'otherwise disposed of by the
Almighty', had to be provided from the regimental profits.[2] If
the gaps were not filled the regiment was, of course, respited
not only for the subsistence, but also for the 2d. per day off-
reckonings, most of which had, in all probability, been already
contracted away for clothing. Such losses could not be eliminated in advance by, for example, drawing money for the entire regiment before it was completely recruited; not only was
the officer, as Hutcheson pointed out, 'sworn to the day of
enlisting soldiers', but, in the case of newly raising regiments,
the warrant always laid down a minimum number of men who
had to be enlisted before mustering could start at all. Existing
regiments were bound, in principle, to meet any recruiting
costs, including levy money, out of the Stock Purse Fund, i.e.
the balance of the off-reckonings before clothing had been paid
for. When war, or other casualties, increased the cost beyond
what regimental funds could be expected to bear, relief was,
however, frequently, and perhaps normally, given, either as an
allowance from respites, or out of the Vote for 'extraordinaries'.[3]

[1] There was no Recruiting Act in 1712, and the Mutiny Act was the first of its
kind to cover peacetime conditions in Queen Anne's reign.

[2] Hutcheson claims that the Queen also met the cost on drafting, but the very
large number of warrants in existence which ordered regiments receiving drafted
men to pay the equivalent of levy money and ancillary costs (normally £3) to the
drafting regiment makes it difficult to accept his claim without further evidence.
The theory and practice of Levy Money, however, are as complicated matters as
any in the reign: there are few generalizations to which an exception cannot be
adduced. Many examples of payment of equivalent of levy money for drafted men
are in the Secretary at War's Entry Books (WO 26).

[3] Clode, ii, pp. 2, 3.

As early as 1594 the Privy Council had ruled that, although captains were responsible for the immediate replacement of men 'departed for any reason', a month's pay would be allowed to help meet levying, transporting, and equipping expenses.[1]

The Mutiny Act of 1703 laid down that all money arising from respites (i.e. the money representing the pay of the difference between establishments and strengths) might be applied for recruiting. The money was not necessarily, however, drawn by the regiments according to their establishment figures, but was distributed as laid down by the Queen, the Prince Consort, the Lord Treasurer, the Commissioners of the Treasury, the Captain-General, or (for marines) the Lord High Admiral.[2] Thus, money saved on respites in the West Indies, for example, was ordered by a Secretary at War's Establishment Warrant of 16 April 1704 to be applied as levy money in such proportions as the Queen, the Generalissimo, the Lord Treasurer, or the Captain-General might lay down.[3] Unless some such theoretically exceptional step was taken, levy money, so far as reinforcements were concerned, represented merely an advance of pay to the regiment, rather than a bounty. When Parliament in the Recruiting Acts stipulated a specific sum for levy money, this did not necessarily represent a claim by regiments on the Treasury, but indicated an obligation on the part of the regiments towards recruits. In the case of entirely new regiments, there was an actual grant, so that the colonel might meet the initial outlay.[4] Later in the reign, when Recruiting Acts raised the levy money payable, 40s. of the cost was met by the Government, but by that time recruits for the Peninsula, for instance, were reckoned to cost at least £6 (rising to £9) more than their levy money on account of the cost of transport, clothing, and feeding until the first muster—and if the recruit died before the muster, there was no levy money at all.[5] In general all levy money had in the first instance to be paid by the officers on the spot, many

[1] Cruickshank, pp. 18–19.

[2] Annae 2 and 3, cap. 17.   [3] Ests. WO 24/37.

[4] Forbes, p. 85. See the report by St. John in September 1704 on a proposition to raise a regiment at private expense. In calculating the saving, he includes levy money for 658 soldiers at £3 each. Letter Book 133, p. 77, quoted at Clode, ii, pp. 581–2.

[5] Examples are PGO WO 71/3/12–13: meeting of Board of General Officers, 19 June 1714, and *Journals Commons*, xvii, 2 Apr. 1714.

of whom were still hopefully claiming refunds years after the war had finished. Conversely the possession and payment of this money from regimental funds could involve the individual recruiting officers in difficulties. Hutcheson claimed that more officers were 'disgraced, broken, and cashiered' on account of recruiting than from any other cause. If he was recruiting while the regiment was abroad, desertion was so expensive that his whole pay could not make good the cost. Only by raising money through the sale of his commission (i.e. by realizing, in effect, his life's savings) could he meet the charge. He might do all in his power, but ''tis no excuse . . . you had the Levy Money, Sir, and if you have not your men, your commission must answer it'.[1]

The raising of recruits and, latterly, the amount of levy money were dealt with in the Recruiting Acts; the source of the levy money, when mentioned, was covered in the Mutiny Acts. Annae 2 and 3, cap. 17, laid down that the money from respites was to go towards the levy money 'as the whole charge . . . for such recruits, except for men or horses killed or taken by the enemy or lost at sea'.[2] An example has been given above of one case where similar provision was made by departmental instruction. The distinction between such waivers and the carrying of fictitious men or 'faggots' on the muster rolls was, of course, a fine one. In 1695, indeed, there were 5,747 faggots authorized by Royal Warrant.[3] As early in Anne's reign as 29 January 1703 a petition from America talked of 'the whole army whilst in Flanders being allowed complete without muster rolls, in consideration of the great loss and charge they were at in recruiting'.[4] Regiments which lost their muster rolls or failed for any reason to submit them had to follow a heart-breaking procedure to get their money, which was normally only paid, in fact, if the House of Commons resolved accordingly—usually by a clause in the Mutiny Act. What the troops in America no doubt meant was that the regiments' muster rolls had been

---

[1] A specimen case of selling a commission to pay for levy money is dealt with in Southwell's letter of 11 Nov. 1710. SP Mil. 41/3.

[2] But for its omission of mention of deserters, this would bear out the general rule that the Government met the cost of levy money only on newly raising. It may have been that this specific earmarking of respites represented safeguarding from what rapacious commanding officers regarded as 'very legitimate perquisites'.

[3] Woodruff, p. 279.   [4] *Journals Commons*, xiv.

overruled by orders from the Secretary at War to pay them according to establishment, and not according to strength.[1] In the Secretary at War's papers of the period are many warrants to allow regiments to muster 'as full' in order to meet extraordinary recruiting expenditure.[2]

It was in the Peninsula, of course, that regiments experienced their greatest difficulties. The men hated the theatre, and foot regiments serving there, unless commanded by well-known officers, or of sufficient standing to give additional bounties, found it more and more difficult to function. Horse and dragoon regiments were usually just able to keep themselves up to strength without calling on the Treasury and without levy money. This was due partly to better pay, and partly to prestige. In the case of line regiments, the generals complained repeatedly that, if the mustering rules were strictly applied, recruiting was impossible. Even the Commissary of Musters in Portugal was moved on 18 November 1710 to complain 'the difficulties we lye under in recruiting is very great, and the charge extraordinary; there's not a man comes from GREAT BRITTAIN on this account, but what costs the officer from £6 to £8; and considering how many of them dye on their landing, especially when they are sent over by transports'. Of 300 recently landed, he concluded, not a hundred reached their regiments.[3] Portmore, a few months later, stated: 'Any method of recruiting would be of more service than what is in use.' Every packet, he wrote, brought some recruits so bad that they could not be used, and he had had to order the enlistment of Spanish or Portuguese. Very indifferent recruits were costing £8 to £9 and only a third of those embarked were joining the regiments in the field.[4] It was, above all, this endemic shortage of men in the Peninsula that made the abolition of drafting between regiments impossible despite widespread opposition

[1] Ranelagh, however, did quote one such case in his exculpation where he claimed that troops could, in fact, be paid *without* muster rolls, if the Secretary at War were to issue a warrant accordingly. His example came from the previous reign. *Journals Commons*, xiv, 30 Nov. 1702.

[2] Two examples are at *Dom. Cal.*, i, p. 248, and SP Mil. 41/3, Aug. 1710: e.g. note of 7 Oct. 1710 from Secretary at War's office which states it has been the custom in Portugal for non-effective money to remain, after the monthly reviews, with the Paymaster for recruiting.

[3] Treas. 1/136/13.

[4] *Treas. Cal.*, iv, p. 242: dispatch of 6 Jan. 1711.

to which even the Queen herself paid lip service. One of the most vigorous of all Marlborough's protests was against drafting for the Peninsula as early as 1705, but even he could not stop the practice.[1] At that time the Gibraltar garrison was at half strength, and by January 1706 so weak that officers could not be detached for recruiting. Drafting was necessary, wrote the commander, for the units 'unless speedily recruited will dwindle to nothing'.[2]

Although the Peninsula was the most expensive theatre in terms of numbers of men, the West Indies was, in proportion to the number deployed, the most difficult, primarily due to heavy losses from sickness. At the same time as the Gibraltar governor was calling for reinforcements, the Leeward Islands were complaining that the only companies which were full 'were kept by enlisting inhabitants of the island and servants when their period of servitude expired'.[3] This did not, of course, commend itself to the local population as it meant no real increase in their strength. Not one of twenty companies sent to Jamaica at that time was above thirty strong, and the commander of another West Indies expedition was authorized, in order to fill gaps due to casualties and sickness, to take in local half-pay officers.[4] Over three years, eighty-six reinforcements were sent to New York for four companies whose strength varied from seventy-four to ninety-three.[5] In 1707 the Governor of St. Nevis wrote that the recruits sent out were either old men or boys 'fit for nothing, some so bad the officers are so ashamed of as to discharge'. Those discharged were so bad that they could not even work and were left to beg their bread. The situation, to be sure, does not seem to have unduly perturbed the commanding officer, who, the Governor complained, was taking his pleasure in London with several of his officers. Of the officers remaining, only one captain and very few of the lieutenants or ensigns had seen service. The Governor's confession that he could not work miracles would seem almost to have disqualified him for the post in these circumstances, but he bravely concluded by writing that he hoped he would do his duty.[6]

---

[1] Anne Cal., p. 179.   [2] SP Mil. 41/3/81.   [3] H.M.C.H. of L., vii, p. 261.
[4] SP Mil. 41/3/86: St. John on 23 Feb. 1705. Dom. Cal., i, p. 548.
[5] H.M.C.H. of L., vii, p. 318: position at 24 Feb. 1707.
[6] Treas. Cal., iii, p. 53.

While the need abroad grew greater, in England newer ways of making illicit money were constantly being discovered— release of 'pressed' men for a consideration,[1] enlistment of debtors as a formality, only to secure their release from prison, refusal by local constables to deliver men up without a *douceur*, and enlistment in order to desert with the levy money were only a few.[2] Constables who were allowed 6*d.* a day subsistence for recruits refused to deliver them under 18*d.*, while recruiters like the infamous Colonel Charteris who did very well out of 'thieves, bad characters, and debtor swishing to defraud their creditors' made the customary money 'on the side' by recruiting men under duress and threatening to send them to Spain unless 'compensation' was forthcoming for their discharge.[3] A lucrative form of fraud was to run a 'fake' recruiting party from which the men had to buy their release. The first mention I have seen is for 1703, when Blathywayt replied to an inquiry from the Mayor of Dorchester. Whoever, he wrote, had been recruiting in that area was an impostor with counterfeit orders. 'No officer', the Secretary at War pointed out, 'ought to take upon him to beat up for volontiers without an authority under Her Majesty's Own hand, or an authentick copy thereof attested by the Secretary at War.'[4] Deserters with sham discharges, men who had bribed their way out, or released debtors who never served, were a further discouragement to volunteers and provided the magistrates and other civil authorities with fresh ground for complaint against the military. One of the earliest tasks of the Board of General Officers was to carry out a 'purge'

---

[1] Farquhar's constable did it for 11*s.*, thus making 1*s.* more than the levy money payable to him—but he was unlucky as the magistrates forthwith impressed him.

[2] Taylor, a 'professional deserter' from the Guards, was stated, when finally convicted, to have collected £60 in *one year* by enlisting and deserting.

[3] Fort., pp. 573, 576.

[4] A specimen recruiting order, signed by the Secretary at War on behalf of the Queen and addressed 'To . . . or to the officers appointed by him to raise recruits' reads: 'These are to authorize you by Beat of Drum or otherwise to raise so many Volontiers as shall be wanting to recruit and fill up the respective Companys of our Regiment of Foot under Your Command for Our Service wherein all Magistrates Justices of the Peace Constables or other Our Officers whom it may concern are hereby required to be assisting unto you and in providing Quarters and otherwise as there shall be occasion. Given at Our Court at St James's this 26th day of March 1702 in the First Year of Our Reign.' Entry Books WO 26/11.

against debtors whose names were on the books of the Guards merely to evade their creditors. In their early days they spent a very large amount of time on detailed examination of recruiting abuses, and checking suspect muster rolls.[1]

Officers, who were in such straits that they prayed, like Plume, to have an honest man 'in my company for the novelty's sake', undoubtedly took matters into their own hands, and used combinations of guile and force. The Justices of the Peace exhibited, in general, little sympathy, but Farquhar shows that, where they and the recruiting officer did find each other agreeable, provisions for impressing the unemployed might be interpreted liberally—and coin of the realm may have been as effective a sanction as solicitude for defence of the realm. 'Were you my child, I'd send you to Bedlam first, or the army afterwards', the Justices might declare. The men hailed before them, however, were not their children, but 'a very impudent fellow, fit for a soldier . . . a whoremaster . . . and therefore fit to go', or (this was the captain's own plea) 'a very pretty Fellow, and therefore fit to serve'. Voters irregularly enlisted could get powerful support from their M.P.s and normally did not have undue trouble in securing their discharge, but there were cases which had to go to the Queen's Bench. Random examples of 'routine' cases are Samuel Meales, an elector of Abingdon, ordered to be released by the Secretary at War on 19 July 1706, and three unwilling dragoons who, in 1707, were 'listed in an unjustifiable manner . . . men of good substance, not within the intentions of the Act of Parliament'.[2] In 1707 two Danes were forcibly enlisted, but later discharged.[3] It is not surprising, in the circumstances, to find electors providing themselves with passes—for example two setting out on a journey to London in 1706 had documents certifying that they were 'on lawful occasions', qualified to vote for a Member of Parliament, and, therefore, not liable to be impressed.[4] Less influential citizens had their own means of achieving the same result. The inhabitants of Sussex, for example, were officially described as 'difficult to press', because they 'fly into woods and there form themselves into bodies able to resist the country'.[5] In 1705, in neighbouring

---

[1] PGO WO 71/1.
[2] Entry Books WO 26/13.
[3] Ibid., 10 Jan. 1707.
[4] Ibid., 16 Jan. 1706.
[5] *Dom. Cal.*, i, p. 847.

Hampshire, two sergeants, a corporal, and three privates of Burr's regiment were severely manhandled by a band of twenty people as they were taking a Joseph Cooper, 'enlisted by the J.P.s of Romsey as a disorderly fellow', to Southampton.[1] A large number of the recruits in the Savoy had themselves mutinied early in the previous year, and two were killed when the guard fired to quell the disturbance.[2] In the Recruiting Act of 1708 there is mention of numbers of deserters resorting to Threapwood, near Chester. They had apparently some sort of 'hideout' there, and the Commissioners for the County of Chester and the officers of Threapwood were ordered to apply the Act in that area.[3] Captain Gabriel Crespigny of Lieutenant-General George's regiment, while recruiting in Wigan, met with 'a very barbarous Treatmt from the People who had gathered Themselves together in a tumultuous Manner to hinder his carrying off Recruits, and assaulting him with Stones.' He suffered one broken rib, several bruises, was 'long . . . under Surgeons and Physitians', and had an expensive journey to 'the Bath'. Like many others, he was, by all this, reduced to 'very great necessity and straits', and had incurred such a debt that he was 'unable to subsist without speedy relief'. There is no evidence to show that he was given it.[4]

The story of recruitment and reinforcement during the reign is an epitome of the administrative side of the war—antiquated methods, not always aggravated by corruption, leading relentlessly to a hopeless impasse. Regiments were kept in anything approaching fighting trim only by the diligent work of their own recruiting officers, and the determination of officers and men in the field. The army had a fairly clear idea of what it wanted—subsidized foreign troops in the Peninsula, and a levy on parishes along the lines of that for the militia. The two principal reasons for action and inaction elsewhere were that some things had always been done before, and others had never been done before. They were to retain their validity for many years. The results of the inability to realize changed methods were required

---

[1] SPO 34/6, 11 Sept. 1705.
[2] War Letters WO 4/2, Secretary at War on 13 March 1704. Special legal advice had to be obtained from the Attorney-General to defend the Coldstream Guardsmen who had opened fire.
[3] Annae 7, cap. 2.   [4] PGO WO 71/2: meeting of 10 Feb. 1712.

were a long and costly drain on the country in Spain, suffering and inability to establish settled society in the Plantations, and considerable slowing down of the war in its later stages, even in Flanders which was in the most-favoured position of all the theatres.

The burden of the recruiting fell on England, for Irish Catholics were excluded, and other Irish regiments could only be used with care as they were susceptible to propaganda, especially if opposed by their compatriots of the Wild Geese.[1] The Scots were, to a lesser extent, also suspect. With these two sources restricted, the provision of a large-scale army was a more difficult problem than in succeeding wars of the pre-1914 type, and required bold action, broad minds, and original thought. The M.P.s of Queen Anne's time may have possessed all these virtues: their modesty certainly prevented them from displaying them in their dealings with the army.

[1] Dispatches in the Ormonde papers bracket Scots and dissident Irish, and Trevelyan states that Scottish Highlanders were, in fact, enlisted in the Irish regiments in France. *English Social History*, G. M. Trevelyan (London, Reprint Society Edition, 1948), p. 452. (*Social History.*)

IV

PAY, CLOTHING, AND QUARTERING

PAY

THE change over the centuries in the description of soldiering from a 'trade' to a 'profession' is more in consonance with actual development than might be expected. It is essential, if the tortuous maze of subsistence, off-reckonings, accoutrements, respites, clearings, and muster rolls is to lead towards any degree of understanding of Anne's armies, to grasp that, for regimental officers, soldiering was indeed a trade or business which might show a profit or a disastrous loss. A regiment could fairly be described as a property owned by an unlimited company of which the Commanding Officer was managing director, and the officers partners or sole shareholders. Honest and efficient commanding officers had, with good luck, fair property from which they made a reasonable income; corrupt colonels had bad property from which they made much more. This property could be bought and sold. It represented, for a man of rank, his savings and investment. It was scarcely more corrupt to buy a commission in Queen Anne's time than it was, until 1948, to buy a medical practice. It was a straightforward business transaction with prices governed as much by convention as by supply and demand. Once on the rungs of the ladder, an officer had to pay for every promotion, whether by seniority or by merit. If he had no money, then he got no promotion, unless he were fortunate enough to be promoted to a vacancy caused by death. The only exceptions were officers of the artillery and engineers, 'a peculiar people subject to the Master General of the Ordnance', from whom they held their commissions.

The records of the time do not support the Duke of Wellington's assertion that promotion by purchase 'exempts the British army from the character of being a "mercenary army" '. In the same way, we must modify Clode's contention, 'the pay of the officer cannot be looked upon—having regard to the purchase of his commission—in any other light than as an "honorarium", clearly indicating the policy of employing men of independent means—not mere professional officers—in the military service of the Crown'. It may have been true that, at any one time, 'three fourths of the whole number receive but little for their services besides the honour of serving the King'; a large proportion of those who comprised that three-quarters looked forward to the day when they might join the remaining quarter.[1] The Roundhead Ready-Reckoner, *The Souldier's Accompt*, as befitted a more plebeian army, talked of '. . . profit being one of the chief ends why men undertake the military profession and honour not the only (though the chiefest) of their aims. . . .'[2]

Up to the rank of colonel, there was a regular scale of pay according to rank. It ranged from 8*d.* per day for the private foot-soldier, or sentinel, to 12*s.* per day for his colonel. General officers received no standard 'pay of rank', and had always to be provided for on a special parliamentary estimate along with staff officers. Pay for them ranged, by convention, from £10 per day for commanders-in-chief to £1. 10*s.* for a brigadier. This represented, of course, only a portion of those officers' earnings, since they invariably had a company and regiment in their name for which they also drew pay, and any perquisites for which that appointment made them eligible. Their absence from their regiments was the origin of the quip in *The Recruiting Officer*:

> You shall receive your pay and do no duty.
> Then you must make me a field officer.

Officers drew extra money for forage, and there were further allowances for servants. Detailed rates for all ranks are given in Appendix G.

All pay was divided under two heads—subsistence, and arrears, or off-reckonings. The term arrears was normally restricted to officers' pay, and off-reckonings exclusively applied to other ranks. In Elizabethan times, subsistence had also been known as the imprest—a term still used today with the similar meaning of an advance, although not restricted to pay. Subsist-

---

[1] Clode, i, p. 106.
[2] *The Souldier's Accompt.* By T.R. (London (?), 1647). (*Souldier's Accompt.*)

ence was what its name conveys, a proportion of pay to provide for a soldier's subsistence. It was, in theory, paid in advance without deduction. There may be a record somewhere of this having actually taken place on some occasion in the period considered. I have been unable to find any evidence of such a case. In the 1704 Mutiny Act subsistence was prescribed as 6*d.* out of the 8*d.* of a private foot-soldier, 8*d.* out of their 1*s.* for corporals and drummers, and 1*s.* out of their 1*s.* 6*d.* for sergeants, with corresponding proportions in the cavalry and dragoons. Of the total subsistence, 1*s.* per week for sergeants, 2*d.* a week for corporals and drummers, and 6*d.* a week for private soldiers had only to be accounted for by the commanding officer every two months. The evidence shows that, even in the rare instances when money was available, the figures of cash payments were not (with the exception of 3*s.* 0*d.* of the private soldier's weekly 3*s.* 6*d.*) observed with too great nicety overseas. The subsistence paid to horse and dragoons contained an element (half in the case of a private dragoon) for feeding the soldiers' mounts at dry forage, and the soldier was stopped a portion of the subsistence in summer, when the animals went to grass, to contribute towards the cost of remounts. There is evidence to show that the soldier had not always been restricted in his actual receipts to this 3*s.* 6*d.* per week subsistence. The author of the *Recruiting Essay*, dealing with 'the clipping and pareing the soldiers' pay', claimed that, in Cromwell's time, auxiliaries sent to France received their entire 4*s.* 8*d.* per week (i.e. 8*d.* per day) 'constantly paid . . . on the drum head and no stoppage to be made on any pretence', except for a coat or hat at a cost not exceeding 20*s.* Even this, he added, was, in fact, normally given to the soldier free as a reward for good service. In Anne's armies, on the other hand, although the Mutiny Act laid down that subsistence was to be 3*s.* paid weekly, and the odd 6*d.* accounted for every two months, yet, on foreign service, it was claimed, the man's captain did not account for this money. The officer merely claimed that the 6*d.* was laid out in necessaries. 'The tent [the soldier] lies in, the Kettle he dresses his Victuals in,[1] the canteen he carries his Water in (or Beer, when he can get it), and for the very Exchange of Musquats (made useless by Time and Ser-

---

[1] An unexpected tribute came from the same source, when talking of the bread supplied, he wrote that 'the soldier has no reason to complain of the commissary'.

vice)[1] are stopt out of the odd sixpence a week.' The officer did not lose since he stopped this money both in the field and in the barracks during campaigning. An example of a year's regimental necessaries or contingencies on which the sixpences, &c., would be spent shows (for 1707) 676 spatterdashes and haversacks, 39 sergeants' spatterdashes, 13 camp colours, 26 drum cases 'and charge for painting drums', 200 knapsacks, 130 kettles and flasks, 493 bowls, buckles for sergeants, and buckles and garters for men.[2] The appropriation of the 6d. probably dated from 1687 when an order in the *London Gazette* laid down that 3s. a week was to be paid in two equal portions without deduction. Captains were further to account every two months for 6d. a week 'allowed ... for the providing such necessaries to each soldier to which the off-reckonings or residue of their pay hath not been formerly liable'.[3] At any rate, N.C.O.s and men, unless in a regiment broken up between two clothings, received no cash over and above their subsistence. Normally they would have been satisfied to receive even that. It has been reckoned that the private soldier was relieved indeed if he got 4d. per day to himself.[4]

What did this represent in money values of the age? A useful source of comparison is Gregory King's tables which, referring to the time of the Revolution, calculate yearly incomes from the hearth-tax figures. These show knights with about £650 per year, lesser clergymen £50, 'labouring people and outservants' £15, and cottagers and paupers £6. 10s.[5] Allowing for the continuation of inflation between 1688 and Anne's reign, one

[1] Elizabeth's soldiers who had to pay for the very arrows they fired would have considered him lucky. The Articles of War of 4 Feb. 1717, as recast after submission to the House, laid down (paragraph 43) that a soldier selling or wilfully losing property or stealing from his comrades should suffer a weekly stoppage not exceeding half of his pay. This was the only stoppage permissible except those under Sign Manual, and could be imposed only by a regimental court martial, which could order confinement or corporal punishment in addition. *Journals Commons*, xviii.

[2] Fort. Hist., pp. 189–90.
[3] Walton, p. 652, footnote 1908.
[4] Woodruff, p. 266; see also Walton, p. 681.
[5] Extracts from the Tables are: knights £650; merchants and traders £400; lesser clergymen £50; freeholders £55–£91; shopkeepers and tradesmen £45; labouring people and outservants £15; common soldiers £14; cottagers and paupers £6. 10s. (Quoted in *Social History*, p. 279.) The soldier's pay was actually £12. 4s. at 8d. per day in a 366-day year; a dragoon would get £27. 9s. and a cavalry trooper £45. 15s., but at least one-third of the last two would necessarily be expended on the horses.

quarter can be added to all of these. The soldier's pay, however, remained unaltered. The politician of later years who opposed increases in soldiers' pay because they made the army licentious need not have feared for the morals of Queen Anne's men.[1] In the *Recruiting Essay* it was contended that, if the soldier's pay were to hold its original value, then it would require to be 1s. 6d. per day. Even present-day memories can go back to a time when it actually reached that figure. Hutcheson claimed that, in south England, a footman had £20 per year, and a sailor 18s. per month 'besides his Dyer', even when completely unskilled. Other sources show that a skilled, or able, seaman got 24s. per month, plus a daily victualling allowance of a gallon of beer, 1 lb. of biscuit, and 2 lb. of beef—a substantial nourishment by soldiers' standards.[2] Extra labourers employed by the Ordnance Department got 1s. 6d. per day, including Sundays and holidays.[3] Nevertheless, conceded Hutcheson, the English pay was 'the largest in the world', although it did not carry 'due encouragement to serve in the infantry abroad'. He contended that the rates of 26 stivers (approx. 2s. 6d.) per week, plus bread in the field, and 32 stivers (approx. 3s. 0d.) in garrison, where the soldier had to find his own meat, drink, washing, and repair of arms, were insufficient. There were, in addition, clothing renewals, since the official allowance was insufficient—for instance the soldier received each year only one pair of shoes, a most essential part of his equipment when all movement was on foot. Hutcheson remarked: 'It must be good husbanding if (clothing) does not amount to 4–5 stivers per week'—i.e. just over 6d. As a result of all this, he went on, 'even in plentiful campaigns'—that is, when plunder was good—the soldier's pay was 'not sufficient to support the common necessities of Nature'.[4] He had a scheme by which, to improve conditions of foreign service, soldiers in England should be allowed to work for private employers, and 2d. of their pay diverted to troops abroad.[5] They would then

---

[1] Clode, i, p. 106.

[2] *Samuel Pepys: The Years of Peril*, Arthur Bryant (Cambridge, 1935), p. 129. (*Years of Peril.*) [3] Registers WO 25/336.

[4] He claims that recruiting was stimulated after a successful campaign because the insufficient pay was augmented by 'the gratitude of Friends (rescued from bondage) and the Plunder of Enemies'. Readers of Mother Ross's memoirs will perhaps assimilate the two sources.

[5] It was not exceptional for them to work for the Ordnance abroad—one example was at Placentia in 1713 when an order was issued for them to work on

have clothing, and 6*d*. per week for shoes, shirts, and stockings, or the money at the end of two months, their 3*s*. per week subsistence, and lodging, fire, and candle, 'besides the advantage of working'. Under these conditions, he claimed, the soldier would be as well off as a freeholder of £20–£25.

This was, of course, a flight of fancy. In the meantime, not only had the soldier to be content with his infrequently paid fraction of 6*d*. per day, but had to think himself lucky if that was in money, and not in tallies at such a discount that they would fetch only a fraction of their nominal value. The discount was normally about 30 per cent., but at one time so low did the tallies fall that even the Bank of England and the East India Company, on whom considerable official pressure could be brought, refused to accept them. The terse, if efficient, Godolphin replied to protesting recipients in this case that, since they could not negotiate the tallies, he had better give them to someone else—and did. Colonel Andrew Windsor, again, ventured to point out on 18 April 1711, that, since several of his officers had been arrested for his soldiers' subsistence debts, he would prefer, towards the £570,000 owed him, something which he could use for money, instead of the token sum given in tallies. His petition is feelingly minuted that the tallies were not meant for soldiers' subsistence, but as an advance of the regimental debt to Windsor himself.[1] Meanwhile the officers remained in jail, and the soldiers obtained their bread and lodging as best they could. They no doubt appreciated their good fortune in rising to the heights of tallies. Two years' arrears of payment of any kind was quite normal. The amounts quoted would be incredible were there not the admissions of the Treasury officials themselves on the piteous petitions which poured in throughout the reign. Parliament's self-righteous and repeated assertions that the army must be paid by the State, and not from the Privy Purse, must have seemed mockery to the soldiers who were so often not paid at all. The record is probably held by Colonel Michelbourne's case. While he lay a prisoner in the Fleet for debt, his regiment was still due, at the end of the reign, over £198,000 owing since

the fortifications and barracks at 6*d*. per day. Entry Books WO 26/14. In other cases they were hired out and the Commander pocketed at least part of the proceeds. In Newfoundland, the soldiers appear to have recompensed themselves by a series of robberies. *APC Col. II*, p. 634, report from Newfoundland.

[1] *Treas. Cal.*, iii, p. 456, and iv, p. 264.

the siege of Londonderry in 1690.[1] In 1706, the officers and men of Harvey's regiment were still petitioning the House for their pay for the years 1689–92. They were, it was noted, 'reduced to great necessities and the publick service is greatly prejudiced by their clamour'. The House does not appear to have been greatly impressed either by their necessities or by their clamour.[2]

Those colonels who did manage to obtain their men's pay were due, after payment of the soldiers' subsistence, £3. 0s. 10d. per private as 'gross off-reckonings'. This again was a paper entry. From it there were deducted 1s. in the £ (on the total pay) for the Paymaster (poundage[3])—12s. 2d.—and a day's pay for Chelsea Hospital. This left £2. 8s. 0d. per head as 'net off-reckonings' from which there had to come £2. 2s. for the Commissary for each troop or company passed at musters—i.e. six times per year—one-third of a day's pay for the Commissary-General of Musters, 30s. for the auditors, 'fees to the exchequer, fees to the treasury, fees for the issue of pay warrants, fees to every greedy clerk who could make himself disagreeable'.[4] The remaining balance went into the Stock Purse Fund, to which was charged clothing and all other expenses, including, for example, the recognized deduction of 2d. per month from each man's pay for the doctor. Even in Elizabeth's day sample costs of clothing for privates were £3. 5s. 3d. to £4. 2s. 6d., so that no lavish surplus was likely to remain.[5] The fund was made up annually, and, after deducting £5 for each man deficient, to be carried forward as a credit, any balance was available for division among the officers of captain's rank and above.[6] It is comforting to know that this system did not last in its entirety beyond the French Revolutionary wars.

A pay office clerk who sought to find out in 1702 the authority for some of the deductions was told by the Secretary at War that

---

[1] *The Deplorable Case of the Londonderry & Inniskilling Regiments*, by a Member of Parliament (London (?), 1707). (*Inniskillings.*)

[2] *Journals Commons*, xv, 14 Jan. 1706.

[3] Originally introduced, said Hutcheson, 'on pretence' of facilitating 'advances' of pay (i.e. payment at reasonable intervals) so that the soldier might not be perpetually in the hands of creditors. No one, to my knowledge, ever seriously claimed that the money was so applied after 1684.   [4] Fort., p. 317.

[5] Yet the colonels deducted £4. 2s. 6d. ostensibly for two suits of summer and winter clothing. Cruickshank, p. 77; Fort., p. 156. Part of the explanation lies in the larger amount of off-reckonings for N.C.O.s without a proportional increase in cost of clothing.   [6] Clode, ii, pp. 2–3.

off-reckonings were covered by the Royal Warrant of 17 June 1695, and the others by 'common usage'.[1] In fact, 'common usage' had already been reinforced by a warrant of 1 June 1702 which ordered the poundage deduction for the Paymaster, and deductions for the office of the Court of Exchequer, and for Chelsea. Another warrant later reaffirmed the deduction for Chelsea.[2] This was thereafter reaffirmed in each year's Mutiny Act which declared hopefully that there was to be no other deduction. Deductions for rations, dating back to 1678, were made when bread was issued, and on board ship there was a similar deduction, equivalent to the daily subsistence.[3]

The money the colonel was due was calculated on the regimental musters held as a rule at home every two months. Supervision of these was the duty of a Commissary of Musters, or Muster-Master, who had to sign the three copies of the muster rolls[4]—one on parchment for the Paymaster, one on paper for the Comptroller of Army Accounts, or the Muster-Master-General, and one for retention. Overseas forces each had their own Commissary-General of Musters—responsible to the Muster-Master-General—who was also sometimes the

---

[1] Treas. 1/11/28, 27 Oct. 1703. Until about 1669 there was a theoretically voluntary deduction of a tithing to the clergy. Walton, p. 660.

[2] Ests. WO 24/26.

[3] Walton, p. 659.

[4] A specimen muster roll bound with the Regulations for Regiments in the West Indies is laid out as follows:

Names of each officer and soldier in Coll Thomas Handasyde's company.	Days of Death Desertion or Promotion.	Present at the Muster of 61 days from the . . . day of . . . to the . . . day of . . . 170 .	New men admitted.
Coll Thomas Handasyde, Coll and Capt	——————	Coll Thos Handasyde	
Steph Jacks, Chaplain	——————	Steph Jacks	
Jno Smalwood Chirurgeon	Dead the . . .		
—			
—			
—			

1. Sentinell
2. Sentinell

This Docket to be placed at the end of the roll in the usual form.

(Ests. WO 24/37 dated 10 Apr. 1704.)

Deputy Judge-Advocate (e.g. establishment for Spain, 15 November 1710.)[1] The Commissary-General nominated for the projected 1702 expedition[2] to the West Indies was voted £400 per year, and the appointment for the home forces in 1704 carried £1. 5s. 8¾d. per day, of which £150 per year was to come from the one day's pay per year subscribed for Chelsea.[3] As noted in Chapter I, a post of Paymaster of Marines was created in 1702, and there was in existence a Muster-Master-General of Marine Forces in 1709, if not earlier—filled by Samuel Lynn.[4] There were various provisions for supervision of the muster-masters. Godolphin, in his instructions to the Comptrollers of Army Accounts, ordered them to check that paymasters and muster-masters were performing their duties, and that muster rolls were being forwarded to the Paymaster's office.[5] The only printed set of rules I have seen for muster-masters is dated 1645, but they must have remained substantially unaltered. These provided for monthly musters when the roll was to be called as per the previous muster and officers or soldiers dead, absent, or recruited were to be noted. They had to view anyone recruited between musters, and there were various provisions regarding sick, leave, and horses.[6] It was the muster-master's duty to make sure that no falsified muster rolls were submitted. The various devices for drawing money to which regiments were not entitled do tribute to the ingenuity of the officers of the time—having a man 'stand-in' while the muster was taken, declaring a man to be sick and unable to attend,[7] mustering servants (of whom the officers were allowed a certain number as perquisites),

---

[1] Ests. WO 24/75.
[2] This expedition did not actually sail, and on 28 Aug. 1704 both Marlborough and the Lord Treasurer reported against the appointment in the West Indies of a Deputy to the Commissary-General on the grounds that the appointment would delay rather than hasten submission of rolls. Treas. 1/83/8.
[3] Dom. Cal., i, p. 272; Journals Commons, xiv, 11 Nov. 1704.
[4] Dom. Cal., i, p. 484, letter of 10 May 1702 appoints Whitfield Paymaster of Marines. Audit Office enrolments, xv, p. 429, quoted at Treas. Cal., iii, p. 20, show the appointment from 16 May 1702. Lynn's appointment is at Dalton, vi, p. 200.
[5] Clode, ii, p. 669.
[6] Rules and Instructions to the Muster-Masters of the Army, 1645. (Muster-Masters' Instructions.)
[7] The Mutiny Act of 1713 provided that, within ten miles of London, sick men excused musters were to be seen by the surgeon or his mate. This may have been a special provision on account of the large number of debtors who enlisted in the Guards with no particularly serious intention of serving.

or, in the case of foreign troops at least, mustering the same man
in the grenadier company, and later as a foot soldier, were only
a few of the more obvious.[1]

The penalty for making a false muster was cashiering and a
fine of £100, with the same punishment for the muster-master
conniving. The person mustered falsely (i.e. the man who did
not 'pass muster') was sent to the 'house of correction' for ten
days and 'deemed to be enlisted'. The penalty for mustering
servants other than those allowed, or mustering someone by
the wrong name, was the same as for a false muster.[2] The Dutch
and the Scots took a rather more serious view. There is a case on
record of a Robert Stuart having been hanged for passing off
six sailors at a Scots Brigade muster.[3] Precautions against false
musters at home included the provisions in various Mutiny Acts
that the local mayor or a J.P. (two in Westminster or Southwark)[4]
should be present at the muster. Overseas, of course, there could
not be the same supervision, and it is undoubtedly the case that
regiments were frequently mustered without even a muster-
master being present. For the men deficient on a muster, and
not otherwise excused,[5] the colonel was 'respited' of their pay—
i.e. had it deducted from what he was entitled to on establishment.

Obviously this involved a certain amount of complicated
accounting. No staff was provided to deal with it while the
colonel got on with his job of fighting until, eventually, the
authorities allowed regiments a clerk or agent—with no allowance of money.[6] By and large, these regimental agents were
probably the biggest rascals living off soldier-men in an age of
very keen competition. The normal method of payment was
that they drew from the off-reckonings 2d. in the £ of the total
regimental pay,[7] but some drew a fixed sum, equivalent to, or

[1] SP For. 109/1, dateless report by Commissioners for Inspecting the Army
Abroad.
[2] Annae 2 and 3, cap. 17.   [3] Scots Brigade, i, p. xxix.
[4] J.P.s in these places appear to have been somewhat remiss in their duties, as,
in the Acts from 1705 onwards, it was provided that if, after due notice, they did
not appear on the parade, mustering might proceed without them.
[5] Warrants are not infrequent allowing men absent or recruiting to appear on
the rolls as having mustered. Registers 25/3180.
[6] Except in the case of the 1st and 3rd Guards—see Chapter III.
[7] CM Warrants 30/105, Minute of 25 Apr. 1772: The Customary Practice of
the Army concerning Off-reckonings.

more than, a captain's pay,[1] and some a man's subsistence from each company. An unsuccessful attempt was made during the reign to have their salaries fixed uniformly.[2] The bulk of the income of many undoubtedly came from bribes for clothing and other contracts, by swindling people of their pay or allowances, and even by judicious conspiracy with the colonel, by which, for example, they themselves supplied the clothing.

The agents were recalcitrant in their dealings with State officials as they claimed that they were private servants of the colonel,[3] and no one else could interfere. Eventually, as the result largely of clamour by officers who demanded their trial by court martial, provision was inserted in the Mutiny Act 1708 which bound them to obey the orders of the Queen or Lord Treasurer, but in 1710 we find the Comptroller of Accounts still complaining that the agents pay no attention to repeated instructions to submit their accounts. The convention grew up that regimental agents were appointed by the Colonel-in-Chief, and approved by the Secretary at War, while agents to independent companies were appointed by the Secretary at War.[4] No student of the period will feel ill-disposed to the three officers who, in 1712, took matters into their own hands and placed an agent under arrest. The Board of General Officers censured the three concerned—not for arresting the agent, but for doing so while the Board were considering a case in which he was involved.[5] Their example was, however, repeated, it will be remembered, by Captain Douglas in 1714, who, declaring to the Board 'in open contempt of their authority' that he would not wait for their decision, set out to prosecute an agent, Captain Evans, whom he arrested, and was in consequence suspended from his half-pay.[6]

Of fifty-eight regiments detailed in the *Commons Journals* for 19 May 1702, eleven had officers as agents. Of these, the majority were probably 'reformed' officers (i.e. from disbanded

---

[1] In the 'Abstracts' it is claimed that it was £1. 2s. 6d., and that colonels were in the habit of selling the agencies. Contemporary records seem to bear out the second contention. *Abstracts of the Numbers and Yearly Pay of the Land Forces*, by a Member of Parliament (in fact, A. Hutcheson) (London (?), 1718). (*Hutcheson.*)

[2] *Treas. Cal.*, iii, p. 279, Comptroller of Accounts, 15 July 1704.

[3] An 'Agent and Solicitor' to the Invalides was appointed by Royal Order on 17 June 1714, but this is the only case of its kind I have seen, apart from the Guards SP Mil. 44/173/396. [4] Clode, ii, p. 261.

[5] PGO WO 71/2, 15 Apr. 1712. [6] PGO WO 71/3, 8 July 1714.

regiments), but Brigadier Colembine and the Governor of
Portland were at that time acting as their own agents. There
is further evidence of at least one case of a serving officer filling
—or rather, being absent from—the post.[1] There is also one
case on record of a clerk in the Pay Office working as an agent,
which seems to present greater opportunities for fraud than
were normally required.[2]

Such was the general arrangement. It remains to consider its
failures in detail, and to examine modifications to rule, of which,
on account of the haphazard system of recording in the Secretary at War's office, and the indiscriminate use of terms whose
meaning is nowhere clearly defined, it is quite impossible to
make a full and assured catalogue. Off-reckonings will be explained in more detail when dealing with clothing, but some
consideration is required here. The minute of 1772 already
quoted states quite clearly, and study of the accounts bears out
the contention, that the off-reckonings were *intended* purely and
simply for regimental expenses. No colonel had a claim on them
for any other purpose, or without the authorization and direction of the Crown which 'hath been sometimes withdrawn'. The
whole tenor of the age, however, and the attitude towards a regiment, bear out the assertion that colonels nevertheless 'esteemed
that balance . . . a very legal perquisite . . . to which' they 'were
thought to have as good a right as to any part of their personal
pay'.[3] The author of the 'Abstracts' put it quite forcibly:

The . . . off-reckonings are to pay for . . . Cloaths, and if any Thing
remain, it is for the Benefit of the Colonel: and I believe it will not
be pretended, that they are Loosers in this matter, it being very well
known, that considerable Gratifications are given by Clothiers of
Regiments to the Colonels on this account: and is no small Perquisite
in the value of a Regiment, and indeed by Long Usage, it is now
become esteem'd a Right, as to any part of their Personal Pay.

He states that Lieutenant-General Wood was said to have distributed any money left over among his men, but that he had a

---

[1] *Journals Commons*, xiii; Board of General Officers: Out Letters, many references
to agents with military ranks. (*BGO: Out Letters WO 7*.) The absent officer was
Captain St. Eloy, addressed in Secretary at War's letter of 30 Sept. 1703: Marching
Orders WO 5/11.   [2] Marching Orders WO 5/11, 23 Jan. 1703.
[3] *Hutcheson*.

'very nice conscience in this Particular'. Lord Raby, as colonel of the Royal Dragoons, made, while the regiment was in Spain, and he a diplomat in Germany, £100 from his troop in six months, plus his pay as colonel and captain, plus his servants'.[1] In the *Recruiting Essay*, the author of the 'Abstracts' states:

> . . . he that sees the English Army, will easily distinguish a vast Difference in the Goodness of the Soldier's Clothing; tho' I believe no Colonel in the Army neglects the Perquisit wholly got by it; for which they have at least Twenty-five Years' Prescription to plead for.

Remarking that nothing was more reasonable than that colonels should have salaries 'answerable to their character, the great Trust repos'd in them, and the Equipage they are oblig'd to keep', he made the somewhat revolutionary claim that perquisites out of the soldiers' pay should not be the way to do it. It has been estimated that in the dragoons, for example, colonels normally made a profit of £1 per man per year, which was accepted as legitimate so long as stoppages did not eat into the soldiers' subsistence.[2] There was, on the other hand, the duty imposed on the commanding officer by regulation: 'The sole responsibility of the Colonel for the Pay and Equipment of his Regiment is the principle of Military Finance, who is held responsible in his fortune and in his character for the discharge of his duty in providing the supplies of his Regiment.'[3] It was, however, not only the commanding officer, with his duty and responsibility, who had perquisites. An officer who had officiated as an adjutant appealed in 1709 to the General Officers for the pay of his appointment, but was told he had no right to it, as he did well enough to get 'the perquisites of the office'.[4] Without being unduly insulting, one may assume that quartermasters did no less badly, but their tracks have, not unexpectedly, been covered.

What had an officer to invest for this return? To become an ensign of the line cost, according to regiment, from £200 to £500 upwards: a company sold for a minimum of £250, and a regiment seldom went for less than £400 or £500. A company

---

[1] Captain-Lieutenant Sheldon's letter quoted at Woodruff, pp. 779–80.
[2] Woodruff, p. 266.
[3] Regulations of 14 Jan. 1707 quoted at Clode, ii, pp. 568–9.
[4] PGO WO 71/1, 22 Mar. 1709.

in the Guards might cost £1,600.[1] There were considerable possibilities of loss on this investment. The officer had to reckon with two major hazards apart from the risk of being killed, maimed, thrown on the streets when the need for him had passed, or of not being paid at all (which, to be sure, he shared with most Government servants, except those who handled money or stores).[2] These hazards were, excessive losses of men through death or desertion, and losses of equipment.

Raising of recruits was the most expensive task a regiment had to undertake, and there was little 'return' on a man until he had put in at least a year's service. While the Board of General Officers confirmed that a man recruited in a 'small clothing year' need only receive the items issued then, and not a complete outfit, some provision over the scale had to be made for reinforcements who must mostly have been poor wretches with little of their own.[3] Not all colonels had the heart to equip them by stripping dying men, although the practice was not unknown,[4] and, even if no clothing was provided, recruits most certainly had to be given arms and accoutrements. The only free grant of equipment was, in general, on first raising. Nor did all colonels have at their disposal the entire off-reckonings. Many had to meet prior commitments for pensions for widows, children, or ex-officers, who were a continuing burden over and above the normal expenditure of war. One of the best known of such claims is that of William Theresa Douglas, goddaughter of William III, and captain in Gustavus Hamilton's regiment, who was dealt with in Chapter II, where the cases of Lieutenant Samuel Breton and Colonel Joseph Johnson were also mentioned. When the marine regiments were disbanded towards the end of the war the cost of £738 for thirty-five marine officers'

---

[1] Dalton, v, p. xxx; Colonel Burton's case, p. 62; *Treas. Cal.*, iv, p. 251, Kane's company of foot; PGO WO 71/1, case of Viscount Charlemont; PGO WO 71/2, 25 Apr. 1711, Sankie's regiment; Murray, ii, p. 441. These figures are minima rather than means. Viscount Charlemont spurned an offer of £500 for his regiment in Spain in 1706; Sir Richard Temple's regiment sold in Flanders in 1711 for £1,000: in 1711 Blackader got £2,600 for his lieutenant-colonelcy in the Cameronians; and companies in Flanders fetched £500 in the previous year. PGO WO 71/1; Murray, v, pp. 20, 67; Blackader, p. 428.

[2] Marlborough himself was £1,300 in arrears at one time. *Dom. Cal.*, i, p. 13.

[3] PGO WO 71/2, 9 Feb. 1714.

[4] Marching Orders WO 5/11, 1 Dec. 1702.

widows 'exposed to starve' due to cessation of the marine widows' fund was allocated to various army regiments.[1]

An example of a most unprofitable investment was Barrymore's regiment. While in Spain all its private soldiers were incorporated into a regiment of dragoons, and, on return to Britain, the commanding officer was ordered to re-raise it. On applying to the Ordnance Office for arms, he was told that, having been 'once Arm'd out of the stores of Our Ordnance, it was quite contrary to the Rules and Practice thereof to issue Arms . . . a second time'.[2] Barrymore, therefore, had to re-equip the battalion at regimental expense, and it went off on the Hill expedition to North America, where no one had much success. On its return, the rumour got about that it was to embark for Dunkirk. The chance of going to this plague spot produced such heavy desertion among the troops that the regiment was plunged even more deeply in debt, and the C.O. had to petition for special treatment.[3] Other unlucky shareholders were Lieutenant-Colonel Bastie and a number of his officers in Count Nassau's regiment. Serving in both William's war and the Spanish Succession, they were eventually captured at Almanza after twenty years' service. They remained in prison for three years, and were welcomed on release with the news that the money voted for their regiment had been used to raise and maintain another. Due, at the time of their petition to the House, £3,703, they were in the routine language (and condition) of the day 're-duced to the utmost extremities'.[4]

Excess of zeal could, of course, be just as costly as bad luck, as many a conscientious officer experienced. One such was Captain and Adjutant Matthew Poole, who, between May 1706 and January 1707, on his trip to Spain, and in the Peninsula, spent £301 from his own pocket for the regiment on such things as shoes and stockings, wine and brandy for his men on board ship, and for the men's subsistence; £2. 10s. to bury two of them; and £1. 10s. for two rolls of tobacco. He was still petitioning

---

[1] Entry Books WO 26/14, 5 Nov. 1713.

[2] Registers WO 25/3180. There appears, from a reference in 1704, to have been occasions on which newly recruited MEN were armed initially by the Ordnance. It was not the general practice, and the reference may be to new regiments only, although the Board states 'new men'. Ord. Letters WO 46/6, Mar. 1704.

[3] *Treas. Cal.*, iv, p. 432.

[4] *Journals Commons*, xvii, 13 Feb. 1712.

for the money, plus his own pay, in 1709.[1] He should, of course, have learned from the captain captured at Camaret Bay who paid his starving men 2*d.* per day while prisoners in order to prevent them accepting service with the French for food. He had only his own sense of duty to blame when the Treasury minuted his claim for refund, 'My Lord can do nothing in this'.[2] They must have heard with envy of the commanding officer of the British Fusilier Regiment of the previous reign who not only failed to pay his men for four years, but declared, when challenged, that he was quite in order, as it was a 'custom of the service, and the king was cognisant of his proceedings'.[3] Unless one took this colonel's way out, the making of money was a slow, albeit risky, business in which the profits were far from as good as they appeared to the onlooker. When Stanhope, for instance, was in 1695 given his company in the Guards, his father wrote that he should collect '£600 to £700 a year, and honour equal to the degree of a colonel'.[4] Writing two years later, Stanhope himself did not deal with a soft currency like honour, but stated that, as far as cash was concerned, he was receiving 10*s.* per week.[5] Exalted rank brought no relief. When he went to Spain as Commander-in-Chief, not only did he surrender his £10 per day pay, but paid £1,362 for a diamond-hilted sword presented, by order of the Cabinet, to Starhemberg.

Barrymore's regiment, mentioned above, was eventually given some relief by being empowered to carry on its muster rolls for the period 25 October 1706 to 13 May 1708 six fictitious names, a practice so widely followed that it requires fuller consideration.[6] The British soldier has, throughout the centuries, shown a surprising ability to live under conditions, and for wages which, on the outbreak of war, his fellow citizens, who are, in the last resort, responsible for his conditions, appear to find quite intolerable when they themselves must exist under them. The regular soldier then finds, for the period of the temporary soldier's service at least, that some alleviation is possible without involving the nation in a deadful cataclysm. This was no less the case during Anne's time than in others. Similarly, too,

---

[1] Treas. 1/119/13.   [2] *Treas. Cal.*, iii, p. 131, Mar. 1702.
[3] *The Story of the British Army*, C. Cooper King (London, 1897), p. 88. (*Cooper King.*)
[4] *Stanhope: A Study in 18th Century War and Diplomacy*, Basil Williams (London, 1932), p. 60. (*Stanhope.*)   [5] Stanhope, p. 16, footnote.
[6] Registers WO 25/3180.

improvements were so made that their 'temporary' nature should not be obscured. This was done by 'stretching' existing, instead of introducing new, regulations. The most convenient, and therefore favourite, method of doing this was to allow colonels to draw money for non-existent men. Throughout the reign, every Mutiny Act contained special provision to ensure, in Marlborough's own words, that 'no more are allowed and mustered than are actually in the Service'.[1] Yet the practice of 'allowing and mustering' men who were most certainly not in the Service was officially sanctioned time and time again.[2] Clode lists (incompletely) the fictitious men borne on regimental establishments by royal authority—two for widows' fund, one for loss of clothing by desertion, one for burial expenses of soldiers, or for the captain's losses due to desertion, and one for the agent.[3] Other instances were of five fictitious men allowed for arms spoiled in the West Indies, or lost by shipwreck, and seventeen for the 'better pay and maintenance of hautbois' (a rather wry provision since these fictitious men were often themselves known as 'hautboys'). Regiments were also allowed 'as full', despite deficiencies at musters, in order to meet special recruiting expenses, and Galway once allowed his C.O.s in the Peninsula a man's pay per company to meet extraordinary charges.[4]

The best-known cases of uniform application were, of course, the provisions for a specified number of men per company towards widows' pension funds, but the more frequently applied flexible allowance was for recruiting expenses. At first, provision for special recruiting expenses—e.g. to wipe out debts due to replacement of heavy desertions or casualties—appears to have been made when the colonels appealed for this. The allowance could be in the form of so many men for a specified period, but was probably more frequently granted as a discounting of 'respites'. Under this provision, the regiment would be credited either with its full pay, irrespective of the deduction previously debited against it, as being under strength, or with repayment of a specified sum—e.g. Heyman Rook had a special allowance

[1] Murray, iv, p. 7.
[2] It was, of course, a practice of considerable age, stamped out during the Commonwealth, but revived under Charles II.
[3] Clode, i, p. 105.
[4] Warrants (specimens of many) in Registers WO 25/3180, 6 Apr. and 6 July 1706; *Dom. Cal.*, i, p. 248, Sept. 1702; Treas. 1/83/107, 1 Apr. 1703.

of £102. 4s. from his respites in 1705 to compensate for desertion losses on his embarkation march.[1] Later, particularly in the Peninsula, which presented, as might be expected in any matter concerning reinforcement, special problems, the provision of extra allowances on a universal scale became almost routine. In 1710 Walpole had all the regiments in Spain mustered complete in order to raise a fund for levy money. This money did not go necessarily to the regiments themselves, but was probably allocated according to the custom in Portugal, where the forces were 'reviewed', or mustered, monthly, and the subsistence issued accordingly. The 'non-effective' money then remained with the Paymaster to form a fund for recruiting.[2] According to the Audit Commissioners, the Deputy Commissary in Flanders was directed by Marlborough at the start of the war to muster troops complete when defective. This was justified by the application of the non-effective money to recruiting, since the officers had to recruit their troops and companies, and accept this payment in lieu of a recruiting fee. The Commissioners disapproved, nevertheless, as provisions, transports, clothes, and other necessaries were provided according to the full establishment, while troops remained only half complete.[3] It scarcely required the Attorney-General's opinion (17 August 1711) to tell that such provisions were quite contrary to the Mutiny Acts' provisions against false musters, but presumably it would have been pedantic to quibble when so many regiments carried their 'faggots' or 'warrant men' for the agent's or colonel's benefit.[4] In all cases, there was still a fee payable to the muster-master for 'removal of respites'.[5]

The authorities undoubtedly remained interested in mustering offences even when technical breaches of the law became routine. In the years 1712–13, for example, numerous advertisements appeared in the *Gazette* giving the initials of people who had written to the Secretary at War to disclose 'ill practices in mustering'. In each case, the informants were asked to report to the Secretary when they would receive 'all due encouragement and protection'.[6] The sudden rush of such information was probably due to demobilization of disgruntled or righteous-

[1] Entry Books WO 26/13. [2] SP Mil. 41/3, 4 Aug. and 7 Oct. 1710.
[3] Clode, i, p. 123. [4] *Treas. Cal.*, iv, p. 301. [5] Walton, p. 660.
[6] Entry Books WO 26/14.

minded soldiers. A glimpse of the usefulness of knowing of such offences—even when merely an accepted 'custom of the service' —is given in a letter from Southwell, Lord Lieutenant of Ireland. Wishing to remove certain politically unreliable officers, he suggested that this might be done without undue fuss as 'just cause may be found to break them for false musters, and not completing their companies, etc.'.[1] Her Majesty could not, constitutionally, have been dealt with under this head, but it was, no doubt, a reassurance to her advisers when Parliament included in the Mutiny Act of 1708 that the writing-in of 'widows' men' under her warrant did not constitute a false muster. Technically, no doubt, another 'false muster' was the allowance of officers' servants. The Mutiny Acts repeatedly prohibited the mustering of servants, and on an expedition we find them restricted as follows:

Colonel as colonel and captain	4	(later amended to 6 at sea)
Captain	2	
Lieutenant	2	
Adjutant	1[2]	

This did not signify an outburst of egalitarian sentiment, but was part of the war against perquisites. Hutcheson, in his 'Abstracts', traces the history. The custom was that each officer had an allowance of a specified number of servants which he considered a source of additional personal pay. He was not compelled to arm or clothe these men, and usually avoided their appearing at musters, although their names were on the rolls. King William (who knew sufficient of English financial practices to order that his Dutch regiments receive their pay complete in bulk, without deduction, for his own officers to sub-allot[3]) reduced these by four per regiment, and later ordered that they should appear in the ranks at musters, duly clothed and equipped. In 1698 three servants per company were cut.[4] In the course of time the officers won back the lost ground. First the servants appeared on muster parades as servants, which meant, no doubt, certain latitude as to equipment. Then they ceased to parade at all. Eventually, by 1712, the officers reached the

[1] *Dom. Cal.*, ii, p. 230.   [2] *H.M.C.H. of L.*, vii, p. 205.
[3] *Journals Commons*, xiv, 30 Nov. 1702.   [4] Walton, p. 687.

stage of not even putting their servants on the muster rolls by name—which meant that they drew pay for them *and* for the men taking their places in the ranks. The prohibition against servants being mustered had been to meet precisely this case. Parliament's intention was not to prohibit servants mustering, but to prohibit them mustering *as soldiers*, when officers could draw pay twice for them. Hutcheson claimed that the conventional allowance of servants was seven for each troop, five for each company, plus three for the colonel, and, in foot regiments, one for the quartermaster. 'By long usage', he comments, 'this has been esteemed part of their personal pay.' A report by the General Officers to Marlborough in 1708, later issued as a Royal Proclamation, allowed nine men per troop, and seven per company as servants,[1] while St. John said (of Almanza) that officers and their servants were 'a full fourth part of the whole' army strength.[2]

All these added up to exceptional provision for the regiment as a whole—or for the colonel, according to his morality. So far as the private soldiers were concerned, it was soon found that the subsistence allowed them was not always sufficient to live on—particularly in the case of mounted men who had also horses to feed, shoe, and care for—and even then extra deductions for clothing might be made from subsistence.[3] Presumably, also, if a soldier were in a regiment like Tedcomb's which was not clothed for three years on account of its indebtedness he had to spend some of his subsistence on buying a minimum of covering for his body.[4] This might be all very well for regular soldiers, but when honest citizens were serving something else was required. As a result, there grew up a maze of special allowances, granted according to the pressing needs of the moment, and no doubt influenced by the ripeness of any particular regiment to mutiny, but without any guiding principle. These ranged from the grant to some regiments of the cost of postage on their muster rolls from the West Indies[5] to an extra $7\frac{1}{2}d.$ per day to troopers in Portugal to pay for bread and forage.[6] In another case in Portugal, it was ordered that troopers should be

---

[1] Treas. 1/11; PGO WO 71/1, 19 Jan. 1708.

[2] *Journals Commons*, xv, 18 Feb. 1708.

[3] e.g. deduction of 6d. per week in Catalonia. SP Mil. 41/3, 3 Dec. 1705.

[4] *Dom. Cal.*, ii, p. 59.   [5] *Treas. Cal.*, iii, p. 272.   [6] Ibid., iv, p. 258.

charged 6*d*. per day for subsistence, while the Government met the rest, including shoeing and accoutrements, estimated to total 8*d*. per day.[1] Special provision was made at one time for the foot at Gibraltar, where the practice was that 'when the price exceeded what could be reasonably charged upon the subsistence, a portion has been paid from thence, and the overplus provided for as the nature of the service would admit'.[2] From Colonel Joseph Benet's report of 15 August 1711, the service does not appear to have admitted much, for, he complained, the soldiers had had to destroy their own quarters for want of fuel to cook their meat.[3] An attempt to reduce costs on the Rock had been made by Galway in 1708 when he arranged for the construction of two windmills for corn grinding. The savings thus brought about, he reckoned, would enable the men to pay for their own bread.[4]

Other 'non-standard' sources of money were sea pay, slope money, forage money, and pinchgut money. Sea pay amounted to 1*s*. per day, out of which approximately 8*d*. per day was liable to be stopped for provisions,[5] which, however, the Mutiny Act of 1708 admitted it was not customary to deduct, except on carriage to the Low Countries and the Netherlands. As soldiers, understandably, made quite a custom of refusing to set out for overseas without payment of arrears, it became customary to give them an 'advance' of six weeks' sea pay immediately before embarkation. There were normally considerable deductions from this for its intended purpose of purchase of 'sea accessories', such as caps, frocks, or water bottles.[6] Slope money was a billeting and victualling allowance for officers actually present with the regiment. A minute of the Board of General Officers for 14 August 1713 states 'Non-effective slope money, being no part of the pay, but given for the officers present', it was in the colonel's power to dispose of a company's money

---

[1] Treas. 1/121/1. Troopers, of course, were not always so well considered. When without a horse, they were stopped 12*d*. per day of their subsistence to raise the price of a new one. PGO WO 71/3, 25 June 1714. If, again, a dragoon found himself fulfilling the role of cavalry he was in danger of being stopped 3*d*. per day 'mounting money'. PGO WO 71/2, 11 July 1713.

[2] *Treas. Cal.*, iv, p. 550.

[3] Ibid., iv, pp. 299–300.

[4] Ibid., iv, p. 98.

[5] PGO WO 71/2, 16 Oct. 1713.

[6] SP Mil. 41/3, 18 Apr. 1705.

(also called slope-gilt) drawn for those not present.[1] One set of accounts for Churchill's Marines shows £925 paid to the men for subsistence, and £502 to the captains for 'slops and regimental clothing' between 25 March and 24 December 1710, and £2,892 and £1,300 under the same heads for 25 December 1710 to 24 March 1712.[2] Soldiers, of course, could be so far behind in their ordinary subsistence that their advance of sea pay was entirely swallowed up before embarkation. This may have been the origin of Grenville's request to the Secretary of State on 23 December 1710, that a regiment, sailing from Ireland on a man-of-war, being unable to pay the 8d. per day, should be supplied 'as sailors' by the Commissioners of Victualling.[3] Forage and waggon money was an allowance to general and staff officers, and to regiments in the field, calculated in terms of so many rations[4] and the rations then expressed in money, with different scales for general and staff officers, horse, and foot.[5] This allowance was intended 'for carrying the soldiers' tents and other necessaries of the campaign',[6] but gave a substantial proportion to the staff. There must, undoubtedly, have been an appreciable amount left over after the bills had been met. Further to this there was an allowance of actual waggons—Marlborough had 27 with 3 carts and 20 baggage horses—which, of course, brought the need for further horse rations.[7] The detail of a junior officer's account submitted to the Board of General Officers on 5 June 1714 shows an item 'mule money'—£14. 5s. for 497 days—which may have been some form of sub-allotment

[1] PGO WO 71/2; *JSAHR*, vol. xxxi, no. 126, p. 94; vol. xxx, no. 124, p. 188.
[2] Treas. 1/167, 10 Dec. 1713.   [3] SP Mil. 41/3.
[4] A specimen vote shows:

Forage Money: rations per day—General of Horse 40; ADC 4; General of Foot 40; Lieutenant-General 30; Major-General 24; Brigadier 12; Brigade Major 3; Quartermaster-General 6; Deputy Paymaster 6; Judge-Advocate 4; Provost Marshal 3; Waggon-Master-General 2; Dragoons 60 per troop; Foot 60 per battalion. The total cost of this for 200 days was 174,600 guilders—i.e. £16,634 at approx. 10½ guilders to the £.

Waggon Money. In addition, £4,000 waggon money was voted for 20 battalions. (From *Journals Commons*, xvii, 20 Feb. 1712.)   [5] Treas. 1/137.

[6] *Journals Commons*, xiv, 1 Feb. 1703. It was not issued between 1695 and the Spanish Succession War.

[7] Treas. 1/157, where Ormonde asks for the same allowance. Numerous other instances in Treasury papers: *Treas. Cal.*, iv, p. 291, gives an example for foreign troops.

of the regiment's forage and waggon money.[1] I have seen only
one official reference to pinchgut money. This seemed to indicate it might be money which men could receive by under-
drawing their rations at sea—a rebate, in short, from the 8*d.*
taken from their sea pay. This, however, is guess-work; Private
Deane's remark does not necessarily bear it out: 'we bid adieu
to the wooden world, being translated from Purgatory to Parre-
dise, and from pinch gutt to whole Allowance.' Soldiers who
escorted prisoners of war on moves in England were given an
allowance for travelling, and extraordinary expenses in quarters.[2]
There is also an indication in one document that the clothing
of drummers may have been at least defrayed by the Treasury.[3]

Whether soldiers of those days were as alert as others of a later
date who profited by exchange vacillations, we do not know,
but the parliament of Anne's time was certainly quicker off its
mark. Soldiers in America, it was pointed out in 1704, were
not allowed to profit from a favourable exchange, as any surplus
arising on that account was to be applied for payment of a chaplain, for contingencies, and towards fortifications.[4]

A source of valuable additional income was bounties, such
as those voted after Blenheim and Oudenarde. After the first
battle, a total of £64,013 was distributed, of which £4,142 went
to general and staff officers (including medical); £4,000 to disabled men; £31,292 for horses killed and cavalry arms and
accoutrements lost in action; £5,600 for infantry arms and accoutrements similarly lost; £3,013 to the widows; and £436 to
the hospital. The remaining £33,530 went to the train, and
cavalry and infantry regiments. Marlborough himself received
£600 as Captain-General, and a further £117 as colonel of his
regiment. Brigadier Cadogan was given £60 as Quartermaster-
General, and £120 as colonel of his regiment of horse. The other
ranks drew sums ranging from £1 to £2. 10*s.* according to rank,
approximately one month's subsistence.[5]

CLOTHING

What remained of the off-reckonings after deductions and the
Chelsea contribution was, strictly speaking, expendable solely

[1] PGO WO 71/3.   [2] War Letters, WO 4/2, 19 Oct. 1703.
[3] *Treas. Cal.*, ii, p. 420.   [4] *Journals Commons*, xiv, 22 Feb. 1704.
[5] Dalton, v, part ii, Blenheim Roll.

on the soldier's clothing.[1] Off-reckonings were credited to a regiment according to the establishment, and not according to effectives, in the first instance.[2] Since the colonel was liable, however, to be respited for those not present, the credit, was, in effect, for those mustered. The system, of course, went back to the beginnings of armies when commanding officers were responsible for providing, mounting, arming, and clothing their men. The more modern principle was effectively stated in Regulations for Clothing dated 14 January 1707, already quoted:

> The sole responsibility of the Colonel for the Pay and Equipment of his Regiment is the principle of Military Finance, who is held responsible in his fortune and in his character for the discharge of his duty in providing the supplies of his Regiment.[3]

As the first commanding officers were company commanders, so clothing was originally their concern. Thus, in early days, the balance of the money left after purchase of clothes was regularly paid to the soldier. This excess of 'twopences' over the cost of his clothes amounted frequently, claimed Hutcheson, to 20s. or 25s. in the year. He went on to claim that 'some time after the Tangier campaign', in the course of a domestic dispute, the colonels took over the commitment. 'To show their good Husbandry', he remarks, they included in items chargeable to the soldier's off-reckonings, bandoliers, swords, and belts. 'Then', he concludes, 'accounting was at an end.'[4] The steady fall in the value of money not only affected the amount the soldier could buy with his subsistence, but also meant that money previously adequate for his clothing would not now meet the cost with the same ease.[5] It was probably more this depreciation than changed

---

[1] The Household Cavalry, the Ordnance Corps (including artillery and engineers), and Colonial Regiments (except the West India Regiment)—these a later development—did not subscribe to this system. Clothing for the Ordnance Corps was obtained by centralized contract, and distributed under a system akin to the present method of Ordnance Depots, after inspection at the Tower of London. Forbes, p. 111; Clode, ii, p. 569. The stoppage of off-reckonings from the pay of others was authorized under a Warrant of 1695. Warrant for the Regulation of Off-Reckonings, 1695. (*Off-Reckonings*.)

[2] PGO WO 71/1, 11 Mar. 1709; Clode, ii, p. 569.

[3] Quoted at Clode, ii, p. 568 et seq., but I have been unable to trace the Regulations themselves.   [4] *Recruiting Essay*.

[5] When the system was abolished by Royal Warrant of 6 June 1854, the colonels were, nevertheless, given compensation ranging from £450 to £1,000 per annum. Clode, i, p. 108.

standards of morality which enabled the *Recruiting Essay* to compare Anne's days unfavourably with Cromwell's when the auxiliaries sent to France had 4*s*. 8*d*. 'consistently paid on the Drum Head'. By the turn of the century, at any rate, matters had so changed that, far from receiving a balance from the off-reckonings, the soldier frequently found himself due for further cuttings from his subsistence. This, understandably, did not lead to contentment, and various regulations were introduced to ameliorate the situation. A number of them have been mentioned above in the section on Pay.

It was customary to clothe a soldier in two 'cycles'. Although there was, certainly until the Clothing Board was functioning properly, a 'vast Difference in the Goodness of the Soldier's Clothing', the procedure was theoretically the same in all regiments. There was a 'first year's clothing' which fitted out a soldier complete, and a 'second year's' which was more or less a renewal of the more expendable items—one shirt, one pair of shoes, a hat, and so on. The issue was made, however, on a regimental, and not on an individual basis, so that a man who was unlucky enough to enlist in a 'second year' did not get a complete issue of clothes until the following year.[1] With the 'vast Difference in the Goodness' which prevailed, it is not possible to state authoritatively what the soldier received, just as the sums made and lost on the clothing by bad and good colonels can only be guess-work. The author of the *Recruiting Essay*[2] quotes a scale (given in full in Appendix I) which shows a first year's clothing costing £2. 10*s*. 1*d*. and a second year's 14*s*. 4*d*. This was approximately half of what the colonel received as off-reckonings, but the figures seem strange when placed against the estimate of £3. 5*s*. 3*d*. and upwards in Elizabeth's day when prices were much lower.[3] The official report quoted in the Appendix shows £4. 7*s*. 4*d*. for what appears to be a large clothing year. Although, too, Hutcheson takes account of sword and belt, he does not add bayonet and cartridge box, which, says Fortescue, had been added by this time[4]—but the official report includes none of these. He himself included bandoliers as one

---

[1] PGO WO 71/2, 9 Feb. 1714.

[2] By no means, of course, an infallible witness. In one of his calculations in the pamphlet he uses an establishment figure for 1707 which is 17,000 (more than 25 per cent.) short of the correct total.

[3] Cruickshank, p. 77.   [4] Fort., pp. 317–18.

of the items added 'after Tangier', but does not quote them in his costs. No doubt those were to be paid for by colonels—but how, without deduction from off-reckonings, he does not indicate. Colonels of marine regiments had, in addition, to provide 'bedding and other necessaries' for the sea service.[1] The Ordnance Department supplied bedding to the Marshal of the Savoy, but left the marshals of regiments to make their own arrangements.[2] The first official scale was in the report by the General Officers to Marlborough early in 1708, embodied in the Royal Proclamation of 19 January. Starting off with the 1708 campaign as a 'first year's clothing' it prescribed the cycle from then onwards. It was on the same system of a full issue the first year, and renewals the second, but provided that a waistcoat should be issued in the first year only in the case of newly raised regiments and recruits, who would also get two pairs of stockings. Swords, belts, cartridge boxes, and drum carriages were to be met from off-reckonings. Those lost in action or worn out were to be replaced by colonels, those spoiled by negligence by the company commander—which may have meant from the soldier's subsistence.[3]

The scale prescribed the following:

TROOPERS

For 1708 campaign	*For second year*
New coat well lined with serge.	New coat well lined with serge.
New waistcoat.	New waistcoat.
New laced hat.	New laced hat.
Pair new boots.	Pair new boots.
Pair new gloves.	New breeches.
New horse furniture.	New horse furniture.
	New grenadier accoutrements.

DRAGOONS

For 1708 campaign	*For second year*
As for Troopers' second year.	As for Troopers.

FOOT SOLDIERS

For 1708 campaign	*For second year*
Good full-bodied cloth coat well lined.	A good cloth coat well lined.

[1] *H.M.C.H. of L.*, vii, p. 200.   [2] Ord. Letters WO 46/6.
[3] Treas. 1/3; PGO WO 71/1, 19 Jan. 1708.

'Which may serve for the waist-coat the second year.'	Waistcoat of former coat.
Pair of good Karsey Breeches.	Again.
Pair of good strong stockings.	Again.
Pair of good strong shoes.	Again.
Two good shirts and neckcloths.	One again.
Good strong hat, well laced.	Again.[1]

It will be seen that in this case, for troopers 1708 was really a 'second year' and the 'second year' a large clothing year. For dragoons there was no difference. In none of the cases is the difference between the years commensurate with the difference in costs quoted in other sources.

The scale seems to have remained substantially unaltered, save for the special provision made for the West Indies on 18 August 1709:[2]

First year	*Second year*
One coat double breasted half way down, faced yellow serge, unlined.	
Two waistcoats of good double ticking.	One waistcoat as before.
One pair of breeches of good double ticking.	One pair of breeches as before.
Two pairs of shoes.	One pair of shoes.
Two shirts.	Two shirts.
One pair of stockings.	One pair of stockings.
Two cravats and neckcloths.	Two cravats.
One hat.	One hat.
One pair of gaiters and garters.	

This scale included certain additions to the normal, since the remainder, being of lighter material, was less expensive.[3]

If issued, these scales provided a fair basis for the soldier, but quite obviously did not keep him completely 'kitted'; one pair of stockings, for instance, could hardly be expected to last an infantry soldier for a year.[4] The soldier might hope for provision of these from the portion of his subsistence not paid to him, but 'accounted for' every two months—but he would usually have to contribute towards them in the end. Estimates and figures

---

[1] Treas. 1/111.   [2] PGO WO 71/1.   [3] Treas. 1/126.

[4] Matthew Bishop tells how, about the time of Oudenarde, 'the greater part of the Welch Fusiliers marched without shoes'.

for his contribution vary immensely—from four to five stivers per week in the Low Countries for clothing, to deductions in Catalonia (always an expensive zone) of 6*d.* per week for clothes in 1705, and the same in 1710 to cover clothes and camp necessaries.[1] On the other hand, Hutcheson, pleading his case for a special 'clothing allowance' for those abroad, reckoned that with 6*d.* per week for shoes, shirts, and stockings, plus his subsistence pay, a soldier would be as well off as a freeholder of £20–£25.

Overlooking the transmutation of the soldier's entire off-reckonings into a colonel's perquisite, there were several flaws of practice, as opposed to morality, in the scheme by which the soldier lived on his subsistence, and hoped to receive his clothing in lieu of the balance of his pay. The first was that in many cases he was not clothed. In the Flanders campaign of William's day, the British troops' outfit was reported on by Waldeck as: 'shoes bad, clothing miserable, and arms defective'. In the Irish campaign a few years earlier, the men were without greatcoats, cloaks, boots, or belts, and practically without shoes. The custom was slow of dying. In accordance with the tradition of treating worst those who deserve best, the authorities had brought the companies of Chelsea Invalides by 1709 to the position where six had not received any clothing since they were formed, and another four companies had received none for two years.[2] This was the result of two years' gestation of a report by the Paymaster of the Guards and Garrisons that the clothing was 'as bad as was possible to imagine'. £5,000, he had reported, would clothe the four companies then involved at the scale of one coat, one pair of breeches, one hat, one pair of shoes, one pair of stockings, two shirts, two neckcloths, and sword and belt for each soldier every two years. The total issue on the previous clothing, he remarked, had been one shirt and one neckcloth per soldier. The Lord Treasurer's minute was not very helpful; it ordered the author of the report 'to contract for clothing in the best manner that may be'.[3] Major Archibald Patton's remonstrance of 14 June 1704 concerns another case as representative as any, particularly of regiments consigned to the West Indies. The Major claimed that, ordered overseas on 13 May

[1] *Recruiting Essay*; SP Mil. 41/3; Treas. 1/136.
[2] Treas. 1/117, 11 Feb. 1709.   [3] *Treas. Cal.*, iii, p. 511.

1702, he was authorized six weeks' advance of pay to make up his equipage, but this the Colonel did not hand over. The men received only one week's subsistence, and in the next two and a half years were issued with one pair of shoes, two pairs of stockings, two shirts, two neckcloths, and one blue 'linsy-woolsy' shirt without lining, and a 'cap of the same to keep their clothes'. This was stopped from their weekly subsistence, and, wrote the Major, 'noe Christian could doe otherwise than Pitty the Poore men to see them Mount the Guard before the Face of an Enemy bare footed and bare leg'd'. Returning home in the following year, the men received no clothing, so that the officers had to produce shoes, stockings, and other necessaries from the weekly subsistence. 'If the officers had not ordered old suits to be cut down for waistcoats, breeches and stockings the soldiers . . . must have landed naked.'

The second disadvantage, quite often coexistent with the first, was that due to bad luck, bad management, rascally agents, or greedy colonels, regiments ran up enormous debts on account of clothing. As a result, their off-reckonings were pledged for many years ahead. In cases where such debts were partly attributable to losses, one could understand the commanders who were reproved for taking away from sick soldiers 'their Regimental Clothing insomuch that even when their Lives are dispair'd of they are left naked'.[1] The first audible note of alarm on the subject of debts was sounded by the Comptrollers of Army Accounts in a long report to the Lord Treasurer on 24 November 1704. Of the off-reckonings of the foot regiments to be clothed in the spring, only five, they reported, would be clear. The total debt for the remainder for which they had records was almost £32,000, and they believed that the figures for regiments whose returns had not so far been received were the same, or worse.

'It is our humble opinion', they wrote, 'that if some remedy be not immediately applyed, it will be next to impossible either to cloath the Army well, or bring it out of Debt as manifestly appears by the exorbitant Prices in many of the contracts exhibited to us.'

[1] Marching Orders WO 5/11, 1 Dec. 1702. The value of a man's clothing and accoutrements (apart from his intrinsic 'price' as a soldier) is indicated by the cases where regiments to which men were drafted were ordered to pay not only £3 drafting money, but compensation for clothing and accoutrements. Entry Books WO 26/13, 10 July 1706, is one example of many.

Despite regulations, they said, the debts were increasing because colonels had no check over the making of contracts. The rule that the cost of clothing was not to exceed the off-reckonings was valueless because it did not specify the period of off-reckonings intended! Their recommendation is particularly revealing by the way in which it shows that, even in the eyes of those anti-militarist gentlemen, the off-reckonings had come to be regarded as not, fundamentally, part of the 'poor soldier's pay', but as a sum of money invariably to be deducted *in toto*. They asked that the off-reckonings be treated as a deduction 'like poundage', to be paid only to clothiers with a regular assignment. When there was no such assignment, the off-reckonings should remain with the Paymaster until a new contract was signed.[1] Marlborough himself was obviously thinking along the same lines when, in January of the following year, he recommended to the Lord Treasurer, who accepted the principle, that clothing debts be satisfied before any other assignment in order to preserve 'the credit of the army'.[2] This meant that tailors with a contract for clothing would be paid before such claimants as miscellaneous creditors of the colonel, retired officers, or widows entitled to a payment from the regimental funds, and before, presumably, agents took their fees. To what extent this actually took place it is impossible to say. There was nothing, at any rate, to prevent commanding officers, or agents, with the pressure they could bring to bear on clothiers, from making their own arrangements to receive at least some of the money from the tailors once they had drawn it. The problem of claims on off-reckonings was, of course, not a new one, and had been the subject of regulations in the previous reign. An item in the Royal Warrant of Regulations for the Payment of the Army published on 17 June 1695 dealt specifically and in detail with the disposal of off-reckonings. After deduction of those due to officers' servants, and their own percentage of the pay of N.C.O.s and private soldiers, the agents were to pay so much of the remainder to the clothiers as had been contracted for. As regiments had, in the past, exceeded the off-reckonings on clothing, the amounts thus payable were stipulated. They ranged from £155. 16s. 11d. for an independent company at Upnor, to £3,516. 4s. 10d. for each troop of Guards. After these

[1] Treas. 1/92/48.   [2] Treas. 1/93/8.

payments, the agents were to pay each field and staff officer, and then give the captains the men's money before finally taking out any more money due to themselves.[1]

A further thorough report on regimental debts was in June 1708, by Commissioners appointed by the Board of General Officers. This showed that, on an average, approximately six months' off-reckonings were pledged. Out of twenty-four regiments, thirteen were fairly substantially in debt. The highest figure was for Northumberland's regiment, which will be mentioned separately, and the next £1,383. Allowing for the provision of the current year's clothing and issue of the off-reckonings the number in debt would be reduced to ten. For those in debt, the Commissioners recommended approval of assignments of the off-reckonings up to 29 April 1710, when debts outstanding would, it was estimated, vary from £14 to £200. They reported that seven regiments actually had money in the bank varying from £118 to £1,335. They gave a special report on Northumberland's regiment, whose debt a month before Northumberland took over had been £2,088 pledged per year for three and a half years, plus a disputed debt of £984. Shortly after Northumberland took over, a new contract had been entered into for just over £9,626. This would have taken off-reckonings up till 29 January 1711 to wipe out, even had the original debt been ignored. The Commissioners calculated that the £9,626 was excessive and could be well reduced to £4,290. They accordingly recommended that sanction be given to assigning of the off-reckonings only until 24 March 1710. The balance, they recommended, should be negotiated between Northumberland and his creditors, 'being of opinion that the off-reckonings ought not to be further charged therewith.[2] The Clothing Commissioners wrought better than even they had anticipated. By 21 February 1709, largely as a result of their supervision and pressure, the situation had so improved that only two regiments remained in debt—one for £436 and one for £1,269.[3] The situation again deteriorated, so far as numbers of regiments were concerned, between then and the close of the reign when fifteen out of ninety-three disbanded regiments were in debt (over and above arrears of off-reckonings) to a total of £17,825.[4]

[1] Treas. 1/42/18.   [2] Treas. 1/107.
[3] PGO WO 71/1.   [4] Journals Commons, xvii, 2 Apr. 1714.

The third difficulty was one experienced even as recently as the war of 1939–45 by forces which tended to carry over into war conditions arrangements for any 'private' supply either by men themselves in return for cash, or by contractors and civilians operating with the army. This was the breakdown of the system in overseas theatres, particularly in difficult country such as Spain or, of course, in that neglected stench-pot of the times, the West Indies. In the end, as is described in another chapter, the Ordnance Department did in some cases step in, and in others shrewd general officers commanding made arrangements for supplies of such necessities as shoes.

The first two difficulties of the system—non-clothing of the soldier owing to corruption, or owing to mismanagement and debt—were tackled remarkably thoroughly when due allowance is made for the prejudices and pockets that had to be touched. The Mutiny Act of 1704 enacted that for the 'encouragement and well-clothing of the army' money due for clothing might be issued at the end of two months even if muster rolls had not been returned. Deductions of off-reckonings and their payment, however, were to be made only to someone with a regular assignment. If there were no assignment, the colonel or agent was not to gobble the money (openly at any rate), but it was to remain with the Paymaster until a new contract was made. This was only the start. Marlborough himself took a keen interest in the clothing of his troops, and, although it is not correct, as is often claimed, that the Board of General Officers was set up by him to rectify the clothing muddle, he, nevertheless, very early saw that this was a suitable body for such a task. St. John and Churchill, the Duke's brother, formed a drafting committee which in the course of 1705 investigated the position. They drew up the outlines of a scheme to lay down rules for patterns, allowances, and deductions with an over-all control over contracts. It may have been as a result of this investigation that, in 1706, an act was passed to permit the making up of clothes with cloth buttons for the army, despite the general prohibition against the manufacture of cloth buttons.[1] When the Board of General Officers was properly under way, the Duke had them consider the problem, and early in 1708 they submitted the report which contained the clothing scales mentioned above. They recommended that a

[1] Ibid., xv, 18 Jan. 1706.

board should examine all the debts for clothing, and where these appeared to be the fault of the colonel, should re-allot the contracts where they considered it desirable, and, where necessary, clear debts by stoppages from commanding officers' pay. Patterns were to be produced by regiments and sealed by the General Officers when approved. Contracts were to be submitted for inspection, and assignments of off-reckonings were not to be more than two-thirds of two years for the first clothing for infantry, while, in the case of cavalry, two years' money might be assigned except for a sum to be retained for supply of accoutrements in the second year. The General Officers were to inspect the clothing,[1] to make provision for arbitration between regiments and contractors, and to report regularly to the Captain-General and the Lord Treasurer. They also recommended that clothing of foreign troops should be by tender, but this was not accepted. Finally, in the best traditions of an ascending bureaucracy, they asked that provision should be made of an office and clerks for the Board. With the exception of the paragraph about foreign troops, all these were incorporated in the Queen's proclamation of 19 January 1708.[2]

The recommended Clothing Board itself was established as a sub-committee of the Board of General Officers. It was decided on 12 February that it should consist of one general, two lieutenant-generals, two major-generals, and two brigadiers, with a quorum of three. The senior in London was to preside at the first meeting, and thereafter they were to work down the list in seniority. This body was normally referred to subsequently as the Commissioners for Clothing, or simply as the Clothing Board. A proclamation by Marlborough in the Queen's name (actually signed by Cardonnel 'By His Grace's Command') two days later further modified this by ordering that the General Officers would elect the Board which would have a tenure of office of two months. The first Board so elected comprised Generals Steuart, Ingolsby, Earls Orkney and Stair, Viscounts Shannon and Temple, and Brigadier-General Tatton. These Boards examined clothes, approved patterns, vetted contracts,

---

[1] They had proposed as early as 1706 that inspection be entrusted to six general officers. Entry Books WO 26/13, 4 Feb. 1706.

[2] PGO WO 71/1; the proclamation is also available in draft at Treas. 1/133, date 14 Jan. 1708.

and by and large kept a close watch on the handling of off-reckonings. It was the Board elected for the two months commencing
14 April 1708 which made the report quoted above of regimental debts. This report, made in the first instance to the Board of
General Officers, and forwarded by them to the Lord Treasurer,
showed that the Commissioners had certified the assignments
of off-reckonings and asked that the Paymaster comply with no
other assignments or deductions. This set of Commissioners also
started the lengthy period of thinking about special provision
for uniforms in the West Indies. The Board took particularly
seriously their duties of inspecting patterns and clothes. Previously inspection had been the task of the Comptrollers for
Army Accounts, who were responsible for inspection of all army
stores, but it had been on rather a 'catch-as-catch-can' basis,
whereas the Clothing Board made it a yearly ceremony. Expeditions going overseas had often had their inspections waived in
the past (e.g. Secretary of State's letter of 19 October 1703 on
the Portugal expedition)[1] and in 1707 the system collapsed when
one of the Comptrollers died and the other resigned.[2] When the
Office got under way again, its role regarding clothing was appreciably modified. The Clothing Board had clothing for each
rank demonstrated, when feasible, before the senior officers, and
in the succeeding reign the King himself was frequently present at these inspections. The general procedure was that the
Board examined contracts in conjunction with the Comptrollers
of Army Accounts to see if the regimental account would stand
the cost. Firms who obtained contracts submitted samples of
what they proposed to supply, and these were compared with
the regimental sealed patterns kept in the office of the Comptrollers. If the samples were suitable, they were sealed with the
seals of three of the Board, and the office seal. When the clothing
was eventually ready, each consignment was examined by at
least one member of the Board on the contractor's premises.[3]
Just as inspections by the Comptrollers of Accounts were in
their day suspended, so no doubt was the Board's examination
in the case of Jack Hill's Canadian expedition. The cost of
clothing for this was £27,000. The actual price paid, Harley,
who had access to the figures, alleged later, was £7,000.

[1] *Treas. Cal.*, ii, p. 161.
[2] Treas. 1/179.   [3] Forbes, p. 137.

As one of the not numerous bodies of serious-minded men of the age, the Clothing Commissioners were bound to run into difficulties. One problem which particularly worried them over a period was that of clothing Scottish troops after the Union. Their report of 21 February 1709 put the problem in a nutshell:

> Your Commrs observe there is a peculiar Cloathing for the Three Highland Companies in North Britain, not at all Military, but like the Cloathing of the Natives there, that they may the better discover any Designs or Machinations against the Government of the Country.

Requesting orders to sanction plaids, tartan coats, trousers, hose, pumps, bonnets, shirts, cravats, shoulder belts, broad belts, powder horns with belts and measures, broad swords with basket hilts, targets, and pistols, they concluded by asking plaintively how they could be expected to view this clothing when it was only available in the Highlands—where, presumably, no over-civilized Sassenach would, even in those rougher days, trust himself. Even the viewing of the normal clothing in more refined parts of Scotland presented them, they said, with considerable difficulties in the year under report, the first after the Union.[1] They persisted in their good work, however, with very regular meetings extensively and accurately minuted. Their hand was seen in the Regulations for the Better Government of the Forces issued on 1 May 1711. Paragraph 7 laid down that not above fourteen months' off-reckonings would be allowed for the first year's clothing so that ten might remain for the next year's refit.[2]

The Commissioners were concerned with payment for clothing, its scale, patterns, and quality. They were powerless in the matter of supply, and it was in this that overseas commands suffered most. The general officers commanding had to take matters into their own hands when troops went out of the country. Marlborough, for instance, on the march to the Danube, arranged for a complete issue of shoes at Frankfurt, and there is another reference to a supply of 1,000 pairs at a cost of £97. 18s. 4d.[3] The Orders and Instructions issued to 'Thomas Castle, Gentl, Commissary of the Stores of Warr for Our Forces in Spain', on 15 December 1705 by the Secretary of

[1] PGO WO 71/1.   [2] SP Mil. 41/4.   [3] Dom. Cal., i, p. 691.

State, deal very largely with clothes. He was to take with him 20,000 hats, 20,000 shirts and neckcloths, 20,000 pairs of shoes, 20,000 pairs of stockings, and clothing for 1,000 dragoons and 4,000 foot, primarily to equip the optimistically estimated numbers of Spaniards coming over. These were to be charged to the troops at 3s. 6d. for a hat, 3s. 7d. for a shirt and cravat, 4s. for a pair of shoes, and 1s. 6d. for a pair of stockings.[1] In spite of this the Peninsula troops were perpetually in rags. A memorial on 2 September 1707 showed Galway in desperation for clothing and accoutrements, especially for the horse. Money seems to have been in part the difficulty at this time, for the memorial makes a point of his suggestion that the clothiers be paid half their bill immediately on delivery,[2] this to be debited to extraordinaries in the current year, and afterwards transferred, if approved, as part of the subsistence of fresh troops for the following year. The balance, it was suggested, might be given in warrants until money became available.[3] This may have had some immediate effect, but it was not lasting, for, in the following year, Galway wrote that, on account of the late arrival and non-arrival of clothes from Britain, he had instructed his colonels to fit out their men from government stores or otherwise, and asked that accounts should be adjusted accordingly. His need to have something done and the Clothing Board's desire to keep the business as clean as possible clashed. The Commissioners very justly pointed out that the system would mean the setting up by private persons of 'magazines of ill clothes'. They suggested that if such a system were necessary (i.e. dumps of clothes), then reserves should be established by the colonels themselves and special advances of off-reckonings made to meet the cost.[4] The suggestion does not appear to have been pursued any further. It was presumably not feasible to raise sufficient money to make an advance of any magnitude. On 31 July 1709, however, the Lord Treasurer approved a proposal by Galway to lay up a store of shoes, stockings, shirts, and cravats at Lisbon at a cost of £3,000, 'there being no such things to be had there'.

---

[1] Treas. 1/96.

[2] Delivery is an ambiguous term and here means delivery by the tailor, and not to Galway. The actual shipping of clothes when ready was a matter calling for much thought and organization as can be seen from the letter-books of the period. Officers home on recruiting frequently collected and escorted clothing.

[3] Ord. Letters WO 46/6.　　　　　　　　　　　　　[4] PGO WO 71/1.

They were to be charged to regiments as issued.[1] There is, indeed, evidence that stores of some kind were established in 1707, but the financial arrangements are obscure, and the stores themselves were not always popular with commanding officers. The Lieutenant-Colonel of Raby's Dragoons, writing from Spain in 1707, commented, '. . . wee might (have) the hats made here, for there is no depending to have them out of England, and half of them when they come are eaten with the ratts, besides I fear much that my Lord would order us to take them out of the stores, as he hath done to Peper and Pierces. I could not endure to see the regiment with white, or yellow tape laced hatts, with a little white cony skin for a cockade.' A year later he was able to write with relief: 'It was well wee had hatts made on purpose for we had been obliged to take nasty Foot hatts out of the stores; these are very good, do not come to 10s. each. . . .'[2] In Ireland, on the other hand, which knew barracks before they were accepted elsewhere, the State invariably provided a store of clothing from which regiments drew on payment. In 1712 Argyll, taking over command in Minorca as a bristly new broom, was soon reduced to despair by the complete lack of supplies or clothing of any kind.

Technically, there could, in law, be no question of local supply. The 1702 Mutiny Act laid down, and the provision was repeated in each renewal, that all arms, clothes, &c., were to be bought in England. How this was circumvented in, for example, Marlborough's provision of shoes at Frankfurt, I do not know. In the case of arms, as is shown in another chapter, the provision was made less burdensome by giving arms from foreign sources to troops on the *Irish* establishment, and there was a certain amount of sleight of hand over foreign troops in English pay, but there is no suggestion that such procedure was adopted in the case of the 'shoe magazine' at Frankfurt. Under any circumstances, however, the troops in the West Indies would no doubt have retained their leadership in all forms of suffering, neglect, and mismanagement. Bearing in mind Major Patton's remonstrance, we can well accept Fortescue's statement that they were 'reduced almost to nakedness' as the literal truth. It was not always the fault of the colonels. Frequently the commanding officers themselves were ignorant of their destination

---

[1] *Treas. Cal.*, iv, p. 42.   [2] Woodruff.

on dispatch, and did not know whether to equip themselves for warm or temperate climes. It took a long time for an official scale to be considered (early 1708), longer to be laid down, and still longer, we can be sure, for it to be implemented. Of the patterns which were presented at the Board meeting on 18 August 1709, those for shirts and neckcloths were rejected, but, in the absence of these fripperies, the soldiers would no doubt appreciate the 'little leather cap with a peak to it which serves on occasion to drink out of' added by one clothier.[1]

Such tenuous bureaucracy as existed in those days could weave a most effective red-tape cocoon. One unfortunate Irish regiment in Jamaica ordered cloth to be sent from Ireland. This had to be shipped via Bristol which it reached only after considerable delay. From there, being of Irish origin, it could not be discharged without a Treasury warrant, and, to obtain this, the clothing had eventually to be dispatched to London.[2] There is no evidence to show that it failed in the end to reach its destination, but, knowing the health record of the West Indies, we can be sure that the number of the original garrison surviving to receive it cannot have been large.

QUARTERING

Several methods were chosen for the attempted ruination of Britain's army and her soldiers—starvation or poisoning with bad food, rendering the troops mutinous by failure to pay them, killing them off through exposure in inadequate clothes, murder in troop transports, or slaughter in the charnel-houses designated hospitals. One of the more subtle, but probably more nearly successful than all the others, was debauching through lack of proper accommodation.

There were few barracks . . . and the soldiers were scattered in small detachments in scores and hundreds . . . of ale-houses . . . municipalities and inn-keepers fought bitterly against the inclusion of troops within their borders.[3]

In 1697 there was calculated to be accommodation for 5,000 infantry in the country.[4] Even accepted at its face value, this

---

[1] Treas. 1/136. [2] Fort., p. 561, footnote. [3] *Last Post*, p. 20.
[4] The estimates for the year included provision of tents for a further 6,000 infantry and 4,000 horse. *Journals Commons*, xii, quoted at Clode, i, p. 221.

was inadequate. Throughout Anne's reign, the establishment for guards and garrisons alone ranged between 7,000 and 12,000. At the same time, one of the rights upon which sturdy Englishmen took a firm stand was the refusal to allow billeting of troops in their houses:

> To the grievous and insupportable vexation and detriment of many counties and persons in particular [ran the Petition of Right of 1628], a new and almost unheard-of way hath been invented and put in practice, to lay soldiers upon them, scattered in companies here and there, even in the heart and bowels of this kingdom; and to compel many of your Majesty's subjects to receive and lodge them in their own houses, and both themselves and others to contribute towards the maintenance of them, to the exceeding great disservice of your Majesty, the general terror of all, and utter undoing of many of your people.[1]

Protection against visitations by such demons had to be put higher than the merely negative one of defence against trespass. Quartering of soldiers in private houses without permission of the occupants was made a specific offence under the Mutiny Acts.[2] Officers committing a breach of this section, or bringing pressure to bear on civilians or civilian officers to have men so quartered, were liable to be cashiered. In the face of all this, the Government had to make shift for their dangerous charges by visiting them upon the other criminal class—inn-keepers. Officers who excused, illicitly, an inn-keeper from having soldiers billeted on him were also liable to cashiering. Thus troops were scattered in tiny detachments in squalid little ale-houses in back streets and out of the way hamlets—unlettered men without supervision, subjected—and succumbing—to the temptations of idleness and dissipation. That they remained serviceable as soldiers at all is probably in measure due to the business acumen of the inn-keepers who undoubtedly knew to the last halfpenny for just how much debauchery their brutal and licentious guests could pay.

Quartering, even on inn-keepers, had to be done through constables or J.P.s who were empowered under the 1703 and

---

[1] As quoted at Clode, i, p. 20.

[2] Annae 2 and 3, cap. 17, and subsequent Mutiny Acts. The 1703 Act was in its title designated 'An Act for Better Paying of the Army and Quarters. . . .'

subsequent Mutiny Acts to quarter in 'inns,[1] livery stables, ale-houses, victualling houses, and all houses selling brandy, strong waters, cyder, or metheglin by retail to be drunk on the premises, and in no other, and in no private houses whatsoever'. Although the Act very clearly stated 'in no private houses', a limited amount of such billeting did go on with the consent of the owners. The Justices, when billeting, prescribed prices, for payment of which the officers were held responsible. The same Act detailed the maximum rates: an officer of horse below the rank of captain, 2s. for diet and small beer; officers of dragoons under the rank of captain, 1s. for small beer, hay, and straw; officers of foot under the rank of captain, 1s. for diet and small beer, plus 6d. for any horses or ponies; lieutenants of horse 1s. for diet, small beer, hay, and straw; lieutenants of dragoons 9d. for the same; foot soldiers 4d. Receipt of subsistence was to be announced and inn-keepers' bills cleared before the men were paid. Officers disobeying the law were to be *ipso facto* cashiered. Uncleared debts could be deducted by paymasters from the officers' arrears, or, if there were none—unlikely event—from the regiment's subsistence. If no cash had been received by the time a detachment left, certificates were to be given to the inn-keeper for his debts.[2] A few hundred government creditors more or less could make little difference.

In Ireland there was some provision of barracks, 'but these were small and widely scattered, being in fact police-barracks, to hold down a hostile population.[3] Dublin was an exception—until the formation of the camp at Aldershot in 1855, Dublin was the only quarter in the United Kingdom where, at normal times, there were enough troops assembled for a brigade field day.'[4] The detachments were so small that they had no cohesion as military bodies and were wasted away by boredom and their sullen surroundings. The normal strength of a cavalry barracks, for example, was a troop.[5]

Although not quite so disordered as Ireland, Scotland, especially after the Union, was also looked upon with suspicion.

---

[1] Inn-keepers at Epsom 'or similar places' were exempt since they 'lodged or received water takers only'.

[2] Mutiny Acts.

[3] Parliament voted £25,000 for barracks in Ireland on the conclusion of William's campaign. Clode, i, p. 225.

[4] *Last Post*, p. 20.   [5] Numerous references in *Dom. Cal.*, e.g. ii, p. 102.

As a result the country was, comparatively speaking, heavily garrisoned, but the troops were not so widely dispersed as in Ireland. Scotland received one of the biggest and earliest allocations of money for barrack accommodation when £9,300 was granted just after the '15. This was to provide quarters on the scale of one bed per two men.[1] Five beds per room 18 feet by 17 feet was the authorized scale, and the 1718 estimates justified the expenditure as 'preventing the robberies and depredations of the Highlanders'.[2] It was not the custom in that country to quarter troops in specific inns, but to assign localities to units or sub-units. The farmers, by direction of the Commissioners of Supply, then brought in forage for which '(units) payed little or nothing'—a rather surprising arrangement for that particular part of the kingdom.[3] In the Mutiny Acts passed subsequent to the Union, it was provided that, so far as quartering in Scotland was concerned, the pre-Union laws should stand. The Lord Treasurer was even authorized to exceed the money allocated for payment for quartering if the provision entailed this, provided the total did not exceed that voted for subsistence.[4]

The comparative few who were in barracks in England were not luxuriously accommodated. An English Military Dictionary of 1702 gives a definition of Barracks:

A hut like a little Cottage, for Soldiers to lie in the Camp. Once, only those of the Horse were called Barracks, and those of the Foot Huts: but now the name is indifferently given to both. These are made, either when the soldiers have not tents, or when any Army lies long in a Place in bad Weather, because they keep out cold, heat, or rain better than tents, and are otherwise more commodious. They are generally made by fixing four strong forked Poles in the ground, and laying four others across them; then they build the Walls with Wattles, or Sods, or such as the Place affords. The Top is either thatch'd, if there be straw to spare, or covered with Planks, or sometimes with Turf.[5]

Where permanent barracks, as the term is used today, existed, the standard was no doubt a trifle higher, but not strikingly so. At Sandown Castle there were 'no beds, but a nasty Court of Guard were a sutler lived within a partition made of boards, with his wife and family'. At the Horse Guards in 1662: 'I was

---

[1] Hampden Gordon, p. 148.   [2] Clode, i, p. 222.
[3] Treas. 1/169.   [4] Annae 6, cap. 18.   [5] Walton, pp. 716–17.

had into the Guard Room which I thought to be hell; some therein were sleeping, others swearing, others smoking tobacco. In the chimney of the room I believe there was two bushels of broken tobacco pipes, almost half one load of ashes.'[1] St. John, again, wrote in 1707 to the Treasury that a memorial by the captains of Lord Paston's regiment had been presented 'setting forth that immediately after the regiment was raised and reviewed by His Royal Highness in the year 1704, they were ordered into the garrison of Portsmouth, where, by reason of their continuance near a year and a half, the sickness of the place, want of firing, and the badness of the barracks, the regiment was reduced by death and desertion to about one half of their number'.[2]

Surprising as it may seem, the Board of Ordnance, under whom barracks came, made some provision for fuel and lighting, and for furniture. This did not always keep up with requirements. The garrison at Portsmouth had to petition on 12 October 1709 for fire and candle since they suffered 'extremely from want' and 'several have perished'.[3] This was speedily put right by an order on 23 August 1711 that the cost should be inserted in the estimates.[4] There is, of course, no conclusive evidence on the date of actual payment of the money or provision of the light and fuel. An average figure for the total cost of fuel and candle for the whole of Britain was £1,900 per year, ranging from £10 at Calshot, Portland, and St. Mans to £450 for the Foot Guards.[5] At Woolwich each entitled room was allowed 1½ pecks of coal and one candle of eight per lb. from 29 September to 25 March. For the remainder of the year the allowance was half a peck of coal and no candle—which is, indeed, more coal than is allowed at the time of writing.[6] In those days, however, shortages of fuel were perhaps not so easily compensated for, as the bedding scale was one sheet per soldier and one bed, rug, blanket, and bolster between two.[7] Rooms entitled to fuel were calculated on the basis of the following per room:

[1] Ibid., p. 717.
[2] W.O. Order Book 136, p. 3: quoted at Clode, i, pp. 221–2.
[3] *Treas. Cal.*, iv, p. 139.
[4] Ibid., iv, p. 304.   [5] Treas. 1/130.
[6] The fuel of Anne's days would, of course, have to serve for cooking as well as heating.
[7] Ests. WO 24/45; SP Mil. 41/4: Wyndham's letter of 10 Apr. 1713.

captains 1; lieutenants 2; fireworker-lieutenants 7 per 3 rooms; cadets 2; sergeants 1, corporals 1, and bombardiers 4—total 6; privates 6. Each captain's room had, for furniture, one round table, one square table, and six chairs. The lieutenants got only four chairs, but otherwise the same, and the seven fireworker-lieutenants were entitled to three of each type of table and twelve chairs. Each room at Woolwich was also furnished with—one ferrett, one coal box, two iron candlesticks, one fleshfork, one hand-hook, one frying-pan, and one bucket hooped with iron. Detachments received one wooden bushel, and one wooden half bushel, plus one shovel shod with iron 'for which', notes the clerk in familiar tones, 'the commanding officer's receipt is to be taken, and he is then answerable'. A further note states that articles such as 'bellows, wooden dishes, trenchers, cans, ladles, or chamber pots are liable to be broken without due care,' and storekeepers were, therefore, to allow £2 per year and no more, to furnish these to N.C.O.s and private soldiers.[1]

For those not in permanent barracks or billets the picture was, of course, rather different. St. John, for example, wrote to Colonel Morgan on 18 October 1707 about troops in the Isle of Wight:

Great complaints being made of the ill condition which the two regiments . . . are in from their long encampment there, and especially at this season of the year, His Royal Highness directs me to recommend it to you to provide the best accommodation you can for such of them as cannot be quartered upon public houses in the Island, by hiring either barns, or empty houses whereby the soldiers may be kept from perishing through the severity of the weather, until Her Majesty's further orders shall be given concerning them.[2]

Progress may be judged from the report of March 1711 concerning a detachment sent to Standgate Creek:

The places where they keep guard are two or three miles distant from each other, and as far from any house, and they are forced to stand in the open marshes to do their duty, which is so deep that they are up to their knees, so that it is impossible for them to live unless there be some guard house made or tents provided to keep them from the severity of the weather.[3]

[1] Ests. WO 24/45.
[2] Letter Book 136, p. 28: quoted at Clode, i, p. 223.
[3] SP Mil. 41/3.

There is no evidence of provision of tents or making of guard house.

Overseas garrisons were, of course, in worse state:

> Since... troublous possessions boasted neither inns nor inn-keepers, the problem of providing the garrisons with food, fuel, and shelter was too high for our military administrators. Even in New York ... one third of the garrison perished from sheer cold in a single winter. In Newfoundland and Nova Scotia—not genial climates—the barracks fell to pieces over the soldiers' heads.[1]

Even when troops arrived with the consent, or indeed in response to the pleas, of the local inhabitants, they were not necessarily better treated. In 1706 those sent to the Leeward Islands were provided with quarters by local Government Ordinance. On the expiry of the immediate emergency, they were evicted and left to fend for themselves. It was some considerable time before the local government could be prevailed upon to renew the Ordinance. In America, when billeting became no longer legally permissible, a barrackmaster-general was appointed to provide barrack accommodation under the orders of the commander-in-chief. The cost was borne upon the extraordinaries.[2] Progress was not impressive. Given an incentive, troops could contribute to their own difficulties. It was not normal for them to be given overseas the chances they had in public houses in Britain. In Jamaica, however, the planters had the right to refuse to have soldiers quartered on payment of an allowance to those affected. The Council of Trade and Plantations, reporting to the House of Lords on 30 November 1704, noted that this 'occasioned the debauchery of the soldiers by spending that money on strong liquors instead of applying the same to provide themselves with quarters'. The agents, according to the Council, were endeavouring to persuade the islanders to provide quarters instead of cash in lieu. It appeared, however, to be well worth 10s. per officer and 5s. per man per week to keep them out of one's home. The Council, therefore, recommended the building of barracks 'as in Ireland ... wherein the officers may have due care of the health of their soldiers by restraining them from many extravagancies they are subject to, in open and distant quarters'. On construction of these, fresh

---

[1] *Last Post*, p. 20.   [2] Clode, i, p. 228.

provisions might be distributed daily from stores to be brought from the northern plantations 'either by undertakers' (an appropriate term in view of Jamaica's mortality record) 'or officers ... appointed for that purpose'.[1] There is no evidence that this was done.

When campaigning in the field in Europe, quarters had, as in all wars, to be taken as they came—perhaps under hedges, perhaps, if fortune smiled, in an empty or a damaged house. In the winter, the men were billeted, but it was not the pernicious system which operated in the U.K. since units as a whole were more concentrated, and there would often be considerable numbers of men actually living and cooking in the one building, if suitable. Fending for themselves while fighting, and, no doubt, exercising considerable latitude in 'scrounging' and 'improvising', the troops had fewer grumbles than casualties, although not many were as bizarre in their allocation of credit as Blackader who declared:

> I bless God for the good accommodation I have had at this siege [Dendermond] which has been so gentle and cheap to us. I got lodged in a house near the town, and exposed to the fire of the batteries, but I can lay me down in peace and sleep for the Lord makes me to dwell in safety.[2]

Some damage was always inevitable:

> I bless the Lord for his mercies to me. I have got the accommodation here of a cottage though it is like to be pulled down about my ears by the soldiers searching for wood and straw.[3]

The responsibility for quartering on campaign or on the march was that of the Quartermaster-General who, in this respect, was the successor of the Harbinger. Prior to the institution of the appointment of Quartermaster-General in 1689, the Harbinger's tasks in quartering had fallen to the Scoutmaster-General and Provost Master-General. The Harbinger's duties had been laid down in Henry VIII's time. He was to 'appoint for the lord general the chief lodgings, and next after him his two lord lieutenants . . . the master of the ordinance and all other mean officers to be lodged as near to the council as he conveniently may . . . and after he must reserve certain of the

---

[1] *H.M.C.H. of L.*, vi, p. 102.   [2] Blackader, p. 113.   [3] Ibid., p. 407.

best lodgings for the captains and men of worship . . . delivering
to every man's servant . . . one billet'. He worked under the
High Marshal, or second-in-command, and had a number of
subordinates under himself to every one of whom he was to
'deliver . . . a book, dividing the lodgings in the town in four
parts, appointing to every clerk one part of the town to make
lodgings in, which clerks must appoint no lodgings but such
as the harbinger appointed by billet'. The Harbinger and his
servants had

to give their attendance upon the high marishall when he goeth to
view the ground where the camp shall be pitched. And after that the
high marishall hath appointed the ground for the camp, then the
provost marshall maketh division of the quarters of the camp, assigning a place for the market, or place of assembly, and the streets
for the same; and the harbinger being made privy thereunto must
remain upon the same ground ready to answer all such as come
before, to know where they shall pitch their tents and discharge
their carriages.[1]

The best description of the 'mechanics' of camping in the field
comes a century later from Kincaid, who accompanied Wellington's armies which undoubtedly showed few changes in this respect from a century previously.

The quartering of our division, whether by night or by day, was an
affair of about five minutes. The quarter-master-general preceded
the troops, accompanied by the brigade-majors and the quartermasters of regiments; and after marking off certain houses for his
general and staff, he split the remainder of the town between the
majors of brigades; they, in their turn, provided for their generals
and staff, and then made a wholesale division of streets among the
quarter-masters of regiments, who, after providing for their commanding officers and staff, retailed the remaining houses, in equal
proportions, among the companies; so that, by the time that the
regiment arrived, there was nothing to be done beyond the quartermaster's simply telling each captain 'Here's a certain number of
houses for you'. . . .

When a regiment arrives at its ground for the night, it is formed in
columns of companies at full, half, or quarter distance, according to
the space which circumstances will permit. . . . The officer commanding each company then receives his orders; and, after communi-
cating whatever may be necessary to the men, he desires them to

[1] Walton, pp. 623-5.

'pile arms and make themselves comfortable for the night'. . . . The soldiers of each company have a hereditary claim to the ground next to their arms, as have their officers to a wider range on the same line, limited to the end of a bugle sound, if not by a neighbouring corps. Each individual knows his place as well as if he had been born on the estate.

. . . When the light baggage and provisions come in at the head of the regiment . . . the first thing to be done is to make some tea. . . . We then proceed to our various duties. The officers of each company form a mess of themselves. One remains in camp to attend to the duties of the regiment; a second attends to the mess; he goes to the regimental butcher and bespeaks a portion of the only purchaseable commodities—hearts, livers, and kidneys; and also to see whether he cannot do the commissary out of a few extra biscuits, or a canteen of brandy; and the remainder are gentlemen at large for the day.[1]

Allocation of winter quarters was a more tricky business. The men had to be reasonably well lodged, if only to obviate deaths from exposure. The standard of accommodation varied from district to district, as did desirability from the point of view of supplying, foraging, and so on. When numerous allies and auxiliaries were involved, much thought and diplomacy, even on the highest level, were required. It was, in fact, in the course of correspondence in which Marlborough was emphasizing that each country should accept a due proportion of the worse and more expensive quarters that even his smiling patience snapped with 'it is grown too much in fashion to canvass and reflect on what I doe without any consideration of the service':[2] this, with his comment on Walpole's dismissal as Secretary at War, are the only two irritated remarks in his dispatches.

With experience, staff and regimental officers and men probably found it possible during the reign to alleviate some of the worst evils of the lack of a proper barracks and quartering system. There was no fundamental alteration, however, nor even a change in approach, by those in authority, and it was to be many years before any serious attempt was made to construct barracks in England. It cannot yet be said that everywhere are soldiers housed in a civilized manner.

---

[1] *Wellington's Men: Some Soldier Autobiographies*, W. H. Fitchett (London, 1900). (*Fitchett*.)
[2] SP Mil. 41/3/121, dispatch of 11 Oct. 1710.

V

ARMS AND SERVICES

IN addition to its responsibility for Crown fortresses, the Board of Ordnance was charged with the provision of siege trains for the field army. These trains consisted of three elements, artillery, engineers, and stores for both, with provision for over-all control of transport. As these stores were so much greater in amount and bulk than any required by the rest of the army, and since the train had this machinery for store handling and also a transport organization, it followed that, when the time came for some central supply of stores other than those required for trains, it was executed by the Ordnance. The place of the train in the field army was predominant. No army could function decisively without it, and it was a shrewd observation on Sergeant Millner's part when he calculated campaigns from the time of the train going out of winter quarters until it returned 'it being the metropolitan ensign of an army in time of war'. Its pace determined the progress of the army—in normal times we might say retarded. It was Millner again who wrote that on the Danube march, the army as a whole could march as much in one day as the artillery could in two. The magnitude of the problem is indicated by the figure of 16,000 horses to drag guns and ammunition for the siege of Lille in 1708.[1] Only a small proportion of the horses, of course, was on the permanent strength. Most were hired, often with drivers, from the countryside in which the army was operating. Wyndham declared to Peterborough in Spain in 1706: 'I have not one cart or mule for the train in this place, so that, if I march, all the guns, powder, and ball must be left behind in an enemy's country.'[2]

Within the train, civilians and officers were mixed. The guns were under the charge of the 'Gentlemen of the Ordnance'.

---

[1] *The Royal Army Service Corps. A History of Transport and Supply in the British Army,* J. W. Fortescue (Cambridge, 1930), p. 22. (*Fort. RASC.*)

[2] *H.M.C.H. of L.,* vii, p. 498.

The working and use of them was committed to officers of artillery, while their movement was the responsibility of the Controller of the Train, assisted by his waggon-masters, commissaries of draught horses, and conductors, who have left behind the name of their rank in the present Royal Army Ordnance Corps.[1] The present Corps of Royal Engineers was represented solely by officers, as the artisans were entirely civilian.[2] Sea transport for the train was arranged direct by the Board of Ordnance without the participation of the Secretary at War, and probably without that of the Secretary of State.[3] The train was self-contained in practically every respect, and had its own Paymaster, who was responsible to the Board in the first instance.[4]

The stores staff was mainly civilian, and on at least one occasion the civilian commissary and the military officer in command did not see eye to eye. Major Borgard complained from Portugal in 1704 about his commissary, Mr. Jackson, who was said to be unacquainted with his business and to leave everything to the major, who complained he had to be everywhere at once and was 'fatigued for want of a proper person to assist him'. The people and stores were divided in three parts with Jackson in 'Lisbon etc' from where the major could get no word of what he was doing. Jackson, who was paid 8s. per day, countered with a request for an increase in pay because he had been ordered by Major Borgard to keep a horse. He complained that he had been ordered to march with the train 'which was very hard with so small a pay', that he received no encouragement, was at his wit's end, and was so uneasy with the major he would stay on no account. Marlborough's comment that if Jackson remained at his post 'Her Majesty's service may suffer further inconvenience' seems reasonable. He ordered Jackson's removal, but at the same time asked the board to find him another post 'where he might be more useful in the service and have some little subsistence'.[5] The orders issued to the Commissary of the Train on Peterborough's expedition, 'which are the general instructions to all commissaries',

---

[1] Walton, pp. 701–2. [2] Forbes, p. 110.
[3] But cf. p. 209 below. Entry Books WO 26/11: Secretary at War's Letter of 13 May 1702.
[4] *Treas. Cal.*, iv, p. 580. [5] Ord. Letters WO 46/6.

show him to have been the direct ancestor of today's Ordnance officer in his responsibilities for receipt, issuing, and accounting for stores.[1]

Trains, of course, were not standard in size, but were designed for the expedition on which engaged. One specified in *The Souldier's Accompt* in 1647 is commanded by a General of Ordnance (at £4 per day), assisted by a lieutenant-general. There are a chief engineer, and six engineers 'for ordering of trenches, fortifications, and approaches'. For the guns and their transport and ammunition, there are twenty gentlemen of the ordnance, matrosses, a waggon-master, assistants, and conductors, commissaries, and an ammunitionary. There are miners, and 600 pioneers with officers, 100 matrosses 'to work about rivers', and a miscellany of tradesmen from cooper to blacksmith. Finally, there are a paymaster, a provost marshal, and three under-jailers. A train formed in 1688 was commanded by the gunner, Sir Henry Shere, with special provision for Sir Martin Beckman, the Chief Engineer, to take command in Shere's absence. In 1692 in Flanders there were a lieutenant-colonel as second engineer, a major, and three engineers. There were several gunner officers, gunners, a 'captain of the tin boats', a mortar detachment of one petardeer, four firemasters, and four bombardiers, and the usual ancillaries and tradesmen. Six hundred horses were required for the guns and tin boats, and 600 horses and 200 waggons for the conveyance of stores.[2] The first peace-time train was formed in 1698.[3] A typical train of 1703 carried 14 sakers, 10 three-pounders, 4 ten-inch and 6 eight-inch guns, and cost £34,806, plus £10,630 for wages. It had two companies of gunners with engineers in the form of pioneers and pontoon men, as well as an Assistant Commissary of Stores, wheelwrights, collar men, and tinmen.[4] The high proportion of machinery, its transport, and skilled manpower always made the train expensive. By 1708 the cost in Flanders was £45,000 and in Spain £12,254.[5]

It was perhaps the high cost that made the Board cautious at times in fitting out. It came in for severe criticism from Methuen,

[1] Treas. 1/84/35, issued 1 May 1705.
[2] *History of the Corps of Royal Engineers*, Whitworth Porter (London, 1889), vol. i, pp. 54–56. (*Porter*.)
[3] Ibid., p. 61.   [4] *Journals Commons*, xiii, 21 Jan. 1702.
[5] Ibid. xiii, 19 Jan. 1702; 25 Nov. 1703; xv, 18 Nov. 1707.

Ambassador to Portugal, who had obtained assistance for the King of Portugal from Britain, in 1703. Not only, he wrote, were the miners, gunners, and bombardiers unworthy of their names, and without officers, but the train was sent out without attendants, smith, wheelwrights, or any artificer 'into a country where is none'. On inquiring why the Board had sent the train thus, he had been told that 'these things were not in the treaty ... neither was it mentioned that there should be a captain, lieutenant, or ensign in a foot company, and I had hoped that in the execution of this great enterprise more regard would have been had to what was necessary to succeed in such an undertaking than the literal perfection of the articles'. The representatives of the Board were duly ordered to appear before a Committee of the House of Lords, but there is no evidence that this perturbed them unduly.[1]

Although divided into different categories within the train, the officers moved from one branch to the other with ease. The engineer officers, in particular, were frequently drawn in the first instance from infantry regiments. Richard King, originally a captain in the Royal Scots Fusiliers, made, it will be remembered, more or less a compote of his entire service at the siege of Menin. There, he brought forward the victuals, guns, and ammunition, did duty in the trenches as an engineer, with the batteries as a gunner, and finally with his own regiment of foot (p. 65). Engineer officers working with and paid as artillery continued to draw half pay as engineers, but a move towards absentee holding of gunner companies was firmly discouraged.[2] Very many of the artillery and engineer officers continued, nevertheless, to draw their infantry pay although they never saw their regiments.[3] Indeed it would have been surprising had they not done so, for in the case of junior officers their infantry pay and perquisites were frequently more than their pay from the Board. There were no doubt a number of Ordnance perquisites. Money could apparently, for example, be made from recovered shot. Although Marlborough was reluctant to allow this in 1705 to Colonel Benet at Gibraltar, for whom he

---

[1] Ord. Warrants WO 55/343.
[2] Particularly notable, as it was Pendlebury, the Master Gunner, who was refused the company. Ord. Letters WO 46/6, 13 Feb. 1711.
[3] Marlborough himself took steps to stop this.

appears to have had a distaste, the Board of Ordnance allowed £164 for it in 1715.[1] Brigadier Shimpton was a man of swifter action. He removed in 1706 ten brass cannon from Gibraltar and sold them in Lisbon the 'protests of the engineer notwithstanding'. He was made a major-general when he defended himself by saying he sold 'about 10 tons of broken brass guns for 500 and 20 odd pistols'. This 'broken brass' he said had been given to him as a 'recompense of his Service', without specifying by whom.[2]

Artillery

'When the catapult was first seen at Lacedaemon,' recorded William Camden in *Remains concerning Britain*, 'Archidamus cried "Now mankind has come to an end".'[3] And, as mankind came to an end, so came the gunners into existence. Their formal existence in England, however, is normally considered to date from 27 November 1715 when a warrant created two companies of matrosses and gunners to deal with the rebellion. In 1716 the plan attributed to Michael Richards, Chief Engineer, to constitute the Royal Regiment, and the Corps of Royal Engineers, was put into operation.

In earlier days the task of looking after the engines of war had also involved siege and field works. As gunpowder and guns developed, the men responsible for them in the field had remained a scratch crew with little specific organization of their own. The New Model, as might be expected, aspired to a separately designated body of artillery which, also not unexpectedly, disappeared with the break-up of the Commonwealth. Guns were, at the Restoration, once more allotted to infantry battalions, where they were frequently manned by specially trained fusiliers. So far as the national garrison was concerned, the Board of Ordnance had long been charged with the care of Crown fortresses and armaments. Until 1667 it was left to local governors of these fortresses and defence works to cut Crown timber for, and to repair them, but, as the result of abuses, the Board of Ordnance was, by Order in Council dated 26 April 1677, authorized to call all governors and

---

[1] Ord. Minutes WO 47/23, and Porter, p. 69.
[2] Ord. Letters WO 46/6, 15 Feb. 1707 and 13 Dec. 1707.
[3] P. 267—quoted in *AA.*, p. 92.

commissioners to account. In the fortifications were placed very small military forces, and gunners and master gunners who were appointed to particular places for life. Their status was ill-defined, and they were considered not even to be subject to such military law concerning discipline as might be in force from time to time.[1] The first sign of a reawakening of interest in artillery came, familiarly enough, when James, Duke of York's influence was felt. Under the Royal Warrant of 1682, the duties of the Master Gunner were restated, and the appointment given to Captain Richard Leake, R.N., at £190 per annum. He claimed the following fees—for examination and certificate of proficiency 10s.; for taking gunner's oath 5s.; for admitting on muster roll 2s. 6d.[2]

Leake's warrant instructed him

to profess and teach his Art to our Under-Gunners in the exercise of shooting of Great Ordnance, Mortar Peeces, etc., in such Publique Place or Places as by the Master of Our Ordnance shall be allotted and appointed for the Purpose and therein to Exercise them once a moneth in Winter and twice ev'ry Moneth in Summer. . . . To certify to Our Master of Our Ordnance or Our Principall Officers the Ability of Any Gunner or Scholler. . . . To keep a Register of all gunners that receive any Fees from us. . . . To keep likewise an Extract List of All our Great Guns as well Brass as Iron belonging to any of Our Ships, Forts, Castles, Blockhouses, or Garrisons.[3]

The inclusion of responsibility for the guns on board ship helps to explain the appointment of a naval officer; the Board of Ordnance was responsible for gunning the fleet. In the following year, in the new warrant for the Board of Ordnance, also inspired by the Duke of York, the Lieutenant-General of Ordnance was made directly responsible for the Master-Gunner. He was to 'direct and oversee the Master Gunner, Fire Master, Mates, Gunners, and Fire Workers, and frequently to require an account of the Master Gunner and Fire Master of all . . .

---

[1] Clode, i, p. 8. In 1702 the Solicitor-General gave as his opinion that matrosses and gunners came within military law for quartering. Marching Orders WO 5/11. They were not, however, automatically subject to military discipline, and as late as 1783 were still reckoned in the Ordnance Establishment Warrant as part of the 'civil' establishment. Clode, i, p. 8.

[2] Walton, p. 663.

[3] *Army Quarterly*, liv, no. 10 (London, 1947), 'The Master Gunner, St. James's Park', by J. T. Edwards. (*Army Quarterly*.)

gunners, fireworkers, practitioners, and scholars of their proficiencies'. The staff in the gunnery branch was to consist of: Master-Gunner of England at a salary of £190 per year; three mates at £45. 10s. each; Firemaster at £150; Firemaster's mate at £80; four Fireworkers or Petardiers at £50 each; two Proof Masters at £20 each; and sixty gunners at 1s. per day.[1]

In the field, however, in spite of these fine titles and reasonable salaries, the gunners, with their cumbersome transport and mountains of ammunition, did not receive the deference which they probably thought their specially arrayed status merited. After Sedgemoor, Henry Shere, the Master-Gunner (later to suffer such mental agonies of conflict between loyalty to his king and loyalty to his religion) was moved to complain that he had been 'secretary of War, Governour of Carriages, of Sick and Wounded, and a Commissary of Provisions'. Yet, in spite of all, there was 'no deference for the artillery as (is) practised in other armies'. The infantry, complaining that the guns hindered movement, put them in the rear with the baggage, and then, somewhat unreasonably, demurred at their arrival three hours late on the battlefield. The artillery were, not unexpectedly, hurt at being late, not only for the fight, but into camp, and for food.[2]

William III found his artillery officers in the first campaign 'ignorant, lazy and cowardly, and a week's easy work rendered the guns unserviceable'. For the campaign after that, he brought gunners from Holland.[3] In the large-scale disbandment of 1697, only four companies of thirty with one officer per ten men were retained as a regimental train.[4] The lack of appreciation persisted. In Anne's reign, a master-gunner sent with two mates to train the Jamaicans, but recalled for lack of employment, reported that the local commander set him and his mates to do duty as 'common gunners', and sent his artificers into the country to find work. There were eight culverins mounted with nothing under the wheels or train of the carriage, and one of the thirteen-inch mortars was dismounted with a rotten bed. The Council had refused him 70s.

---

[1] Ord. Warrants WO 55/536: warrant of 25 July 1683.　　[2] Fort. *Marl.*

[3] An interesting 'throw-back'. The early Master-Gunners were nearly all Flemings and 'the Gunners have no other bookes but such as were written by them'. Bourne, 'Art of Shooting'—quoted in *Army Quarterly*, op. cit.

[4] Fort., i, pp. 343 and 389.

(which he later reduced to 50s.) to build a shed to protect the guns of the field train, mounted before the governor's door. In Kingstown, on the other hand, the tumbrils were dismounted and had lain exposed to the weather for twelve months.[1] As the war progressed, however, the status of artillery in the field rose, and the Board took a steadily growing direct interest. The Master-Gunner's post became more and more a sinecure, and Pendlebury, appointed in 1710, was the last 'Master Gunner of England'. In 1716, the post was redesignated 'Master Gunner of Whitehall and St. James's Park', which emphasized its ceremonial nature.

The artillery were, on the whole, better paid than the infantry. In the case of the officers, however, this was so only when they drew the extra money paid for accompanying the train, and they had, of course, no profit from off-reckonings. The commander of a train was normally, though not necessarily nor always, an artillery officer, as opposed to an engineer. His pay depended entirely on the size of his command. A captain of artillery received £60 per year, but 10s. per day in addition when with a train, 1st lieutenants £50 and 6s. per day, mates £45. 10s., 2nd lieutenants £40, and sergeants £20 and 2s. 6d. in the train. Bombardiers received 2s. per day (the Chief Bombardier for England had £54. 15s. per year), gunners 1s. 6d. per day—the same as labourers—and matrosses 1s. 3d. The matrosses were, one might say, gunners' mates, or even apprentice gunners. The Chief Firemaster for England had £150 per year, his mate £80, and two Firemasters under him £60 each. The seventeen fireworkers in England had £40 apiece (those in the train had 4s. per day), and the Firemaster for the Fire Ships £60. The Firemaster in a train had 8s. per day. The Chief Petardeer in England had £54. 15s. per year, and the four petardeers under him £36. 10s. apiece.[2] The Master-Gunner in the Tower of London had 2s. per day, and 'the usual fees' which in a post of that nature would be not inconsiderable. The Master-Gunner at Jamaica had 5s. per day, and his mate 3s. The Master-Gunner at Margate had £20 per year. A number of these figures were an apparent advance on

[1] Ord. Warrants WO 55/343.

[2] *Dom. Cal.*, i, pp. 579–80 (this shows matrosses at 1s. per day), ii, p. 448; *Journals Commons*, xiii, 21 Jan. 1702, xiv, 19 and 29 Nov. 1703, 15 Nov. 1704.

those laid down in the warrant of 1683, but it is difficult to be precise how much in the way of final earnings the original figures really represented as there were various means of supplementing them. The warrant ordered that bombardiers, gunners, and matrosses should have 6*d.* per day, but this must have been a 'basic' figure of some sort, and cannot have been the real final pay, if only because of the lack of differentiation between ranks. Artificers who went with the train were to have their gunners' and matrosses' pays made up to 2*s.* 6*d.* 'if they deserve it'; otherwise they were not to receive more than an additional 1*s.* Men in the trains certainly made additional money in normal times, as it was laid down that the Ordnance Department should take as many of its employees as possible from the trains, and make their pay up to the correct rate.[1]

The bulk of the horses and wagonners was found locally on an army's march. They were levied on the countryside. On the Danube campaign, for example, Franconia provided 340 horses with harnesses, and 16 waggons at six sols per day for every man leading a horse.[2] There was an intermediate category of horse between the 'full time' and the 'casual'. This was provided by contractors and accompanied the army throughout a campaign. In Blenheim year Marlborough particularly instructed Blood to be careful of these horses and draw extensively on the country. At times the contractors suffered severe losses. In his dispatch of 19 July 1704, Marlborough forwarded a petition from the artillery horse contractors who had lost 688 horses in the previous campaign at an estimated cost of 80 guilders a horse. They had had additional expenses due to having to pay for their grazing, and had been disappointed in expectations of an extraordinary allowance on the march into Germany. 'These great losses,' they went on in familiar language, 'will unavoidably ruin your Supplicants, being now above £3,000 sterling in debt, besides all their great trouble and fatigue of the three last Campagnes.' By tacking on various odds and ends, they inflated their losses to 88,960, which Blood proceeded to whittle to 35,400 guilders. He reckoned that, of this smaller figure, the contractors should themselves bear 'one third, a half, or two thirds', which would seem to indicate that he knew of considerable profits in better times.[3]

---

[1] *Army Quarterly*, liv, No. 10.   [2] Murray, i, p. 425.   [3] Ord. Letters WO 46/6.

While the number of horses which could be harnessed to the limbers at any one time was constant, the number required per gun naturally varied with the terrain, and the necessity for reliefs. A fair figure is that of 470 horses for 25 pieces of 24-lb. shot, or 200 for 10 of 24-lb. given in Marlborough's dispatch of 1706. Pontoon horses could be used in an emergency to help in the drawing of guns, and, by employment of spare harness, the waggon horses could also be switched.[1] Men were also used on occasion to drag the guns, and the M.G.O. held special harness which could be issued for such service.[2]

Technically the guns were unimpressive. They are stated to have been 'deficient alike in accuracy, in range, in penetrative power, and in durability'.[3] The Board of Ordnance was not, however, a body to be afflicted with lack of confidence. When, for example, a G. Ramendon in 1705 offered them a system of shooting by night for a reward of £1,000, they noted: 'In our opinion the shooting by night as well as by day is not a very difficult thing'—and added that it had been done before.[4]

Marlborough, for his part, had a keen realization of the importance of artillery on the battle-field, in spite of its technical imperfections and the problems of movement and supply which it brought literally in its train. In his usual fashion, he got successful results, not by sweeping innovation, but by unremitting personal effort (in many of his battles he himself saw to the precise placing of the guns), and by skilful choice of subordinates. His intensive and extensive use of artillery—in the Netherlands he had 1·16 guns per 1,000 men against the French 0·91[5]— inspired his gunners. Their new-found enthusiasm and pride helped to bring increasing skill and an *esprit de corps* which led logically to the developments of the next reign.

The cost of providing and maintaining artillery in the field cannot be precisely calculated because it appeared in the estimates as part of the total cost of the train. Since, however, a large part of the engineers' work was on behalf of the guns

[1] Murray, iii, p. 15.
[2] *Dom. Cal.*, i, p. 384. No doubt the ammunition loads could have been lightened had more soldiers been like John Jones of whom Corporal Matthew Bishop wrote. This soldier had such an appetite that, to make money for extra food, he used to gather up cannon balls from the battle-fields and sell them to his artillery comrades.
[3] Atkinson, p. 12.   [4] Ord. Letters WO 46/6.
[5] Atkinson, p. 505, footnote.

(construction of siege positions, bridges for limbers and waggons, and so on), undoubtedly the major proportion of the cost of the train was, directly or indirectly, for artillery.

Engineers

At the turn of the eighteenth century the engineers were, like the artillery, an arm of the Office of Ordnance only part military. In the case of the engineers the civilian element was present throughout in all categories, and was not, as was largely the case in the artillery, restricted to specific tasks. Not only was there extensive employment of local unskilled labour for digging, but many of the higher appointments, such as chief engineers with overseas garrisons, were held by civilians.[1] The Surveyor-General, under whom they were placed by the Warrant of 1683, was not necessarily a soldier by origin, but, although junior to the Lieutenant-General of the Ordnance, he was very powerful. Not only did he wield great influence by his regular attendance at Board meetings, whose minutes show that he himself frequently comprised the 'meeting', but he was also, by virtue of his appointment, an officer of State. Originally he had under him an assistant, but this post, which had been created by William, was abolished by the Warrant of 3 July 1702.[2] The organization then reverted to the form laid down in the original instructions of 25 July 1683, i.e. a Surveyor, a Principal or Chief Engineer, a Second Engineer, and a Third Engineer. The original salary of the Surveyor-General was £400, but this was later raised to £500. An additional perquisite fell to him when he was designated Assistant to the Lieutenant-General of the Ordnance. This brought a further £300 (the Lieutenant-General drew £800), with no real addition of work. When Brydges was appointed surveyor at £500, the additional £300 was not approved, but in 1709 the Board pressed that another £200 should be paid to him with effect from his original date of appointment seven years previously.[3] The Assistant Surveyor, while the post

---

[1] The lack of distinct army rank caused frequent disputes over the engineers' share of prize money. A Royal Warrant of 16 December 1692 gave them 15 shares each. Porter, p. 59.

[2] Ord. Warrants WO 55/342/234.

[3] Ord. Letters WO 46/6, 29 Nov. 1709.

existed, drew £250, the Principal Engineer £300, the Second Engineer £250, and the Third Engineer £150.[1] It was stipulated that the Chief Engineer was to be a 'person of considerable scientific attainments, to be skilled in all the principles of attack and defence, to be well versed in the strength and cost of material, and to be competent for the construction and superintendence of fortifications and works'.[2] There was also provision for 'two ordinary engineers or young men to be bred up in the Art and Knowledge of Fortificacion' at £100 apiece.[3] Under William, the Chief Engineer, Alexander de la Martinière, had also been nominated Director of the Trenches, but the officer apparently got little profit from this. In a petition dated 17 June 1702, he claimed that he had entered the engineer service on Queen Mary's promise of 10s. per day, and engineer pay until promoted lieutenant-colonel. He had served from May 1692 until the disbandment of the army, had never been promoted lieutenant-colonel, and had received only £75. His claim for a further £1,184 was minuted in 1702 'No fund for this debt . . .' and in 1704 'Nothing can be done on this'.[4]

Master Workman of Her Majesty's Stores and Fortifications was a sinecure appointment which the Board of Ordnance itself declared in 1705 carried no duties.[5] The Workmaster for Building and Repairing All Forts was paid £120 per annum,[6] and a report quoted by Nottingham (in a letter to the M.G.O.) in 1702 suggests that this may not have been hardly earned:

Portland Castle is in a very ruinous condition, and will be totally rifled unless some speedy care be taken by appointing some fitt person to look after the same . . . there is not one grain of powder in the Castle . . . the Gunner being very necessitous was forced the Sunday before for fear of his Debtors[7] to quit the Castle, and shift for himself . . . he has left in possession of the Sutler's office which is in the Castle Yard, a miserable poor fellow that sweeps chimneys for his living, and two Porters as soe rated in pay, but live not in the castle which is the only Garrison . . . although the said Mr. Langrish has the Keys of the Castle, Yet the Windows are open, so that any person may get in and cut away the Leads

---

[1] Ord. Warrants WO 55/536, *Journals Commons*, xiv, 15 Nov. 1704.
[2] Clode, i, p. 265.   [3] Ord. Warrants WO 55/536; 55/342/234.
[4] *Treas. Cal.*, iii, p. 27.   [5] Ord. Letters WO 46/6.
[6] Ord. Warrants WO 55/342/283.
[7] *Sic*—presumably an error for 'creditors'.

that cover it, which will certainly be done, if timely care be not taken, as Weymouth Castle by neglect was demolished.[1]

These appointments were all in the permanently established 'headquarters staff' of engineers. The engineer officers in the trains were drawn from line regiments, and commanded miners, pioneers, pontoon men, and local labourers. In overseas garrisons (and even occasionally on continental service) the engineer could be a civilian. Civilian engineers frequently exercised their freedom of choice and refused to go to the more unpopular stations.[2] Such refusal was, indeed, not confined to civilians. In 1697 Colonel Wolgang Romer refused to go to New York on the grounds that £365 a year, which he was already getting in England, was too little. Romney, the Master-General, suspended him, but the King increased his pay by 10s. per day, and he took up his post. The Board of Ordnance exercised their usual restraint when they commented that the King's action 'may give great encouragement to such practices and very much prejudice the service'.[3]

Whether military or civilian, however, the species, anticipating the reputation of 'methodist, married, or mad', appeared to call for special treatment.

It is no easy thing [wrote Galway from the Peninsula] to find good engineers, and a Commission from the Board of Ordnance is not sufficient to make one . . . good engineers are so scarce, that one must bear with their humours and forgive them because we can't be without them.[4]

Even Marlborough, himself the M.G.O., had to complain from Lille in 1708 to Godolphin: 'It is impossible for me to express the uneasiness I suffer for the ill-conduct of our engineers at the siege where I think everything goes very wrong. It would be a cruel thing if . . . we should fail of taking it by ignorance of our engineers.' Before the end of this siege engineer casualties were over sixty.[5]

---

[1] Ord. Warrants WO 55/342/186–7.
[2] Parkes, the governor of St. Nevis who complained so bitterly in 1707 about absentee officers and poor-quality recruits, included in his catalogue of woe that he was without an engineer. *Treas. Cal.*, iii, p. 353.
[3] Porter, pp. 136–7.
[4] Ord. Minutes WO 47/22, 30 November 1704.   [5] Murray, ii, p. 312.

In the field a captain of pioneers drew 4*s.* per day, while the
bridge-master, serving with either the company of pontoon
men, or with the artillery, had 5*s.* per day. Sergeants of pioneers
had 2*s.* per day, and the pioneers themselves 1*s.* Corporals in
the pontoon company had 2*s.* per day and the pontoon men
1*s.* 6*d.*[1] Pay for officers or civilians not in the train depended,
in general, on the appointment and not on rank. The First
Engineers at New York and Jamaica drew 20*s.* per day, and
the Second Engineers 10*s.*[2] Lieutenant-Colonel John Armstrong
is referred to in one of Marlborough's dispatches as succeeding
Colonel Michael Richards as an 'engineer on the establishment
of Ordnance at £100 per year'. There are also warrants showing grants of £100 to captains for 'encouragement to perfect'
themselves in engineering.[3] As all these payments would be in
addition to the officers' regimental pay, it was not entirely
illogical that they should not be directly related to rank. There
was a tendency for a time to regard some engineer posts at
fortresses as sinecures which would provide additional money to
officers serving with regiments or otherwise unable to perform
their duties. Marlborough set his face steadfastly against this.
He attacked the problem in two ways, both by refusing to create
posts 'which would be pensions', and by making engineers
actually required at fortresses leave their regiments.[4] The case
of Colonel Benet and Gibraltar showed him at his most determined. Benet, as a captain, had been the first into Gibraltar
(on 25 November 1704) after the siege was over. His work there
brought him a lieutenant-colonelcy, a Queen's gratuity of
£200, and an Ordnance Minute (31 May 1705) 'that a letter
be writ to Captain Bennett to acquaint him that the Board
are sensible of his great services at Gibraltar, and doubt not
but that the Duke of Marlborough will consider them'.[5] The
Duke was, however, adamant that Benet should surrender his
infantry command, and rejected the Board's plea to the contrary.[6]

A note may be made here of a body called the King's Com-

[1] *Dom. Cal.*, i, pp. 579–80; *Journals Commons*, xii, 21 Jan. 1702.
[2] Ibid. xiv, 15 Nov. 1704.
[3] Murray, v, p. 503; SP Mil. 44/173, 17 Mar. 1704 and 17 Feb. 1710.
[4] Ord. Letters WO 46/86: dispatch of 28 May 1708.
[5] Porter, p. 66. On this occasion Benet's name was spelt as shown.
[6] Ord. Letters WO 46/6, 11 May and 5 June 1710.

pany of Engineers of which little appears to be known except that it was under the monarch's direct control without interference from the Board although some of the company were on the Ordnance establishment. Lieutenant-Colonel Blood was made Director and Commander-in-Chief of this body of twenty-seven officers in 1696. The members had no grading, but pay ranging from 5s. to 10s. per day was made by special warrants from the Treasury. In the same year, the King appointed Blood Second Engineer of England over the head of a senior.[1] This may have been part contributory to the dispute between Blood and the Board six years later. He appears to have taken offence that the post of Commander of the Train in the Flanders expedition was first offered to an officer who had served under him in Ireland. Commenting to the Master-General on a letter of Blood's which has unfortunately not been traced, the Board wrote that they had just heard he refused to take command of the train 'in the manner you doth propose'. This

considering his status of being an engineer upon the establishment is of Such ill consequence and so far intrenches upon your Lordship's authority, that it justly deserves the utmost punishment, and it is our opinion Colonel Blood should be forthwith discharged from any employment in the office. . . . The commission you intended Colonel Blood . . . cannot . . . give any occasion to be ridiculed or laughed at, and certainly Colonel Blood making that interpretation of it is a high reflection upon your Lordship and the Board.[2]

The Colonel flourished rather better under the next Master-General. He has already been mentioned as artillery commander at Blenheim. He was promoted Brigadier-General, and remained as the Duke's artillery commander until his death at Brussels in 1707.

ORDNANCE STORES

The branch of the Ordnance Department concerned with provision and distribution of stores did not start Anne's reign at a high level of efficiency. The organization introduced by James II while Duke of York suffered considerably during the revolution, and even in William III's first Irish campaign the department was of assistance to its former Master-General

[1] Porter, p. 60.   [2] Ibid., p. 111.

rather than to the new Sovereign. Later, William was to dispatch Marlborough, although not at that time Master-General, to improve the situation in Flanders; Waldeck's report concerning the English and their equipment there has already been mentioned. The Board displayed at least a certain robustness of spirit, when, despite the previous six years, it claimed in a letter on 28 April 1696 that 'noe publick complaint' had ever 'been made against our office'.[1] Any improvement Marlborough may have managed to bring about in Flanders was lost in the great reductions after the Peace of Ryswick. In 1702 at the time of Ormonde's projected expedition, one regiment was reported as having arms 'twenty four years old . . . and most of them unserviceable'. In the following year's campaign, men fought with swords because 'the officers find it not safe for them to use their firearms'.[2] On 20 February 1711, however, Marlborough, moved perhaps by irony or discretion, wrote to the Principal Officers, 'you have hitherto performed all the Services relating to the Office of Ordnance very agreeably to Her Majesty's interest, and fully to my satisfaction'.[3]

Marlborough's influence as M.G.O. was, as in other spheres, limited by the fact that he was commander in one theatre of operations while technically responsible for much more. The day-to-day running of the service was inevitably the responsibility of the Lieutenant-General, assisted by the Board of Ordnance. The office as then constituted was of such recent growth that it cannot really be said that the conception of a Master-General serving abroad was a new one. Marlborough himself while abroad consistently gave responsibility and power to the Board as the men on the spot. With only rudimentary means of communication, this was the only way anything approaching speedy decisions could be reached. He was very loth to intervene even when he was directly referred to, such as in the case of the remonstrance by Mr. Lowther in 1790. 'As you know,' he replied to the Board, 'I leave matters in my absence to your decision, and . . . I shall always be of your

[1] Ord. Letters WO 46/6.
[2] Entry Books WO 26/11, 7 May 1702; *Dom. Cal.*, ii, p. 162, 19 Oct. 1703. Yet only a year later, Prince Eugene declared of the English troops who marched to the Danube: 'I never saw better harness, better clothes, finer belts and accoutrements.'
[3] Ord. Letters WO 46/6.

opinion.'[1] Always remarkably careless of his prerogatives, he encouraged his subordinates in the Ordnance to deal direct with outsiders. To Erle, he wrote in 1705 on the Lieutenant-General's taking office, that he should on arrival in England call immediately on the Lord Treasurer 'who will give you all the information necessary while I am absent'.[2] One of the few cases where he would not accept the Board's advice was that of Colonel Benet, already referred to.

As a commander in the field, the Duke, although M.G.O., was as dependent on the functioning of the Board as other commanders, but, inevitably, no matter how good or how bad the office as a whole might be, the Flanders theatre received preferential treatment. The Duke declared that the Principal Officers had performed their duties 'fully to my satisfaction'. The commanders in Spain or of neglected garrisons in the West Indies had another tale to tell. The office could supply only one theatre adequately. The fact that that was Flanders was not necessarily due exclusively to personal bias. Marlborough was in Flanders precisely because it was the vital theatre. Despite the cries of 'no peace without Spain,' responsible people realized that, while the war might be lost in many places— including Westminster—it could be won only in the Low Countries and in the North of France.

The channels through which the Board might receive their orders have been dealt with separately. A recurrent difficulty, inevitable perhaps in the early stages of the war, was the receipt of incomplete or contradictory orders without appreciation of the time required to fulfil them. The Board was particularly tried by Nottingham when he was Secretary of State. On one occasion, for example, having omitted bayonets altogether from a demand, he later asked for 5,000 to be included, and shortly afterwards increased this to 6,500. In ordering swords he failed to stipulate whether scabbards were required, and so favoured the Portuguese envoy as to let him pick and choose from stock in the midst of the rush to meet his orders. The Board, having already turned all cutlers on to production of the 6,500 bayonets, and having no swords in stock, protested strenuously against 'the confusion this office is put into' and the increase in expense caused by short notice and 'by so often changing

[1] Murray, iv, p. 524.   [2] Ibid. iv, p. 614.

measures'. About the same time, they gave the Secretary an elementary lesson in 'staff duties' by pointing out clearly where a responsibility belonged, and why. In reply to an inquiry, they wrote to him that they could not decide whether it would be 'to Her Majesty's prejudice to sell 5,000 muskets to Portugal. ... We cannot take upon us to judge ... not knowing what other necessary demands there may be.'[1]

The original instructions laid down that stores were only to be issued by the Principal Officers 'under particular warrant in writing under our Sign Manual, or Order of Our Council, or letter of Our Lord Admiral, or Lords Commissioner of our Admiralty' for the sea service, or on 'signification', from the M.G.O. thereupon.[2] This the Board reiterated early in the reign when they declared that 'no stores are to be issued but by Warrant from Her Majesty, the Privy Council or Lord High Admiral'. Although, they said, they had lately obliged the Secretary of State in the absence of the Queen in order not to cause delay, the practice could not continue. This, among other things, indicates the status of the Board, which was prepared, if necessary, to argue with the Secretary of State, a very powerful Cabinet Minister, who was, in fact, responsible for countersigning the Queen's warrants for such issues.[3] It will be remembered that on 24 March 1703 Blathywayt wrote that, when arms were required, he customarily signified requirements to the Officers of Ordnance 'whereupon a warrant has been procured from the Secretary of State'.[4]

It is not easy to disentangle from the records of the day what proportion, or indeed what types of stores, were supplied under private arrangements, what the Ordnance Department supplied 'on repayment', and what was 'issue'. The basic rule appears to have been that new regiments were armed free by the Ordnance, but 'after once a Regimt is Armd they are for ye future to take care to keep their Arms in good Condicon ... if any Regimt is willing to pay for new Arms Wee have no objection to their haveing ym'.[5] Ammunition, including powder

---

[1] Ord. Warrants WO 55/343, 1703.   [2] Ibid. 55/536.
[3] Ibid. 55/342.   [4] War Letters, WO 4/27.
[5] Records show such deliveries on repayment between, for example, 5 Nov. 1688 and 24 Dec. 1699: 'An account of arms and other habilments of war

for training horses 'to bear fire' was no longer paid for by the individual soldier;[1] the guns of the artillery were provided by the Department which also supplied the ammunition; transport was provided within certain limits, although officers paid for their own horses, and, broadly speaking, the carriage of them. Forbes claims that, for the supply of muskets, the colonel and the Board made a contract—but this appears to have been a 'contract' only inasmuch as it was a custom of the service. The colonel, he adds, was bound to keep his arms in good condition, and, if required, to return them to store in the same condition as when issued; this was certainly not a firm rule. Concessions were granted as time went on, and undoubtedly arms expended on service were frequently replaced free of charge.[2] There were various justifiable reasons for modification of the rule about free initial supply followed by repair or replacement at regimental or individual expense. The universally disliked, but eternally popular, system of drafting men *en bloc* between regiments was one. An example in point was Barrymore in 1706, whose case was dealt with in the previous chapter.[3]

Then there were the cases of men taken prisoner with their arms. There is a reference in the House of Commons Journals to a claim by a committee that such cases could be met by a special contingent warrant from the commanding officer, but the procedure does not seem to have been widely followed, as this is the only reference to it which I have seen.[4]

The Board, nevertheless, repeatedly took its stand on the principle of repayment for all replacements. On 21 August 1703, it wrote to the Secretary of State, Nottingham,

. . . it is not usual for the Office of Ordnance, after they have once armed a regiment, ever to change arms, as, if that should be brought

---

delivered out of store to regiments between 5th November and 24th December and charged to their accompts to be deducted out of their pay' shows: 600 carbines at 26*s*.; 800 pistols at 25*s*.; 537 snaphaunce muskets at £1; 8 halberds at 1*s*.; 475 French tents at £1; 13 bells for arms at £1. Ord. Letters WO 46/6, 9 Jan. 1705.

[1] While this was undoubtedly the general principle, there is a notable series of items among the flood of petitions submitted to the Board of General Officers on demobilization in 1713. These allege that certain men paid for ammunition but did not receive it. The Board, so far as I can see, did not even comment on these particular pleas, and I have not so far been able to find any explanation of them. PGO WO 71/2.   [2] Forbes, p. 105.

[3] Registers WO 25/3180: warrant of 13 Nov. 1706.

[4] *Journals Commons*, xvi, 4 Feb. 1706.

into practice, it would prove a new and very great charge to Her Majesty. And not only His late Majesty King William, but His Grace the Duke of Marlborough since upon several applications . . . always refused to order their arms to be changed.[1]

Later in the same year they reiterated:

. . . the colonels of each regiment are expected when once armed to keep them at their own expense in good condition. . . . If every regiment has liberty to change what arms they please, we take it for granted every regiment will desire to be entirely new armed, which was never allowed by His late Majesty, nor is there any provision made by Parliament for new arming regiments which have been once armed.[2]

And again, a little over a month later:

We must again repeat to your Lordship that this frequent arming of regiments puts Her Majesty to greater expense than was ever formerly ordered . . . and if encouragement is given to demands of this nature, it may be expected to arm as often as clothe.[3]

It is, for all that, still difficult to claim with confidence that any rule was strictly applied. In a minute of 15 May 1708, for example,[4] the Board of General Officers quite firmly claimed that it was the custom in the horse to replace old arms as soon as they were worn out. Whether this was a provision applying specifically to the horse as distinct from the dragoons or infantry, whether the General Officers were incorrectly advised, or whether it hinged on some contested interpretation of an Office of Ordnance rule, I have been unable to determine.

The Board's attitude seems to have remained quite firmly as stated on 3 June 1702:

The Office of late have been at a Prodigious charge in supplying the Army with Armes, for which noe consideration was made by Parliament, and our Stores are very much exhausted. We cannot judge of the necessity for arming them, but his late Majesty would never arme any Regiment that had been once armed but expected all losses and repairs to be made good by the officers, and we doe not know any extraordinary reason for granting of it.[5]

---

[1] Ord. Warrants WO 55/343.   [2] Ibid., 11 Sept. 1703.
[3] Ibid., 19 Oct. 1703.
[4] PGO WO 71/1.   [5] Ord. Warrants WO 55/342/230.

In the previous reign, troops had been subject to stoppages for purchase of regimental arms. A rule issued in Dublin on 2 September 1697 stated that the Colonel of the 8th Dragoons (Conyngham's) had stopped each dragoon 24s. for the provision of pistols. The King, however, had ruled against this. The Colonel had, therefore, issued each dragoon with 'a good broad sword value 12s.', and now intended to use the remaining 12s. 'towards the better arming that regiment with fuzees'. These arms became regimental and not individual property, for 'no dragoon who shall hereafter be discharged at his own request or be broke . . . shall have any challenge or pretence to his arms; but if any troops shall be disbanded each Dragoon shall carry off his sword and receive the 12s. stopt towards buying his fuzee'.[1] In 1704 the Board were asking Marlborough to use his influence against a proposal for supply of pistols to Brigadier Ross's dragoons because hitherto they had not been 'burthen'd' with such provision for Dragoons.[2]

A complication present throughout the reign was that many regiments were initially armed with pikes which had to be replaced by bayonets. The cost of this was normally met by allowing fictitious names for a specified number of musters.[3] The Board wrote in 1706:

all the regiments raised since the disuse of pikes have provided bayonets . . . at their own charge. Few of the officers agree in the sort of bayonets fit to be used or in the manner of fixing them as may appear by the various sorts there are of them in the Army.[4]

Confused preferences had already meant that, two years earlier, the Board had had to make special arrangements to send socket bayonets to Portugal while they still had 3,000 plug bayonets in store in the Tower.[5]

There were, of course, no scales or inspections, and repair was essentially a regimental matter. Since the cost of the repair had to be paid from the off-reckonings it was obviously to the colonel's advantage to keep it as low as possible. No spares were allowed,[6] and in time of war the costs must have risen

---

[1] Walton, p. 854.   [2] Ord. Letters WO 46/6.
[3] Registers WO 25/3180 contain many examples
[4] Ord. Warrants WO 55/353/148.
[5] AA., p. 75.
[6] Ord. Letters WO 46/6, 14 Mar. 1704.

considerably. It seems, in these circumstances, quite likely that the author of the *Recruiting Essay* was correct in claiming that the 'very Exchange of Musquats (made useless by Time and Service) are stopt' out of the 6*d*. a week subsistence accounted for at stipulated intervals as distinct from that to be paid 'on the drum head'. In the end, of course, costs got completely beyond the normal methods, and, as in most other cases, the rules were relaxed, not so far as payment for arms was concerned, but by provision for what were technically false musters. One example is the special Royal Warrant allowing six fictitious names on rolls for the period 25 October 1706 to 13 May 1708 to meet such charges.[1]

In general, accoutrements and equipment other than arms were a charge against the regiment, although it is claimed by Forbes that the Ordnance supplied regimental drums and tentage for general purposes, as distinct from camp equipment on service.[2] A decision of the Privy Council in 1703, however, appears to make it quite clear that regiments normally paid for tentage, but that in exceptional cases there was free replacement for any lost on service.[3]

For loss or destruction of arms or accoutrements by negligence, the individual soldier was held responsible. Until a debt so incurred was cleared he had, when on foreign service, to live on bread and water, not so much as a punishment, but in order that the money so saved on his subsistence might be applied towards the cost.[4] Article 42 of the Articles of War laid before Parliament in 1717 stipulated that a soldier spoiling arms or ammunition should run the gauntlet, while an officer, storekeeper, or commissary of provisions embezzling, selling, or wilfully spoiling them should be cashiered. Article 43 stipulated that any soldier selling or wilfully losing property or stealing from his comrades was to be placed under weekly stoppage not exceeding half of his pay in addition to confinement or corporal punishment. This, significantly enough, was the only stoppage permitted except under Sign Manual, and was to be imposed only by court martial.[5] With muskets at 20*s*. to 22*s*. and car-

---

[1] Registers WO 25/3180: warrant of 13 Nov. 1706.
[2] Forbes, p. 105.
[3] Ord. Warrants WO 55/343.
[4] SP For. 109/1. [5] *Journals Commons*, xvii, 4 Feb. 1717.

bines 26s. apiece, the soldier must have had a prolonged spell on short pay or plain fare to clear the debt. National taxation remained, however, at a level considerably lower than that to which two wars have accustomed us today.

The trains were clothed through depots in a method not unlike today's. This was yet a further advantage to soldiers and civilians in the Ordnance, for in no other respect was the Department responsible for free clothing issues.[1]

To watch issues in the field, and keep account of debits, the Ordnance had their Commissaries, and there were also appointed, by the Treasury, on 26 June 1703, two Comptrollers of Army Accounts, who had, among other duties, 'to keep account of arms, provisions, tents, and other things delivered out of store to regiments, troops, or companies, and in cases where deductions are to be made for any of them, to see that the value is duly charged to account'.[2]

While muskets, pikes, tents, and so on may have been the principal concern of the office in time of war, it still had peacetime commitments in the shape of an item which bulks even larger today in the Ordnance Corp's calculations—barrack furniture, and fuel and lighting. This has been dealt with in the previous chapter.

How successful was the procurement and supply of Ordnance stores? Generally speaking, English arms had been better until this time than foreign, although a trifle dearer. During the war, however, arms manufacturers in England seem to have been unable to expand their production sufficiently, and not to have been above accompanying inflated prices with deflated quality. The Department were seriously hampered in providing all types of stores, including arms, as well as clothing and equipment, by the law that none for British troops was to be bought overseas. In 1704 prices for 10,000 muskets were approximately £11,000 in England, but £8,000 in Holland. In view of the low stocks, an Order in Council, issued on Marlborough's representations in 1706, authorized the purchase of 10,000 muskets for Ireland in Holland. The English gunmakers were said at that time to be unable to supply more than

[1] Clode, i, p. 108; Forbes, p. 110.
[2] Treas. 1/84/35; Clode, ii, pp. 668 et seq.

2,000 per month.[1] In the following February breast arms (for the horse) which were required at the rate of 60 per week were costing £1. 5s. in England, while the Dutch could make them for 15s.[2] The trouble led to a debate in the House of Commons in March 1707[3] when the Master Wardens and Company of Gunmakers of the City of London submitted a petition. The Ordnance Office admitted a debt of £30,000—a side-swipe at the House rather than a damaging admission—and the purchase of 18,000 arms in Holland, of which 10,000 were for Ireland. The gunmakers' representative claimed that they could supply 70,000 arms a year and guaranteed 30,000 every six months. They had, he claimed, already offered to do this if they were paid some part of their debts in order to let the men have their wages. Since the accession, he went on, they had had only one year's work for the English Government, although they had made 40,000 arms for the Portuguese. They had no quarrel with the rates laid down, but asked to be allowed interest on their debts. In conclusion, the witness referred darkly to the act requiring troops in Her Majesty's Service in English pay to be equipped from England and the provision for cashiering offenders.

The Ordnance representative replied that they had had continually to press the gunmakers, who had never offered more than 10,000 arms in six months. He referred specifically to a delay in the supply of locks, tenders for which were 20s. from Holland, and 40s. in the United Kingdom. (There was one of 26s. from England, but unfortunately it was not to pattern.) The petitioners had been paid in their turn 'and are no more in arrears than other artificers'—which meant, of course, no less. One lot of arms purchased abroad, he went on, was not for English troops, although they were under Rivers, and the other lot went to Ireland for troops on the Irish establishment. He then counter-attacked by calling witnesses to give evidence of widespread complaints in Flanders four years previously about arms which men were afraid to fire for fear of bursting them.

After an inconclusive debate, the House extended the ban

[1] Treas. Cal., iii, pp. 383 and 414; Anne Cal., p. 276.
[2] Ord. Letters WO 46/6, Feb. 1707.
[3] Journals Commons, xv.

on purchases of foreign arms to troops in 'Her Majesty's pay *or* service'—but simultaneously negated the provision by saying this should apply 'as far as is consistent with the service'.[1]

The type of armament manufacturer dear to a later-day political cartoonist was more thoroughly portrayed by the saltpetre and gunpowder dealers. Saltpetre was a big problem, even without complications of profit and loss. Its supply depended on the safe running of the East Indies Fleet, whose uncertain arrival more than once caused Marlborough himself anxiety, and led to purchases in Holland. The East India Company was under obligation to supply 500 tons of saltpetre per year at £53 per ton in war, and £45 per ton in peace.[2] This had then to be put out to contract for manufacture into gunpowder. The rate paid was 16s. per barrel, but the manufacturers not only pushed this up during the war to 18s., but also increased considerably their allowance for 'refraction' or wastage through impurities, which eventually reached a figure 1 per cent. higher than that allowed by the East India Company to the Board. When the Board refused to raise the refraction further, the manufacturers demanded 20s. per barrel, and the troubled Principal Officers were driven to consider the possible supply of 15,000 barrels per year by one man. This they eventually rejected lest, once they had put themselves in his power, their last case be worse than their first.[3]

It was fortunate the Board's prudence had led to building up large stocks, for the drain in the early part of the war was heavy. Starting 1701 with 36,558 muskets in store for the land service, the office found itself by the following January with under 10,000. By mid-1704 they had issued 45,000 for the land service and 11,000 for the sea service. Fortescue claims that, two months before Blenheim, the supply of firelocks and socket bayonets was exhausted, but the report to the House on

---

[1] Ibid., 19 Mar. 1707.

[2] *Treas. Cal.*, iv, p. 451.

[3] Ibid., iii, p. 449; iv, pp. 151/3; Ord. Letters WO 46/6. An offer they had less difficulty in rejecting was from a Richard Jones who was willing to save them £2,000 to £3,000 by the use of old metal. He claimed in his letter that, having made shot and shell for five years, he had saved the Government between £15,000 and £16,000. The Board gave less weight to all these claims than to the necessity for him to explain 'how it was he erased certain words from a debenture'. *Treas. Cal.*, iv, p. 260.

13 November 1704 claimed 15,662 snaphaunce muskets in stock on 1 June of that year.[1] A letter to Marlborough on 9 January 1705 stated that small arms stocks had fallen from 50,000 at the beginning of the war to 6,000.[2]

Much the severest drop was, however, in stores of saltpetre. Stocks fell quickly from the minimum of 1,000 tons laid down in Charles's time to 170 tons in 1705.[3] I have not seen any figures for 1705 for gunpowder, expenditure of which was 13,000 to 15,000 barrels per year, and, as the drop in all stores seems to have been most severe between 1704 and 1705, previous figures are probably not of much value. They show, however, 14,000 barrels in stock in 1701, rising by 1704 to over 19,000.[4]

At the same time the Board suffered the familiar harassments from people with 'bright ideas' such as the vociferous efforts in 1702 to get them to supply the troops in the West Indies with 'buccanneering muskets' because they would be lighter. Those familiar sponsors of anything unmilitary for adoption by the army were coldly received by the Board, who replied to the pressing demands to produce out of the air some of those remarkable weapons that 'until we see a pattern of what is desired, we know not how to give any directions to the gunmakers thereupon'. When a sample of the revolutionary musket was eventually produced it turned out to be heavier and less serviceable than those already in use.[5]

Their most serious handicap was, of course, that with which most offices of State were familiar—lack of money. It was a difficulty which inevitably affected the Board particularly severely because of their dependence on large numbers of civilian suppliers. In 1702 their debt for contracts was nearly £166,300.[6] The most remarkable point about the events from then onwards is the way in which the Board kept the enormous debts under control. Credit for this must, no doubt, be shared with the Lord Treasurer. In 1683 the Ordnance estimates had been £10,653; in 1712, when the peak of the war had been passed, the

[1] Fort., p. 584; *Journals Commons*, xiv, 13 Nov. 1704.
[2] Ord. Letters 46/6.
[3] There were 800 tons in stock in 1702. Ord. Letters WO 46/6, letter of 9 Jan. 1705.
[4] *Journals Commons*, xiv, 13 Nov. 1704.
[5] Ord. Warrants WO 55/342/287 and 288, 22 Oct. 1702.
[6] *Journals Commons*, xiv, 6 Nov. 1702.

train alone in Flanders was costing £53,000 per year; yet the 1702 debt of £166,293 (against which they had received only £115,952) had been reduced nine years later to £163,000.[1] The highest figure reached was in 1708, when the office owed over £230,000, of which nearly £200,000 was for stores and services, and £16,000 for freight of ships.[2] The difficulties to be surmounted were exemplified in the estimates and votes for 1703 and 1704, already mentioned in Chapter II. For the first year the estimate was £104,478; Parliament voted £70,973, and the Department actually received £60,000. In the following year the estimate was £176,169; £118,362 was voted, and £91,728 actually paid. As a result of this their cash in hand had dropped by January 1705 from £110,000 to £36,000, of which £20,000 was reckoned to be earmarked for the following year.[3]

There was persistent difficulty over the Board's responsibilities to the navy.[4] It was the custom that 5s. per month per man was payable to the Ordnance for their services. This, at least, was said to be Parliament's intent, but in 1705 the Board complained that, since there was no specific appropriation in the Act, they were receiving only 4s.[5] This was in spite of their plea in the previous year for 6s. because of new works at Plymouth, and a claim put forward in a minute at that time that Parliament had actually determined 7s. per man in the vote of 30 November. At the time they raised this matter, the Board gave fairly convincing evidence of the justice of their claim by assigning £32,000 to pay off 'great debts' due as navy arrears and £10,900 for army. On 15 November 1705, in voting £120,000 against a cost of nearly £174,000 for Land Ordnance Services, Parliament also significantly allocated a total of £104,000 for the Sea Service estimates at 4s. per man per month.[6] In the following July a memorial by the Commissioners of Ordnance to the Lord Treasurer stated that their artificers' pay was 1¼ years in arrears, and there was not half the powder in store which was considered necessary.[7]

---

[1] Ibid.; *Treas. Cal.*, iv, p. 270; Treas. 1/82.

[2] *Journals Commons*, xvi, 11 Dec. 1708.

[3] Ord. Letters WO 46/6.

[4] Out of the moneys voted to the Ordnance Department for 1701–2, £105,000 was paid out for Sea Services as against £71,000 for Land. *H.M.C.H. of L.*, vi, pp. 70–76.   [5] Ord. Letters WO 46/6.

[6] *Journals Commons*, xiv.   [7] *Treas. Cal.*, iii, p. 520.

By 1709 the arrears had mounted to two years', and the Department was tried severely when instructed to provide stores to the value of £60,000 for an expedition, but was not voted any money by Parliament. In addition the tallies which they did have were acceptable to few. The artificers, it was declared, were 'reduced to the last extremity'. They were still two years in arrear in January 1710 when the debentures held by the office were at 30 per cent. discount.[1]

Typical of the small, almost token, payments which had to be made from time to time to keep things going was the passing by the Lord Treasurer of £12,000 for each of the Land and Sea Services against an Ordnance demand of £77,000 and £50,000.[2] By 1711, a note of alarm was creeping into correspondence which had hitherto been conducted more in hope than despair. The artificers—contractors and workmen—were insisting on being paid in ready money instead of practically worthless tallies, but the Treasurer had to work the latter off somewhere. By April the Board was petitioning 'it would be much for Her Majesty's Service that as much favour should be shown (the artificers) as is possible, and if their Lordships could conveniently order them a quarter's payment (about £30,000) it would give them fresh credit'. It was apparently *not* convenient to their Lordships, for no payment was made.[3]

The debt at 30 November 1711 was £104,582, of which the biggest item was £41,000 for powder for Portugal, and the next £24,000 to artificers and others for stores and services. Flanders was due £17,258. To meet this debt, the Board had tallies, stock, and assignments on revenue of £14,500, but out of this they had also to pay £42,000 for land fortifications. In 1712 the officers of the train in Spain and Flanders were three years in arrears, and such payment as they were receiving was in South Sea stock at a heavy discount.[4]

A typical year's estimates included: Holland train £45,000; routine expenses £28,273 (this included salaries, rents of storehouses, repairs of storehouses, barracks, platforms, carriages, artillery stores in garrisons, and maintenance of stores—all

---

[1] *Treas. Cal.*, iv, p. 160.   [2] Ibid., p. 115.
[3] Ibid., pp. 261 and 263.
[4] *Journals Commons*, xvii, 17 Dec. 1711; *Treas. Cal.*, iv, p. 353.

under the heading of 'ordinary of the office'); saltpetre
£10,600; Jamaica £511; New York £182; powder for Portugal
£10,954; Gibraltar £3,631; 'the charge of replenishing the
stores which are very much exhausted by several expeditions'
£40,000; increases and repairs to Gibraltar fortifications
£18,000; Spain £12,254; and carriages and draught for cannon,
ammunition, and stores for train and army £64,000.[1] A non-
recurring item appears to have been the ten gallons of salad
oil for Jamaica at £4 in 1703.[2]

Under such conditions, it is not very surprising to find the
Board complaining in 1702 that 'too often the bombs and shells
have been filled with sand instead of proper ingredients', or
that Brudenell going abroad in 1704 complained that arms
delivered to him were 'old barrels with new furbishings' and
when used in firing most of them were 'found to have holes in
them'.[3] In the previous year the Antigua garrison reported
that the arms there were very bad, that there was no small
powder, and only 50 flints were serviceable out of 1,000.
Musket balls had to be improvised from cartridge cases.[4] A
survey of the Barbados defences in 1702 showed that in 28
forts and batteries there were 58 serviceable guns out of 308.[5]

Nottingham based part of his case for the repeated instructions for exchange of unserviceable arms, to which the Board
objected, on the bad state of arms issued. He claimed on 19
October 1703 that 'arms in Flanders this year have been so unserviceable, and the Duke of Marlborough has been sensible
of it, that upon occasion the men have fought with their swords
only, the officers finding it not safe for them to use their fire
arms'. The Board's riposte was that they were not surprised,
as the arms had not been properly looked after, and that they
knew of one case where the arms had been taken over in 1696
with no evidence of their having been repaired or replaced
since.[6]

Neither the Board nor the contractors were entirely to blame
for shortcomings in the tropical stations or in the Plantations.
The effects of tropical climate on equipment took those directly

[1] *Journals Commons*, xv, 18 Nov. 1707.
[2] Ibid., xiv, 25 Nov. 1703.
[3] Ord. Warrants 55/342/299; Ord. Letters WO 46/6.
[4] *Dom. Cal.*, i, p. 718.   [5] *APC Col.*, ii, p. 405.
[6] Ord. Warrants WO 55/343.

responsible as much unawares as in a more recent war, and the colonists, like a body of their successors some seventy years later, displayed no enthusiasm for expenditure on their defence, or for good husbandry on their behalf. A representation, for example, from the Lords Commissioners of Trade and Plantations on 2 April 1703 stated that at New York the forts were in a ruinous condition. Most of the gun platforms and carriages were quite rotten, many of the guns dismounted, and some honeycombed so that they could not be safely fired. The arms of the four foot companies were very bad. In the two companies stationed in New York itself there were only 27 muskets fit for use, and in no company were there more than 12 swords and 12 bayonets. A demand was put in for stores estimated to cost £5,568, which, said Ordnance, they could supply, but there was no financial provision by Parliament since it had always been thought that the 'plantations were to provide themselves at their own expense with what stores they had occasion for'. From January 1700 to date, the Board added, there had been dispatched to the plantations nearly £20,000 of stores with no return.[1] Nevis Isle was another representative case. In 1706 the islanders complained that of 500 muskets sent them only one in five was fit for service, 'which', they remarked with some restraint, 'was a great disappointment at the time of the late attempt of the French'. The Board's reply showed that 500 muskets had been sent to the Leewards in 1694, followed by 340 in 1700, but that there had been no complaint till now, six to twelve years later.

'Arms, in these parts', they explained patiently, 'will become rusty and unserviceable in a short time if great care be not taken to keep them clean, which the (local) government ought to do since there is no Officer of the Ordnance there.'[2]

Packing was a further problem, as indicated in the Privy Council instruction of 22 January 1708 to send to Newfoundland bedding for eighty men with due precautions 'that the supply be not again rendered unserviceable by its usage on shipboard'.[3] The cumbersome nature of supply is demonstrated by the apparent inability or inadvisability of obtaining a simple item like eighty sets of bedding locally.

---

[1] *H.M.C.H. of L.*, vii, p. 201.
[2] Ibid., p. 261.
[3] *APC Col.*, ii, p. 537.

TRANSPORT

The only overall army organization for transport was that
coming under the Ordnance Department which was not answerable to the Secretary at War or to any military commander as
such, but to a Secretary of State through the Master-General.
The officer responsible for transport was the Lieutenant-
General who exercised his functions through the Waggon-
Master-General,[1] but his responsibilities were confined to the
trains. For other movement in the field, each commander had
to solve his own transport problem, which was, indeed, one
which required a large part of his personal attention. This was
true right down to battalion level where, indeed, the most
costly item in any commanding officer's budget next to reinforcements was horses, either for transport or remounts.
Commanders themselves had to see to bread waggons, ammunition waggons, carriages for the sick, baggage waggons, and the
bulk of the artillery horses, although in the latter case they had
the assistance of the appropriate officers of the train. The only
permanent supply was a nucleus of artillery horses in the train
(with civilian drivers), the officers' chargers which the officers
themselves provided, and, of course, the horses of the cavalry
and dragoons. Other transport came from contract or impressment. Normally the bread and forage contractors did some
transport contracting, but could not meet the total requirements.

Pack animals were largely used, although, when available,
and when the roads would carry it, wheeled transport was,
naturally, preferred. Frequently the owners themselves accompanied horses and waggons as drivers, and, except for the
bread and artillery horses, transport seldom moved more than
three marches from its 'home'. There is reason to believe that
extensive hiring by relatively long-term contract, as opposed
to sporadic hiring and impressment, owes much to Marlborough.[2] Much of the transport other than in the train continued, however, long after Anne's reign to be considered a
civilian problem, which was, like the Commissariat, primarily

[1] At a pay of £100 per year under the Warrant of 1683 which designated him
Waggon-Master-General for England.

[2] *The Predecessors of the Royal Army Service Corps 1757–1888*, C. H. Masse (London,
1948), p. xiv. (*Masse.*)

the concern of the Treasury. Treasury representatives (deputies or commissaries) oversaw it, including even transport for the sick and wounded.[1] The Commissioners for Transport, although primarily interested in sea transport, were involved in the transport of the sick, particularly in Spain, and largely because no one else was specifically charged with the responsibility.

There was, naturally enough in the circumstances, no 'scale' of transport. The stipulation of an 'allowance' of transport for general officers—Marlborough's was 27 waggons, 3 carts, and 20 baggage horses[2]—did not necessarily mean that this was provided in kind. Peterborough in Spain is said to have had 17 waggons, over 50 mules, and several valuable horses, which, with the baggage, were estimated to be of a total value of £8,000 (say over £80,000 in 1965 currency),[3] but commanders-in-chief of more modest tastes are unlikely, even with their 'pilgrim bottles, silver vessels . . . and special staff of servants with stewards and controllers' to have used their entire allowance. It represented, in greater or less degree, a cash perquisite. In the same way, there was an 'allowance' of transport to battalions. This represented neither their needs nor what was provided; it was an entitlement, for which they received a credit to set against the cost of any transport actually obtained. There was also voted as part of the estimates every year a sum for bread waggons. Bread waggons were used for many tasks other than carrying bread, but any cost over and above the vote was met from the soldiers' subsistence. Specimen figures for these various moneys are: Flanders 1705—waggon money (i.e. general officers and battalions) £18,259; bread waggons (for 40,000) £39,822; and half the cost for the augmentation (of 20,000) £5,880. As the total budget for Flanders for that year was just over £670,000 it can be seen that even such transport as the Government did pay for was a considerable item.[4] The number of animals and vehicles used varied according to the

[1] Fort. *RASC*. Up to 1870 the duties of Commissary-General for Commissariat Services, Purveyor in Chief for Hospitals, Superintendent of Barrack Department, and Commander of Military Trains were nowhere co-ordinated under a Secretary of State. They were in that year centralized under the Surveyor-General. Memorandum of 24 Apr. 1884 on the Administration of the Supply and Transport Services—Reports and Miscellaneous Papers WO 33/42. (*Misc. WO 33*.)

[2] Treas. 1/157.

[3] Fort. *RASC*, p. 23.

[4] *Journals Commons*, xiv, 3 Nov. 1704.

terrain and availability. On the march to the Danube there were 2,000 horses, including the artillery teams. On 31 July 1704 the Duke wrote that he was trying to give four waggons per battalion for bread, but two years later (on 22 June 1706) he allowed only 'two or three' waggons per battalion to be levied from the villages, exclusively for the use of the sick. In 1707 Wackerbart, one of his subordinate commanders, shocked the Captain-General by bidding for a scale of 200 per 4,000 men, when the allocation for others at that time, according to Marlborough, was 50 per 10,000. The latter seems a very low figure, which must have entailed considerable pack transport, and seems unlikely to have taken account of supplies. It excluded, of course, the train.[1]

With provision so largely a matter of local arrangement, abuses were inevitably frequent. Junior, and not so junior, commanders fought vigorously for their own hands, and, when not closely supervised, commandeered extensively. A good commander attempted to provide sufficient transport on a regularized basis, and retained the sympathy, or at least passive acquiescence, of the local population by putting down unauthorized levies as strongly as he curbed plundering. Marlborough was relentless in this and his vigorous pruning of baggage was an innovation as novel in those days as his conception of mobile warfare.

Spain found practically all the weak spots in the army system. Transport under Peterborough in particular collapsed almost completely. It was through no lack of energy on his part, for, said Colonel Andrew Bissett, giving evidence for the Lords inquiry on 11 February 1708, the Earl was 'very indefatigable from morning till night' in buying mules to let the army march 'which could not have been compassed without his Lordship's fatigues below the character of a general'. This evidence was confirmed by other officers, one of whom added that his commander's efforts had also extended to horse waggons and other necessaries.[2] Peterborough himself described the problem in a letter to Archduke Charles on 10 June 1706: 'I have not been able to get one horse . . . we have no more yet than 60 mules instead of the 800 which we want. I begin to feel

---

[1] Murray, i, p. 371; ii, p. 619; iii, p. 468.
[2] *H.M.C.H. of L.*, vii, pp. 509–11.

that some private persons must profit . . . and that the public must loose.'¹ Whoever profited it was not commanders like Wyndham who, on his march from Requena in July 1706, had to leave his ammunition behind for want of carriage, and complained to Peterborough that, when the mules did arrive, he had no money to pay for them.² Commenting that the scarcity was 'incredible', Peterborough explained that those sent were cast animals 'unfit to . . . be bought, but . . . to perform any drudgery (and) only to be provided with forage till the troops were (better) supplied'.³ Major-General Wills who commanded marines in Spain in the previous year spent £3,163 in buying and maintaining mules. He was still petitioning for the money in 1709.⁴

As in all other departments, there was persistent troublesome delay over payment. Even contractors like Medina and Vanderkaa, working under Marlborough's careful eye, were often exceedingly short of money, and due quite incredible sums from the Government. Once again, however, the palm for outstanding debts goes to an obligation from the previous reign. John Bingham and Katherine Dunbar petitioned on 27 January 1703 that in 1691 they had spent over £1,036 in fulfilling a contract to Ginkell for thirty horses 'with all manner of equipage, and pay for all drivers, carmen, and all necessary attendants, and to carry ammunition from the magazines into the field'. They had received up till then £299. 17s. 2½d.

In the United Kingdom, impressment of transport was provided for in the Mutiny Acts. Under the 1703 Act the duty of provision fell on Justices who had to receive cash on the spot from commanders. The rates were 8d. a mile for a five-horse waggon and a six-ox, or four-ox and two-horse waggon; 6d. for a four-horse cart. This impressment was no more popular than overseas and provision had to be made in the 1705 Act for punishment of anyone obstructing provision of carriages. This clause was, in fact, aimed primarily at constables, who were, presumably, subject to bribery by local owners. Under the 1708 Act, the Government went into the bribery business itself by authorizing treasurers of counties to increase carriage money

¹ H.M.C.H. of L., vii, p. 481.
² Ibid., pp. 497–8.
³ Ibid., pp. 483 and 500.   ⁴ Treas. 1/113.

paid to constables. At the same time it was provided that no waggon should carry more than 20 cwt.[1] Impressed carriages were not to be taken more than one day's journey, and no soldiers, servants, or women were to ride on the waggons. Impressment of saddle horses was forbidden.[2]

On the march, experience had produced an efficient system which reduced congestion to a minimum. Every regiment of horse or foot had its waggon or baggage master, who might be officer, sergeant, or corporal 'to act and see that every officer's baggage from highest to lowest march according to the dignity and precedency of him to whom it belong'. These waggon masters received their orders daily from the Waggon-Master-General,[3] who had to attend on the major-generals of cavalry and infantry to receive the order of march and routes. Baggage waggons followed their own regiments, and if any tried to overtake others, the Waggon-Master-General was authorized to make them and their loads a prize. The Waggon-Master-General normally had two assistants to aid in marshalling the transport for the march, and, if two roads were used, one was available to supervise transport on each.

It may be said, in brief, that, while procurement and provision of land transport were among the more rudimentary forms of army organization, administration and policing on the march were normally of a fairly high standard. On a well-ordered campaign, it was seldom that baggage physically impeded movement, although it might set its pace.

Sea Transport

Despite the fervour with which, in the wet canteen, the troop-ship which left Bombay has been hailed, sea transport has never been popular with army other ranks: nor has it maintained standards which might impugn the soldiers' judgement. Wellington's warrior, Kincaid, who noted his comrades as 'rosy cheeked, chubbed youths after three months' feeding on ships' dumplings', would have been regarded with at least reserve on troop-decks had he voiced his opinions there at any time between the Hundred Years and the Korean Wars. In modern

---

[1] The provisions obtaining in Scotland prior to the Union were left unaltered.
[2] Annae 2 and 3, cap. 17.
[3] He had 7s. 1½d. per day for himself and his assistant in Flanders.

times, troopships have been squalid, uncomfortable, and even unhealthy. In Anne's day they were floating slaughter-houses. The degradation on board ship surpassed that of hospital, prison, or barracks. Even Private Deane, a douce, well-behaved soldier, not given to grumbling, described his experience as 'continual destruction in the foretop, the pox above aboard, the plague between decks, hell in the forecastle, and the devil at the helm'. In further detail, he wrote of 'labouring under many inconveniences, having only the bare Deck to lye upon, which hardship caused abundance of our men to bid adieu to the world'.[1]

As might be expected, responsibility is difficult to determine. Both the Secretary at War and the Lieutenant-General of the Ordnance had some hand in the business—as was evidenced by their presence at the embarkation in 1706.[2] Whether, however, they were there to supervise the actual embarkation only as far as the ship's side, or whether their responsibility continued once the troops were aboard, it is harder to say. The Lord Treasurer, as the controller of the purse, and no doubt because he was Godolphin, was most certainly involved. The Secretary of State played a considerable part. The immediate authority rested with a body called the Commissioners of Transport, the Committee of Transports, or Commission of Transportation, who no doubt owed their origin to the special officials appointed in Elizabeth's time to supervise arrangements at the ports in connexion with embarkation. These duties included 'hiring of the transports, provision of food, payment of the troops prior to embarkation, and mustering and disembarkation on arrival'.[3] The Commissioners presented their accounts direct to the House of Commons, where their representatives also appeared when their conduct was being examined. The organization of army and navy was so different that comparison with Pepys's famous appearances is probably inept, and the latter cannot be considered as conclusive evidence against the impression that the Commissioners' dealing direct with the elected representatives might imply a status in their own right. The bulk of the orders

[1] *A Journal of the Campaign in Flanders*, Private John Marshall Deane (issued privately by the Rev. John B. Deane, London, 1846), p. 4. (*Deane.*)
[2] SP Mil. 41/3. See p. 19.
[3] Cruickshank, p. 31.

issued to the Commissioners appears to have come from the Secretary of State, but this is not decisive evidence, since troop movements, other than internal relief marches which tended to pass into the Secretary at War's jurisdiction, were the responsibility of the Secretary of State. I have also seen one case—and there are no doubt others—where the Secretary at War gave direct orders to the Commissioners to take recruits on board (at Portsmouth). On this occasion, the Commissioners, remembering their Elizabethan responsibilities, asked the Commissioners of Victualling to put the corresponding rations on board, and were refused 'without proper orders'. The Secretary at War had then to ask the Secretary of State to issue the necessary orders to the Victualling Officers.[1]

Yet again, the Board of Ordnance, which was technically responsible for its own 'transportation',[2] had on one occasion at least to write to the Secretary at War for the issue of necessary orders for shipping and provisions when it wished to send officers, men, and horses with the train.[3] There seems to have been less a division than a confusion of responsibility. The Board of Ordnance sometimes got transports for their stores through the Commissioners, and sometimes by direct contract. The Secretary of State dealt not only with transport, but, even, on at least one occasion, postponed an embarkation on 'domestic' military grounds—'that it will not be fit' for the men 'to lie aboard their ships' at Portsmouth on account of the inevitable sickness.[4] Fortescue claims that transport, like the Commissariat, came under the Treasury, and there is evidence to support this in the implementation of Coleby's reforms in 1705—see later. It is probable, indeed, that the situation was not finally cleared up until the reforms of 1870 when the Commissary-General, the Purveyor, and the rest had their wings clipped and were lodged in the Surveyor-General's aviary.[5]

---

[1] SP Mil. 41/3, 14 Mar. 1711.   [2] See p. 174, n. 3.
[3] Ord. Warrants WO 55/342/163, 18 Apr. 1702.
[4] *Dom. Cal.*, ii, p. 110.
[5] See p. 204, n. 1. In 1796 the Commissioners themselves requested that all orders should come through the Secretary at War, owing to the difficulty of satisfying conflicting demands. Secretary at War: In Letters, WO 1; Letter of 29 Dec. 1796 to Dundas. (*War Letters, WO 1.*) On 29 Jan. 1799 they described themselves as 'this branch of the Naval Service'. War Letters, WO 1/850.

The evidence for the Lord Treasurer's control over the Commissioners, including their civilian responsibilities,[1] is strengthened by the handling of the memorandum put forward by Coleby when he took over the running of the office of 'the Committee of Transports' in 1705. The proposals indicate the state of the Office:

That the Committee have fixed meeting places and times, and keep minutes; that money be assigned for transport; that the cashier inform the other commissioners when money has been received; that there be a ledger kept for charges and bills; that 'some of the gentlemen of Trinity House, or an Eminent Shipwright' measure and appraise transports before sailing in order to avoid swindling if lost; and separate mustering of the ship's company and troops 'for the better saving of Her Majesty's Treasure'.

The monthly freight bill at this time, when there was apparently not even a ledger, was £13,826. 12s. 6d. Understandably, in presenting his recommendations, Coleby abjured responsibility for anything arising out of the past. His proposals were approved by the Lord Treasurer, and issued by him as an instruction.[2] Although the memorandum is primarily concerned with 'saving Her Majesty's treasure', it is reasonable to assume that it is simply one visible sign of a reform in progress: it hardly requires stating that, whoever may have done well out of any wasting of the royal treasure, it would certainly not be troops.

The actual provision of ships was, of course, by contract. The navy occasionally helped, with a bad grace, in the transport of men. On such occasions, all concerned invariably agreed that this was a bad thing, but equally that the present was an exceptional occasion. When the Prince Consort himself as Lord High Admiral protested in January 1702 against the practice, he advanced the unusually solicitous reason that it was bad for the health of the seamen.[3] There is more than one incident on record of the Secretary of State issuing orders direct to the navy to take men—apparently without any objection being raised.[4]

---

[1] *Dom. Cal.*, ii, p. 167.
[2] Treas. 1/83/77, 7 Mar. 1705; 1/84/41, 3 May 1705.
[3] *Dom. Cal.*, i, pp. 532–3.   [4] e.g. *Dom. Cal.*, ii, p. 108.

In 1708, in addition to the 5,000 troops brought hastily from the Low Countries, in 'leaking, rotten, and pest ridden transports', 1,700 were carried in men-of-war. It is at least unlikely that they fared any better than those who had the vermin for company on civilian ships. One attraction of navy transport, so far as the officers were concerned, was the more reasonable cost. Lieutenant-General Ingolsby, for example, when complaining of extravagant rates for transport of arms from Holland to Ireland in 1706, asked specially, on these grounds, that the navy should carry out the task.[1] There was never, however, any question of free transport. Even the Board of Ordnance, which persistently complained of the cost of its obligations for 'the sea services', had to pay full rates for transport of officers, men, and stores.[2]

For the regimental officer the transport of his troops was, like clothing or equipment, a charge against the regimental funds, but there were certain concessions, such as free sea provisions except on the journey to the Netherlands, and, for a time, free transport for twenty-six horses per battalion. There was also limited free transport for recruits on the packet-boats (665 were carried on the journey Harwich–Holland between September 1711 and January 1712),[3] which also carried maimed soldiers and recruiting sergeants who held passes.[4] The packet-boats appear also to have provided a very efficient service for deserters bound for England. Provisions on men-of-war, on the other hand, could prove more expensive. There was sometimes an adjustment of subsistence allowance or methods to compensate for this.[5]

The costs of the ships to the Government seem to have varied widely, and depended not only on the length of voyage and type of ship (for men or stores), but also, of course, on the state of the market. In 1703 store ships ranged from 10s. to 50s. per ton per month, while in the previous year, a Commissioners' representative, Van Homugh, a shrewd bargainer for transport,

[1] Murray, iii, p. 529.
[2] Several references in dispatches, e.g. Murray, i, p. 139, 12 July 1703. Also *Dom. Cal.*, ii, p. 15.   [3] Treas. 1/143.
[4] *Dom. Cal.*, i, p. 507.   [5] Secretary at War's letter of 26 Dec. 1710.

hired vessels at 12s. per ton in Ireland, at a time when they were reckoned to be not at all plentiful.[1] Van Homugh's performance is all the more remarkable when viewed in the light of his letter a little afterwards which stated that 'without money, provisions, and the needful orders, it is impossible for me to proceed'.[2]

In 1702 the transport of three troops of horse (approximately 300–400 men and horses) and two troops of dragoons from Ireland to England—a short voyage—cost £778, while in 1711 the Commissioners contracted for overseas transport at £4 per man including bedding and necessaries.[3] The scale at this time was 1¼ tons per man.[4]

Logically enough, the Commissioners' responsibilities did not end with the provision of bare ships and sailors to man them. Elizabeth's officials, as noted above, had feeding and pay responsibilities, and early in Anne's reign provisioning of horses in transit was added to their duties—in a Board of Ordnance letter.[5] Rationing of soldiers on board was, however, the task of the Commissioners of Victualling, to whom, when they were on their dignity, the Secretary at War had, as we have seen, to give orders through the Secretary of State.[6] They were primarily responsible for Navy Victualling—they were sometimes known as the Victuallers of the Navy—but fed soldiers at sea and in port awaiting sailing. They also gave orders for the preparation of victuals against arrivals.[7]

Food represented a large item in the cost of transport of horses. An estimate dated 28 March 1702 for 285 animals shows £3,311 for feed, £1,781 for water casks, £427 for flooring stalls and slinging the horses, and £40 for incidental charges.[8] As this was a Transport Commissioners' estimate of other than charter costs, it does not show the hiring fee. Oats at 14s. per quarter and hay at £3. 10s. per 13½ cwt. load seem a little dear, but it is at least an indication of the incidence of charges. The Com-

[1] Dom. Cal., ii, pp. 104 and 106.   [2] Letter of 8 Aug. 1703.
[3] SP Mil. 41/3.   [4] Various references, e.g. Dom. Cal., ii, p. 58.
[5] SP Mil. 41/3, 25 Mar. 1702.
[6] See St. John's letters of 10 Apr. 1705 and 2 Mar. 1706 in SP Mil. 41/3.
[7] State Papers (Domestic Entry Book), p. 105. (SPO.)
[8] The space for horses ordered by the Secretary at War in 1704 was 25 inches between rails, but is also claimed to have been 1½ tons on a long voyage. War Letters WO 4/2, 17 Feb. 1704, and SP Mil. 41/3/237.

missioners' bill for £586,468 for 1 to 30 March 1707 contained £24,906 for hay, oats, bread, beer (presumably not for the horses), and such other 'non shipping' items.[1] Incidentals which appeared in the total year's bill of £160,000 for 1711 included hay, oats, bread, beer, cheese, bedding, cabins, cradles, stabling, cooperage, lighterage, labourers' travelling charges, repairing returned bedding, and office charges. Interest charges for that year, in which the highest month was June at £23,173 expenditure, totalled just under £6,100.[2] There were at times, of course, additional problems like the Prince of Hesse's 25–30 tons of baggage *en route* to the Peninsula,[3] or less pressing matters like the beds ordered to be provided in 1702 in all men-of-war carrying land forces. These were to cost 11s. each at Portsmouth and created a disturbance and hullabaloo which up-ended a number of departments of state for many months.[4]

As a sample of the 'balance' of an expedition we may note the twenty-five transports detailed at SP Mil. 41/3/251. There was one store-ship, one baggage ship, and one victualling ship— a total of 8,591 tons at 16s. per ton. The hospital ship was 567 tons at 18s. per ton, and victualling cost 13s. 3d. per man per month for the cavalry and infantry, while 180 of the train cost £137. 5s. The fitting out of 138 officers' cabins cost 6s. 6d. each, and 5,450 men's 4s. each. The hospital ship cost £170 to fit out, 211 cradles 12s. 6d. each, and 5,680 beds a total of £3,131. The agent's salary was £32.

Places more unsuitable for women could hardly be imagined, but they numbered at times more than 10 per cent. of the complement—for example St. Clair's 5,013 men had 583 women with them.[5] St. John eventually took action and claimed to have 'broken' the practice in 1705 when Peterborough went to Spain.[6] It was, however, in full swing again in Wellington's time—and for that matter obtained while troopships lasted, although rarely in war. It would, of course, be inaccurate to suggest that the troopships of the second half of the twentieth century showed no improvement over the charnel houses of other days.

[1] *Journals Commons*, xvi, 1 Dec. 1709. [2] Ibid., xvii.
[3] *Dom. Cal.*, ii, p. 130. [4] Ibid., i, pp. 130 and 134.
[5] SP Mil. 41/3/249. Southwell wrote to Nottingham in 1703 about 'the necessary allowance of 4 women to a company . . . which is the least that has been provided and cannot be avoided'. *Dom. Cal.*, ii, p. 102. [6] SP Mil. 41/3/17.

While the women apparently clamoured to go, there had been, on the other hand, a recognized charge since Elizabeth's days at least on all transport expenses of a fee for watchmen to keep the husbands from deserting once on board ship. Men with inclinations to desert were normally given plenty of time to consider the project. The Jamaica garrison relief of 1705, for example, lay on board ship five months, and were, in the end, dispatched on the West Indies packets in batches of sixty. Sickness figures are, mercifully, not available, but we do know that forty-eight perished in one day when overtaken by a storm in port.[1] Some six years later complaints were made of danger to officers' and men's lives on transports at Portsmouth from the 'prodigious heat of the corn'. The Commissioners of Transport, pointing out that the contract was for £4 per man, including provision of bedding and necessaries, explained that the ship was also permitted to carry corn as a private arrangement —with, no doubt, fees for the employees of the Office of Transport. This corn, they added, 'having been a long time on board, there is great reason to believe its heat will very much endanger the men's lives'. They suggested the soldiers might be put on another ship.[2] Two years later, when Colonel Nevil complained about overcrowding on the Spanish run, he was told that in time of war room never exceeded two tons per three men (which was, of course, nonsense—see p. 212, above), even although it was anticipated they might be on board from three to five months. When the hold was full of provisions, men had to be carried between decks, where it was no doubt a great consolation to them to know that the ship had been measured by the rules of Ship Wrights' Hall, or even, in the case of the luckier ones, by an elder brother of Trinity House.[3] An example of the conditions on the Peninsula trip was provided by Galway's force which in 1706, between Lisbon and Valencia, had its effective strength of 8,000 halved.[4] Out of the famous 29,000 who dwindled to 9,000 at Almanza, over 4,000 were put out of action at sea. On a journey from Portsmouth to Lisbon in 1710/11, sixty men out of five regiments died and a further 200 were incapacitated by sickness.[5] Even the Paymaster's watchdog, the Commissary of Musters, was moved to report

---

[1] Fort., p. 570.   [2] SP Mil. 41/3.   [3] Treas. Cal., iv, p. 46.
[4] Fort., p. 559.   [5] Anne Cal., p. 661.

from Portugal on 18 November 1710: 'Of 300 men that came ashore some time since, not a hundred ever got to the regiments.'[1] In the matter of killing off soldiers, however, the West Indies could not be deprived of its pre-eminence. Five regiments moving thence to Newfoundland in 1702/3 were caught in fog and bad weather. Fevers and tropical sickness then very quickly reduced them to 1,038 men.[2] One might indeed suspect a gently irony when the Commissioners, in these circumstances, recommended that, on the Scotland–Flanders voyage, since it was longer than that from Harwich, the men should have 2 oz. of butter, ½ lb. of cheese, and 1 lb. of bread added to their daily allowance 'for the better preservation of [their] health'.[3]

As in practically all spheres, the government was, of course, in the not very strong position of being permanently in debt to the shipowners—although some officials did a little towards balancing the account. One, Mason, for example, owed £5,887 when relieved.[4] In 1708 the shipowners were over two years in arrears, and had not even received a payment on account for nine months; by early 1711 the total debts for the service ran to over £45,000, plus nearly £2,500 interest. In spite of their difficulties over money, it was no doubt appropriate, in view of their wide experience on the subject, that the Commissioners should, at one time, have been given the care of the sick and wounded.[5]

SUPPLIES

'The troops I have the honour to command', wrote Marlborough immediately before Blenheim, 'cannot subsist without bread, and the Germans, that are used to starve, cannot march without them.' The gently sardonic comment is a guide both to the character of the Commander-in-Chief himself, and to the custom of the times which normally permitted generals to turn their troops loose, rather like (very hungry) nomadic flocks, to find their own food.

The English . . . are the best soldiers in the world so long as their Beef and Pudding lasts . . . that the People of other Countries can

[1] *Treas. Cal.*, iv, p. 224.   [2] Dalton, v, p. xvii.
[3] SP Mil. 41/3, Feb. 1711.
[4] *Treas. Cal.*, iv, p. 544.   [5] Fort, p. 562.

live harder than the English is not so much a Virtue in them, but from a necessity made habitual to them . . . and there is no Nation under the Sun where the meaner people are bread up with such substantial nourishing foods as the English; Flesh, Fish, Bread, Butter, and Cheese, and malt liquors being the General Diet of Her Majesties labouring subjects . . . and 'tis the great wages at home that enables the English to support this well eating.[1]

'Englishmen', Pepys had remarked some years earlier, 'love their bellies above everything else.'

This multiplied the problems of a Commissariat sufficiently harassed by incompetence and corruption, and already branded in the words of its own officials as 'an office which appears to have been . . . managed under the greatest Confusion of Accounts, No Journals or Ledgers being found, by which to charge or discharge, no Course of Assignments in the Payments of Bills, but some of them paid in a few Days, Weeks, or Months, while others of the same and preceding Dates remained for several years unpaid'. Here, it must be noted, the complainants added adroitly, if perhaps righteously, 'This concerns the Conduct of our Predecessors'.[2] This was not really news to a Parliament already surfeited with tales of mismanagement and corruption. In March of the same year the Commons had resolved that the 'late Commissioners of the Victualling . . . have been guilty of a breach of trust', and requested Her Majesty to direct 'an immediate and effectual Prosecution' against the Cashier.[3]

This organization had, in the 1689 Irish campaign, produced scarcity rations at famine prices in Dundalk while stocks rotted in Belfast. A departmental quibble about responsibility for transport intensified the scarcity of all items except those which yielded easy profit, such as salt, which the commissary Shales supplied at 4s. per lb.—only $5\frac{1}{5}$ times the price he had paid for it.[4] Any who survived the campaign must have raised puzzled eyebrows fourteen years later when the Irish Parliament (in the winter of 1705) represented that, during the years 1689–91, the army obtained 'large quantities' of food from the countryside 'to the utter ruin of many families'.[5]

---

[1] Recruiting Essay.   [2] Journals Commons, xiv, 21 Nov. 1704.
[3] Ibid., 14 Mar. 1704.
[4] Fort.   [5] Dom. Cal., ii, p. 235.

Yet, typically, without any radical recasting of the system, Marlborough, by strict supervision through a Commissary-General with purveyors, commissaries, munitionaries, and selected sutlers, commanded, under more difficult conditions, better-fed soldiers than any of their predecessors except Cromwell's men.

The idea of 'rationing' soldiers' food is said to have been first applied in Elizabeth's reign because the English soldiers were considered to be so improvident that they would not keep several days' food, but ate it all on the day of issue.[1] The official supply of items of diet fell naturally into the hands of the Commissariat whose responsibilities then covered pay, movement, and supplies of all descriptions including, in the field, munitions. The High Treasurer had authority over the provost master, the muster-master, the commissaries, suppliers of food and clothing, paymasters, the pioneers, carriage master, and thus delineated some vague co-ordination. His powers fell away with the change in character of the commissaries after the Restoration, when the departments became independent, save for some supervision on active service by the Commissary-General who also on occasion overlooked the Judge-Advocate.[2] In Charles I's and parliamentary armies the title of Commissary-General as already noted was not restricted to the supply services. The Commissary-General of Horse was roughly equivalent to the Major-General of Foot. It is doubtful, however, if the Commissaries-General of Musters or of Victuals held any command, although they received precedence as staff officers.[3]

After the Restoration, the lucrative posts drifted into the hands of courtiers and civilian favourites, and the commissaries, although the military command became extinct, retained their precedence in military courts and councils of war. The less rewarding posts continued to be held by army officers of the Commissariat, with military commissions, and subject to military law.[4]

By Anne's time, the organization of supplies was in the hands of the Commissioners of Victualling, who had serving under

[1] Masse, pp. xiii–xiv.
[2] Walton, pp. 631 and 632; Fort. RASC, p. 17.
[3] Walton, pp. 633–5.
[4] Masse, xii–xiv; Walton, p. 635.

them in the field their commissaries-general and commissaries. They were charged with the supply of such food and forage as the Government produced, and were reimbursed either by parliamentary votes or by the traditionally more normal method of deductions from subsistence. The status of the Commissioners was at times in doubt owing to the constitutional shift taking place between the Secretary of State and the Secretary at War. It has already been noted how in 1705 and 1706, for example, St. John asked Hedges, Secretary of State, to issue instructions for rations to be put on board ship for soldiers; but in 1710 when the Commissioners were in contact with Dartmouth with inquiries concerning ports at which victuals for Spain were to be shipped, they asked that the directions should be issued through the Admiralty.[1]

An entry of three years later shows, however, that, so far as appointments in the lower branches were concerned, it was recognized that the business was one primarily of military concern, for it is the Secretary at War who intimates to Dartmouth that Her Majesty has approved the appointment of a Commissary of Provisions at Gibraltar.[2] A letter of Walpole's to Boyle in 1708 seems to indicate that local collectors of customs acted on occasion as representatives for provisioning of troops.[3] In garrisons overseas, and in naval bases, there may have been interlocking—integrated would undoubtedly be too strong a term—systems when the local victualler, with somewhat the status of a naval purser, catered for both sailors and soldiers. These victuallers could be ex-servicemen, like Colonel Thomas Erskine, governor of Scilly, ex-commander of a man-of-war for twenty-three years 'and at the same time purser and victualler of many of them', who petitioned for the Gibraltar and Port Mahon contracts.[4] These posts were seldom well paid, and there was never any serious denial that abuses and corruption were widespread, chiefly among 'underlings, particularly those in posts with little or no pay', of whom pursers appear to have been the biggest offenders.[5]

However provided, the commissaries had a dual respon-

---

[1] SP Mil. 41/3/11 and 41/3/75 dated 10 Apr. 1705 and 2 Mar. 1706; Anne Cal., p. 640.

[2] War Letters WO/4, Secretary at War's Letter of 27 June 1713.

[3] Anne Cal., p. 466.   [4] *Treas. Cal.*, iv, p. 430.

[5] Treas. 1/130, memorial of 1710.

sibility—to the Commissioners of Victualling and to the field commander. This is exemplified in the instructions issued on 8 November 1702 to Martin Llwellyn, on taking up office as Commissary-General of the Provisions to the Forces in Portugal:

> You are to receive the provisions from the Commissary or officer of the King of Portugal in such quantity or proportion as our General or the Commander-in-Chief of our forces shall direct; for which you are to give your receipt and charge yourself therewith in a book kept for that purpose under several distinct heads, which you are to issue out weekly to each company or regiment as directed by the General or Commander-in-Chief, taking the officers' receipt of each company or regiment to whom you shall deliver the same which shall be entered in the same book on credit side. Once a month you shall prepare an account of what you shall receive and issue for our General or the Commander-in-Chief by which it will appear what remains in your custody.
>
> In case you are required to supply the army with provisions you shall do it with all good husbandry and frugality best for our service, taking receipts from the persons from whom you buy the same. You are to charge yourself with such provisions and issue them as aforesaid.
>
> You are with what provisions you shall be furnished with, and what bills that you draw to pay them, to charge yourself debtor in account, and take credit in the said account of provisions bought, giving frequent account thereto to our Commander-in-Chief. You are to take care that the provisions that you receive be good and fit for our service.[1]

For this, Martin received 20s. per day plus 5s. for each of his two clerks.[2] The course of his business may be judged from items in his petition of 5 January 1706 when he asked for reimbursement of expenditure as follows:

weights and scales for bread 9s 6d; certificates of false weight 9s; two years rent £25; printed receipts £2 15s: charges in hireing of Mules for my Baggage to Quarters and severall times from thence to Lisbon £15.

His total demand was for £108. 11s. 6d.—all in a quite ill-educated looking hand.[3]

[1] *Dom. Cal.*, ii, p. 192.
[2] Ibid., p. 162, 29 Oct. 1703.   [3] Treas. 1/97/15.

In principle the soldier paid for his food with the money issued to him as subsistence. Bread was frequently provided through commissary channels, and the money deducted from the men's subsistence before issue. Procurement of the remainder, either from local inhabitants, or from the sutlers who accompanied regiments, was normally the soldier's own responsibility. There was normally one grand sutler for every regiment, and one petty sutler for each troop of horse or company of foot. These sutlers were private civilian traders, and the major in the regiment was charged with supervision of quality and sale by fair weight and measure. In this he was assisted by the adjutant. When closely supervised, the sutlers had to carry out their responsibilities conscientiously. It was ordered that men should have bacon 'or other flesh meat' twice weekly, in order, it has been said, to prevent them spending all of their subsistence upon drink. Commanding officers were further ordered to encourage butchers to follow regiments with sheep and cattle on hoof, and to see the men had meat 'so that they should have no excuse for falling back upon liquor'.[1] As for vegetables, the men were sent out to gather roots for themselves.[2]

It is doubtful how far the subsistence allowance ever went towards feeding the troops. When the discrepancy between the cost of food and subsistence grew too great, extra money was on occasion voted. In William's time, provisions for regiments transported abroad were stated to be given and not charged to accounts. A later example of such a case, which I have actually seen, was the debit to the Irish revenues of a £1,000 debt of Brigadier Selwyn's regiment in Jamaica. The reason for this was the 'dearness of provisions and all other necessaries'. £1,000 was reckoned to be the cost of rations supplied before starting out.[3] The principle, however imperfectly observed, seems, nevertheless, to have been that on board ship stoppages were to be imposed equivalent to the total daily subsistence, i.e. 8d. not 6d.[4] One of the concessions most prized by the

---

[1] Cf. The *Recruiting Essay*: '. . . certainly there is no People in the world so extreamly negligent and careless of themselves as the English raw soldiers; they mind not what they eat, or what they drink, so it but gratifie their present craving Appetite, though never so destructive to their Healths; which it is the Officers' Duty as much to prevent.' [2] Fort. *RASC*, p. 20.
[3] *Dom. Cal.*, i, p. 166. [4] But see Chapter XV on the subject of Sea Pay.

Ordnance was that they received full rations as of right while on board ship with no stoppage, but, in practice, stoppages do not appear to have been regularly imposed on the others except on journeys to and from the Low Countries.[1]

The rules regarding payment were, in fact, frequently relaxed in Anne's time: rations were costing so much more and soldiers were so much the more valuable that there was little option. Costs beyond what the troops 'could allow of their subsistence' were met by various means, but usually from 'extraordinaries of war'. A marginal note to such a charge of £7,338 in the Military State Papers for 1711 in Portugal indicates that it at least was debited to the subsidies payable to Portugal.[2]

A 1709 report on Newfoundland opened '. . . it having been found that Beer Brewed there with molasses is much more Wholesome and better than that brewed with malt . . .', and went on to ask for an augmentation of an amount certified by the Commissioners for Victualling as reasonable so that enough could be bought 'as also that a competent Proportion of Flower and oatmeal be sent and less biscuit, which is more beneficial to the soldiers'.[3]

The Comptrollers of Army Accounts noted concerning wheat at Gibraltar that 'the practice has been that when the price exceeded what could be reasonably charged upon the subsistence, a portion has been paid from thence, and the overplus provided for as the nature of the service would admit'.[4] In Gibraltar they had, of course, a very cogent reason for such a procedure. No less than Bolingbroke himself informed the Lord Treasurer in March 1714 that the garrison had had to be changed because the regiments might mutiny if deductions were made out of their pay for provisions delivered.[5]

Initially a proportion of the subsistence was intended to cover transport of the bread, but the large figures for bread waggons[6] which appear in estimates throughout the reign, show that this, even when deducted, by no means met the full cost.

In Portugal again, in Galway's day, each trooper was allowed

[1] Walton, p. 659; Forbes, p. 110.   [2] SP Mil. 41/4.
[3] APC Col., ii, p. xxxi, 23 Mar. 1704.
[4] Treas. Cal., iv, p. 550, 4 Feb. 1714.
[5] Ibid., p. 560, 5 Mar. 1714. See also p. 229 below.
[6] £20,000 out of a total bill of £833,826 for 40,000 troops in Flanders in 1702, for example. Journals Commons, xiv, 6 Nov. 1702.

$7\frac{1}{2}d.$ per day above his pay to meet the costs of bread and forage
—that is an increase of 30 per cent. of his subsistence. Bread
seems to have been the most expensive item in the Peninsula,
but Galway himself reported in 1708 that the regiments might
bear the expense out of the subsistence 'since the Queen gives
them other provisions'. In addition, two mills were ordered
to be built to reduce the cost of corn,[1] although six handmills
issued to each regiment or battalion in Flanders two years
earlier were never used.[2]

The handmills were indicative of the problem confronting
the armies. They had grown too large to live systematically off
the country if they were not to estrange the local populations,
but had no organization of their own either for bringing food over
the long distances which their renewal of mobility created or
for handling anything but the 'finished article'. The difference
between a bad and a good system of supply was that the latter
catered by firm agreements with contractors to produce bread
and with sutlers to 'tail' the regiments, while under the former
the men bought or extorted their own food.

In the field there was an entitlement to 'forage and waggon
money' which always bulked largely as a separate item in the
estimates. This was an allowance to general and staff officers,
and to regiments or battalions in terms of so many rations, and
dated back at least to William's time, when a general of foot,
for example, had been allowed 40, and a lieutenant-general 30.
The figures for units depended on establishment, but were
about 60 per battalion or regiment. The cash value of the rations
also varied from time to time. In November 1703, for example,
it was 6 stivers for a general, 4 stivers for a cavalry troop, and
6 for an infantry battalion. The rate of exchange at this time
was 16 gilders 11 stivers to the £, so that the general and the
infantry battalion had between $4\frac{1}{4}d.$ and $4\frac{1}{2}d.$ per ration. In
1712 the exchange was quoted at approximately $10\frac{1}{2}$ gilders
to the £, which gave nearly $7d.$ per ration.[3] The *Recruiting Essay*,
on the other hand, claimed that the soldier's subsistence was
equivalent to 26 stivers (1s. 6d.), plus his bread in the field,

[1] *Treas. Cal.*, iv, p. 98.
[2] *Select Documents for Queen Anne's Reign*, G. M. Trevelyan (Cambridge, 1929),
p. 134. (*Select Docs.*)
[3] Treas. 1/87, 19 Nov. 1703; *Journals Commons*, xvii, 20 Feb. 1712.

and 32 stivers (1*s*. 10½*d*.) in garrison, where he had to find his 'meat, drink, washing, and mending, etc.'[1]

It has been said of Marlborough that he was the first to establish 'the modern principle of payment for supplies in the theatre of war, and appointed men of local importance to provide supplies and transport'.[2] This, of course, cannot be accepted in its entirety as no English army overseas had ever lived exclusively by levies or plunder.

In William's time, after all, the allowance in the field was two pounds of bread, one pound of meat or cheese, and one bottle of wine or two of beer. The Proviant Master-General was later ordered to provide also 'corn, grain, and lea of several kinds, stock-fish, herrings, and all other salted fishes, salted and hung fleshes, especially beef and bacon, cheese, butter, almonds, chestnuts, and hazel nuts, wine, beer, malt, honey, vinegar, oil, tobacco, wood, and coal for firing, and as many living oxen, cows, sheep, and swine, hens, and turkeys, as can be conveniently fed'.[3] Even in William's army it is possible that this was, in fact, done on some exceptional occasion, but it is most certain that any of the items which reached the soldier would be paid for by him.

One of the earliest records concerning direct provision is a warrant of 1689 authorizing the Commissary-General to issue rations, as directed by the general, against stoppages not exceeding 4*d*. per day for infantry soldiers, 7¼*d*. for dragoons, and 1*s*. for light horse. Marlborough's achievement was to systemize the procedure, principally by making much greater use of the local knowledge and resources of indigenous merchants and contractors. He undoubtedly obtained striking results in the improvement of quality of the soldiers' food and increased regularity of supply.

Bread remained the staple, although the ubiquitous biscuit was also, of course, issued. The Duke may well wince at the irony of history which remarks on his work for the troops' bread only because of the notorious '2½ per cent.' allegations in the peculation charges. The Commander-in-Chief himself, a man not given to talking of his own deeds, is a fair and dignified witness:

---

[1] The author's figures, of course, require at least interpretation—compare, for example, the figures for the ration contract quoted below, pp. 224–5.

[2] Masse, op. cit.   [3] Walton, p. 695.

. . . our troops all along have had as much and as good bread as the States' forces. . . . If England has had bread as cheap as the Dutch, they have had it as cheap as possible . . . everything has been so organised, and there has been so little cause for complaint, that all know our army in Flanders has been regularly supplied with bread during the war, and has received it with an exactness that will be hardly thought consistent with the secrecy and suddenness of some of the moves.[1]

Even the *Recruiting Essay* admitted that the issue of bread was a good bargain: 'the soldier', it said, 'has no reason to complain of the commissary'.

The soldiers themselves bore this out:

As we marched (to Blenheim), [wrote one], commissaries were appointed to furnish us with all manner of necessaries for men and horse. These were brought to the ground before we arrived, and the soldiers had nothing to do, but to pitch tents, boil their kettles, and lie down to rest. Surely never was such a march carried on with more order and regularity, and with less fatigue to both men and horse.[2]

Hare tells how it was done:

And to make things yet more easy both to the Armies and the Countries it marched through, his Grace was not unmindfull to provide money and order Regular payments for everything that was brought into the camp; a thing hitherto unknown in Germany . . . and to prevent any failure herein he order'd the Treasurer of the Army to be always in cash to answer Bills, and daily to have a Month's Subsistence before hand, and that the supplies should be laid from Frankfort to Nurenberg, and that he should lose no time in sending credit to these places.[3]

The contracts were, as would be expected, for the supply of so many rations—i.e. rations for 10 men for 10 days would be the same as for 2 men for 50 days. Rates varied according to the nationality of the troops, with the English the most expensive. The winter quarters ration contract for 1710, for example, provided for Hanoverians at $7\frac{1}{4}$ stivers per ration, Saxons 8 stivers, and Danes and Hessians $8\frac{3}{4}$ stivers; Marlborough turned

---

[1] *The Life of John, Duke of Marlborough*, J. W. Lediard (London, Wilcox, 1736), ii, pp. 371–2. (*Lediard*.)   [2] Parker, p. 95.
[3] British Museum Add. MSS. 9114; quoted in *Select Docs.*, pp. 100–1.

down an offer of 1,844,500 for the British from the Dutch contract, because, he said, he could get them cheaper than 9¾
stivers per ration.[1] Part of the variation of cost while in winter
quarters was undoubtedly due to the different locations of the
troops, and the problems of transporting, but a proportion
represented differences in standards of living.

Once contracts were made, Marlborough sought for fair play
for both contractors and troops. The few stern words in his
dispatches are almost all reserved for defaulting contractors. In
1704 he wrote to Vanderkaa, the bread contractor:

We are in precisely the same state as we have been practically
throughout the campaign with Solomon Abraham. I am astonished
that you should leave us entirely at his mercy, when you know very
well that he has neither credit nor judgment in these affairs; such
are things, that, if you do not remedy them immediately, I can see
we shall lack altogether.

Machado, another bread contractor, earned the following:

I deeply regret that I find myself obliged to point out to you the
trouble and embarrassment I have had throughout this campaign
on account of the little care you have taken to satisfy your bread
contract. This, without regard for the public service, you farmed
out to Redonde, and he to Solomon Abraham, who has neither
credit nor judgment for an affair of such importance. As a result,
had it not been for the trouble taken by Vanderkaa, the army would
undoubtedly have perished.[2]

The pillars of his contracting system were the brothers
Solomon and Moses de Medina, who, despite his greatest
efforts, had their own money troubles, mentioned in Chapter I.
Marlborough not only always did his best to ensure payment,
but tried to see that the contractors were not put upon unduly
by the troops who were, as has been known on other occasions,
adroit in the matter of ration drawing. He noted with displeasure during the siege of Lille that the numbers of bread
rations drawn, instead of going down 'as they should in reason'
(due to casualties) 'are increasing', and ordered that, in future,
commissaries were to get the numbers required by regiments
before issue, and to ensure these were not more than was

[1] Murray. Cf. figures quoted in *Recruiting Essay*, as shown above at p. 223.
[2] Murray, i, p. 516.

absolutely necessary.[1] Lille presented, indeed, a particularly difficult problem, and at one point the issue ration was reduced by one-third, and money given in lieu.[2] When this was ordered, the Duke particularly charged Cadogan with seeing that the money actually reached the men. The troops themselves accepted the procedure gladly enough, but it is to be doubted if they welcomed it as heartily as did the later warrior, Anton, of Wellington's time. He was to write of his militia days that he received $\frac{1}{2}$ lb. of beef or meat daily, which was $\frac{1}{4}$ lb. less than the allowance. Of this he entirely approved, since 'if we did not get it, we did not pay for it. Indeed, small allowances of provisions are always best. Why force upon us more than is barely necessary for subsistence, when, in brief, more meat in the platter means fewer pence in the pocket?' It is scarcely necessary, perhaps, to add that this occurred in Aberdeen.[3]

Provisions other than bread were in large part supplied by the sutlers. The trade was hazardous, and, if profits could be large, they were equally uncertain. In the event of the defeat of the army followed, they risked the loss of all their stock. Conversely, they were among the most voracious of plunderers, who did not confine their depredations to the sphere of supplies, although these yielded the quickest profit as they could be turned to cash immediately in the field. Both sutlers and the troops themselves could inflict much loss on the local inhabitants. Mother Ross considered a position with the 'Forlorn hope' or camp colour-men well worth the extra danger, because of the chances of additional plunder 'as there are but few to share it'. Her garnerings from farms ranged over fowls, pigeons, sheep, faggots, hay, straw, barrels of beer, feathers from a bed (to protect her mare's back from hot bread taken from an oven), beef, bacon, butter, brandy, vinegar, and such concealed articles as she could fish from wells whence the unco-operative peasantry had removed the buckets.

When Marlborough found it necessary to purchase or to requisition at a fixed price, he took great pains to cause the least possible ill will. Avoidance of excessive demands on the country people was always one of the factors in his planning, and he frequently marched in several columns, purely to avoid

[1] Murray, iv, p. 264.   [2] Ibid., p. 292.   [3] *Fitchett.*

excessive concentration of demands. He was at particular pains to 'spare' the country of his allies. There were no doubt numerous cases where the advantages to be gained by leniency could be other than political. The Assistant Quartermaster-General who received the following—written from Malines on 7 June 1709—would undoubtedly appreciate to the full how damaging it would be to his country's prospects to ignore the request—or the invitation:

Sir, I hear that you are on the march with the Palatine troops, and are likely to pass by this town. In that case, sir, I beg you to remember that we are interested in Bonheyden where we have meadows which may be greatly damaged by the passage of troops. So, sir, if you can avoid that route we shall be eternally grateful to you. Remembering all your kindnesses in the past, I hope that you will not refuse me this favour; and if you pass by Malines yourself give us at least the pleasure of making use of our house,

I have etc,
La Comtesse d'Avelin.

P.S. The Comte, who is absent, will gladly assure you of the pleasure that it will give him to see you.[1]

While enlightened or shrewd commanders tried to 'spare' the countryside as much as possible, it was, nevertheless, recognized that those who had the honour to have their country fought over owed an obligation to the troops on their territory. If the army belonged to a hostile state, then the terms would perhaps be harsher, but in either case there would be allegations of military oppression, and of civilian overcharging. In the case of legitimate contracts, the Netherlanders were, characteristically, a canny people. This was particularly true of the Belgians who represented a potential 'fifth column'. By and large, however, so long as Marlborough was in command of the armies, difficulties were smoothed over, and both sides probably got as fair a deal as was possible in those days and circumstances.

Not unnaturally, after the cessation of hostilities by the English, when the Dutch considered they had been deserted, the atmosphere became much pricklier. In 1713 the Dutch lodged a very strenuous protest against foraging in the vicinity of Ghent as 'a great burden upon the country in time of peace'. The

[1] Fort., *Hist.*, p. 180.

English general, Wyndham, pointed out to his Government that contracts for forage had expired and 'no further provision can be made in time of peace'. The British, he added, were at the further disadvantage that they could not form magazines like the Dutch who had 'a considerable revenue from the country'.[1] Failing the co-operation of the local inhabitants it was, of course, quite impossible in those days to form magazines with or without money. In the same year, Wyndham strenuously defended Brigadier Sabine who was involved in trouble with the Dutch for foraging. Obviously the general knew his Treasury, for the strongest argument in defence of his subordinate was that the demand made on the inhabitants was 'absolutely necessary to save Her Majesty the expense of forage'.[2] Brigadier Preston, involved in a similar complaint, not only claimed on 11 July 1713 that he had paid for everything alleged to have been plundered except for one bill for 250 faggots outstanding, but retaliated by complaining of excessive prices— for example $7\frac{1}{2}$ stivers (9d.) for a loaf of less than 6 lb. against 6 stivers ($7\frac{1}{4}d$.) for fully 6 lb.—and, further, that the Dutch were erecting Customs Houses where excessive duties were being levied.[3]

John Millner who discovered 'bosom friends turned hated enemies' in his march under Ormonde from Cambresis to Ghent, recorded that no man was permitted to cut down any corn nor scarce to tread on it. There was to be no damage nor meddling with anything on any pretence without paying full value. The troops were not allowed into garrisons, and at the few places where the local people handed articles over the walls, they insisted on prior payment. It may have been these experiences, or, more probably, just the English tradition, which made the Government rather kinder towards their ex-enemies than Wyndham and Preston to the Dutch. At any rate, the demolition force dispatched to Dunkirk had orders that the town should not be involved in expense, and that the cost of bedding, firing, and other necessaries formerly borne by France should be borne by Britain.[4]

---

[1] SP Mil. 41/4.   [2] Ibid.
[3] Ibid. The rate of exchange at this period was approximately 10 gilders 10 stivers to the £. *Journals Commons*, xvii, 20 Feb. 1712.
[4] SP Mil. 41/4.

Spain, with its record, at the worst, of bitter hostility, and, at the best, of non-co-operation towards any occupying army, friend or foe, and its specialities in wines, has always been renowned as a country of plunder. Remarkably enough, in this war, when the inhabitants were, by and large, hostile and sullen, foraging was much less than in Wellington's day, and wanton plundering, of course, bore no resemblance to the excesses of the Iron Duke's hordes. The principal reason appears to have been good discipline, but an indication of the ameliorative measures adopted is Stanhope's order in 1708. This laid down that, to obviate oppression of, or exactions from, the local inhabitants, individual local purchase was forbidden, and men had to do all their buying from army stores. The shaky nature of the system is disclosed by his further provision, that, to meet the additional expense which would be thus incurred, company commanders might carry fourteen extra vacancies in their companies.[1]

The Gibraltar case referred to at p. 221 was an interesting example of the military commander vainly pleading for action by the civil authorities before it was too late. Earl Portmore wrote in 1710 that, prior to leaving England for Gibraltar, he had asked for an establishment for fortifications and other 'extraordinaries'. He was told this existed, but discovered later it made no mention of either fortifications or soft bread, for which the debts were already £57,000. The Lord Treasurer therefore ordered soft bread to be charged to the soldiers' subsistence, but this proved to be so unpopular that 'the garrison mutinied and that place had like to have been lost'. Since he was 'loath to see Her Majesty's troops perish, and a place of that importance lost', Portmore took it upon himself to sign warrants, but was very unhappy about the business, as in these times he was quite likely to be himself charged with the expenditure thus authorized. The Secretary at War kept unsuccessfully pleading with the Secretary at State and Lord Treasurer (meanwhile at times skilfully, if unpopularly, conniving at naval rations going to the troops) until the garrison was eventually changed three years later, and arrears debited to 'extraordinaries'.[2]

[1] *Stanhope*, p. 70.
[2] SP Mil. 41/3 and 41/4.

What could the troops hope actually to see in terms of 'beef and pudding'? They could not all be as easily catered for as Blackader who, after remarking 'This night was an unpleasant uneasy night to our regiment for they have wanted bread these five days and are faint', went on to write that he slept sound 'for God sustained'.[1] For those requiring more solid fare, there was the standard indicated by Mathew Bishop who wrote that during the sieges of St. Venant and Aire, 'we got two to three bushels of beans, and a bushel of wheat at a time: so some days we had boiled beans, and sometimes when we mounted the trenches we made ourselves dumplings which we thought good living'. He seems, however, to have been as interested in drink as in food. In the wet trenches he had sustenance from geneva, brandy, and brotherskeys. In the mornings he appears to have preferred coffee (black, no doubt) which he found 'very refreshing after a night's duty on the cold ground'.

In Elizabeth's time a day's 'basic' ration had been reckoned to be:

1 lb. bread and biscuit	$1\frac{1}{2}d.$
3 oz. butter	$\frac{3}{4}d.$
6 oz. cheese	$1d.$
$\frac{3}{4}$ pint oatmeal	$\frac{3}{4}d.$
transport charges	$\frac{1}{2}d.$
	$4\frac{1}{2}d.$

It was reckoned, however, that there also entered into the rations at one time or another peas, beans, rice, pork, bacon, and fresh and salt beef, fresh Dutch ling, dried Newfoundland cod, and herring, beer (otherwise the troops fell sick), ranging from a quart to half a gallon, and sometimes half a pint of sack, topped off with half a pint of whisky every other day.[2] In Anne's time there was probably more salt meat, and slightly less fish eaten, and I have seen no references to whisky, although the troops in Spain undoubtedly had more wine than was good for them.[3]

[1] *Blackader*, pp. 145-6.   [2] Cruickshank, pp. 55-56.

[3] An idea of the proportions may be gained from the figures of a shipment of provisions for a company in Newfoundland (80 men) in 1702:

biscuit	24,752 lb.	malt	93 qr. 4 bushels	flour	3,536 lb.
beef	2,538 pieces	suet	589 lb.	hops	$2\frac{1}{2}$ cwt.
pork	3,536 pieces	pease	110 bushels 4 gals.	butter	13,626 lb.
cheshire cheese	1,772 lb.	oatmeal	165 bushels 6 gals.		

When supplies were available the men did, by the standards
of the time, feed reasonably well, as can be judged from the
action of even the thrifty Netherlanders who, when the Brussels
garrison was threatened with siege in 1708, issued a daily
allowance of one lb. meat, two quarts of beer, and four glasses
of brandy. In measuring progress over the years, this may be
compared with Kincaid's fare during the retreat to Torres
Vedras under Wellington—'a pound of raw beef drawn fresh
from the bullock, a pound of biscuit, and a glass of rum' daily.[1]

At sea, the soldiers were not reckoned to feed well, even if
not always as badly as Uncle Toby and Corporal Trim who
had:

putrid salt beef to which the sailors gave the name of Irish horse,
salt pork of New England which, though neither fish nor flesh,
savoured of both, bread from the same country, every biscuit whereof, like a piece of clock work, moved by its own internal impulse
occasioned by the myriads of insects that dwelt within it; and butter
served by the gill, that tasted like train oil thickened with salt.

Towards the end of the war, the Commissioners of Transport,
supported by Marlborough, recommended that on the voyage
Scotland–Flanders, since it was longer than Harwich–Flanders,
each man should have 2 oz. butter, $\frac{1}{2}$ lb. cheese, and 1 lb. of
bread added to his ration 'for the better preservation of (his)
health'. I have been unable to confirm whether St. John (then
Secretary of State) took any action on the representation, forwarded to him by Grenville as Secretary at War.[2]

(Sailors at sea fared better as a rule than the soldiers. When
Pepys overhauled the victualling contracts, as a supplement
to the triple Establishment for Manning, Gunning, and Officer-
ing the Service at the close of 1677, it was passed that the victuallers were to have 6d. per day for victuals in harbour, $7\frac{3}{4}d$.
at sea, and 8d. south of Lisbon. For this, every seaman was to
get 1 gallon of beer, brewed under clearly defined conditions,
1 lb. of clean, sweet, wheaten biscuit, and 2 lb. of English salted
beef, or of bacon and pork four days a week, with cod, haber-
dine, or Poor John, and 2 oz. of butter and Suffolk cheese on

Presumably even a government department would not ship salt fish to Newfoundland. *APC Col.*, ii, p. 401.
    [1] *Fitchett.*   [2] SP Mil. 41/3, 4 Feb. 1711.

the other three. There were special provisions for south of latitude 39.)[1]

Owing to wide differences in prices from year to year, and from theatre to theatre, it is not possible to give any 'average' cost to the Government, and the best that can be done is to quote a few representative figures.

In 1703 Colonel Quary offered to be contractor 'at more easy terms than any other man in America' with 'very good ship's bread' at 9s. 6d. per cwt., flour 11s. per cwt., best pork 40s. per barrel, best South Carolina beef 24s. per barrel, rice 15s. per barrel, and English peas 3s. a bushel.[2] In 1712 a review by the Commissioners of Victualling compared prices on the 'old course' with those on the new. I have quoted here the highest on the old system, and the lowest on the new, which was uniformly more economical:

beef per cwt.	£2 and £1. 1s. 6d.
pork per cwt.	£3. 3s. and £1. 8s.
bread per cwt.	£1. 3s. and 8s. 6d.
wheat per qr.	£3. 4s. and £1. 8s.
flour per cwt.	£1. 2s. and 10s. 6d.
oatmeal per cwt.	£2. 9s. 6d. and £1. 7s. 6d.
butter per lb.	9d. and 3¾d.
cheese per lb.	4½d. and 1¼d.
oil per gallon	7s. and 4s.
peas per qr	£2. 10s. and £1. 6s. 6d.
beef per tun	£4 and £2. 10s.
malt per qr	£2. 9s. and 18s.[3]

Irish meat was recognized to be generally cheaper than English, but was disliked by the troops. The oxen in Ireland were small, and not stall fed, so that the salt 'penetrates into and eats out the heart and nourishment of the meat', while Irish pork had a fishy taste because the hogs fed on the sea coast.[4] An indication of the amount of salt there was 'to eat out the heart and nourishment of the meat' is in the figure of 30,000 bushels to cure flesh for 40,000 men.[5] In 1714, 8,000 bushels were said to be required for 10,000 men: this cost 10s. per bushel in France, although it was reckoned to be available elsewhere at 9s.–9s. 6d.[6]

[1] *Years of Peril*, p. 190. [2] *Dom. Cal.*, ii, p. 147.
[3] Treas. 1/52, 18 Sept. 1712.
[4] *Treas. Cal.*, iv, pp. 218–19, Commissioners of Victualling, 25 Oct. 1710.
[5] *Treas. Cal.*, iv, p. 135. [6] Ibid., p. 559.

An estimate for three months' rations for the Edinburgh garrison in 1711 comprised:

300 bolls meal at 10s. a bol, ⅓ biscuit	£150
67 bolls malt at 11s. 8d. per boll	£39. 1s. 8d.
6,000 cwt. cheese at 3½d. per cwt.	£87. 10s.
3,000 cwt. butter at 6d. per lb.	£75
5 bolls salt at 5s. per boll	£1. 5s.
3 barrels soap at £4 per barrel	£12[1]

Victualling at sea was reckoned to cost 15s. 3d. per man per month.[2]

Prices were, in many cases, barely relevant since the victualling system laboured under the chronic difficulty of the day— lack of finance. Peterborough himself complained to Charles of Spain in 1706: 'I never had the money to make magazines in Valencia', and later advanced lack of money as the reason for refusing Charles's Aragon project.[3] At home in 1711, the position was so acute that the merchants were claiming they could only dispose of government bills at upwards of 35 per cent. discount.[4] It was not surprising that, in similar circumstances in 1689, a contractor had complained of being compelled to issue 16 oz. to the lb., whereas it had always been the practice to issue only 14 oz. The Controller and Commissary-General's decision was overturned, and he was allowed to revert to the old system.[5] Others took care to anticipate Her Majesty's favour, like the sea captain who, admitting to use of government transports for private trading, was further alleged to have flung so much water on the corn that when it was taken ashore at Barcelona 'the inhabitants could not endure the smell of it'. Corn intended for Charles of Spain's troops provided, *en route*, rations for ambassadors from Sardinia with all their servants, and a 'large quantity of oxen, sheep, and most sorts of poultry'. Little wonder that the seamen themselves 'abused' the master 'for thirteene days'.[6]

A contrasting picture was that of Colonel Bennet, Bennett, or Benet, the engineer,[7] who claimed to have fed the horses of Gibraltar garrison and about forty oxen for six months out of

---

[1] Treas. 1/169. [2] SP Mil. 41/3/251.
[3] *H.M.C.H. of L.*, vii, pp. 470 and 473.
[4] *Treas. Cal.*, iv, p. 306, Commissioners of Victualling, 30 Aug. 1711.
[5] Walton, p. 696. [6] Treas. 1/135, 1708.
[7] Whom Marlborough made surrender his infantry company, p. 186.

his own pocket, and could only, in return, 'hope to deserve Her Majesty's favour'. Her Majesty's favour was such that already, with forty-seven chaldrons of coal required at £7 a chaldron, the troops had destroyed two-thirds of the town including 'even their own quarters for wood to dress their meat'.[1]

When provision of supplies for men represented a burden on the countryside, and a more than troublesome problem for the army organization, it was only to be expected that horse forage, so much greater in quantity, should be correspondingly more difficult. The redeeming feature so far as the horses were concerned was that a certain amount of feeding could be had more directly from the countryside, although farmers were no more willing to see their ground cropped clean by hungry cavalry and baggage animals than to surrender their grain to ravenous soldiers. Just, too, as man does not live by bread alone, so horses cannot survive on grass only: the consumption of grain at the siege of Lille, for instance, has been rated at 1,000 sacks per day. Forage in this case was said to have been made particularly difficult owing to the flight of the local inhabitants. As a result, threshing had to be carried out by the troopers themselves at a rate of a crown a sack.[2]

Consumption of hay per horse on board government transports was reckoned at 15 lb. per head per day, and oats at one peck. So far as home purchase was concerned, prices appear to have varied as widely as 50s. and 70s. a ton for hay, and 11s. to 14s. a quarter for oats.[3]

With such large quantities involved, it was inevitable that small shifts in price should have considerable effects on the troops required to maintain horses out of their pay, and it must be remembered that a considerable part of the large apparent difference between an infantryman's and a cavalryman's pay represented subsistence for the horseman's mount. Even when the trooper was without a horse, it was normal to stop him 12d. per day subsistence to go towards the purchase of a new one.[4] Thus, through the war, among the items of 'extraordinary charges', forage allowances are frequent, and in at least the 1711 estimates, forage for the entire Peninsular army (including

[1] *Treas. Cal.*, iv, pp. 299–300.   [2] Taylor, ii, pp. 225–6.
[3] *Dom. Cal.*, i, pp. 13–14 and 134.
[4] PGO WO 71/3, 25 June 1714.

13,000 foreign troops) appeared with waggon and baggage money for the officers as normal expenditure.

In the United Kingdom the position was a trifle easier, no doubt because of the considerable civilian horse population, but Scotland, as an exceedingly poor country, presented special problems. Not only was an extraordinary allowance made on account of the price of forage in the north, but the modification of practice after the Union introduced complications.[1] After the Revolution, it had been ordered by Parliament, as a result of widespread complaints, that no officer was to have the foraging of his own troop. Contracts then laid down a rate of 6*d.* per night for dry forage and 2½*d.* for green per horse, plus 12*d.* in the £ poundage on the pay of the entire Standing Army—representing about £4,000. After the Union this was altered once again, and the Queen ordered, in place of the poundage, an additional 3*d.* per night dry forage, and 1*d.* grass —figures considered to be considerably below those previously obtainable. A contract dated 24 August 1710 with an Edinburgh merchant shows 3½*d.* for green forage, and 9*d.* for store hay or cut straw, plus a Scots peck of oats. In this case, the cost was first deducted from the men's subsistence, but, on subsequent representations, 1*d.* per horse was repaid for the period 15 May–14 October, and a further 3*d.* per horse for the period 15 October–14 May of the following year.

In the same year General Echlyn presented a memorial— apparently unsuccessful—that foraging of dragoon horses be the officers' responsibility, as the supply in the previous year by commissaries had been most unsatisfactory.[2] In 1712 the rates in Scotland were 7½*d.* per night dry forage, and 3*d.* grass.[3]

MEDICAL SERVICES

It is safe to say that the medical services of Anne's armies were remarkable for mismanagement, brutality, inhumanity, and, possibly, corruption. The best medical science of the time was not good, and the army could not expect to have anything but the worst. There was little to tempt doctors into the army. There was, for that matter, little enough to tempt anyone. In the case of a doctor, however, it took him away from his practice,

[1] Treas. 1/169.   [2] Ibid. 1/121.
[3] *Treas. Cal.*, iv, p. 399, 28 June 1712.

and, as Dr. William Neilson said in his petition, lost them 'all opportunitys . . . of making Friends to live by (their) Profession'.¹ Yet the very fact that they had a civilian 'trade' was considered ground for not granting to doctors when they left the service the half pay for which the regimental officers could qualify. It was, nevertheless, not necessary for a doctor to be professionally qualified to obtain employment in the army.² This held good for almost two hundred years more. There is a case on record in 1745 of a private soldier being taken from the ranks and appointed to the medical charge of his unit because he was reputed to have been 'bred a surgeon'. On the other hand, there are numerous cases of military surgeons being appointed to combatant commissions. One commanded a company of artillery for eighteen years, and in 1809 a Surgeon to the Forces was Intelligence Officer and A.D.C. to the Officer Commanding Troops on a West African expedition.³

Pay was not princely in the lower medical ranks, and poor in the higher: the Physician, the Surgeon, and the Apothecary-Generals to the Forces had only 10s. per day.⁴ There was some compensation for poor pay in the profit from supply of medicines. Doctors might supply these either by fixed allowance or by detailed charge to the Government. Paymasters required in the latter case a detailed list with the exact quantity of each drug taken by each patient together with the date. As the bills were normally referred to a senior military doctor for checking, professional jealousy and variations in price stimulated voluminous correspondence. It was nevertheless generally conceded that the supply of drugs was 'a good pecuniary speculation'. In 1691, in fact, the Apothecary-General in Ireland had specifically petitioned to be allowed to supply medicines as a perquisite of his office.⁵

The organization of Medicine was almost exclusively regimental. Hospitals were, in the early stages of the war, improvised with the aid of the local inhabitants, such as the Beguine

---

¹ SP Mil. 41/4.

² Readers of *Roderick Random* will remember that even when, in the case of the navy, there was inquiry into capabilities, it could hardly be called rigorous.

³ 'Army Doctors in the 18th Century', A. E. S. Laws in *Royal United Services Institution Journal*, vol. xcii, no. 571, Aug. 1948 (London). (*RUSI*.)

⁴ In 1690 the Physician and the Chirurgeon-General had had 20s. per day. Walton, p. 651.   ⁵ Ibid., p. 759, and *RUSI*.

who had looked after Corporal Trim in an earlier war. Any co-ordination was as a branch of the staff, rather than a service; that is to say, although there were physicians, apothecaries, and surgeons-general, there was no Army Medical Corps. Any troops taken for medical employment had to be roughly equivalent to what is today termed extra-regimentally employed, although they continued to count against the strength of their parent units. This, of course, was one way of helping to ensure that, in the normal course of events, the worst men would be available.

In the course of the reign, the pressure of events, particularly in the Peninsula, brought about a change not generally noted in studies of the period. In Spain, in the latter years of the war, hospitals were authorized out of either contingencies or 'extra-ordinaries of war'. They were normally commanded by 'directors'.

The Commissioners for Sick and Wounded had responsibilities, but their precise role in army medicine is not clear. They were technically a body for dealing with seamen, but, as with prisoners, they took part in matters affecting soldiers, but normally only those at home. There is, however, a Secretary at War's letter of 1702 in which he wrote that he had been employing the Commissioners' Apothecary-General overseas, and recommending him to the Commissioners' favour that 'he may not suffer . . . by his necessary absence'.[1] This anticipated the letter conveying the information that the Prince Consort had ordered the Commissioners to take the same charge of soldiers brought home sick or wounded as they did of seamen.[2] The execution of this threat may be deduced from Lord Shannon's letter of 29 October 1710 which stated he had been obliged 'to bring away all the men that there was a possibility to remove from the hospital in the Isle of Wight to prevent losing 'em quite from service'.[3]

When the Secretary at War, on 17 August 1703, ordered 'Mr. Teal and other Apothecarys' to prepare eight double chests of medicines for chirurgeons proceeding to Portugal, the order to the Commissioners to inspect the medicines came from another authority—the Lords of the Committee of the Privy Council—on 9 September.[4] The statutory provision for inspec-

---

[1] Entry Books WO 26/11.
[2] Marching Orders WO 5/11.
[3] SP Mil. 41/3/122.
[4] War Letters, WO 4/2.

tion of medicines which was made seven years later did not put
the responsibility exclusively on the Commissioners. The Mutiny
Act of 1710 prescribed that, in order 'to supply good and wholesome medicines internal and external, and for preventing loss
and sufferings of many of Her Majesty's officers and soldiers
thereof', examinations of medicines should be carried out in
public by the Master and Wardens of the Company of Apothecaries, accompanied by the Physician or Surgeon-General of
the Army, or physicians nominated by the Commissioners for
Sick and Wounded, or the College of Physicians.

The three chiefs of the medical service in the army were the
Physician to the Forces, the Surgeon to the Forces, and the
Apothecary to the Forces. Although they were designated 'to
the Forces', the same qualification is true of them as of senior
commanders or staff officers that they were normally confined
in their activities either to one theatre or to the home garrisons. The charter for the Apothecary laid down that he was 'to
furnish the several Regiments of the Army with medicines, and
from time to time to observe such orders and directions as he
should receive from his Superior Officers, according to the
Rules and Discipline of War'.[1] There were disputes about
division of responsibilities between him and the Physician. As
early as 8 December 1702 the Society of Apothecaries in London
complained about 'poaching' on their preserves by physicians.[2]
Abroad, apothecaries were appointed only to the larger theatres,
and were normally designated Apothecaries-General 'to the
Forces'. The surgeon and physician, who were more widely provided, were usually appointed not 'to the Forces' but to the
Commander-in-Chief. These appointments do not seem to have
been dependent on the rank of the expedition commanders;
there are several cases of their being appointed to brigadiers.
Their pay was 10s. per day—3s. 4d. more than the corresponding chaplain.[3]

When, at a later date, hospital establishments were sanctioned, physicians and surgeons to the commanders-in-chief
were given also the appointments of physicians and surgeons of

[1] *Journals Commons*, xiv, 19 Feb. 1705.
[2] *Dom. Cal.*, i, pp. 334–5.
[3] e.g. to Whetham on 13 May 1709; Dalton, vi, 239.

all the hospitals in the theatre.¹ Surgeons and apothecaries were apointed to garrisons also, including Gibraltar, and there was a Physician to Chelsea Hospital.

The backbone of the service was the regimental chirurgeon (appointed by the colonel), and his mate in the infantry battalions, and the chirurgeon in the cavalry regiments. The regimental chirurgeon received 4s. per day, 8d. less than the chaplain, plus 2s. for his horse in the cavalry, and normally a horse for his chest in the infantry. His mate normally received 2s. per day, but sometimes 2s. 6d. The Ordnance were allowed a master surgeon in their trains. He received 5s. and had, in place of a mate, an assistant surgeon who received 3s. per day.²

The total number of doctors present at Blenheim was seventeen, or approximately one per 600 men. This was approximately the figure for regimental medical officers alone in 1939–45, exclusive of those in hospitals, field ambulances, and other medical units and establishments. Nor had the doctors of Marlborough's day other ranks of a medical or nursing corps to back them up.

There was no establishment of field hospitals, and no medical transport. Regiments had to provide carts for their wounded until the Commissioners of Transport took over.³ Sick or wounded who could not thus accompany their regiments were disposed in villages and towns, sometimes with a surgeon, and one or two officers or N.C.O.s, and money for their subsistence. The inadequacy of this solution in a war of movement was made obvious after Blenheim when the problem of the wounded was almost as overwhelming as that of prisoners of war. Campaigning among a hostile population in Spain, the setting up of bases in places like Port Mahon, and the presence of troops in the Plantations,⁴ which were without even the inadequate local

¹ e.g. Smallbones and Labonge with Argyll in Spain in 1711; Dalton, vi, p. 182.

² Specimens at *Journals Commons*, xiii, 21 Jan. 1702.

³ See Marlborough's dispatch of June 1706, which, although strictly prohibiting levying of waggons on the countryside, makes an exception in favour of two or three per battalion for the sick; Murray, ii, p. 619.

⁴ In 1702 the building of a hospital in Barbados was recommended 'when other more pressing services are provided'. *APC Col.*, ii, p. 405. In the same year the Privy Council sanctioned money for a surgeon's mate for the company at Newfoundland who was 'represented as necessary' although there was no establishment for him. He was voted £36. 10s. for a year's subsistence plus £25 for his

resources of Germany and the Low Countries, compelled in time more orderly provision for disposal of sick and wounded. Unfit men were, in days when regiments were a business to be run at a profit, a double hindrance to commanding officers. Unless they recovered very quickly, they had to be cast aside as soon and as cheaply as possible. On 11 June 1706 Stanhope, the Ambassador at Barcelona, wrote to Peterborough that he had been obliged to give subsistence to several sick men left without any money.[1] On at least one occasion a shipload of invalids from Portugal was turned loose in the United Kingdom to beg in the streets (of Penrhyn).

The soldier did not, for all that, have his medical facilities, either in or out of hospital, provided free. Towards the regimental doctor's services there was a stoppage of 2d. per man per month from the off-reckonings; how far this went to supplement the doctor's pay, how far it was claimed by the Treasury, or how far it represented a recompense to the colonel, who in turn was responsible for paying the doctor, is not clear.[2] The hospital charge was at first fixed as the patient's full subsistence, but this was later superseded in some theatres by an 'insurance' system of $\frac{1}{4}d.$ a day for private soldiers, and 6d. in the £ or one day's pay per annum from officers.[3] That neither of these amounts was adequate is evidenced by the grant of 12d. per man per day to the Commissioners for Sick and Wounded for hospitals in Britain.[4] The excess costs in the field, as well as those of medicines, were met by deductions at source from the total pay of the army, and thence no doubt in due course came from subsistence. This could not continue in the face of rising costs, and, as early as 3 May 1703, the Secretary at War asked the Lord Treasurer if it was not possible to meet the cost of the yearly chest of medicines for Newfoundland, about which the Privy Council had debated the previous year, out of the normal poundage deduction or from contingencies.[5] On 4 February 1708, Galway, writing home from the Peninsula, said that a hospital was so important it was quite impossible to do without one. By the treaty the King of Portugal had

medicine chest. *APC Col.*, ii, p. 401. Detachments were frequently left without medical attention and had to obtain the services of a civilian, or, if available, naval surgeon.   [1] *H.M.C.H. of L.*, vii, p. 477.
   [2] *RUSI.*   [3] Walton, pp. 656–7.
   [4] SP Mil. 41/3/122.   [5] Entry Books WO 26/11.

undertaken to supply necessaries, but the Portuguese were quite unable to fulfil their obligation, and a great number of men were lost 'owing to our dependance upon (Portuguese) assistance'. He forwarded an establishment, and asked that provision be made out of extraordinaries as the subsistence money was inadequate.[1]

In the previous reign the experiment had been made in Flanders of making a contractor 'Intendant' of the hospitals who had supplied everything except the pay of the staff. Subsequently, in 1693, there had been a contract for the whole care of the sick at 9¼ stivers (approximately 4½*d*.) per man per day, but by 1696 the doctors were complaining that they were without pay from the contractors, because these in turn had received no money from the Government.[2]

The estimates for Spain for 1708 gave a physician to the hospital at £1 per day, a master chirurgeon at 10*s*., and a director at £1. The apothecary got 5*s*. per day, and the chaplain 6*s*. 8*d*. In Portugal the physician to the hospital had only 15*s*. per day, but the two master chirurgeons had 10*s*. each, and their four mates 5*s*.[3] The estimates presented to the House on 5 December of the following year included in extraordinaries charges for hospitals 'occasioned by the great numbers of sick and wounded . . . and the excessive dearness of all sorts of provisions'.[4] Establishments of hospitals varied, but they almost always had a 'director' with clerk, a surgeon, physician, and apothecary. Portmore in Portugal in 1711 had what looks like one of the earliest mobile hospitals—called by him a 'flying hospital'—where the director had two clerks, and there was also an assistant apothecary.[5]

The establishment laid down in the warrant of 10 October 1712 for Dunkirk, and met out of poundage, was:

four physicians	at £1 per day each.
one director and clerk	£1
one comptroller	10*s*.
one chaplain	6*s*. 8*d*.
two master chirurgeons	10*s*. each.
three chirurgeons' mates	5*s*. each.
three apothecaries	5*s*. each.

—a total cost of £8. 6*s*. 8*d*. per day.

[1] *Treas. Cal.*, iv, p. 95.   [2] Walton, p. 756.   [3] Ests. WO 24/47 and 24/48.
[4] *Journals Commons*, xvi.   [5] *Treas. Cal.*, iv, p. 258.

The hospital at Nieuport, established by warrant of 30 June 1714, had a director and clerk at £1, a physician at £1, a comptroller at 10s., a master apothecary at 10s., a mate at 5s., and a surgeon's mate at 5s.[1]

The best that can be said of the hospitals is that the standards may have varied. One author said they were places 'from whence (by the cursed management . . .) 'tis well if one half ever comes out till carried to the grave'.[2] The hospital at Port Mahon, although strictly a navy establishment, was as representative as any. From it a surgeon's mate wrote on 10 June 1711:

> The wounded men . . . are intirely neglected . . . the Agent will not comply with giving them the Provisions You (Dr. Stewart) order, and continually employs the Nurses about his own Private Affairs—such as Washing his Linnen, Scouring his Pewter, looking after his Horses and Cattle, So that the Sick Men are without any Assistance.

Men ordered a quart of milk and half a pound of flour were getting a pint of milk and three ounces of flour without anything else.

> Yesterday [continued the writer], One of the Men . . . showed Me a Piece of Beef, the Allowance of four Men for One Day, it was not half boyld and it weighed but two Pound two Ounces. I tasted the Broth which had no other Relish than Hott Water, the Agent not allowing any Salt or anything else to season it, neither does he allow any Utensills to the Sick Men to bring and eat their Victuals in. Those that has not Money to buy necessarys very often wants their Victuals for want of a Dish to put it in. Several others has shown me their Victuals which was of a piece with the former (viz) little and ill boyl'd, the Wine for the most part is so bad that it is not fit for a Xtian to drink, and is the occasion of so many Men falling into Fluxes. . . .
> The Sick Men are without Light or anybody to assist them, the ill consequence of which I dayly see by the Bruised Stumps, when these poor Creatures are obliged to rise in the night in search of a little Water. Neither is there Water enough at any time to serve the Sick Men halfe a day.[3]

---

[1] Ests. WO 24/75.   [2] *Recruiting Essay.*   [3] SPO 109/1.

In the same month four surgeons' mates from the hospital petitioned the Commissioners for Sick and Wounded:

The men . . . have generally Allow'd them . . . a pint of Wine (very often so sower that it does them more harm than good) and one small loafe of bread, 12 or 14 ounces of beefe, mutton, or goat boil'd without any greens or even as much as a little salt in the Broath. This is served them so Irregularly that very often it is dark before they have it . . . there is neither pott, dish, spoon, or any other utensil whatever allow'd . . . soe that those poor men that have no mony to buy these necessaries suffer miserably for want of them . . . as to poor Sick men that can't make use of this diet there is no regard, he (the agent) not allowing them as much as water gruell without stopping all their allowance for that day.[1]

On 27 October of the following year, three surgeons' mates further petitioned that, while food was charged for at the rate of bread 2d., meat $3\frac{3}{4}d.$, and wine $\frac{3}{4}d.$ per day, the flesh was generally old goat. The Queen had provided cradles, beds, blankets, sheets, dishes, bowls, spoons, and kitchen utensils, but, for the want of dishes, men often lost their dinner. At the issuing of wine in the morning, they frequently had to drink their day's ration from the steward's measure for want of a dish to keep it in till the evening. The agent was allowed 10s. for each burial, but normally wrapped up the corpses in a hammock and threw the 'Bodys into the Ground without Christian Burial, and so carelessly that Wee have seen the Doggs and Hoggs tare the Bodys out of the Ground'. One former patient reported that in his time at the hospital, only one man was buried in a coffin: he, exercising considerable foresight, had bought it himself.[2] The doctor who forwarded the mates' petitions was sent home and the Admiral, parading the complainants, warned them that, if there were a repetition, he would suspend them all.

Unless a man served in Flanders, the odds against him missing these delights were heavy. Peterborough wrote from Spain on 13 June 1706: 'our men, especially the newcomers, are most of them sick and in hospital . . . they will not be able to bear the marches through the burning mountains.'[3] Wyndham wrote in the following month: 'The weather is so excessive hot that our foot drop down dead on their march. We have a great

[1] Ibid.   [2] Ibid.   [3] H.M.C.H. of L., vii, p. 473.

many sick men that I take the best care I can to bring along with me.'[1] In another letter Peterborough declared: 'The heats (together with the strong wine which they cannot forbear drinking) have reduced all the new troops to such a condition that they are almost lost and useless.'[2] There is no record of anything being supplied which would have helped to prevent the men from drinking the strong wines. Conditions did not improve with the passing of time. A detachment of 300 landed at Valencia in 1711, for example, was reduced to 100 by the time the men reached their regiments.[3] It was no relief to go from the field into a garrison like Gibraltar. There, in 1706, more than half the men were disabled through disease from exposure. It was four years before orders were received for construction of barracks destroyed in the siege, and in 1711 the men were still burning for fuel such quarters as remained.[4] Worst of all, of course, were the West Indies, where, wrote Colonel Daniel Parkes (who had brought the good news from Blenheim to Windsor), he had 'endured more fatigue than if he had been anywhere else, and had had the plague, pestilence, and bloody flux, and had endured a hurricane which was as dreadful as possible for human nature to have an idea of'. Little wonder he reminded his correspondent of 'yr promise to me (when I had the honour to make your heart glad by telling you the news of the glorious victory at Blenheim), the Duchess and your Lordship bid me go home and take care of myself, and you would take care of my fortune. I had the honour to hear the same thing told me by the Queen at Windsor.'[5] Another letter of 5 May 1710, commenting on the 'great misfortune in the loss of men', remarked that every fifth or sixth man was dead of 'a fever with sore throat'.[6] Yellow fever reduced the strength of the West Indies battalions by about 40 per cent. per year, and one writer has remarked that 'one principal function of the

---

[1] H.M.C.H. of L., vii, p. 498. [2] Ibid., p. 483.
[3] Treas. Cal., 18 Nov. 1710.
[4] Ibid., 18 Nov. 1707 and 15 Aug. 1711.
[5] Ibid., iii, p. 542. His misfortunes were not at an end. He was later killed by a Captain Rokeby whose disobedience also led to considerable damage on the island. The case, after much preliminary procrastination, dragged on interminably before the Board of General Officers until Rokeby was found guilty of 'disobeying the Governor's orders, and encouraging his soldiers to do the same'. He was sentenced to be discharged the service. APC Col., ii, p. 650.
[6] Treas. Cal., iv, p. 171.

white soldiers in the West Indies was to die of the yellow fever'.[1] In 1703 Lord Donegall's regiment lost three out of thirty-six officers between 12 March and 6 May, and between the following 1 November and 6 July a further seventeen. Eight regiments stationed in Guadaloupe lost over 10 per cent. of their strength by death between 12 March and 6 May 1703, and a prohibition against the use of ships from the West Indies for fear of infection was issued in that year.[2] In 1707 Handasyde reported from Jamaica that because many of his soldiers had been carried off 'by a raging mortality' he required 300 to bring him up to strength.[3] These conditions detracted from the value of the ruling (not, of course, observed) that West Indies regiments should do only three years abroad, during which they were to 'be duly and fully satisfied every week, or as often as possible in money or provisions', and the officers to receive not only full subsistence, but full pay, subject only to the usual deductions for clothing, poundage, and one day's pay for Chelsea.[4]

The prohibition, mentioned above, against the use of West Indian ships for movement of troops appears bizarre in the light of the routine massacre which took place on naval transports and troopships—men coming ashore 'so sickly that the number ... was as large as after the greatest engagement'.[5] The description in *Tristram Shandy* was no doubt as valid in this reign as in the previous:

The sick and wounded were squeezed into certain vessels which thence obtained the name of hospital ships, though methinks they scarce deserved such a creditable title, seeing few of them could boast of their surgeon, nurse, or cook; and the space between decks was so confined, that the miserable patients had not room to sit upright in their beds. Their wounds and stumps being neglected contracted filth or putrefaction, and millions of maggots were hatched amidst the corruption of their sores.

Roderick Random was to work among similar scenes in a subsequent war.

A surgeon employed by the Commissioners for Sick and Wounded protested on 9 January 1703 that it was not true,

---

[1] *Last Post*, pp. 20 and 33.   [2] *Dom. Cal.*, ii, and SP Mil. 41.
[3] *APC Col.*, ii, p. 516, 20 March 1707.
[4] SP Mil. 41/3/53; *APC Col.*, ii, p. 420, Nov. 1702.
[5] *Treas. Cal.*, iii, p. 282.

as had been alleged, that men suffered because he was sick. 'We
have not', he adduced in refutation, 'lost 40 out of (the) 300.'[1]
At Deal, reported the Commissioners on 21 November 1702,
there were 400 sick—but there had been 'only 16 deaths in 10
days, and these of men who were ill-accommodated in their
ships, and past recovery before they landed'.[2]

Home stations could sometimes emulate the records of those
overseas, and even be placed in the same class as shipboard.
St. John wrote in 1707 to the Treasury about Lord Paston's
regiment which, after being ordered into garrison in Portsmouth, 'by reason of their continuance near a year and a half,
the sickness of the place, want of firing, and the badness of the
barracks . . . was reduced by death and desertion to about one
half of their number'.[3] Lest soldiers in such surroundings should
be deprived of the benefits of a sea journey or serving in the
salubrious overseas stations it was for some time the custom to
incarcerate all destined for abroad in Tilbury Fort, or at the
Savoy under the Provost Marshal, but the unhealthiness of
these places occasioned fevers 'by which . . . the numbers will
be very much decreased and the officers great losers'.[4]

Considering the circumstances in which the men lived, sickness in the northern European battle zone was not, compared
with other theatres, heavy. The most unhealthy place was
Dunkirk, which was not, of course, occupied until the armistice, when troops were sent there under Jack Hill to demolish
the defences, and a hospital was established. There was a
notorious sickness, known as Dunkirk fever, which may have
been a species of malaria, and records show that, in the early
days of the occupation, at least 2,400 men were sick at one time,
and the cost of medicines between 1 August 1712 and 5 April
1714 was nearly £12,000.[5] Apart from the French port, and
incidents such as the siege of Lille, which so overstrained the
hospitals of Menin and Courtrai,[6] isolated spots like Bergen-
Op-Zoom, of whose dangers Marlborough was fully cognizant,[7]
or the outbreak of typhus during the siege of Douai in 1710

---

[1] *Dom. Cal.*, i, p. 535.   [2] Ibid., p. 306.
[3] WO Order Book 136, p. 3, as quoted at Clode, i, p. 221.
[4] Evidence of Lords Commissioners for Trade and Plantations before House of
Lords on 19 Nov. 1707, *H.M.C.H. of L.*, vii, pp. 268–71.
[5] *Treas. Cal.*, iv, p. 603.   [6] Taylor, ii, p. 218.
[7] Murray, dispatch of 23 Nov. 1703.

(which seems to have been confined largely to the civil population), the armies in the Low Countries enjoyed reasonable health. These troops were the best fed, the most strictly disciplined, and most regularly paid, and, in addition, special commissioners for the sick and wounded were attached from the fourth campaign onwards.

There were some devoted men among those designated as doctors, but, as was the case with the devoted in many spheres, they received scant help or sympathy. There was little incentive to doctors to put themselves about when there were cases like those of Charles Angebaud, Apothecary-General to the Army in Ireland during William's wars, who, at the commencement of the reign was still due nearly £500 paid by him for medicines (and for which the regiments had actually been stopped), or of Samuel Fenner, former Governor of Hospitals in Ireland, still due over £1,000 in 1703.[1] Anne's Commons were reasonably expeditious in Fenner's case. They passed a bill for his recompense in eleven days less than three years later, although it would be rash to declare, on the strength of that, that Fenner in fact received the money.[2] Another fourteen doctors who raised and manned a hospital for William in Ireland were still petitioning in 1708 for almost £2,000 due to them,[3] while Major-General Wills, marine commander in Spain, went out of his way in a petition in January 1709 to state that he was not charging for hospitals he had maintained at his own expense in that country.[4] In conclusion there was the case of Dr. William Neilson. He was Master-Surgeon to the Hospitals, and Surgeon-General to the Army in Spain under Peterborough; Physician to the Hospitals under Galway; Director to the Hospitals in Portugal by a commission from home; and Physician-General to the Forces in Portugal under Portmore. He was stated to have done 'signal services in the absence of the Physician of the hospital and the sudden death of the Master Surgeon . . . without any reward expending all his own Money and engaging his Credit as much that he was almost ruin'd by his charitable preserving the lives of the Poor Soldiers which

[1] *Journals Commons*, xiv, 2 and 27 Jan. 1703.
[2] Ibid., xv, 16 Jan. 1706.
[3] Ibid., 20 Jan. 1708.
[4] Treas. 1/113.

must otherwise have miserably perish'd in a strange country for want of necessarys'. After receiving 10s. per day half pay on his retirement, he was cut off with nothing on 25 December 1714.[1]

REMOUNTS

In battalions, remounting was an expensive item. All officers—cavalry, dragoon, or infantry—supplied, and bore the cost of, their own horses. Originally the trooper and dragoon were on the same footing. The horse was the soldier's own property, paid for out of his own money, and his to take away with him on discharge. (Trouble over variations in this practice during the Protectorate is mentioned on p. 324, footnote 2.) He normally brought his mount with him on enlistment, but on occasion was supplied with it, and the price (approximately £15) deducted from his pay.[2] The requirement that the trooper should provide his own horse was not always to the benefit of the service, for, if it were lost, and he were unable to replace it, he had to leave as he was disqualified from further service. The rule was modified in 1697. Henceforth each man was stopped 4s. per month during the 'grass' or summer months when his outlay on subsistence of his horse was less. Each 1st of May the captains accounted to the men for the preceding year's stoppage, which was absorbed for the greater part in remounting. Any surplus after remounting was to be divided among the men with the exception of those given fresh horses who, in addition, had to pay double stoppages in the subsequent year.

By this method [the Regulation declared], the horses being in common to the whole troop, such trooper as shall be discharged upon his own desire, or shall be broke . . . shall have no pretence of challenge to his horse, neither is to have any money for him, but the horse is to remain in the troop for His Majesty's service, and to mount the trooper that shall be listed in his room; for which reason no Captain shall stop or make any deductions for the horse from the new enlisted trooper, neither shall any Captain discharge any man without first acquainting his Colonel, and giving the reasons thereof.

---

[1] SP Mil. 41/4. The petition is undated and calendared as 1713. This date, taken from extracts of Portmore's letter and the Queen's warrant, which are attached, is obviously wrong, as, in the body, reference is made to the (past) date 25 Nov. 1714, and the petition itself is addressed to King George I.

[2] Walton, p. 708.

And if it should happen that any of the troops should be disbanded, the several horses of such troops are hereby declared to belong to the troopers that ride them, and not to the Captain, and each trooper shall carry off the horse on which he served.[1]

The statement that the trooper should have no claim to a horse for which he had helped to pay, becomes understandable when it is borne in mind that a large part of the subsistence, from which the stoppage was being made, was recognized to be for his horse.

The levy money for newly raised horse or dragoon regiments was greater than for infantry regiments, and part was earmarked for mounting. A warrant issued in 1699 ruled that, after a non-commissioned officer or trooper had served for a year, the horse 'which His Majesty has paid for by the levy money' was to be given to him on discharge. If he had served less than a year, then the horse was to be sold, and the money credited to the Government.[2] When the troopers were without horses it became the custom to stop them 12d. from their 2s. per day subsistence to go towards the purchase of a remount.[3] The muster-master inspected horses on musters, and saw that the proper number was produced. He ordered defective horses to be disposed of for the benefit of the State, and their replacement by others fit for service. Horses killed or expended in the course of a campaign were replaced by the State, and the records show, for instance, regular payments by Monk in Scotland in 1654 of £8 to troopers 'for one horse lost on actual service' in order to remount themselves. Horses dying of disease or falling below standard, on the other hand, had to be replaced by the trooper himself. A passage from his Order Book dated 10 October 1656 reads: 'Order to Commissary John Clarke to give notice unto such troopers of the respective troops he musters who had small or bad horses, that they provide themselves with better or more sufficient horses, against the muster of the 25th November, or he is not to pass them.'[4]

The system was reviewed in 1714, and a new set of orders

[1] Rules in a Code of Regulations published in Dublin on 13 Aug. 1697, and quoted at Walton, p. 709.

[2] Walton, p. 710: warrant of 11 Mar. 1699.

[3] PGO WO 71/3, 25 June 1714.

[4] *Cromwell's Army*, C. H. Firth (London, 1902), p. 246. (*Cromwell's Army.*)

issued to deal with the remounting of dragoons in Great Britain 'whose horses are or may be lost or rendered unfit for Service by Accidents'. The dragoon, it was pointed out, had 14d. per day subsistence, of which 7d. was for the maintenance of the horse at dry forage, and 7d. for himself, keeping his accoutrements in order, and shoeing his horse.[1] (The soldier normally purchased horse-shoes from the regimental store, as the Government contracted for them wholesale and supplied regiments.)[2] Under the new system, the horse was to go out to grass at 3d. per day from 1 May to 31 October, both dates inclusive, and the dragoon was to be stopped 2½d. per day for that period. This would raise £61. 6s. 4d. per troop, and the dragoon would still be 1½d. per day better off than on dry forage, which would give him 'a due encouragement'. The snag, which necessitated this 'due encouragement' being brought to notice, was presumably that, in the summer time, the trooper would seldom pay 7d. per day for forage in any case. The Paymaster was ordered to pay the 2½d. per day to the colonel of each regiment, who was responsible for remounts. This should have been done by distribution of the money to the captains, who would then account to the men.[3]

The levy money on newly raising a regiment was probably sufficient for the horses, but, of course, cavalry horses were more expensive than dragoon horses. If there was a change of role—even if not of designation—during a regiment's life, difficulties arose. A system akin to that officially sanctioned to deal with losses by accident seems to have operated under the name of 'mounting money'. Such, at any rate, appears to be the most reasonable interpretation to put upon the case considered by the Board of General Officers on 11 July 1713. Four dragoons complained to the Board about the stoppage during the summer of 3d. per day 'mounting' money. The Board commented that this 'for the last war has been in a more than ordinary manner reasonable' since dragoons had been acting as horse. Having been opposed to the best of the French troops, it had been necessary for the officers to buy horses at a price not much inferior to that paid by the cavalry and the officers

---

[1] Entry Books WO 26/14, 10 June 1714.
[2] *Cromwell's Army*, p. 245.
[3] Entry Books WO 26/14, 10 June 1714.

had been 'left ... yet more considerably out of pocket'. No doubt the N.C.O.s and men appreciated the honour of being allowed to share this expense.¹ Peterborough's difficulties became understandable: 'I have made the finest regiment that ever was seen', he wrote to Charles III in June 1706. 'They are clothed, armed, and want nothing but horses.'² Three years earlier, prices for mounts in Portugal had been £12 for troopers' horses, and £18 for officers'.³ In 1706 officers of Rivers's regiment in Holland who were ordered to hand over dragoon horses to the Dutch, who had lost theirs *en route*, were recompensed at £12 per animal.⁴ By 1712 the usual levy money was stated to have risen to £15, although there were cases of £12 being paid.⁵ The cost had undoubtedly risen to the higher figure. Although, as in the infantry, levy money was, strictly speaking, payable only on first raising, there were, similarly, exceptions. In 1705 fairly large payments were made to officers of horse, dragoons, and foot, and to horse and dragoon regiments for horses killed 'passing the enemy lines, or dead of distemper'.⁶ Added to this source of loss was the enemy practice, which it is surprising the British did not, in the circumstances, copy extensively—the organization of horse-stealing parties.

Flanders was expensive in horses owing to the high incidence of sickness. On top of that, there were the murderous conditions in the ship transports. While sickness might occasionally be compensated for, there was no such redress for losses on shipboard, and the two together often made the levy money a mere token.⁷ Conditions for animals on board ship were probably worse than for men, and a sea voyage was a grave financial threat to any officer. The case of Conyngham's Dragoons who crossed from Cork to the Peninsula in 1704 is only a more extreme example of not unusual happenings. Conyngham embarked 286 horses, of which 141 had died when he presented his memorial of 18 December, and another 8 to 10 were feared for.⁸ The 141 included 27 horses 'of officers not in a position to

¹ PGO WO 71/2, 11 July 1713.   ² H.M.C.H. of L., vii, p. 483.
³ War Letters WO 4/2; Secretary at War's Minute no. 6, 10 Nov. 1703.
⁴ Entry Books WO 26/13, 10 Aug. 1713.
⁵ Treas. Cal., iv, p. 356.
⁶ Journals Commons, xv, 19 Nov. 1705.   ⁷ Fort., pp. 575–6.
⁸ He still could not quite equal the record of the Queen's Bays who, in 1690, lost every charger and troop horse in crossing from England to Ireland.

remount themselves'. The horses, he stated, were 'beate to pieces and stifled for want of rome'.[1] He and his regiment must have viewed somewhat cynically the proposal made in the same year that horses for Portugal should be purchased in Ireland 'on the grounds of cheapness, and ease of transport'.[2] The space allowed on board ship was officially laid down as 25 inches between rails, but the war was well advanced before the Commissioners of Transport had reached the stage of even inquiring into the erection at Harwich of a place for horses awaiting embarkation, or just disembarked. The cost for such a work for 400 horses was estimated at £1,200 to £1,300.[3]

How the armies were in the circumstances kept mounted at all, even at excessive cost to the officers, it is barely possible at this distance of time to discover. It was probably due to the firm allocation of individual responsibility, the greater popularity of the horsed arms which made recruiting simpler—and probably the fear of the mounted man that if he were left unhorsed he would have to join those who churned in the mud or sifted the dust below him.

[1] SP Mil. 41/3/237.
[2] SP Mil. 41/3/81, 19 July 1704.
[3] War Letters WO 4/2, 17 Feb. 1704; Treas. 1/82.

VI

DISCIPLINE AND MORALE

HE secured the affections of his soldiers by his good nature, care for their provisions, and vigilance not to expose them to unnecessary danger, and gained those of his officers by his affability; both one and the other followed him to action with such a chearfulness, resolution, and unanimity as were sure presages of success. . . . As no indecent expression ever dropp'd from his lips, so he was imitated by the genteel part of the army. . . . Cursing, Swearing and Blustering were never heard among those who were reckon'd good officers, and his Army was beyond all contradiction the best academy in the world to teach a young gentleman wit and breeding. The poor soldiers who were (too many of them) the refuse and dregs of the nation became . . . tractable, civil, orderly, and clean, and had an air and spirit above the vulgar. . . . He gave particular directions to the Provost Marshal to chase away all loose women. . . .[1]

This is a sad corps I am engaged in; vice raging openly and impudently. They speak just such language as devils would do. I find this ill in our trade, that there is now so much tyranny and knavery in the army, that it is a wonder how a man of straight generous, honest soul can live in it. . . . Armies which used to be full of men of great and noble souls, are now turned to a parcel of mercenary, fawning, lewd dissipated creatures, the dregs and scum of mankind.[2]

Thus, on the one hand Marlborough's biographer, on the other one of his best officers, on the state of his armies. There had been no such conflict of opinion in the previous reign. Waldeck said of the English armies in Flanders that their officers were ill paid, the colonels ill conducted, the men sickly, listless, undisciplined, and disorderly.[3] One of their generals declared he had not known 'among all the nations I have served with, any officers so remiss on duty as the generality of our own countrymen'.[4] Yet cavalry from the same stock was to be rated by Prince Eugene as the best appointed and finest he had ever

---

[1] Lediard, i, p. xviii.   [2] *Blackader*, p. 76.   [3] Fort., p. 338.
[4] General Kane quoted at p. 171, *A Review of the History of Infantry*, E. M. Lloyd (London, 1908). (*Lloyd.*)

seen. Further, he added, although 'money (which you don't want in England) will buy the fine Clothes and fine Horses . . . it cannot buy that lively air which I see in every one of these Trooper's faces'.[1]

Blackader, the officer quoted above, passing over for a moment that the army remained 'a sad place to be in on the Sabbath where nothing is heard but oaths and profane language', wrote on 26 July 1711:

> We have reason to admire (our General's conduct), and to believe he knows a thousand times better what is to be done than we do. Submissive obedience is our duty, and I give it heartily. If any man deserves implicit obedience I think he does, both in respect of his capacity and his integrity.[2]

On another occasion he warmed sufficiently to declare 'this is the finest army just now in the world', although he still remained wrathful against 'what I fear and hate in this trade, viz, cursing, swearing, filthy language, etc'.[3] Yet it seems that even the language did improve. 'Swearing terribly in Flanders' was not necessarily in itself evidence for or against good discipline any more than being bearded like a pard. It is a measure, however, of the Duke's influence on all ranks that his 'profound distaste for licentiousness either in language or in action' undoubtedly affected in some degree even this almost immutable characteristic of the British soldier. Study can lead, in fact, to only one verdict on his armies. The unflagging series of victories in the most successfully fought war in our history could have been achieved only by a well-disciplined force of good morale.

Whatever the talents of an army's officers, or the standards of its men, the enforcement of discipline requires a special code of laws and regulations. There are two distinct considerations in the provision of this framework. There is, on the one hand, the need to recognize offences which concern only members of the forces, such as mutiny, desertion, or making away with arms. The second consideration is that it is 'requisite for the retaining of forces in their duty . . . that soldiers . . . be brought to a more exemplary and speedy punishment than the usual form of the

---

[1] Hare's Journal as quoted in *Select Docs.*, p. 101.
[2] *Blackader*, p. 411.   [3] Ibid., p. 122; *Select Docs.*, p. 145.

Law will allow': that is, there has to be a special procedure for dealing with offenders.[1]

It was not until the period between the Revolution and the Hanoverian Accession that the law recognized any necessary connexion between these two complementary requirements. They had been dealt with separately in earlier years. Definition of offences was a matter for Parliament—desertion, for example, was made a felony under Henry VI, Stat. 18, cap. 19; the special procedure had been implemented by use of the Royal Prerogative. The two are conjoined today in the Army Act, which also makes provision for certain quasi-military offences by civilians, such as harbouring of deserters. It is now on the Army Act that, by constitutional convention, the army's existence and discipline in the last resort no doubt depend. The army did not depend to the same extent on the Act's progenitors, the Mutiny Acts, which are perhaps more important in constitutional than in military history. There were armies in existence prior to the first Mutiny Act of 1689,[2] and armies continued to exist between then and 1714 despite the numerous periods when there was no Mutiny Act in force.[3] The earliest Mutiny Act to stipulate the number of troops to be maintained was that of 1712—the first peace-time Mutiny Act of Anne's reign, Annae 12, cap. 13 (British troops were withdrawn from Flanders in June 1712, although the Treaty of Peace was not signed until April 1713). This did not become the invariable custom until 1721, although it was usual to declare in the preamble the purpose for which the army was maintained. Each Mutiny Act declared, to be sure, 'the raising or keeping a standing army within this kingdom in time of peace unless it be with consent of Parliament is unlawful', but the history of England is the record of unlawful deeds hallowed by time and custom. It dealt with military and associated offences, and sanctioned special legal process: but it was not—and the Army Act is not—the only Act under which soldiers could be punished for military offences. Other Acts

---

[1] e.g. Annae 2 and 3, cap. 17.

[2] Passed as the result of a mutiny in the Royal Scots when ordered to embark for Holland.

[3] There were no Mutiny Acts in the following periods: 12 Nov. 1689–10 Dec 1689 (28 days); 12 Dec. 1690–20 Dec. 1690 (8 days); 20 Dec. 1691–10 Mar. 1692 (2 months, 20 days); 10 Apr. 1698–20 Feb. 1701 (2 years, 10 months, 10 days); 25 Mar. 1713–25 July 1713 (four months); 25 Mar. 1714–5 June 1714 (2 months, 10 days).

passed in the sixteenth century for the better government of troops have not been repealed. They set forth penalties for mutiny, desertion, making away with arms, and so on. If at any time the present-day Army Act were to lapse before a successor became law, members of the forces would be liable, in theory at least, to the older Acts. The significant distinction is that as these earlier Acts do not provide for special process, trials would have to take place before civilian courts.[1] The Mutiny Act was not even, in strict law, the only authority under which special process could be employed to try soldiers. A military court recognized in 1380 under 13 Richard II, cap. 2, is still claimed as the only *permanent* legal military court in the kingdom; courts martial under the Army Act are legal only during the validity of the Act. The court of Richard II was to take cognizance of contracts touching deeds of arms and of war 'out of the realm, and also of things which touch war within the realm, which cannot be determined or discussed by the common law'. The limitation to matters not covered by common law does not hold good provided the Earl Marshal and Lord High Constable sit conjointly.[2]

This court seems, however, to have played no part from at least the seventeenth century onwards. Even James II, in all the shifts to which he was reduced through lack of legal sanctions, sought rather to pack the King's Bench, before which military offenders had to be tried, rather than revive the ancient tribunal. In his reign it was directed that even captured deserters were to be handed over to the civil magistrates for prosecution as felons.[3]

Apart from special sanctions or tribunals authorized by Parliament, however, the Royal Prerogative was exercised from the earliest times to frame arbitrary regulations for the maintenance of discipline. These regulations were known as Articles of War and prescribed both special punishments and special process. Information on the Articles is not plentiful, but the earliest extant set of general validity is that of 1673. Others of local application dating back to 1639/40 are known. The Earl

---

[1] Walton, p. 531.

[2] Since there has been no Lord High Constable since Henry VIII's reign, such a proceeding might justly be described as unusual in modern times. Walton, pp. 536 and 538.

[3] *JSAHR*, xxix, no. 118 (Summer 1951): Geoffrey Davies quoting WO 4, letter 10, of 20 Jan. 1687.

Marshal's Law and Ordinances of War, promulgated in 1639 to cover the expedition engaged on the Bishops' War with Scotland, were taken as the pattern for many years, but during the period 1660–89 there was a significant change. The Articles of 1673 and 1677 were close copies of the Ordinances of 1639. Monk's first commission as Commander-in-Chief gave him power to make rules for discipline, and to ordain pains and penalties, including 'loss of life or member'. In 1678, however, a note of the Commander-in-Chief's duties and powers expressly stated that he was empowered to exercise martial law 'provided that the same extended not to the taking away of life or limb'.[1] This became the convention, and in the 1686 Articles there appeared a paragraph to become familiar in subsequent issues that no punishment amounting to loss of life or limb should be inflicted in time of peace. The provision was written into the first Mutiny Act (1689), whose preamble stated that no man was to suffer loss of life or limb by martial law. Later Acts restricted the prohibition to the kingdom in time of peace. It has been claimed, and no doubt by convention it became so, that the Articles had the force of law only 'in so far as they were for the good Government of the Army: any Articles which infringed rights of the soldiers as citizens would have been *ultra vires*'.[2] There are, nevertheless, Articles of War extant which purported to interfere with civilian administration of justice. Essex's Ordinances in 1642, for example, included a provision that no magistrate should imprison any soldier except for a capital offence. Although this might be explained as an exceptional measure in time of war, the same explanation cannot be advanced for the somewhat similar provision in Albemarle's Articles of 1666.[3]

It was quite firmly asserted during Anne's reign that the Sovereign's power to convene the courts martial which administered these Articles derived, not from Parliament, but from common law, and the courts were convened under the Great Seal.[4] The Mutiny Act of 1703 (Annae 2 and 3, cap. 17) specifically stated that it did not extend to nor abridge Her

---

[1] Walton, p. 535.
[2] *A Constitutional History of England*, Mark A. Thomson (London, 1938), vol. iv, p. 297. (*Thompson*.) [3] Clode, i, pp. 444 and 448.
[4] Opinion of the Attorney-General 21 Jan. 1712 at SP Mil. 41/4.

Majesty's power of making Articles of War. If the Articles really were issued by virtue of the Royal Prerogative, such an abrogation would seem unnecessary, just as was the provision in the 1713 Act that Articles of War might be continued by the Queen beyond the seas, except in Ireland, 'as in time of war'.[1] The Mutiny Act 3 Geo. I was the first to give the Crown in express terms the power to make Articles of War for the better government of the forces within the kingdoms of England and Ireland. It is almost certainly true to state—it can be put no higher—that, at least until the passing of this Act, the disciplining of troops by special procedure did not entirely depend upon the somewhat erratic Mutiny Acts. A very large field was covered by Articles of War, issued by the Sovereign on the recommendation of the Commanding General. Once, however, Mutiny Acts were passed, then any Articles of War issued had to conform to the law as thus laid down, just as today the Army Summary Jurisdiction Regulations issued by the (former) Army Council have to conform with the Army Act. In a sense the Mutiny Acts gave legal sanction to the extra-legal processes and punishments prescribed by the Articles of War. There was no reference to the Articles in the early Acts, but the special procedure laid down by these Articles was adopted for special tribunals convened under the Mutiny Acts. The constitution and formation of courts martial dealing with offences created by the Mutiny Acts were thenceforward governed by the provisions of the Acts. For lesser offences there was, for many years, no interference with the special tribunals or their proceedings.

With this tacit legitimation of the Articles of War was associated a differentiation between home and overseas, rather than between peace and war, although the distinction in definition was small in days when troops were in general not overseas unless 'on active service'. After the passage of the Mutiny Acts, the provision of special process to deal with serious offences at home depended on the Acts, and not on Articles of War. Overseas, Articles of War continued to be issued. There were thus two sets of law to reconcile. The dichotomy was brought to notice as early as October 1702. Discussing the procedure for punishing participants in the disorders and plundering at Port St. Mary, the Attorney-General gave as his opinion that Martial

[1] Annae 13, cap. 4.

Law[1] could be applied to try overseas offences other than those specifically detailed in the Mutiny Act (mutiny, sedition, and desertion). Parliament's declarations against military law did not, he stated, apply outside the realm. The sanction in general's commissions to impose military law overseas 'according to the late Act of Parliament' did not mean that their powers were confined to offences under the Mutiny Act, but merely that action had to follow the *procedure* laid down in the Act. On the other hand, offences committed overseas could not be tried by court martial in England. They could not, indeed, be tried by the civil courts either, unless they had transgressed the common law. Once a man returned to England, special process not sanctioned by Parliament was abrogated, save in minor military matters. Even in the case of correspondence with the enemy while abroad (made a felony by Annae 2 and 3, cap. 17), for example, it was reiterated that, when tried in England, a man should come before his peers. The only exception to this rule was that, under the same Act of 1703, deserters coming into this country from overseas might be returned abroad for trial by court martial. As, under the Act, the penalty for desertion at home or abroad was death, this savoured of a distinction without a difference. So far as can be judged, Parliament seems to have accepted that its powers did not extend beyond the kingdom. The Mutiny Acts declared: 'Whereas no man may be . . . subject in time of peace to any kind of punishment *within this realm* by martial law. . . .' This was, after all, in keeping with members' solicitude for the liberties and well-being of their constituents, and their belief that soldiers out of sight overseas might, for consistency's sake, be kept also out of mind. Times have no doubt changed.

The categories of members of the forces to whom the Mutiny Acts were made applicable varied from time to time. In William's time the Acts applied to 'persons mustered and in pay as officers or soldiers'; but—in order to remove doubts about

---

[1] i.e. 'law promulgated under Articles of War'. 'Martial Law' was at that time frequently synonymous with what we term Military Law. Much of the political opposition to special disciplinary provisions for troops was due to inability to appreciate that it was possible to have two systems of law—civilian and military operating side by side. Military courts which tried civilians for offences such as espionage were called Courts Martial. Several examples in CM Warrants WO 30/18: the earliest on record there during Anne's reign is 4 Dec. 1704.

gentlemen volunteers serving without pay—Annae 6, cap. 18, amended this definition to persons 'mustered *or* in pay.' 1 Annae, Stat. 2, cap. 20, made officers and men in the artillery trains liable, but this was not invariably enacted until the Act of 1739, although after 1702 they were always liable while serving with the field army. Others of the Ordnance Corps were not detailed in the preamble to the Act until 1855.[1] It was also customary to make special mention of 'marines on shore' in any Mutiny Act which applied to them.

The means employed to bring soldiers to 'a more exem-plary and speedy punishment' were those familiar today—courts martial, and commanding officers of units. The powers of the commanding officers originally stemmed from the Articles of War, although there seems no reason to doubt the truth of Fortescue's assertion that disciplinary measures were applied at all times in the forces whether there was formal sanction or not.[2] The necessity, likelihood, and limitations of such measures are equally obvious. The legal conception of a Martial Court, as distinct from a Martial Judge, goes back, as we have seen, to the time of Richard II. By the seventeenth century there were apparently two types of court functioning—the Regimental Court Martial for the less serious offences, and the General Court Martial. The Regimental Court Martial was almost ex-clusively a disciplinary body. The General Court Martial could deal, in addition, with wider matters referred to it. The Regi-mental Court could award corporal punishment only if approved by the commanding officer, under whose orders it assembled. It consisted of five officers, plus a President not under the rank of captain, all from the regiment concerned. The Articles of War published in 1718 defined its sphere as the punishment of neglect of duty, disorders in quarters 'or other such crimes' (Article 17). Besides trying offences, however, it could be con-vened as the equivalent of today's Boards of Inquiry, and, as shown in the draft Articles of War laid before Parliament on 4 February 1717, could serve as a kind of Arbitration Court 'to judge disputes between soldiers and officers, and soldiers and soldiers'.[3]

The General Court Martial was a more versatile and power-

---

1 Clode, i, pp. 86 and 178. 2 Fort., pp. 313–14.
3 *Journals Commons*, xviii, 4 Feb. 1717.

ful body whose disciplinary functions were subordinate to its main role, in the same way as the other duties of the Regimental Court Martial were subordinate to its disciplinary activities. Trial of capital offences was reserved to the General Court Martial in the Articles of 1717 (based, no doubt, on others no longer extant). It was to consist of thirteen officers with a President of field rank, or the commander-in-chief of forces in a garrison. The Mutiny Acts in Anne's reign laid down that the death sentence required a minimum of nine in favour. This could be passed only between eight in the morning and one in the afternoon, and the provision was later extended to prohibit 'proceedings, tryall, or sentence of death' outside these hours.[1]

Originally the General Court Martial was either a standing court composed of the general officers of the army, or a court specially summoned by the Commander-in-Chief, or the Sovereign, to consider matters referred to it. One was appointed by Royal Warrant on 18 June 1670, for example, to deal with matters arising from the death of Albemarle. It consisted of the colonels of regiments, and was to assist the Duke of York in consideration of 'several particulars relating to military affairs, and the well ordering our forces, as well Guards as others'. Further such courts were convened by warrants of 7 February and 11 March 1688 to 'sit at the Horse Guards' every Friday for the 'redress of all disorders and grievances'. The warrant of 19 February in 1695 ordering a similar body described it simply as a meeting of the chief officers of the army: this may have been because by then the term General Court Martial was beginning to assume its more restricted meaning.[2] A Standing Court Martial of General Officers, presided over at first by Marlborough's brother, was convened in the Spanish Succession War to examine 'great abuses and disorders... by several officers and soldiers ... as well as ... disputes that have happened between officer and officer, and more especially . . . the ill-practices of some officers employed in recruiting. . . .'[3] This court was the progenitor of the notable Board of General Officers, already discussed in Chapter I. Although created to investigate 'great abuses and disorders' in connexion with recruiting, it soon did not so much extend its field as have territory bequeathed to it.

---

[1] Annae 2 and 3, cap. 17, and Annae 7, cap. 4.
[2] Walton, p. 543.   [3] CM Warrants WO 30/18.

A problem with which it was much engaged at one point, for example, was the failure of officers to turn up to sit on courts martial for which they had been detailed. The most extreme action it seems to have been moved to take was ordering, on 15 March 1709, that such absentees should be put under arrest 'during the pleasure of the Board'.[1]

Once the Mutiny Acts came into force, punishments were to some extent regulated by them. For those actions which they declared crimes, they prescribed either maximum or mandatory punishments. It was also accepted that, in time of peace and at home at least, no punishment affecting life and limb could be imposed for offences other than those for which it was prescribed in the Mutiny Act. In general, punishments were expressed as maxima; for example, for desertion in war time, 'death, or such other punishment as the court may determine'. Punishments for officers were death, imprisonment, or cashiering, which, the Articles of War laid down, could be imposed only by a General Court Martial.

The Act of 1712, as a peace-time measure,[2] dispensed with the death penalty, but authorized punishment 'not extending to life and limb' for mutiny, desertion, or striking a superior officer. The death penalty was restored, for the first time in peace, in 1717. The subsequent controversy had a topical ring. One of the offences for which the penalty could be imposed was refusal to obey the 'military orders' of a superior officer. As this appeared to make the soldier punishable for disobedience to an unlawful command, the wording was altered in the following year to refusal 'to obey any lawful command'.[3] The 1712 Act further prescribed corporal punishment 'not extending to life and limb' for immorality, misbehaviour, or neglect of duties. The Articles of 1717 specifically confirmed corporal punishment for selling or wilfully losing or stealing comrades' property —presumably even the colonel could be a 'comrade' within the meaning of the Article. A stoppage not exceeding half pay could

[1] PGO WO 71/1.

[2] Although the English troops were not withdrawn from Flanders until some months after the passing of the Act, it was quite apparent to the Government at the time of its enactment that they soon would be.

[3] 3 Geo. I, cap. 2; 4 Geo. I, cap. 4.

also be imposed, but only by court martial—the only stoppage legally permitted except under Sign Manual.

Although some of the punishments which remained seem sufficiently brutal today, the prohibition of those affecting 'life and limb' was no mere token. The 1639 'Lawes and Ordinances of Warre' had laid down, for example, that, for a second offence of blasphemy, the soldier should have a red-hot iron thrust through his tongue before being ignominiously dismissed the service.[1] This punishment is believed to have persisted at least until Charles II's time, when murderers or brawlers could have M or R branded on their right hands, and anyone guilty of mutilation was liable to have his ears or nose cut off.[2]

The Articles of War of 1717 laid down that blasphemers were to be handed over to the civil magistrates for punishment, and mutilation is not specifically mentioned.[3] In the large number of cases, however, where 'death or such other punishment' as might be determined is laid down, it may be taken that punishment 'extending to life and limb' could be imposed.

There were two officers concerned exclusively with military law and the administration of discipline, the Judge-Advocate and the Provost Marshal or Master. The office of Judge-Advocate-General dates from before the standing army, and the post was originally filled by lawyers. Responsibilities and powers were wider than today. Not only had the Judge-Advocate-General's representative to attend courts martial as legal adviser and clerk, but he was also responsible for bringing suspected offenders to trial. In due course, the office became responsible for the conduct of the prosecution in court.[4] The numbers of Deputy Judge-Advocates-General in the U.K. fluctuated, but they were normally to be found in Ireland and the Channel Islands at least.

The Provost Marshal was responsible not only for the apprehension and custody of all offenders, but also for execution of sentences, maintenance of order in camp or quarters, and, to a limited extent, on the march where he was particularly concerned with the baggage trains. He had also to see to the detail of courts martial, such as warning witnesses, preparing accommodation, etc. He was also responsible for camp sanitation. The

[1] Clode, i, p. 430.
[2] Walton, pp. 565–6.
[3] *Journals Commons*, xviii, 4 Feb. 1717.
[4] Walton, pp. 551–2.

Provost-Marshal-General in the field had a very small staff—three or four other ranks. His representative in regiments disappeared about 1680 when his duties were taken over by the Quartermaster.[1] It was part of the Provost Marshal's duty to supervise the sutlers, and he had the invidious task of ensuring that their prices were fair both to them and to the soldiers. Mother Ross says:

> As some of my readers may not know the provost's office, it will not be amiss to tell them that he attends the camp, and all offenders are put under his care, for which reason he commands a strong guard which goes everywhere with him; and the camp colour-men who always precede the army, escorted by the forlorn hope, choose the strongest house they can meet with for his quarters, that he may secure his prisoners. When we march, the less criminals are handcuffed in the middle of a guard; but notorious ones are chained hand and foot, and put into the bread waggons.

When the Quartermaster was assigned the responsibility for provost in regiments, the Drum Major became responsible for the actual infliction of punishments.[2]

The purpose of discipline is to make an army an efficient instrument for the overthrow of the enemy. Hence a commander must know and accept the limits within which he has to work. Each commander and his army are conditioned by their traditions and the social background of the country which has produced these. It will be of little use to a commander, for example, to produce a force of meticulous parade-ground discipline and mechanical obedience if to do so he has had to break its spirit, or has roused needless and deeply felt resentment. He is no better off if, for fear of breaking its spirit, he merely allows disorder and disobedience to flourish. Laws and

---

[1] A reference in the 1685 Articles for the Better Government of the Land Forces (during Monmouth's rebellion) to regimental provost marshals may simply mean the officer carrying out the duties of provost marshal. The foreign troops hired for duty with Marlborough's armies were rather more liberally supplied with provost staff. The Danes had a Provost Master General, three Officers of Justice, and an Executioner on their Headquarters staff; their horse and foot regiments had each a Provost Marshal and an Executioner, and their dragoons a Provost Marshal only. The Prussians had a joint appointment of Provost Marshal and Executioner in each regiment, but the Hessians had no Executioners. Ests. WO 24/46.

[2] Walton, pp. 464–5.

regulations are only the beginning—the bare bones of discipline which would of themselves produce nothing significant. The results depend on the flesh and blood of the junior officers, the men who clothe them, and the spirit breathed into them by their commanders. To appreciate the effects of these considerations, we must bear in mind differences of tradition, social relationships, the state of the military art, and other even more intangible factors. For example, the uncomplaining obedience of Marlborough's non-commissioned officers and men in almost all respects compels astonished admiration, or even a pang of jealousy: but along with this there went, to present-day eyes, appalling ill-discipline in his officers from subaltern to general.

There was more to this ill-discipline of the officers than the independence engendered by a sense of 'property' in the regiment and commission (for which the officer had paid good English pounds). Because of this, he was able and ready to 'sell up' and declare 'I will soldier no more' if sufficiently displeased. Pepys, however, encountered similar difficulties in his attempts to discipline the naval officers, who had not the same organized market for buying and selling commissions.

Officers were, in the main, gentlemen of substance who would view themselves as subordinate to their army superiors only for strictly limited purposes. Social rank, for example, could often outweigh army rank. The frequent 'angling' for honours arose not only from a human desire for honours, but also from a desire to give one the necessary status to handle unruly army subordinates who might be social superiors. The officers were always conscious that in the last resort their obedience was to the Queen, and the Queen alone. This was the rational ground for the intrigue and use of backstairs influence which appear so shocking to present-day eyes. By convention, officers were riotous, quarrelsome, and fast living, just as they were expected to be high-spirited and dashing on the field of battle. They could have been cured of the one set of characteristics by a single commander in one campaign, only at the expense of sacrificing the others. The effort, therefore, had to be concentrated on keeping any undesirable characteristics within bounds which did not irreparably reduce the officers' military efficiency.

The case of Captain the Master of St. Clair is an example of the brutality which was the obverse of dashing high spirits. The

Master, said by Marlborough to have had 'the misfortune to kill two brothers of Sir John Shaw',[1] was alleged by Sir John to have surprised with a concealed stick 'and beat the first brother twice over the head, then gave him a mortal wound of which he dy'd . . . and . . . afterwards shot the second brother before he had time to put himself in a posture of defence'.[2] St. Clair escaped, and Marlborough actually wrote to Raby, Ambassador to Prussia, to recommend him to the court, where, if later days are any evidence, his past was no doubt a useful testimonial.

The Duke was almost as considerate in the case of Cornets Strickland and Smith who, he wrote to Brigadier Palmer in October 1707, had been guilty of some 'expressions' not to taste. Previous allegations had been without proof, but as this time an affidavit was produced and the matter made very public, Marlborough wrote that they could not be allowed to continue to serve. On the other hand, he did not wish to court-martial them in case they lost their lives 'or suffer worse punishment'. There is, unfortunately, no trace of the future of the cornets, or it might have been possible to find out what 'worse punishment' was feasible in these hardy armies.[3]

Fortesque has summed up aptly:

The true saviours of the organised force were its officers . . . They had the peculiar qualities for good and evil which belong to the ownership of land—the pride of possession, the jealousy of greater neighbours, the instinct of friendliness and of protection towards humbler neighbours and workmen, initiative, readiness to accept responsibility, and . . . . independent spirit.[4]

It was undoubtedly of the officers General Bland was chiefly thinking when he wrote '. . . the English possess courage in an eminent degree, but at the same time . . . want . . . patience, and consequently that which it produces, obedience'.[5] It was the legendary convention of the Cavalier which persisted for the officers:[6] the soldiers provided the obverse—the stubborn, grim-

---

[1] Murray, iv, p. 499, 29 May 1709.   [2] Dalton, vi, p. 401.
[3] Murray, iii, p. 616.   [4] *Last Post*, p. 22.   [5] Lloyd, p. 171.
[6] But cf. Blackader: 'I am never easy among a club of English officers; but I have got all the English sent from me to other parts, and I keep the Germans; for they are not such bold profane sinners, and do not swear so much; and when they do it does not make my flesh creep, or sound in my ears with that hellish ringing echo that English oaths do.' It is doubtful if his preference for battlefield allies was the same.

fighting Roundhead. No good commander would try in the course of one war to effect a revolutionary change in those, even if he thought it desirable. Blackader, for his part, complained: 'Most captains of the army know nothing but to curse and swear at their men. I ordinarily every day put them, by prayer within the circle of God's protection'.[1] Yet he himself was to complain of ill-will from many officers for punishing 'immorality and scandals . . . so far as military law allows'.[2]

Just as the officers came from strata of society whose conduct had nothing in common with those from which the soldiers came, so the ill-discipline of the officers did not necessarily result in ill-discipline in the ranks. It might be proper, or indeed a point of honour, for a gentleman to query and dispute the orders given to *his* regiment: it was the duty and privilege of the soldiers to do precisely as they were told, even by a drunken colonel who regularly plundered their pay. The organization of society was such that the soldiers were initially conditioned to have implicit faith in their officers' judgement. This was no doubt as much the reason for their patient endurance of physical hardship and resolute conduct in the face of peril as the claim that 'there are no people in the world stand so much in need of being compelled to self-preservation as the English Foot Soldiers'.[3] Most of them were simple men. This made their disciplining, in general, easy. It also meant, as with simple troops today, that there were certain matters on which they were as gunpowder, and the normal rules and regulations hardly any longer applied. They endured persistent filching of their pay; but now and again, when matters became too desperate, they would suffer no more. Pay mutinies were so endemic that they were almost condoned. Plundering could be only restricted, not eliminated. When pushed far enough—and it had to be pretty far—they would also mutiny on the subject of food.

The punishments to which they were subjected were almost capricious in their brutality.[4] It is difficult to say how much routine physical ill-treatment took place. In Charles II's time officers had carried a staff about a yard long to correct their

[1] *Blackader*, 27 July 1705.   [2] Ibid., 20 June 1709.   [3] *Recruiting Essay.*
[4] Matched at times by equally capricious clemency. Twenty-five marines condemned to death for mutiny were ordered by the Queen to draw lots. The one unsuccessful man was executed, and the remainder transferred to another regiment, which had to pay the appropriate drafting fee. *Entry Books* WO 26/13, 5 Aug. 1707.

men, while sergeants were to use only their halberds, and corporals were restricted to musket rests. The *Pallas Armata*, indeed, posed the query: 'If a corporal broke a rest in beating a soldier, who should pay for it, the corporal or the soldier?' (The author was a Scot.)[1] It is unlikely, in spite of the clauses in the Mutiny Acts and Articles of War, that some striking did not persist.

The most consistent sentence was for desertion—'to be shot to death at the head of his regiment'[2]—but there is little correlation of severity in others. There were numerous monetary penalties, of which the heaviest authorized was £5 fine for officers and 20s. for men disobeying the provisions for protection of game.[3] There was a large variety of corporal punishments, some of which, although not specifically 'extending to life and limb', might well have as severe incidental effects. Lashing was very common. The most severe on record is the sentence of 12,600 lashes on a guardsman in 1712 for killing his colonel's horse in order to steal the hide. He actually received only 1,800, but did not die.[4] The Strapado consisted of tying a man's legs, then hoisting him to a height by a rope running through a pulley and fastened to his arms behind his back. He was then allowed to drop, and stopped with a jerk. Dislocation of the joints was a frequent result. The Wooden Horse—the normal punishment for drunkenness—was a rough imitation of the animal with planks at an acute angle for its back. The prisoner was mounted on it with his hands tied and his feet loaded with muskets, culverin shot, or other weights. While so seated he might have his crime exhibited on himself—pots and cups hung round the neck of a drunkard, or a wife beater dressed in a petticoat. Artillerymen were, appropriately, sentenced to 'riding the gun'. The cavalry had the 'picquet' in place of the horse. The prisoner mounted a block or stool, and his right hand was secured at full length to a ring driven into the wall, or to a tall post. The block of wood was then removed, and the only rest for his feet was two wooden stumps driven into the ground close to the post, and with bluntly pointed tops. While thus suspended, the offender might be whipped.[5] The power to order running the gauntlet—

---

[1] *Pallas Armata*, 1670/83, as quoted at Walton, p. 546.

[2] Blackader mentions one case in which he pardoned a deserter, only to be a member of a subsequent court martial which sentenced him to death at a repetition of the offence.   [3] Annae 2 and 3, cap. 17.

[4] Fort., p. 586, footnote.   [5] Walton, pp. 564–71.

the mandatory punishment for a sentry quitting his post or anyone selling or spoiling his arms (Articles of War 35 and 37, 40 and 42)—was, like other corporal punishments, reserved to courts martial.

Blackader had unusual ideas of the relative seriousness of offences, but he considered that 'extremes of severity should never be used when the example is not like to serve any good end.... In punishing faults I am sometimes inclined to hastiness. This day I had rather a violent, but short sally of passion, but I must say the occasion of it was just; for it was against the sin I am always angry at, that of swearing. It was soon over, and I am sorry I had shown so much of it.' Shortly afterwards, however, he was to write:

Going out to my post in the afternoon, I found that which I feared was come upon me; for I had the off-scourings of the garrison along with me, both officers and soldiers, most abominable vermin whom my soul abhors. O Lord, how long shall I dwell among men whose tongues are set on fire of hell! O, when wilt Thou deliver me out of this horrid and noisome company? My mind chafed and vexed the whole day with villainy and abominations of all sorts, both against the laws of God and man. Cursing, swearing, drunkenness, robbing, thieving, mutiny, etc. I made some severe examples of punishment, but was ill assisted by some officers, who rather encouraged the villains, so that I believe I shall not be so well liked among many of the English; but I shall be glad to be hated by such. I should be bad enough before such beings would love me.[1]

Punishments are among those things regarded differently according to varying time and place. On a wider view, there are three unchanging, indisputable necessities if a commander is to maintain good discipline. Their fulfilment will not of themselves produce good discipline, but it will not be obtainable without them. The commander must be supported by those above him; he must have adequate powers of punishment and reward; and he must, in turn, support his own subordinates.

Apart from complications involving foreign contingents (a problem we cannot yet be said to have mastered), Marlborough had from the governments in his earlier campaigns all the support and co-operation which he required. In these years, he stamped his personality on the army, and forged a weapon in

[1] *Blackader*, pp. 117–18 and 129–30.

Flanders that was to serve his country well. It was not until the disputes from about the time of Jack ('two bottle') Hill's promotion that serious trouble intruded. The task of stripping him of power and influence was, however, so delicate, and consequently so slow, that his influence was never completely eliminated. So strong was the impress of Churchill's personality and system that, even when the whole higher officer hierarchy became bedevilled with politics, the body of the army itself continued almost untainted. (There was a small bread mutiny after his recall.)

The greatest single item in the 'rewards' list was officer promotion. It was, of course, in theory, as today, the Sovereign's prerogative, with the further complication that the nominal commander-in-chief was the Prince Consort. Formal royal assent was always required for promotions among the higher ranks, but, like much else, the extent to which this was at all significant depended on relations between general and Sovereign. In the early years of the reign Marlborough forwarded lists of general officers and officers to be commissioned, in the tone of a routine matter, even down to the detail of dates for ranks, and pay and allowances. These were sent, not to the Secretary at War, but direct to the appropriate Secretary of State.[1] By the closing years of his office the position was changed. Even his nomination of Cadogan for the post of Lieutenant-General of Ordnance (Marlborough himself was Master-General) was rejected. Forthrightly, but unavailingly, the Duke had to declare in a letter to Godolphin that the Queen must 'in order to bring the discipline of the army back to that happy posture in which it was some time ago . . . let me have in my power to *oblige* the officers, and not to have anybody incoraged to think they can meet with preferment by others'.[2] Although this expressed succinctly one requirement for good discipline, the word 'oblige' shows the attitude of the time which made firm control by the commanding general difficult. In all the quarrels over promotion and appointments which bulked so largely in the latter part of the war—and especially in the Hill–Masham disputes—Marlborough's claim

[1] Murray, i, p. 248, letter of 6 Apr. 1704 shows an example.
[2] *England under Queen Anne*, G. M. Trevelyan (London, 1934), App. to Chapter II, vol. iii. (*Trevelyan*.) The occasion for the comment was a promise that Orkney should be made an English peer, but context and tone make it clear that Marlborough was thinking in general terms.

for power to promote was weakened, because even his Whig partisans looked on it as only a piece of patronage, to be regarded in the same light as rewards to placemen in the Commons, and not as an essential component of the commander's authority and power over his troops.

In 1710 the culminating point in stripping him of this power to 'oblige' was reached when the Ministry transferred control over promotions to a special Board.[1] Among the Board's first acts was the dismissal of all the Duke's brigadiers and others of what those of a similar attitude would no doubt call his 'circus'. The process never went quite as far as Harley wished. His suggestion was that, to make army and navy officers 'dependent on the Crown'—by which he meant dependent on him as the Crown's adviser—the tenure of general officers' commands should be annual, and that the Queen should allow no one but herself to dispose of regiments.[2]

By that time little remained of Marlborough's power over the senior officers who were up to their necks in politics. In 1710, for instance, Orrery, one of the generals in Flanders, wrote direct to Harley for permission to leave camp with a number of other generals, without the Commander-in-Chief's permission 'and return to England . . . when we think fit'. Improving on the occasion, he went on to allege that Marlborough was using his power only to create a faction in his own support, and asked that the writer be promoted major-general. The preposterous request for leave was granted, and shocked even Argyll (no friend to Marlborough, whom he criticized in the House of Lords while technically his subordinate) who was soldier enough to explain to the Commander-in-Chief when the permission arrived that he had not requested it.[3]

Marlborough, of course, had his partisan supporters. Among the most fervid were the old campaigners Meredyth, Macartney, and Honeywood. Like others in their own and succeeding times, they found that, although 'loyalty is a precious jewel many that wear it die beggars'. In November 1710 they were informed upon as having enthusiastically drunk a toast to the Duke's

---

[1] The President of this Board was Ormonde, the future commander-in-chief, to whom Marlborough had in 1704 given a demonstration of loyalty to subordinates by supporting him against a recalcitrant brigadier.

[2] *Cambridge*, p. 470.   [3] Murray, v, p. 172.

health, and 'damnation and confusion to the new ministry and to those who had any hand in turning out the old'.[1] They were cashiered. The orders for their stripping were passed through Marlborough who had to deliver them unopened. Orrery had his reward by being given one of the major-general's vacancies.

From then onwards, senior appointments were determined on political grounds—a procedure which Marlborough had eschewed even when it would have been to his own advantage. In 1702 at the very commencement of his power, he had resisted most strongly and successfully a determined attempt at a political purge by Rochester 'quite through to subaltern appointments.'[2] At the time of his downfall, procedure and tradition had been so firmly established that the Government had to 'go slow'. As a result, the purging was not complete when Anne died.[3] This, in its own way and time, was undoubtedly a substantial contribution to the triumph of the Hanoverian Succession.

No discipline can be enforced in an army if those responsible for it feel that every decision is liable to arbitrary reversal by their superiors. Equally, those to be disciplined must have the sure knowledge that they will be punished for their offences. There is little direct evidence of how much support Marlborough gave to his inferiors in the field, but the free hand he always gave the Board of Ordnance in managing their own business, the support he himself demanded, and the whole cast of his nature would indicate that it was considerable. He was, however, undoubtedly careful of delegating extensive powers of punishment. This is in keeping, in a way, with the character of a man ahead of his time in concern for his troops. On 22 February 1704, for instance, he assured Ormonde that, in granting warrants for court martial, he almost invariably reserved death sentences for his confirmation. Although not, by present-day standards, an exceptional measure, this was un-

---

[1] They claimed in their defence that they merely drank 'a health to the Duke of Marlborough and confusion to all his enemies, a thing usual in all armies, though it happened at the time to be equivocal'. Lediard, i, p. 237.

[2] Churchill, ii, pp. 87–88.

[3] The immediate cause of the failure has been claimed to have been Oxford's slowness in raising the £10,000 required to buy up the commissions of the Hanoverian officers whom Ormonde aimed to compel to 'sell out'. Mahon, *History of England*, quoted at Clode, ii, p. 63, footnote. It was, at any rate, apparently established that there could be no question of widespread arbitrary dismissals or cashiering.

doubtedly then unusual, and if we are to judge, for instance, by the proclamation on plundering (see below), it was not applied strictly throughout the war. The States General on 18 March 1706, in an attempt, no doubt inspired by him, to impose discipline on the foreign troops, laid down that all sentences in armies be remitted to the general-in-chief for approbation, but how literally this was interpreted is not known.[1]

The support Marlborough himself received declined, of course, with his prestige in the Cabinet. The interference with promotions has already been mentioned. While there is no concrete evidence of a specific punishment being rescinded, his own knowledge of the attitude at home undoubtedly made him 'go easy' at times. He dared not, of course, in the later years take any action against those high in the favour of his political rivals. He himself, although feeling this strongly, seldom spoke out on the subject. One exception was his protest to the Queen in 1710 at the proposal to appoint Jack Hill Colonel of Rivers's Regiment and give Rivers himself the post of Lieutenant of the Tower. 'It is, Madam,' he wrote, 'to set up a standard of disaffection to rally all the malcontent officers in the army.'[2] In 1711 he snapped once more when he wrote that if it were not made evident to the officers that he enjoyed the Queen's protection it would be very difficult to maintain discipline—a somewhat obvious truth which has not, however, ceased to be flouted at intervals since then.[3] He had already, in fact, pointed the same lesson in the previous year to Boyle when, as already mentioned, in an otherwise unremarkable letter on winter quarters, he suddenly broke out: 'it is grown too much in fashion to canvas and reflect on what I doe without any consideration of the service'.[4]

When, in 1711, the Sovereign vested power and authority for punishment, and redress of grievances in the Board of General Officers, Marlborough's power was virtually at an end.[5] So too was the war, and the disbandment of the army followed soon afterwards. Its discipline and morale had little time to deteriorate seriously.

[1] Murray, ii, pp. 454–5.
[2] Trevelyan, iii, p. 43.
[3] Churchill, iv, p. 382.   [4] SP Mil. 41/3/121, 11 Oct. 1710.
[5] SP Mil. 41/4: 'Regulations for the Better Government of the Forces', issued 1 May 1711.

In all the theatres there were three major disciplinary problems regarded seriously, but never solved, by those responsible for the English armies. They were—officer 'absenteeism', pay frauds and mutinies, and plundering. Yet one characteristic in which the troops were notably ill-disciplined by present-day standards does not appear to have caused the same concern. This was straggling on the march.

Blackader, with a hardy seasoned regiment, tells how in one of the marches in 1705 'a great many of the army fell down with weariness and several died from the scorching hot weather. . . . A soldier's life is an odd, unaccountable way of living. One day too much heat, another too cold. A bad, irregular way of living.' His comments would hardly serve today as the findings of the inevitable Board of Inquiry. Wyndham, again, in an official dispatch from the Peninsula, was to write:

> The three battalions are all so very much fatigued that though I came in here at ten in the morning, there are still 200 men wanting. . . . The weather is so excessive hot that our foot drop down dead on their march . . . the three battalions do not make above 800 men.[1]

A junior N.C.O., let alone a higher commander, who confessed to having turned up without 20 to 30 per cent. of his strength would today have a difficult time justifying himself. Yet there were circumstances which we are apt to overlook—poor roads, difficulties in feeding, and lack of suitable clothing were some of the factors. Matthew Bishop, as already noted, remarks almost in an aside while telling of a march about the time of Oudenarde: 'I remember the greater part of the Welch Fusiliers marched without shoes.'

Absenteeism on the part of officers was not simply a military offence. It was a tradition.[2] In 1711 it accounted for 174 officers from the Spanish theatre alone. The situation was not as bad in Flanders, but intimation that a regiment was earmarked for the Peninsula, or for such stations as the West Indies, immediately sent up the non-effective figures.

A considerable number of officers succeeded in 'wangling' leave in one fashion or another—one brand of absence they

---

[1] *H.M.C.H. of L.*, vii, p. 498.

[2] Nor was it one confined to the army. Pepys had found the problem in the navy most intractable.

dignified with the title 'Secretary at War's Leave', because they normally by-passed their commanding officers and generals for sanction. Anyone, however, who was really serious about staying in Britain was untroubled by lack of success in obtaining permission from any source. He simply stayed away from his regiment—sometimes for as much as five years.[1] In October 1701 King William had struck fifty-nine officers of the Irish establishment off the half-pay list when they refused to go to the West Indies. Queen Anne, in a burst of accession clemency no doubt, restored them in June 1702, but they did not repent and were finally struck off on 29 January 1703.[2] Officers who were not themselves Irish were not normally so enthusiastic to stay in the Emerald Isle. In September 1708 the Queen had to have special orders issued that all with commands in Ireland should 'repair at once to their posts where She thinks they should be at this time.' There were, of course, exemptions—this time Members of Parliament.[3]

The officers struck off half pay were undoubtedly, by the standards of the times, unlucky. Those sufficiently determined seldom found it impossible to evade overseas service without being put in the position of refusing point blank. The tendency, so outstanding in all officer discipline of the time, to persuade, cajole, and threaten in that order, rather than command and punish, was particularly evident in dealing with absenteeism. Everyone constantly complained of it: yet a biographer considers it worthy of special mention that one of Stanhope's outstanding characteristics while in Spain was that he always *favoured* officers actually with the force over those taking their ease in England. Marlborough, too, never ceased to protect those officers actually in the 'hottest part of the war'. His letter to the Secretary at War on 9 April 1703 was only one of several in which he urged strongly that nothing be done 'which may enforce hardship' upon officers in the field.[4] On 17 March 1705 he wrote that all officers who did not rejoin their units in Flanders by the first boat would be 'respited upon the first

---

[1] Fort., pp. 573-4.

[2] *Historical Manuscripts Commission: Report on Manuscripts of Marquis of Ormonde*, K.P. (London, 1899), vol. iii, p. 468. (*H.M.C. Ormonde.*) Secretary at War: Out Letters (Ireland). (*Ireland WO 8.*)

[3] *Dom Cal.*, i, p. 251: Hedges to Rochester, 14 Sept. 1708.

[4] War Letters WO 4/2.

musters' and their commissions disposed of.[1] In 1709, however, he was still dealing with the same subject. In that year he wrote to Godolphin that he had ordered all to be at their posts by the end of the month, and requested that the Queen should 'show a *dislike* of any that should stay after that time'.[2]

The Board of Ordnance had the same difficulties with their civilian officials. Reporting to Marlborough in 1704 on the refusal of a Mr. Hannaway to go to Barbados, they commented: 'It is impossible to carry on Her Majesty's Service if persons from the Establishment shall pretend to dispute the Commands of the Board, and we therefore hope your Grace will think it reasonable to discharge the said Mr. Hannaway from his present employment which will for the future put a stop to such Practices.'[3] It is indicative of the spirit of the times that it was probably easier to take such disciplinary measures against civilians than against officers holding the Queen's commission. In 1714 absenteeism among the officers was still at least recognized, for there is a reference in a paper of Lord Sempill's to a deduction of 4*s*. in the pound from the pay of field officers absent more than six months in the year.[4] There are cases on record of officers being cashiered for absence, but in all of them which I have seen misspending, or making away with levy money was also alleged. The earliest sentence of cashiering I have found was on 15 October 1709. Two marine officers were court-martialled under a convening order of 5 August 1705 for failing to embark for the West Indies with their regiments, but there were also charges of neglecting to put the regiments' clothing on board—which suggests misappropriation. This court martial is noteworthy in that the President was nominated and ordered to find his own court, not exceeding twelve others. The normal practice was to detail the entire court and President (as today), or simply to order 'the senior member to act as President'.[5]

Any determined attack on absenteeism was, of course, hindered by the existence of conditions which connived at or compelled some breaches of regulations, and facilitated or

[1] Murray, i, p. 608.   [2] Churchill, iv, p. 54: letter of 11 Mar. 1709.
[3] Ord. Letters WO 46/6, 4 Apr. 1704.
[4] *Treas. Cal.*, iv, p. 618: dateless paper probably before 1 Aug.
[5] CM Warrants 30/19 and WO 30/10.

legalized others. St. John ran into the difficulty in 1705. Noting 'with displeasure' the number of absentees from Spain, he discovered that most of them were field officers or children. Since many of the field officers probably had other commands, this was understandable: but precisely such exemptions as these made evasion by others easier. St. John pointed out that the Queen had some time previously ordered that there were not to be more than two officers in a regiment not old enough to serve. When the regiment was ordered overseas these were to be changed with other regiments.[1] In the regiments detailed by him, however, there were five children among the absentees. Out of twelve units in Spain, only two were at that time without absentees. Six of those missing were commanding officers (two had never been with their regiments), three were sick, and three were probably on recruiting parties. The total missing was thirty-six.[2] One would not expect St. John to persist for long in unspectacular drudgery like absentee tracing, and the next time the problem in the Peninsula appears to have been tackled seriously was in 1708 when Walpole found there were eighty-three absentees from seventeen regiments. This included officers on recruiting parties, but 'the recruiting service being over', he asked Sunderland, the Secretary of State, to order them to their posts and that 'examples be made of such as shall neglect their duty'. The confusion of authority is underlined by his comment that there were not more than five fit for duty who had leave of absence from his office. The letter is endorsed (presumably by Sunderland or by his orders) 'all to be broke that don't go immediately to their posts'. On 12 July the Secretary of State, after consulting the Queen, instructed Walpole to issue orders to the absentees to return 'so that in case of disobedience they may be immediately broke'.[3] The figures were down to thirty-nine by August. Most of the remainder had legitimate, or quasi-legitimate excuses; but they still represented a drain on their regiments.[4] By 20 January 1711 the figure had climbed to 174 from thirty-seven regiments. These units were deficient of a further thirty-seven officers who were prisoners of war. Included in the absentees were five chaplains (of whom three had

[1] See p. 337. [2] SP Mil. 41/3/10, 3 Dec. 1705.
[3] SP Mil. 41/3/184 and SP Mil. 41/3/193.
[4] SP Mil. 41/3: letter of 3 Aug. 1709.

substitutes serving), four children, three officers who had never been with their regiments, a few on recruiting parties, some on duty with the train in Flanders, and half a dozen who had not even troubled to think up a weak excuse. Three colonels were missing from the Scots Guards, there was one absence due to gout, and another officer was 'indispos'd and infirm by the gout and palsie'—which does not, however, appear to have indisposed him from drawing his money.[1]

Chaplains always stood high on the absentee list. The Vicar of Kinsale was so consistently employed in deputizing for brethren who should have been with troops in his neighbourhood that the Comptroller of Accounts eventually recommended a deduction of 2s. from each chaplain for whom he acted to be paid to the Vicar.[2] Samuel Noyes, chaplain to the Royal Scots, wrote from the Continent in 1703:

> The 26th (May) was observed strictly as a Fast by the Duke's order, a day or two before which his Grace required an account of what chaplains were absent and the return was made 11 out of 24. They are either in England, Ireland, or the Collonel's Pockets.

On 2 July 1704 he noted that they had only seven chaplains out of twenty-one, and not one with the hospital 'where there is most need'. The Blenheim Roll states that there were, in fact, fourteen chaplains, including Hare, present with the British army at the battle. In a subsequent letter, Noyes reported Hare's arrival on 4 July, and it is possible he was accompanied by others.[3]

There was always a number of officers unable to reach their units for lack of money after recruiting, recuperating, or visiting the kingdom on duty,[4] and we have seen how engineers liked to hold the infantry companies with which they usually started their careers.

The purchase system probably made conclusive action against absentees more difficult than against any other offenders. It made colonels not only commanders but proprietors of their regiments, captains not only commanders but proprietors of their companies. Each regiment was, in fact, a little independent

---

[1] SP Mil. 41/3.   [2] *Treas. Cal.*, iv, p. 73.

[3] *JSAHR*, vol. xxxvii, no. 149 (Mar. 1959), p. 37: no. 151 (Sept. 1959), p. 134: letters of 7 June 1703 and 2 July 1704.

[4] A number of cases in Treas. 1/169; also references in *Recruiting Essay*.

and self-contained possession.[1] Consequently, not only the colonel, but also his superiors felt, to a greater or less extent, that what he did with his independent and self-contained possession, and, above all, how he did it, was, within limits, his own business. In particular, his presence was not a matter of supreme importance so long as the regiment's duty was well and loyally performed.

George Monk, a commander-in-chief not overburdened with faith in human nature, gave his recipe for good discipline in the words: 'if you intend to have a well commanded army, you must pay them punctually, and then your general can with justice punish them severely'.[2] Parliament's inability to heed and learn undoubtedly facilitated Charles II's Restoration. In Anne's reign the same failure was responsible for all the mutinies of any size except the half-hearted outbreaks towards the end, ostensibly over bread, but really due to demoralized disgust at the treatment of Marlborough, and Britain's desertion of her allies. The pay system, and lack of system, it would be little exaggeration to say, were the root cause of all indiscipline. The financial responsibility they bore gained the officers a certain latitude. Pay mutinies by the soldiers frequently achieved what reliance on ordinary justice did not achieve.

The petitions over arrears submitted to the Lord Treasurer, the Board of General Officers, Parliament, the Secretary at War, or anyone who might, by some possibility be less unlikely to act than the 'normal channels', littered the records of the time like a paper chase, and accustomed the army to argument and pleading rather than obedience, and to seek always a new court of appeal, rather than be bounded by one's own superior officer. It was a problem, of course, as old as the standing army, and almost as old as the army itself. Measures for dealing with pay mutinies occupied a hallowed place in the Articles of War. The Mutiny Acts specifically ordered No. 14 of the relevant issue to be read to recruits on enlistment:

... and if any number of soldiers shall presume to assemble and take counsel amongst themselves for the demanding of their Pay or shall at any time demand their Pay in a mutinous manner, any inferior

---

[1] *Last Post*, p. 13. [2] Lloyd, p. 182.

officer accessory thereto, shall suffer death for it, as the heads and very leaders of such mutinous and seditious meetings, and the soldiers shall be punished with death. And if any captain being Privy thereto shall not suppress the same, or complain of it, he shall likewise be punished with death.

Pay was repeatedly used, nevertheless, as a sanction or bargaining counter. The Board of General Officers themselves began their career by requesting and finished by instructing the Paymaster to withhold money from recalcitrant regiments or officers. Little wonder that they found themselves not only swamped with petitions directly submitted, but also being asked by the Lord Treasurer and others to investigate petitions submitted elsewhere. The Board no doubt formed for government staffs a very convenient further excursion upon which awkward missives might be sent in the hope that something might have turned up before they returned. Even it grew impatient as the flood mounted. On 9 February 1713, in a pique at the torrent from disbanding units, it called for punishment of privates who, it alleged, had petitioned falsely regarding non-receipt of pay.[1] It was not, of course, to the irregular method of seeking redress that they objected, but to their being misled by false statements.[2] One of the more intriguing petitions was that submitted to the Lord Treasurer on 7 November 1706 on behalf of the officers of two marine regiments deprived of their pay for nearly eight years, 'in which they have had many assurances' but pay for none except three, 'by which most of them and their poor families are in a miserable condition and are not able to appear abroad'. (They had, in fact, been paid up to 17 February 1697.) This not unusual species of document was distinguished by being signed by thirteen subalterns and the wife of a fourteenth. The prevalence of such neglect was bound to result in breaches of discipline. Ill-organization breeds improvised methods of redress. In addition, of course, there were many matters in which the officers and men felt that they had a right to intervene, since part of their pay was taken to provide the finance. The Paymaster of

[1] PGO WO 71/2.

[2] The Queen herself could be more appreciative of the deleterious effect on discipline of constant 'petitioning' and querying of orders. In Nov. 1712 she sternly 'would not suffer to be read' a petition by twenty-two commanding officers regarding instructions about precedence. They were informed that she 'resented their Proceedings and . . . expected Her orders should be obeyed'. Ibid.

Marines, for instance, was appointed as the result of a petition by five colonels, whose officers themselves subscribed for his allowance in the hope, no doubt, that the investment would save them from their fate of the previous war when 'in a deplorable condition . . . multitudes . . . starved'.[1]

I have come across only two petitions to England from the troops serving directly under Marlborough. One, presented to the House of Commons on 17 December 1706, asked for debentures in payment of their wages for the Irish campaign—a mere fifteen years previously. The House ordered the petition to lie on the table. From a further submission of 22 December 1707 (from 'several officers of Her Majesty's Armies in Flanders') it appears that they eventually received 'some part' of the money, but had the effrontery to ask for more.[2] There are almost bound to have been other collective petitions from Flanders, but their relative scarcity is a tribute both to the way in which Marlborough himself looked after his armies' interests, and to their regard for him as the final source of redress of grievances.

When petitions failed there was always mutiny to turn to: it was seldom unsuccessful. The most persistent mutineers were the marines. There were several good reasons for this. One was that they were often at sea, and once aboard they had little chance of receiving any money, certainly not until they came ashore again. Another was that the physical act of embarkation provided for all soldiers a sort of Rubicon which it became the tradition not to cross until some arrears of pay were eliminated. It was recognized, indeed, that troops about to embark had a priority in claims on such money as the Treasury might have available. Two months' arrears was about the minimum for which troops would compound. One of the most serious causes of disaffection among the marines, however, was bureaucratic pendantry. The Mutiny Acts laid down that, before troops were paid, they must muster. This was interpreted as mustering by regiments. As there were no known cases of complete regiments of marines serving on any one ship, implementation of the order presented certain difficulties. The first solution applied was not to pay the men at all. After representations over a considerable period, and trouble which threatened to be really serious, special permission was issued by the Lord High

<hr />

[1] *Treas. Cal.*, ii, pp. 11, 19–20.   [2] *Journals Commons*, xv.

Admiral to muster by companies.[1] The disturbance with the greatest potentiality of danger was probably when a body of unpaid marines refused to march from St. Albans during the threatened invasion of 1708. The most spectacular was when thirty-nine of them marched out of barracks at Portsmouth to lay down their arms in public.[2] On 28 March 1709 a number of Churchill's marines refused to go aboard at Spithead 'and in a mutinous manner came in a body to the town'. There was considerable alarm over this incident, but troops of the line quashed the revolt.

The earliest mutiny of the reign, whose pattern was followed in the others, occurred in December 1702. Eighty-three men of Colembine's regiment walked out from Tilbury while awaiting embarkation. The Secretary at War, ordering by letter that they should be seized by troops, showed his displeasure in draft, at any rate, by striking out the customary 'Our Trusty and Well-beloved' before Colembine's name. On the same day (11 December), however, he wrote to the Lieutenant-Governor of Tilbury to say he was sending Major-General Cholmondeley with the Deputy Paymaster to give the men their sea pay and further subsistence. Men returning were to be pardoned, and, to deal with the others, two troops of horse and one company of guards were ordered out. Seventy-three men who marched on London with their arms and colours were given a pardon, but the trouble flared up again on 15 December. This time the grievance was such that one officer asked to be allowed to resign his commission. Not so fortunate as his men, he was put in the Tower.[3]

These examples could be multiplied. They were repeated in most theatres, and all throughout the war. The surprise is not indeed that there was this chronic rash of small-scale 'strikes',[4] but that there was no large-scale upheaval. The conditions under which the men served, and the alarmed fashion in which the authorities immediately sought to redress otherwise unheeded grievances once the troops chose to demonstrate that their patience was exhausted, certainly provided ample provocation.

[1] *H.M.C.H. of L.*, vii, pp. 205–7: orders of 16 Feb. 1704 and 14 Jan. 1708.

[2] Ibid., viii, p. 67; SPO, vol. xiv, 29 Mar. 1709.

[3] Marching Orders WO 5/11.

[4] The word, despite military susceptibilities, is the appropriate one, in view of the men's limited objectives and the authorities' reactions.

Pay was a problem to which, if there was no money, there was no answer. It was not so with food which could, in necessity, be provided by plundering, or, on an organized basis, foraging. The besetting sin of armies as they visited themselves on the population was the way in which they swept a country clean, the kind of imposition which led Marlborough to write to the J.P.s of York on 11 April 1708: 'I shall on all occasions use my utmost endeavours that the troops which may be thought necessary for the service and security of the nation do not prove a burden to any part of it.'[1] In hostile countries armies were followed by traders who purchased the soldiers' loot. Mother Ross has left a picture of thoroughgoing pillage.

. . . we miserably plundered the poor inhabitants. . . . We spared nothing, killing, burning, or otherwise destroying whatever we could not carry off. The bells of the churches we broke to pieces, that we might bring them away with us. I filled two bed ticks, after having thrown out the feathers, with bell-metal, men's and women's clothes, some velvets, and about a hundred Dutch caps, which I had plundered from a shop . . . besides the above things, as I was not idle, I got several pieces of plate, as spoons, mugs, cups, etc. . . .

Marlborough realized that this kind of conduct would not normally endear his troops to enemy, allied, or neutral civilians. His dispatches are crammed with injunctions, demands for investigations, and promises of recompense in connexion with plundering. The experienced eye may be forgiven if the constant repetition suggests not only solicitude but a certain lack of success. It is undeniable, nevertheless, that, on the famous Danube march, an army which marched right across Germany won not only plaudits for its military performance, but, probably for the first time in history, the goodwill of the local inhabitants because the soldiers paid their way. The same high standard could not be kept up all the time, but some restraint was observed. Even in Spain, faced with a largely hostile population and dependent on an inapt supply system, an army suffering the greatest demoralizer of all—defeat—produced nothing like the excesses committed under the Iron Duke of Wellington. As a politician Marlborough was aware of the desirability of good relations with the local inhabitants. As a commander, he was

[1] Murray, iii, p. 696.

even more aware of the necessity for feeding his own men. In return, therefore, for keeping down plundering[1] he demanded fairly rigorous levies of food and grain from the districts in which he was operating—but saw the supplies were collected in good order and paid for. He frequently split his armies into several columns while on the march in order to 'spare the countryside'. He saw that his men were fed as well as the standards, and better than the organization, of the time normally allowed. In return, he demanded orderly behaviour from them. Some plundering was, of course, a legitimate perquisite. Samuel Noyes wrote on 2 July 1704:

Our Army were allowed to plunder the countrey, only forbid to meddle with Churches or burn houses, but they did both, and tho the Hussars had been beforehand with them they brought in great quantities of Live cattle, Fowles, and Household Goods. Some strayed so far for Booty that they did not return til next day, and the Duke fearing such looseness might cause half our army to fall into the Enemies hands, gave Orders the 30th that the Officers of every Regiment should call their companies together and tel every man personally that if any One for the future was caught takend any manner of things from the Boors he should be hanged without mercy.[2]

'If any soldier', ran another order which the Duke caused to be read out at the head of every squadron and battalion on the invasion of the Spanish Netherlands after Ramillies, 'shall be taken plundering or doing any other damage to the said inhabitants, their houses, cattle, moveables, or other goods, he shall immediately be punished with death . . . and the more effectually . . . to keep strict discipline', the regiments to which offenders belonged, '. . . shall be obliged to make good . . . all . . . loss and damage . . . without any other form or process than the apprehending such soldiers in the fact, who (as is above said) shall suffer death without mercy'.[3] Which is a standard, at least, to which today we do not aspire. On 30 August 1703 Noyes had written on the subject from St. Tron:

. . . some of our Danes, two officers being with them, barbarously plundering a very pretty church and the Priests House, spoyling

---

[1] See his dispatch of 10 Nov. 1708 to the Earl of Stair ordering a 'careful severe officer' to search all troops and take from them, for restoration to the inhabitants, all plundered goods. Murray, iv, pp. 288–9.

[2] *JSAHR*, xxxvii, No. 151 (Sept. 1959), p. 133.   [3] Lediard, i, pp. 381–2.

everything they could not carry off even to knocking out of the heads of Barrels and such like; Capt. Spotswood, Quarter Master General under Cadoughan [*sic*], saw them all the while, but did not dare speak, for he had like to have been killed once before this year for endeavouring to hinder their plundering, but his party presently coming up he took them all prisoners, and particularly seized the 2 officers comming out of the church with their plunder on their backs. He delivered them to Duke Wirtemburgh who immediately handcufft (them) with Irons at the head of the Regiment and declared the Way of their country was to shoot them without any further tryal or enquiry. Whether any execution has been actually made I can't tel, to be sure, they deserve it, for there has been very severe Orders given out this year against these practises, but which made it worse in this case they violated a Safeguard.[1]

After Marlborough's departure, and in the face of the growing hostility of the local population, standards dropped. In the closing stages of the war, Ormonde actually reached the stage of obtaining permission from the French General to forage in Picardy. This, said Richard Parker, 'nettled our soldiers' who settled matters in their own fashion by waiting till the official parties had gone off, and then organizing their own to which they appointed special officers.

The comparatively good discipline (allied to training and experience) of Marlborough's armies produced the immediately apparent results of a handy army to manœuvre—its night marches, one of the most difficult operations for troops or staff officers, are remarkable. Its powers of endurance were high and it was on good terms with the populations among whom it served. What of its morale? A contemporary, who may have studied Monk, commented:

'tis most certain that he that intends to lead a Military Life, must expect to meet with Cold and Hunger, Storms and Tempests, long and painful Marches, excessive Heats, etc besides the Danger of Battel, but none of them, but what are of short Duration, and the Hopes of them being soon over, has that Effect on the Spirits and Minds of Soldiers, that it enables them not only patiently but cheerfully to bear the greatest Hardships, and surmount the utmost Difficulties. But on the other hand when they find their Pay (even in plentiful campaigns) not sufficient to support the common necessities

[1] *JSAHR*, xxxvii, No. 151 (Sept. 1959), p. 129: letter of.

of Nature, it throws them into that neglect and slothful Despondency, that they care not what becomes of themselves.[1]

Churchill has written that their 'Discipline . . . fighting energy . . . readiness to endure extraordinary losses, the competence and teamplay of their officers, the handiness of their cavalry and field artillery, their costly equipment and lavish feeding, their self-assured unaffected disdain of foreigners, became the talk of Europe'.[2] They were the soldiers who could write of bloody Malplaquet:[3] 'It was the most deliberate, solemn, and well-ordered battle that ever I saw—a noble and fine disposition, and as nobly executed. . . . I never saw troops engage with more cheerfulness, boldness, and resolution. In all the soldiers' faces appeared a brisk and lively gaiety which presaged victory.'[4] Mother Ross's sole complaint was that the bark of the trees, set flying by shot, 'fell on my neck and gave me no small uneasiness by getting down my stays'. After the battle Blackader wrote: 'This morning I went to view the battle field to get a preaching from the dead, which might have been very edifying, for, in all my life, I have not seen the dead bodies lie so thick.' Well indeed might the soldiers 'value themselves too much and think nothing can stand before them'; certainly not the French from whom 'Providence has taken away much of their heads . . . but . . . has left them their heels'. On 24 May 1709 he returned to the subject:

That old tyrant who wasted God's church, is about to be wasted himself. Last war, and for a long time while God was using him for a scourge to the earth, there was conduct in his Generals—strength and courage in his armies. They were a war-like people which their enemies were forced, at their sad expense to confess; but now there is a sensible change, they are not like the men they were. I heard one of their own Colonels who is now killed say 'The only thing he regretted was, that he could not live till he should tell the King that he had his armies composed of Generals without heads, and soldiers without hands.' Our ordinary regiments beat their best troops, wherever we meet them in any equality of numbers.

---

[1] *Recruiting Essay.*   [2] Churchill, ii, p. 480.
[3] A battle whose losses set Westminster in such a scutter of panic that, although at very worst for the English army an inconclusive victory, it marked, as Belloc shrewdly pointed out, the end of the country's absolute supremacy in the war. *The Tactics and Strategy of the Great Duke of Marlborough*, Hilaire Belloc (London, 1933). (*Belloc.*)   [4] *Blackader.*

There can indeed have been no war in which English, or British, morale was higher for a longer time than in Flanders and Germany, and very few in which it ever came up to the same standard.

How far did the methods which produced this English morale conform to those laid down in the standard recipes? There are today certain 'articles of faith' about keeping troops in good heart—they must be well paid, well fed, well looked after, have no worries about dependants, and, recently again much in favour, a soldier should 'know what he fights for, and love what he knows'.

By any standards, Queen Anne's armies were ill, infrequently, and fraudulently paid. Despite the most strenuous efforts, even of Marlborough himself, they were not lavishly fed; their living conditions were quite appalling; their wives starved, and until late in the reign widows had only what the army itself subscribed out of its pay. There were no army welfare services. There is little evidence to show that the troops had any deeper conception of the reason for fighting than the men who won the right to wear the Minden Rose—and, as Earl Wavell commented, if those of that day's battle knew why they were fighting, then their knowledge was superior to that of most subsequent historians. Marlborough's men showed that lavish and good conditions are not essential for good morale. His experience was not unique: George Washington's troops, Napoleon's Moscow Army, and the 14th Army of Burma are only three other examples; but the troops must feel that they are a primary care of their commander, and that he is getting for them the best that can, in the circumstances, be obtained. Poor as Anne's soldiers' fare was, it was, under Marlborough, undoubtedly the best of the age, probably the best ever up till that time. Even the most casual glance at his dispatches will reveal his unceasing care and concern for the troops' bread, which on numerous occasions determined the speed, and even the direction, of a move. This helped to build up the troops' trust in their commander, and was reinforced by continuity of leadership. The soldiers 'knew where they were', and realized there was one master in the house. Once they were able to personalize their leader as Corporal Jack, 'a man of uncommon penetration and presence of mind', the foundations of trust were strengthened.

So far as living and marching conditions were concerned, experience does not lessen, but increases beyond measure, wonder at the conditions under which these men suffered and fought without, apparently, a murmur. No troops of the present day, except the Japanese or Chinese, and, possibly, the Russians have approached their stamina, endurance, and uncomplaining resilience.

When Blackader wrote 'we are not able to stir out of our tents for bad weather, and are lying among mire and dirt. It rains from morn till night so that the artillery cannot be brought forward. . . . We had one of the severest storms I have ever seen, of hail, rain, and wind. Most of our tents were beat down, and torn; and the hollow ways running like rivers . . .', his only comment was, 'What a comfort to have the God of nature to be our protector.' 'The poor soldiers', wrote Marlborough from before Tournai in 1709, 'are up to their knees in dirt, which gives me the spleen to a degree that makes me very uneasy, and consequently makes me languish for retirement.'[1] What it made the poor soldiers languish for is not recorded, but Blackader's reaction when suffering similarly was to remark: 'Those vermin the French are still before us. . . . We marched all yesterday, all night, and all this day. There was a constant heavy rain most of the time, which made the roads very bad, and the march very tedious. We were sometimes four hours marching half a mile. I was thirty hours on horseback, which is the longest time ever I was in my life, either the last war or this.' One who could describe thirty hours of such marching as 'very tedious' must have possessed either a keen sense of humour or high morale. There is no evidence in any part of Blackader's writing to show him a wit. This was not the only march he found tedious.

We left our camp at three o'clock in the afternoon, and marched all night, a tedious and fatiguing march. We continued on our journey till three in the afternoon next day; so that we have been 24 hours under arms. It was sad work for the poor soldiers. . . . This was the worst day for the poor soldiers I have seen. It poured down a heavy rain, and the cavalry had so broken the ways, that the men marched in clay and dirt to the knees almost the whole day, for four leagues. There was hardly a hundred men of a regiment with the

---

[1] Churchill, iii, p. 114: to Sarah, 11 July 1709.

colours that night. . . . I never saw the army so harassed. We came late to our camp. I set up my tent and rested sweetly.

So it could go on indefinitely, the catalogue, as Uncle Toby had put it, of 'the intolerable fatigues and hardships which the soldier . . . is forced (for sixpence a day if he can get it) to undergo'.

The only welfare service to compensate for any of this which I have been able to trace was the dispatch over the two years 1704–5 of 15,500 'soldiers' monitors', of which 7,000 were 'in gold'—supplied at half price through the generosity of author and bookseller. These contained '3¼ sheets' and the binding cost 1½d. Previously the Fleet had benefited to the extent of 1,000 'seamen's monitors' at the 'expense of some private gentlemen'.[1]

It is more important for the morale of troops at war that they be reassured that their dependants and relatives are being well looked after than that they themselves should be cosseted. It would be reasonable to assume that Queen Anne's soldiers, largely illiterate and in civilian life undemanding, felt those home ties more strongly than the more sophisticated troops of recent wars, and much more strongly than contemporary blasé warriors from a background of comfort, security, and civilian welfare. It appears, however, that the pull of the family was in fact less strong so far as the rank and file were concerned. This may have been because most of them were semi-outcasts, many joined precisely in order to cut these ties, and all of them were so effectively cut off in any case that the problem was really irrelevant. So far as officers were concerned, however, Marlborough's army was remarkable for its inception of the great voluntary scheme of subscriptions to provide pensions for widows. The subject is dealt with later, but it is worthy of note here that the pensions became so important that the Government itself had to take over the entire scheme and administer it. Marlborough himself was scrupulous in his solicitude for officers' dependants. On the eve of the Battle of Ramillies, when he could be imagined to have more than enough professional worries, as well as that of physical danger, on his mind, he found time to write a letter to the Court of Prussia on behalf of the widow of one of his officers. In May of the previous year, he had had to take Sir John Wood in hand because his wife and children

---

[1] SP Mil. 41/3/106; *Anne Cal.*, p. 200, 23 Mar. 1705.

were 'represented to be reduced to a very low condition through your unkindness, without any reproach that I can understand on her side'. He advised Wood to continue his allowance of £5 per month, and to pay off all arrears in order to put a stop to further solicitations, 'which, if she should be provoked to carry so far as to Her Majesty or to the States, it is easy to foresee the consequences will prove to your disservice and the dissatisfaction of those who wish you well, among whom you may always reckon, Yours etc. . . .'[1]

There is practically no evidence that English soldiers have, at any time since Cromwell, been deeply inspired by knowing what they fought for and loving what they knew. They have fought implacably and bravely—probably at their best when in small bodies farthest from home—because they have been trained to do it, and to take a pride in so fighting. They have done so for their officers, and, above all perhaps, from pride of regiment. Well-drilled hardy files of muskets were more thought of in Flanders and Spain than soldiery of inspired faith. The Scots and the Irish might be slightly different, and, although this may have given them a dash that the English lacked, they had serious faults. They could be tricky instruments in a commander's hand, and were liable to be touchy. The records of the Scots Brigade in Dutch service show even a Dutch governor requesting a special court martial 'for the accused were Scots to whom they could not say a word'.[2] Too much thinking could be dangerous. The Irish, for example, knew so well what they fought for that it was a rule that, if possible, they should neither be used against their own countrymen in French service, nor be placed in a situation in Ireland where they might have to take part in suppression of disturbances. Confrontation with their compatriots was, of course, sometimes unavoidable, and on one famous field those on the English side very thoroughly routed the Wild Geese; but their superiors preferred it to be done as part of the day's work rather than as a crusade. It was also policy to avoid using Scots in Ireland, and it is on record that it was quite exceptional for a regimental chaplain to be able to carry out his duties in Scotland. Insistence would presumably have 'occasioned great inconveniences' in view of the 'endeavours

---

[1] Murray, ii, pp. 28–29, 1 May 1705.   [2] *Scots Brigade*, ii, p. xiii.

used to subject the soldiers in Scotland to the discipline of their Kirk'.[1] The English sentiments were those of Plume in *The Recruiting Officer*. He hated gentlemen volunteers 'for they are always troublesome and expensive, sometimes dangerous . . . those who know the least obey the best'. Blackader was one who had very firm ideas of what he was fighting for, and they would at times seem to have been more likely to lower than raise his morale:

When I consider this, that we are here assisting those oppressors that have wasted the church and people of God, persecuted and oppressed them, it makes me afraid the quarrel is not right and that we shall not prosper . . . when the carcases of one half of us are dung on the earth in Germany, then, perhaps the other half will bethink themselves. . . . These mouths come to His service hot from cursing and swearing, pretending to thank God for mercies they have no sense of: and when the work is over, return to their trade of swearing and blasphemy . . . I marched all the Sabbath in the midst of an English army. I need say no more to give a notion what hell on earth it is. . . . Every word that our British soldiers speak is a damning of their own blood, and impious swearing by God's blood and wounds. It will be no wonder to see them wallowing in their own blood and wounds.

However exceptional the Cameronian colonel may have been, he undoubtedly epitomized a body of value in the army—the Scots, Presbyterians, and nonconformists who, at best, were engaged in the war on behalf of a cause a shade less bad than the alternative of Popery. For every Tory or moderate Whig whom one can produce to set against such as Blackader, there were dozens who knew no more than that they were fighting under Corporal Jack, against the Frenchies, 'the most easily beat, and cowed of any people in the world'. With a few exceptions, there appears to have been little thoughtful passion among the soldiers. The ostensible dynastic causes of the war were, after all, not apparently such that war aims remained immutable, and the intricacies of the Dutch barrier were unlikely to form matter of urgent principle to debate over an evening's pipe and ale. The combination of instinctive reaction and training, to praise God, honour the Queen, stand by the colours, and chase the Frenchies was as near the fundamental purposes of the war as any, and did not call for an especially righteous body of psalm singers.

[1] SP Mil. 41/4, Brigadier Wightman, 13 Sept. 1711; Grenville to Dartmouth, 30 Aug. 1711.

Morale in Spain, like discipline, was not as good as in Flanders, but disorder was not widespread, and 'difficult' officers like Peterborough could always expend their quarrelling energies on the navy. In the West Indies, discipline and morale, like all else, appear to have been unspeakably bad.

As a whole, however, the army's discipline and morale compared very favourably with its other features. There were no large-scale mutinies, there were few tumultuous soldiers in the streets, cases of outrageous ill-treatment were uncommon, there was little trouble on disbandment, and there were very few cases indeed of reluctance on the battlefield. The good discipline produced a force which, for the first time for many years, won decisive victories on land for Britain. Victory is the best recipe for morale that has yet been devised, and 'thinking nothing can stand before them', those British soldiers, revelling in their unaffected way in their 'great vogue and reputation', felt themselves to be a proud and formidable force. This fostered renewed discipline and *esprit de corps*, which brought in its turn greater victories, and so the chain reaction went on.

DESERTERS

Before, approximately, the middle of the nineteenth century, desertion by large numbers of individual soldiers was a serious problem, not approached in magnitude by even the worst of post-1939 theatres. Throughout every campaign there was a considerable and persistent loss of men who vanished into the surrounding countryside. On the other hand, 'political deserters' seduced from their allegiance on grounds of conscience or belief, either to fight for the enemy, or simply to remain neutral, varied in numbers according to the period and the war. There were, for instance, few during the War of the Austrian Succession, or the Seven Years War, and only on the Russian front in 1917 do they appear to have figured largely in the calculations of combatants between the Napoleonic and post-1918 wars. In Anne's reign this political desertion, as might be expected in a struggle which was to an appreciable extent 'ideological', was considerable. The strain on loyalties was marked on both sides. The Peninsular battle where the French were commanded by the English Duke of Berwick, nephew of

Marlborough himself, and the English by de Ruvigny, the French Earl of Galway, was merely a somewhat piquant example of what was likely to happen, and not a phenomenon contradictory of general experience.

In general, the French seem to have suffered from organized large-scale desertion more than the British—although this may have been in part due to their having no restrictions on Protestants corresponding to those which kept Catholics out of the British army and navy. Although there were repeated injunctions on the use of Irish troops,[1] the French seem to have found even theirs a greater liability than did the English—if we exclude the effort and time spent in the inevitable wrangling which arose over the payment and maintenance of the bodies of Irish persuaded to come over to the English side.

'Normal' desertion from the English armies was not, by the standards of the time, excessive.[2] In Marlborough's armies, in spite of a steady dribble of English back across the North Sea to Harwich and Dover, the total losses through desertion in Flanders were probably smaller than at any previous period, although the German troops were seriously affected from time to time. In Spain, figures were very much larger. This is not surprising in view of the conditions under which the men served, but more remarkable when we consider that it must have been practically impossible for the men—either English or auxiliaries—to get home from the Peninsula. It was prevalent in Britain itself, and was one of the three offences for which the death penalty was provided in the Mutiny Act. It was, further, one of the very few in connexion with which civilians might be punished under the Act (for harbouring deserters, etc.).[3] In his *Recruiting Essay*, Hutcheson wrote that, although there were then thirteen regiments in England, desertion was such that few, if any, could be depended on for immediate service. Although he pressed for

---

[1] e.g. Nottingham specifically forbids use in Portugal of even Protestants from Ireland. *Dom. Cat.*, ii, p. 45.

[2] At the siege of Menin, conducted under unpleasant conditions in 1706, there were: killed, 583; wounded, 2,024; deserted, 21. (Lediard.)

[3] Those who harboured deserters were, under Annae 2 and 3, cap. 17, liable to a £5 fine, half of which went to the informer, and half to the officer from whose regiment the man came. Similar punishment was provided for receiving clothes, ammunition, etc., from deserters, or changing the colour of such clothes. Provision against abuse of this section was that anyone found not guilty on such a charge could recover treble costs.

an increase in overseas pay to stop desertion abroad, his own arguments accept by implication that the greatest relative (and probably absolute) number of deserters was in Britain itself. Declaring—with, no doubt, politicians' or pamphleteers' licence —that deserters almost outnumbered the army, he instanced one regiment which had lost 200 men in a single year. This was all the more reprehensible since, he said, Portsmouth was the only home duty which could be called burdensome. Some of the blame was due to the supineness of the justices, and the 'Indifference, Slothful Negligence, and Connivance of Parish Officers, and the Mercenary and Sordid Covetousness' of har-bourers of deserters.[1] The undeniable major cause, however, was the soldier's own wickedness, abetted sometimes by 'the Insinuation of Friends especially the Female ones'.

In his denunciations Hutcheson was, in his own emphatic way, reiterating a fairly widespread feeling among those with the cause of the war at heart. Only if such feeling did exist could the anti-militarist Parliament of those days have been persuaded to allow desertion as the one offence for which a man returning to England could be hailed abroad once more and there court-martialled.[2]

The Articles of War, under which any deserters returned overseas were tried, not only prescribed the punishment, but also defined the offence fairly rigorously. Article No. 23, as in-corporated in the Mutiny Act, read:

> All officers or soldiers that shall desert, either in the field, upon a march, in quarters, or in garrison shall die for it. And all soldiers shall be reputed and suffer as deserters who shall be found a mile from their garrison or camp, without leave from the officer command-ing-in-chief.

Fortescue states that the punishment for desertion was 'fre-quently 1,000–1,500 lashes or shooting in Hyde Park',[3] but this is an understatement. The routine punishment passed by courts martial sitting in England in time of war—as recorded in the Court Martial Warrant Books—was to be 'shot to death',

---

[1] He throws, quite innocently, a brief flash of light on conditions in overseas theatres by then proposing that the death penalty for desertion should be replaced by posting to the West Indies.

[2] Significantly, this provision was rescinded in the 1712 Act which recognized the virtual end of the war. [3] Fort., p. 569.

normally 'at the head of his regiment'. Even the man who pled at Hull on 23 September 1704 that he had been 'tempted' to York 'by a woman' received no more considerate treatment. Of five deserters from Soames's regiment, tried at Bury St. Edmunds on 12 and 13 July 1705 by a court martial of fourteen, four were sentenced to be 'shot to death'. The fifth prisoner claimed that the Articles of War had not been read to him on enlistment.[1] The court, in 'not guilty—but don't do it again' fashion, agreed that there was 'no positive proof. . . made of it', and let him off with one month in irons during which time he was to be whipped once a week through his regiment.[2] Later in the same year the Queen, extending her mercy to a man sentenced to death, ordered that the Judge-Advocate when laying such cases before her in future was to state whether the case was a fit one for her compassion 'after moving the Court Martial for their directions'.[3]

The vast majority of these cases were of pressed men—i.e. of the unemployed 'deemed to be enlisted'—but, since the bulk of the army consisted of precisely such, this is probably not a particularly valuable observation. The men were of all ages—those in the Bury St. Edmunds case varied from 17 to 40—but it does appear, not surprisingly, that the majority of cases were of recently recruited men. Not only did military service, as it does today, bear more hardly on them in their early days, but, in precisely those days, when they were moving about the country, perhaps unaccompanied, the opportunities to desert were greatest.

In Britain the most harmful and insidious desertion was not, in fact, the straightforward running away of intractable soldiery, but the undeniably large number of deserters nominally on leave. Francis Cusham, tried before a justice in Middlesex on 26 January 1705, said that while in the Guards he never received pay, and did duty only on muster days. He was, he said, only one of several thieves and pick-pockets enrolled in the First and

[1] Reading of the Articles of War about mutiny and desertion were specified by the Mutiny Acts as essentials, ranking equally with receipt or 'tender and refusal' of bounty money, of enlistment. At a trial of Black Watch deserters nearly forty years later, the defence was to plead that the Articles were read in English which the Highlanders did not understand.

[2] CM Warrants WO 30/18.

[3] Ibid., 5 Nov. 1706.

Second Guards but actually at large.[1] Another Guardsman, Taylor, was said to have collected £60 in one year by deserting and re-enlisting.[2] Under the 1708 Act,[3] this form of 'extended furlough' was attacked by the provision that men should have only twenty days' leave in six months without their colonel's permission. Officers signing passes in excess of this were due for the soldiers' debts up to £100. The soldiers, on the other hand, were to be arrested, not as deserters but as vagabonds, the only class in the country liable to conscription. In the same way, officers signing certificates to excuse soldiers from duty for an untrue reason were to be fined £20, of which half was to go to the Queen and half to any private soldier who might give the evidence necessary for conviction. The strength of the temptation to desert was itself emphasized by the provision that such an informer should be entitled to his discharge, if he requested it. The obverse of these provisions in the same Act was a reward of 20s. for apprehension of deserters. The first evidence of rewards for apprehension of deserters occurs, however, six years earlier in Ireland where, on 8 June 1702, a proclamation from Dublin Castle offered a reward of £5 for each deserter from the regiments embarked overseas for that summer's campaigns.[4] In the following year a reward of 10s. per straggling or deserting seaman put aboard ships at Portsmouth was offered.[5] Excessive enthusiasm in pursuit of deserters was restrained by the 1707 Mutiny Act which prohibited officers from breaking in to search for deserters without a J.P.'s warrant. The punishment for breaking this law was cashiering, but, in order to make things not too difficult, the Act simultaneously authorized J.P.s to issue such a warrant.[6]

The need for some restraints was shown by the case of Colonel (later Major-General) Luke Lillingston's 65-year-old cook, who was locked up in the Marshalsea in order, it was alleged, to avoid paying him wages. Referred to obliquely in *The Recruiting Essay* with suitably dark hints about the misdemeanours of those high in authority, this case caused such a furore that there was actually a conference between Lords and Commons over it on 9 March 1706. It was 5 May 1708, however, before the Board

[1] *Anne Cal.*, pp. 183–4.　　　　　　　　[2] *Recruiting Essay.*
[3] Annae 7, cap. 4.　　　　　　　　　　[4] *H.M.C. Ormonde*, pp. 467–8.
[5] Marching Orders WO 5/11, 4 May 1703.　　[6] Annae 6, cap. 74.

of General Officers finally ruled that the man 'appears . . . to have been entertained as a cook, not as a soldier . . . and therefore Colonel Lillingston had no Right to Imprison the said Lacy for Desertion'.[1]

Even troops moving as organized bodies found it quite feasible to leave the service. Heyman Rook, as noted, in 1705 received a special allowance of £102. 4s. from respites as compensation for desertions during an embarkation march.[2] Fortescue says, in fact, that the rule that troop movements within the kingdom should be by ship was introduced in order to reduce desertion on the march. Desire for economy and the traditional preference for any procedure likely to harass the 'poor soldiers' probably ranked equally high. The official practice of shipping recruits to Ireland to avoid desertion can have been only moderately successful, as Hutcheson claimed that the figures there were little better than for England.[3] The threat of a sea passage seems likely to have induced as many desertions prior to embarkation as would otherwise have taken place. Knowledge of the conditions in overseas theatres, the noisome nature of the transports, the appalling time troops rotted below decks in ports, and the facilities presented at such a time of confusion, all combined to make embarkation desertion a convention as firmly established as pre-embarkation pay mutinies. One method adopted to counter this practice was to assemble all troops for overseas on the Isle of Wight, but this had at times to be modified owing to lack of proper accommodation, which resulted in casualties as great as the hypothetical desertions.[4] The magnitude of losses at such times is shown by the case of the four regiments which lay three months at Cork waiting for transports. Owing to their inability to recruit and 'great desertion' they had to be made up to strength, prior to sailing, by drafts of 500 men.[5]

A favourite panacea for desertion for many years has been the amnesty. Once more ahead of the army, seamen and marines who had deserted were offered on 29 January 1703 by Royal Proclamation a free pardon if back on their ships by 1 March. Perhaps the specific statement that they would receive no pay

---

[1] PGO WO 71/1/167. [2] Entry Books WO 26/13.

[3] Entry Books WO 26/13: warrant of 5 July 1704.

[4] See Nottingham and Secretary at War on abandonment of such a plan in 1703: *Dom. Cal.*, ii, p. 110, and War Letters WO 4/2, 4 Oct. 1703.

[5] SP Mil. 41/3, Feb. 1711.

for the period of their absence discouraged potential penitents, but, at any rate, the offer was repeated in February with an extended time limit to 10 April.[1]

In due course the Board of General Officers offered a similar bargain to army deserters. As a result of their proposal, a Royal Proclamation was issued in 1708 pardoning those who surrendered before 25 March in the U.K., 1 June in the Low Countries, and thirty days after publication in Ireland, Spain, and Portugal. In their recommendation, the General Officers also suggested the issue of rewards for the discovery of deserters who did not surrender, but this did not find a place in the proclamation, nor in its successor on 10 May which offered a pardon to all who gave themselves up by 20 June.[2] These proclamations appear to have had precisely the effect they have always had.

Enthusiastic supporters of the idea of forgiveness, although favouring different methods, lived in Devon, according to a memorial by Colonel Rivers. One of his ensigns, Isaac Warner, while in the village of Exminster Longstreet in 1704, met, it is stated, 'a likely young fellow and asked if he would serve Her Majesty'. The youth replied that he already served in General Erle's regiment. 'What brought you hither from your regiment?' asked Ensign Warner, and received the truthful if unexpected reply, 'My legs.' The ensign asked the likely young fellow for his discharge certificate and, when that was not forthcoming, called a constable. Not only, however, would the latter not arrest the man, but the entire town rose with flails and pitchforks 'particularly one . . . who threatened to knock his brains out and called him highwayman and kidnapper'. The man whom Warner had accosted escaped and, in the mêlée, another prisoner under the ensign's charge also made off.[3] The people of Harwich had reason to hold different views. When they complained early in the war about the cost of subsisting soldiers passing through the town, the Secretary at War pointed out to the Lord Treasurer that this complaint, ostensibly about disabled soldiers, was of old standing. It dated, he said, from the last war, and acquired no greater justification with the passage of time. Many of the men were deserters, and most of the others had money. To obviate the trouble, he recommended that in

---

[1] *Dom. Cal.*, i, pp. 560 and 601.
[2] PGO WO 71/1.   [3] SP Mil. 41/3.

future all men coming over from the Low Countries should carry a pass on which entry was to be made of money issued to them before departure. Those without passes were to be arrested as deserters, and any genuine cases to whom subsistence was advanced were to be reported so that the money might be recovered from their regiments.[1] In the following year, directions along these lines were given to the Mayor by the Secretary at War who said that there would be no reimbursement in future for subsistence issued to soldiers from Holland unless paid on Her Majesty's particular directions, or as a result of a certificate from the Captain-General. This he explained, was to help to cut down desertion from the army in Holland.[2] In the following year, nevertheless, Marlborough had specifically to request Harley to make arrangements at the ports for interception of deserters.[3]

The Mayor of Dover was active in securing deserters. The war was barely under way when he received from the Secretary of State a letter applauding his dispatch to London of four intercepted deserters from Flanders. As encouragement, the Secretary wrote: 'I hope we shall find a way to reimburse you' for their upkeep, transport, etc. Thus heartened, the civic chief later produced another twenty-four men whom he was instructed to send to London by ship, and to 'part with them to no land or sea officer, and send(ing) . . . the name of the ship and of the captain who receives them. Send your account that it may be paid'.[4] The injunction about parting with the deserters was to guard against re-enlistment, which most officers were quite prepared to carry out, as one of the few cheap means of keeping up their strengths. The General Officers had, in fact, at their meeting of 26 February 1709, to make special provision to deal with this abuse. Their resolution, later made a standing order, instructed that deserters re-enlisted in other regiments should be returned to their original regiments—provided the levy money was first returned to those who actually enlisted them the second time.[5] Portsmouth, although a seaport, had moments of opinion different from Dover and Harwich. When a party went to a

---

[1] Entry Books WO 26/11, 18 Aug. 1703.
[2] War Letters WO 4/2, Feb. 1704
[3] Murray, ii, p. 99: dispatch of 12 June 1705.
[4] *Dom. Cal.*, i, pp. 27 and 38–39.   [5] PGO WO 71/1.

house there to take over a deserting grenadier from Windsor's regiment, the householder gathered several armed men, and forced the deserter out of custody. Reporting the matter, the colonel was told he might prosecute if he wished. He replied that he would not, owing to the delay and expense. The General Officers passed the ball to the Lords of Committee of Council who seem to have found, without undue difficulty, some other way of taking no action.[1]

There was thus in Britain fairly extensive desertion, chiefly by pressed men, and those about to embark, which met with some sympathy from the population at large. A very few public officials were forward in suppressing it, either because of a particular interest, or out of public spirit.

Overseas, the facilities for successful desertion were less, but the inducements and pressures were greater. Numerous ties of blood and friendship stretched across the battle lines and resulted in considerable contact between the opposing forces, perhaps more notably between the officers than the men. The exceptional circumstances were reinforced by the lingering traditions of chivalry and martial courtesy. Marlborough sent presents to friends within the enemy lines quite openly, and himself received them. Negotiations, involving passage of correspondence and delegates, were constantly in train over forage, prisoners, passes to travel through enemy-held territory, for prisoners to return home during the winter, and so on. Blackader noted one outstanding case of fraternization on the day before the bloodiest battle of the war:

> The French officers and ours, as if it had been concerted between them went out between the two camps, and conversed with one another, and called for their acquaintances, and talked together as friends, as if there had been a cessation of arms, but it was broken off by the generals.[2]

The Irish, with their unprejudiced facility for participating on both sides, were a particularly notable means of contact, between either officers or soldiers. Followers of the career of Mother Ross will remember that on both occasions when she was taken prisoner she encountered compatriots—one of them a cousin who showed that he did not allow ties of loyalty to

---

[1] PGO WO 71/2, 3 May 1711.   [2] *Blackader*, p. 349.

interfere with those of blood—and Corporal Bishop served with a sergeant who had a rendezvous with a sister from the French army at the siege of Douai. Since, of course, England's civil war was marching, one might say, in step with the European War, her soldiers were bound to find themselves taking part, as it were, in a family dispute. King James's queen herself took steps to see that English prisoners were separated from the Dutch and given more civilized treatment than their more stiffnecked allies.

Nevertheless, in spite of the blood ties and the high principles, the ordinary run-of-the-mill traitors still went over for more mundane reasons—normally empty bellies. This was particularly so with men already prisoners. When dependent on their own country, prisoners had a thin time so far as subsistence was concerned, and suffering on this count was judiciously reinforced by the barbarous treatment they frequently received. Reading the records of the time, one can at least understand the plight of the men who declared that, having been prisoners for fifteen months, they were resolved to take up arms for the French king 'rather than die in a prison neglected of their country'.[1] Marlborough himself, when writing to St. John in July 1711, showed an appreciation of the temptations. Dealing with deserters who wished to return to their original loyalty, he described them as being 'under the misfortune' of having gone over to the French and asked that they be assured a pardon if back before the end of August. He added further that the news would be conveyed to them privately lest the enemy, having been appraised, should send then away from the front.[2] Prisoner-deserters were probably most numerous among sailors, but were not particulary rare in either arm if we are to judge from the casual mention of many incidents such as that when fourteen soldiers went over together from prison in 1712 for want of subsistence.[3]

In the Netherlands, Jesuits, friars, and hermits were said to be particularly active in persuading men to desert to the French on the promise of being sent to England.[4] On deserting they were bribed or bullied to join the French and then sent into theatres where they would not be employed against the British.

---

[1] *H.M.C.H. of L.*, vii, pp. 150–1.   [2] Murray, v, pp. 402–3.
[3] *Treas. Cal.*, iv, p. 362: letter of 28 Feb. 1712.   [4] *Recruiting Essay.*

A favourite stratagem to get ordinary prisoners of war to enlist against their country was for the jailers to advance money so that, even should their turn come for exchange, they would not be allowed to leave until they had discharged the debt—which, it was said, they could do only by entering enemy service.[1] Nevertheless, those of them who stood out against bribery or ill-treatment were, it was claimed, actually returned to England by 'underground' means.[2] Bribery does, on occasion, seem to have gone to considerable lengths. One prisoner who escaped from the Spaniards in the West Indies was captured by the French while on his way home. During the five months for which he was kept in jail he was repeatedly offered a commission in the French service, although there was nothing in his record to indicate any special competence.[3]

The men of the Stuart times knew their own weaknesses of organization and finance, and there is no doubt that soldiers who joined the enemy to fill their stomachs were looked upon with more tolerance than would be given today.[4] On the other hand, any Englishman who served the enemy because of his religion was regarded as an unmitigated traitor, while it was accepted (by the English) as only natural that French Protestants should serve against their own country. When instructions were given to prohibit enlistment of French prisoners, they were issued, not because of any high-minded objection to treachery, no matter against whom committed, but on grounds of expediency, or on account of the feelings of the enemy, more closely regarded in those days than now.

The credo that Protestants should automatically serve on the side of the Holy Roman Empire was first openly challenged by the Count de Mornay: 'I do not see that you have any greater rights over Protestants than over Catholics. Whatever faith they may believe, they are all subjects of the King of France.' Up till

[1] *H.M.C.H. of L.*, vii, pp. 151–2.
[2] *Recruiting Essay.*   [3] *Anne Cal.*, p. 431.
[4] Hutcheson talks of soldiers who 'pinch'd with Hunger (the inevitable Effects of Small Pay) grow stomachful and stubborn, and endeavour to revenge themselves on those that induc'd or forc'd them into the Army, by deserting to the Enemy, of which we have too many hundreds of examples'. Marlborough blamed widespread desertion in 1705 on the cold weather, and stated that the English had had 'their share'. Desertion due to bad conditions appears normally to have been greater among the auxiliaries—e.g. the Duke's difficulties in 1711 due to Prussian desertions. Murray, ii, p. 99, and iii, p. 339, 12 June 1705 and 12 May 1711.

then it had been the custom of the Commissioners for Sick and Wounded and Exchange of Prisoners of War to demand of any Frenchman wishing to serve the English a clergyman's certificate that he was a born Protestant. The sceptical de Mornay commented that those capable of paying money for conversion were doubtless equally capable of giving certificates.[1] The Commissioners seem to have been not unduly impressed for, almost immediately afterwards, they stated in reply to a petition that they had no power to release Protestant prisoners 'unless they are willing to serve in the Queen's navy'.[2] As a result, however, of the allegations of ill-treatment bandied back and forth across the channel, the Queen issued an order on 20 April 1703 that the Commissioners were not to accept the service of any French prisoner 'no matter how anxious to enter' so that the 'French may have no excuse for forcing English into theirs'. If there happened to be any among them real Protestants who wished to stay in England, they were not to be returned to France, but, on the other hand, none were to be released without the Queen's special orders. The injunction to give even Protestants every opportunity to return to France was repeated a short time later, and in 1704 the Commissioners, replying to Monsieur de Sulpice, said that, although hundreds of the 3,000 French in their hands were ready to enter the Queen's service, not one had been put on board a ship-of-war except a few Protestants who had refused to return to their native land.[3] This was followed with remarkable speed by a letter of the same day to the Count de Mornay which stated that English officers would not dare to take French sailors into service 'for the Queen has given a positive order that this shall not be done. Not even the poor Protestant prisoners, who prefer captivity in England to the sufferings which they undergo in France' were allowed to enter the Queen's service. It was therefore hoped that the French order against enlistment of English army prisoners would be extended to the fleet.[4] On 14 June 1703 Nottingham wrote to the Commissioners that, although some of the French prisoners had renounced Popery, they must still be detained. They had to be given the opportunity to return to France 'that there may be no ground for the French to say that they have been forced to

---

[1] *Dom. Cal.*, i, p. 591.   [2] Ibid., p. 592.
[3] Ibid., pp. 155 and 689, and ii, p. 14.   [4] Ibid., i, p. 690.

change their religion to avoid the hardship of a prison'.[1] Five days later, however, he himself wrote to the Prince's Council *commanding* the employment of Claude Priget, a French prisoner, on one of Her Majesty's ships, or his discharge. Certificates had been produced, he said, that the prisoner was a Protestant and had prayed to serve on one of Her Majesty's ships or to live in England.[2] One month later, he wrote to the Council concerning two other prisoners who did not wish to return to France: 'if you have no objection they may be taken into the Queen's service on shipboard'.[3]

An English investigator seems to have been not unduly cautious when he reported that there was 'no proof' of the allegation that French prisoners had been compelled to serve in English ships, but admitted that sixty French soldiers recently taken from a packet-boat were deserters from Flanders who had asked to go to Spain to serve King Charles.[4] We know, too, that Marlborough from Blenheim onwards (where he estimated that the prisoners included 3,000 who enlisted with the allies) made persistent, and successful, efforts to recruit deserters.[5] He was more successful than the volatile Peterborough who remarked, during the Lords inquiry into his campaigning, that during the whole siege of Barcelona 'not so much as a lieutenant or ensign' deserted to him.[6] Later commanders in Spain did, however, build up a small force of deserters, which seems, at one stage at any rate, to have been over 400 strong.[7]

Whether his accretion of strength after Blenheim revealed to Marlborough the potentialities of 'political warfare' or whether he did not consider the opportunities proper until then, we cannot, of course, tell. By 21 April 1705, however, he was pressing the home authorities that some of the Irish regiments with the French were likely to be on the Moselle and 'I believe . . . it might not be difficult to influence good numbers to quit that service, if I could be at liberty to give them any encouragement'. He certainly was not the first to think of this method of weakening the enemy, for he asked that the Queen be moved to grant

---

[1] *Dom. Cal.*, ii, p. 14.   [2] Ibid., p. 219.
[3] Ibid., p. 241, 24 Dec. 1703.   [4] *Anne Cal.*, p. 382.
[5] SP Mil. 87/2, part i: dispatch of 21 Aug. 1704.
[6] *H.M.C.H. of L.*, vii, p. 404.
[7] Portmore in Mar. 1711 says he is unable to keep up nine troops of 45, and proposes to reduce to six of 60; *Treas. Cal.*, iv.

him the same power as Schomberg had in Portugal.[1] The power
—which the Lords of the Council pointed out he already had—
to give protection to 'deserting *regiments*' was, he considered,
insufficient. What no doubt weighed heavily with those at home
was, as the Duke pointed out, that it would all result in considerable expense.[2]

Having kept their own Irish from deserting and persuaded
the enemy's Irish to come over, the generals' troubles had only
started. On 8 June 1705 the Duke wrote to d'Aubach that, since
he could not receive the Irish deserters 'coming in daily' into the
English regiments, d'Aubach might have them. If he did so, it
would be necessary to take the officers as well, even though the
material was not up to standard, since they had been in France
for a long time and were not by then very enthusiastic about
serving anyone.[3]

One of the large efforts at suborning was made before Ghent
in December 1708. The Spanish and Walloon troops on the
French side were considered to be vulnerable to propaganda.
'I charged them' (the clergy, magistrates, and commonalty of
the city), wrote Marlborough, 'to declare to the . . . troops . . .
that if they would . . . come over to us, they would be favourably
received into . . . service'.[4]

This offer was embodied in a document signed by the
Captain-General and the Dutch Field Deputies for circulation
among the enemy. While there is no evidence of any considerable positive result, the sudden collapse of resistance may well
be in some measure attributable to the demoralizing effect of
the 'leaflet'. 'Favourably received' was certainly, by present-
day standards, an over-statement. Like many other traitors
before and since, those who came over discovered that their new
masters' solicitude for them declined in ratio to their proximity.
Even although the expense of such regiments was reckoned to
be only half that of an English regiment (apart from the fact
that any English officers employed normally came off the half
pay list), there were constant complaints by commanders that
they were unable, for want of money, to subsist, feed, or clothe
the troops who had come over.[5]

---

[1] SP Mil. 87/2, Pt. i.   [2] Murray, ii, p. 700.
[3] Ibid., p. 83.   [4] Ibid., iv, p. 362.
[5] Ibid., iii, p. 408, and v, pp. 374–5, are only two cases.

That the standards to which the generals wished to commit their governments were not excessive can be gauged from Marlborough's dispatch of 11 June 1711 concerning the terms of service of twenty-four companies of deserters to be in the joint pay of England and the States. Each soldier was to receive 'a pair of slippers, a shirt, and other necessaries . . . and tents of which the cost will not exceed 14 florins per soldier'.[1]

Not all the troops brought over were taken into service. For instance, men surrendering in 1709 were given a pistole each when they surrendered and another when they reached Holland (in order to prevent them going straight to their homes where they would, presumably, have been re-enlisted). England and Holland were sharing this expense, but could not recruit them all and 'the Imperialists' (i.e. the government of the Holy Roman Empire) 'not having one farthing to spare for this service, it is probable the Dutch will encourage some to go to the West Indies'. Only three weeks later Marlborough made particular note of the Queen's directions that no encouragement was to be given to French deserters to go to the Plantations.[2]

The state of morale of deserters, and whether they came over in a body under terms made by their officers (as the Irish seem largely to have done) or as individuals and small parties, no doubt decided whether they were formed into deserters' regiments or recruited as individuals. Deserters in formed regiments seem to have given better service than individuals distributed throughout the army. Marlborough, noting on 26 June 1711 that 'the greater part' of the King of Spain's infantry 'is formed of French deserters', considered it not possible to have any trust in them and suggested that they would be much more useful in the deserters' regiments then forming.[3] Two such regiments still in service at the end of the war were costing England £2,133. 17s. 6d. as her half share.[4] Among the most notable batches were one of 100 French officers sent to Catalonia in 1704, and another of 24 sent to Flanders in 1711, where they took up appointments in various regiments.[5]

In whatever fashion deserters were employed, however, it was

[1] Murray, v, pp. 374–6.
[2] Ibid., iv, pp. 514–15, 24 June 1709; iv, p. 540, 11 July 1709.
[3] Ibid., v, p. 395, 26 June 1711.   [4] SP Mil. 41/4.
[5] Ibid. 41/3, St. John, 11 Jan. 1705; Anne Cal., Grenville, 2 June 1711.

repeatedly admitted that those who came over did not meet with the provision promised them. Even when they came to England in search of relief—'a public faith (which) ought to have been complied with'—they were to discover that they were treated in the same way as the English soldiers in so far as money or justice was concerned.[1] From the sixty or seventy men for whom Marlborough sought even an area where they could get at least subsistence 'till something better turns up'[2] to Captain Mahony who came 'over in a naked condition' and 'is now afflicted with want and ready to perish',[3] there were few who did not have considerable evidence on which to base their valuation of English pledges.

The pledges themselves were usually specific enough. The terms of surrender of Sir Daniel Carroll's Irish regiment in Spanish pay in Portugal in 1710, for instance, as proposed by the officers themselves, and agreed by the English were:

1. That Colonel Luke Keating be Colonel, and Sir Daniel Carroll be Lieutenant Colonel, and the next captain, major, and every other captain take their rank as they are in the Spanish Service: and that Lieutenant Stanton of Lord Barrymore's regiment may have a troop in the said regiment, being agreed to and desired by all the said officers.

2. That the said regiment be formed into a regiment of horse upon the English establishment in England, and paid as such and maintained with any reforms[4] in peace or war in any part of England that Her Majesty may think fit . . . which, if agreed upon, the said Colonel and Captains promise to bring off their several troops or the regiment entire if possible.

The regiment was disbanded in 1712, and the officers were placed on half pay as Dragoons—which was, of course, a breach of faith.[5] This regiment was involved in such a series of wrangles that it was probably worth more to the French when on the English side than on their own. The first move came when, in the course of a dispute over the command, Grenville considered that the terms were not binding since Keating did not actually 'come off (but) . . . was captured'. It was therefore claimed that, the articles having been broken, the commander-in-chief could

[1] *Treas. Cal.*, iv, p. 379. [2] Murray, iii, p. 408.
[3] SP Mil. 41/3, Grenville, 20 Dec. 1710.
[4] i.e. reductions. [5] Dalton, vi, pp. 261–2.

appoint whomsoever he chose to be C.O. It was further alleged that Sir Daniel did not have more than seventy men 'though he took in all deserters of any nation', scarcely any of whom 'but deserted back'. In an endeavour, no doubt, to put the matter quite beyond dispute, it was further alleged that Sir Daniel himself came over only to avoid punishment by the French. Being an Irishman, he was, however, the match of those on the spot, whose evidence, which was substantially against him, was rejected by the Board of General Officers.[1]

The problem of disposal of Catholic officers was dealt with in a proclamation quoted by Grenville in 1712:

> That (officers) should be pardoned for all crimes and offences committed by them in adhering to, or serving under Her Majesty's Enemies ... such of them as should be qualifyd to serve Her Majesty's Forces, should be revived and entertained in the same quality as they enjoy'd in the Service they left, and . . . such, as by reason of their Religion, could not serve in Her Majesty's Forces should be revived and entertained in the Service of the King of Spain, or of such other of Her Majesty's Allies, where they should best like, in the same quality and with the same pay as they enjoyed under Her Majesty's enemies.[2]

Deserters from Her Majesty's Allies were not, however, handed over to their units with great alacrity. Throughout the war deserters from the Scots regiments in the Dutch service were permitted to enlist in the English army in order, it was said, to prevent them going over to the French. After the armistice they were returned to the Dutch, who offered them a free pardon.[3] There does not, on the other hand, appear to have been any measurable desertion by the Scottish Highlanders said to have served with the Irish regiments in French pay.

The most remarkable collection of broken pledges, fraud, and intrigue concerned a 'carry-over' from the Orange campaigns in Ireland. On the surrender of Limerick in October 1691, Lieutenant-Colonel Rice, commander of an Irish regiment of horse, rejected offers to go to France and brought his regiment over to the English 'in pursuance of the public faith and assurances of the English general'. In order to carry this out in the face of his captains' reluctance, and the great efforts being made

---

[1] SP Mil. 41/4.
[2] Ibid., 16 Apr. 1712.   [3] SP Mil. 41/4.

by Sarsfield to persuade them to go to France, he entered into a personal bond for £10,000 to pay all officers and men their full pay, the value of their horses, ammunition, and accoutrements if taken from them, and all other losses and damage should they be disbanded. Had it not been for this, it was claimed and admitted, the captains would have taken their troops to France, as they were entitled to do under the terms of surrender.

The regiment was disbanded the following year, Rice paid it in full, gave each captain £450 for arms, horses, and accoutrements, and had his bond for £10,000 cancelled. The Commissioners of Accounts gave him a certificate of arrears for £8,110. 17s. 6d., and his own troop was valued at £1,066. All suspiciously expeditious; year after year he battled for payment of this money, plus what he was due for his and his captains' troop horses. At one stage a Committee of the House of Commons describing his case as 'singular and unparalleled' and his services as 'extraordinary' admitted his petition: and saw the House pass the whole question to another committee. In 1706, 'after 15 years' painful and expensive solicitation', he was given debentures whose selling value (they were at a discount of 30 to 35 per cent.) was exceeded by his costs. Even then he was not finished. Three of his captains petitioned that he had not paid them and, although he held receipts, the House promptly passed a Bill to make him account for the entire £11,420. 17s. 6d. of debentures, although they realized only £7,980.[1] To ensure justice was done, the colonel was locked up by the sergeant-at-arms and denied access to his counsel. Even the Commissioners appointed to execute judgement were constrained to point out that, if action as instructed by the House under Annae 6, cap. 33, were taken, only £2,600 of woods and lands, a sum vastly exceeded by the colonel's expenses, would remain to him. That seems, however, to have been no concern of Parliament's, which apparently considered this reward quite adequate for 'a singular and unparalleled' case of 'extraordinary' service.

[1] The commissioners who dealt with the case testified that the debentures were realized as £5,380 in cash, and £2,600 in woods and lands. The case was probably reopened after the grant of the debentures as the result, in the first instance, of an anonymous letter whose writer offered his services to 'adjust' the sum, and 'bring the pretensions to far less'. *Anne Cal.*, p. 288.

PRISONERS OF WAR

The importance of taking prisoners varies with strategic aims; their treatment depends partly on social attitudes and partly on the 'ideological content' of a war. If the war is pursued by occupying territory rather than by destroying armies, and if elaborate sieges are the vital events, prisoners are either irrelevant or a burden. In a society where the division between the highly born and others is comparable with that between nations, a camaraderie and respect will, so far as one section is concerned, insinuate themselves across fronts, while there will be ignorance of or indifference to the condition of the others. It will be practically useless to attempt to persuade men of education and honour who value that for which they are fighting to change sides; it will be particularly pointless to attempt to bully them into doing so. Ignorant men, driven to fight by hunger or the law, can be more easily suborned, particularly if their native allegiance is unstable; others, untrained and unfortified, may be amenable to bullying if sufficiently brutal, or to temptation if sufficiently glittering.

Prisoners in Anne's day were, in general, unwelcome. Almost the sole justification for capturing them was to have something to exchange for one's own men in the hands of the enemy. Officers were handled with honourable punctilio and fared, all in all, not unsatisfactorily. Other ranks, swollen in numbers far beyond those hitherto encountered, were at best bodies to be herded, at worst clamorous mouths to be stopped. Stanhope's complaint when in prison after Brihuega was that when he asked his Jesuit jailers for a Demosthenes they sent him a book with Demosthenes on the cover, but inside it was a Tully, 'and it might have been the Alcoran for aught they knew'.[1] Sick soldier prisoners on the move in France were compelled, reported an official English Government investigator, to travel naked and whipped with horse whips 'in a dreadful manner'.[2]

Although warfare ceased, at Marlborough's hand, to consist of sieges and formalized manœuvres, appreciation of the value of prisoners did not increase commensurately. There was, rather, a further objection that they hindered rapid movement. In numbers they far exceeded previous experience. Their own

---

[1] *Stanhope*, p. 116.   [2] *H.M.C.H. of L.*, vii, pp. 151/152.

Government was responsible for feeding them; in the prevailing financial revolution, with its chronic shortage of money, they were naturally among the earliest to go short.

After Blenheim, Marlborough found himself practically apologizing for the number of prisoners he had taken. In his defence he wrote to the States General that he had succeeded in disposing of the prisoners as far as possible in Germany, and only the minority had been brought to Holland, where they were lodged in workhouses and private houses in the vicinity of Breda. Since most of them would be good for exchange against Allied soldiers captured in Portugal, he went on, the expense would not be great.[1] There was, however, at that time no ready-made machinery for exchanges. Marlborough had himself to write home for disposal orders for Tallard, the French commander, 1,200 officers, and 8,000–9,000 'common soldiers'.[2]

'As the charge of subsisting these men must be very great,' he wrote, 'I presume Her Majesty will be inclined that they be exchanged for any other prisoners they may offer.'[3]

As the war progressed, such matters became easier to decide. Commissaries or Commissioners of Prisoners accompanied the armies in the field to expedite exchanges by arranging technicalities such as rendezvous, numbers, rationing, and escorts. These Commissaries did not normally deal with generals or equivalent ranks. Even for these, however, when their exchange was speedily desired, the machinery could work fast. It took only two days to have Cadogan exchanged for Major-General Palavacini—a tribute to the value of the Quartermaster-General to Marlborough. When immediate exchange in the field did not take place, delays could be considerable. In such cases, officers frequently conducted private negotiations. Lieutenant-General Sankey, captured in Spain in 1709, so despaired of the 'normal channels' ever leading him to freedom that he arranged for ten months' leave in England to negotiate his exchange. He does not seem to have been particularly successful as the case was still being argued in March 1712—thirty-five months after his capture.[4]

---

[1] Murray, i, p. 447, 2 Sept. 1704.

[2] His dispatch of 21 Aug. 1704 put the total at 13,000 prisoners—an enormous number in view of the size of the armies involved. SP Mil. 87/2, Pt. i. The generally accepted figure today is about 11,000. Cambridge, v, p. 411. But see p. 314, footnote 1.   [3] Murray, i, p. 490, 14 Aug. 1704.   [4] SP Mil. 41/3 and 41/4.

Delays were sometimes deliberately imposed on the exchange of soldier prisoners, but transfers were simplified by the custom which grew up of releases on a 'man for man' basis. This was hindered to some extent by the disproportion of prisoners held (on the French side at the start of the war, and on the English later), which caused embarrassment to the side left with a number of hungry mouths after repatriation of its own nationals. For prisoners not exchanged there was a 'tariff' of ransoms, but it was not firmly laid down, and it is doubtful how far it was actually operated. In principle, the ransom was approximately one month's pay, although the British showed a preference for a slightly higher figure.[1] Rates suggested for the abortive cartel of 30 October 1702 covered all naval ranks as follows:

Admiral	8,000 livres
Vice-Admiral	4,000 livres
Lieutenant-General, Intendant-General, or Rear-Admiral	2,000 livres
Common Seaman	16 livres
Boys	8 livres[2]

Although this cartel was never formally signed, exchanges were carried out by verbal agreement, including the appropriate amount of wrangling about delay of transports and sufferings of prisoners *en route* to the ports. Again there are indications that the ransom part may not have been strictly applied. In exchanges officers could be 'valued' against other ranks—e.g. the captain of a man-of-war was exchanged for twenty men, and a lieutenant for ten. There was a hitch at one point caused by an involved dispute over the status of ensigns on warships.[3] That this method was not routine for the army at least is shown by a remark of Marlborough's in 1703 that he hoped, if it should be necessary to exchange soldiers, that 'a due proportion will be observed'.[4] In the following year, his personal attention was required in a disagreement over the relative status of corporals and 'marechals de logis'.[5] In March 1705 the Chevalier de Maupeon complained that although he was 'not a pirate nor a merchant but commander of a French ship convoying the fleet

[1] *Dom. Cal.*, i, p. 180.   [2] Ibid., p. 281.
[3] *Treas. Cal.*, iv, pp. 418–19.   [4] Murray, i, p. 509.
[5] Ibid., p. 482: to Villeroi, 25 Sept. 1704.

. . . taken in legitimate war', and, although there were captains of English ships in France, he was not being exchanged.[1]

The 'repatriation' run was normally between the Channel Islands and St. Malo (for Dinan) by packet-boat, or, on special occasions, by man-of-war. Nottingham early in the war turned down a suggestion that all the prisoners held by the French should be concentrated at Calais or Dunkirk. This was, he said, undesirable owing to the long marches required 'and we know by experience in the late war that many perished in so long a march'.[2]

In 1707 Marlborough had a batch of prisoners moved speedily to Britain to avoid handing them over too quickly. Since, he pointed out, the British who would be exchanged for them would not arrive from Spain in time for the forthcoming campaign, it was up to the Allies to ensure that those they were handing over could not take the field earlier.[3] Another occasion on which he procrastinated was, very typically, when he warned against undue haste lest the enemy be provided with a source of intelligence. A modern-sounding intrusion was apparently practised before the end of the war when spies were slipped in among returning prisoners.[4] Such anachronisms, however, rarely affected army officers, who were handled according to the precedents of more spacious and leisurely wars. Parole was regularly given, and seldom broken. A breach in 1712 particularly angered the French who complained to the Secretary at State. Their concern in this case, however, appears to have been caused by the fact that the officer left debts to the local inhabitants unpaid.[5]

As with recruiting, supplies, and transport, the country was not organized for a war on the scale of the one it had to fight. The first report on numbers of prisoners, for instance, shows, on 27 October 1702, only 1,999—1,844 in England, 73 in Guernsey, 82 in Kinsale, 'also some in Jersey, but the agent there was taken by the French whilst coming hither'.[6] The figures rose steadily but very slowly in the next two years to almost 5,000. Then Blenheim produced 11,000—an initial wave which was followed

---

[1] *Anne Cal.*, p. 205. [2] *Dom. Cal.*, i, p. 286.
[3] Murray, iii, p. 438, 23 June 1707.
[4] *Anne Cal.*, p. 782: Mayor of Weymouth's letter to Secretary of State, 15 Dec. 1711.
[5] SP Mil. 41/4, Lansdowne, 12 Apr. 1712.
[6] *Dom. Cal.*, i, p. 279, 15 Feb. 1703.

by a steady flow of comparable magnitude. It was not, of course, routine in those days to ship the prisoners immediately to England, and only about half of the 11,000 were, in fact, allocated to the U.K., but the two figures give a basis of comparison. Owing to the circumstances of the war, the figures *in England* for the first two years must represent practically the entire total —for the most part seamen. The immediate difficulties on the field of battle have been described by Sergeant Millner and Mother Ross who tell how, after Blenheim, the British formed a lane in which the prisoners stood 'some having no shirts, some without shoes or stockings, and others naked as from the womb'.

A conscientious endeavour was always made to 'park' as many as possible of the prisoners on one's Allies, but since the Austrians were normally of little assistance in this—as in most else except Eugene—it was not always successful. The actual apportionment after Blenheim was: the Emperor 5,514; England 5,678: 'besides 3,000 who had taken service with the Allies'.[1] The Emperor's large share on this occasion was partly due to the large numbers of his troops whom the French were ready to exchange, and partly due to the captured troops being on his soil.

The problem of custody of prisoners in Britain presented itself in two familiar ways—lack of money, and confusion over responsible authorities. The navy, in traditional style, was not entirely unprepared. The Commissioners for Sick and Wounded Seamen[2] were charged, under their more comprehensive title of Commissioners for Sick and Wounded Seamen and Exchange of Prisoners of War, with the care and exchange of seamen prisoners. They quite categorically stated on 13 September 1711 that they had 'nothing to do with the Army or the Land Service, our Instructions coming from the Lord High Admiral and relating only to seamen and naval affairs'.[3] They nevertheless had undoubtedly as much to do with soldier prisoners as they did with army sick and wounded.[4] This rebuff to the Treasury

---

[1] Lediard, i, pp. 274–5. Cf. the total (14,192) with the figures on p. 311.

[2] John Evelyn, the diarist, was at one time one of the Commissioners for Sick and Wounded for Kent and Sussex.

[3] Treas. 1/137/28.

[4] Their letter of 12 April 1712 is an example of their writing about prisoners to the Secretary at War—who had most certainly nothing to do with the sea service. This case, concerning an army captain captured at sea, and put in custody of the

concerned inspection of sick and wounded soldiers in Spain, and it is possible that the Commissioners were not restricted within the United Kingdom—even in theory—to seamen and naval affairs.

Within the kingdom prisoners of war were directly looked after by Marshals for Prisoners of War, who worked partly under the Commissioners, partly under the Secretary of State and the Treasury, and partly under the Secretary at War. The first mention of them I have seen is dated 15 February 1703.[1] Rates of pay were prescribed, and they were responsible for feeding their charges according to a scale laid down by the Government, which was supposed to reimburse them. The Marshals shared with the prisoners themselves the results of the country's unpreparedness and shortage of money. On 28 October 1703 the Commissioners were already in debt.[2] By 9 November 1710 their debts had so increased that 'the marshals will be thrown into prison and the prisoners let out'. At that time the Marshal at Portsmouth owed over £6,000 and, having pawned his goods in order to get subsistence for the officers, had reached the stage where 'the prison doors must be opened for the prisoners to shift for themselves or they must be starved'.[3] The Treasury were not, of course, to be moved by familiar tales like these. By the following July, according to a letter from the Mayor, the Marshal was £10,000 in debt, which makes it not surprising that he could not borrow, even at 20 per cent.[4] He asked for directions (which he, naturally, did not get), since Governor Rooke had said that when there was no more subsistence, he would take off the guard and let the prisoners out to shift for themselves 'for that he could not keep a guard on men to starve them'.[5] The comment of the Commissioners was that unless they were 'enabled to pay the bills . . . the service must be at a stand, and the officers must expect nothing but imprisonment and ruin, and the seamen will be exposed to perish in the streets'.[6] In October, Slaughter, the Marshal at Plymouth, re-

---

Commissary at St. Malo, illustrates how the Commissioners' existing contacts and familiarity with the machinery made it almost inevitable that they should be employed whether the prisoners were naval or army. SP Mil. 41/4.

[1] *Dom. Cal.*, i, p. 590.
[2] *Treas. Cal.*, iii, p. 198.
[3] Ibid., iv, p. 221.   [4] Ibid., p. 294.   [5] Ibid., p. 298.
[6] Ibid., p. 300, 15 Aug. 1711.

ported that he had sold all his goods, and borrowed from everyone who would lend.

What to do to subsist the prisoners a week longer, I cannot tell, but will use my utmost endeavours if I sell the bed I lie on. I hope the Government will not think amiss of me, if I set open the prison doors, and let the prisoners shift for themselves, [rather than keep them to starve].[1]

By 23 January 1712 he owed £11,946, had 829 prisoners in his charge, and was receiving more almost daily from privateers.[2] The Dutch privateers, in fact, frequently did their best to lighten his burdens; French prisoners regularly either escaped on board the boats, to be set ashore in France for ransom, or decided to join the ship's semi-piratical enterprises.[3]

About this time the Treasury produced some money and allocated three-quarters of it to Slaughter, much to the Commissioners' annoyance. They protested strenuously that they had other claims, such as £14,138 for the home ports alone. This rose before the following September to £30,641.[4] By 29 January 1713 Slaughter was once more in debt for nearly £3,000.[5]

The upkeep of prisoners was theoretically the responsibility of their parent government. French prisoners, however, fared no better in this respect than Stanhope, who found that the cost to him of his own and fellow prisoners' subsistence was £9,000 per month.[6] This was despite Brydge's claim to have sent him a credit,[7] and a later parliamentary estimate of the cost to the Government was £61,959 for 2,185 horse and dragoons, and £103,754 for the foot.[8] Tallard was given a credit by Marlborough, until such time as money should arrive from his own Government, and actually made a contract for subsistence with the Duke's purveyor, Vanderkaa, but denied responsibility for subsistence for the troops of Spain.[9] Shortly afterwards Marl-

---

[1] *Treas. Cal.*, iv, p. 325, 27 Oct. 1711.   [2] Ibid., p. 352.
[3] *Dom. Cal.*, i, p. 638.   [4] *Treas. Cal.*, iv, pp. 384 and 421.
[5] Ibid., p. 462.   [6] *Stanhope*, p. 115.
[7] *Treas. Cal.*, iv, p. 242, 9 Jan. 1711. Some money was certainly sent—e.g. the bill of credit of 8 Nov. 1707, mentioned in *H.M.C.H. of L.*, vii, p. 157. Another example of dispatch of money abroad for prisoners is at Entry Books WO 26/13 (29 Jan. 1708) dealing with the appointment of Captain John Arnot to visit prisoners in France, investigate their treatment, and distribute subsistence.
[8] *Journals Commons*, xvii, 2 Feb. 1712.
[9] Murray, i, p. 482, 25 Sept. 1704; *Anne Cal.*, p. 726, 30 June 1704.

borough had to complain to Villeroi that the French were costing the Dutch four sols per day.[1]

The official British ration scale for French captives, raised
early in the war from 4*d*. to 5*d*. per day,[2] was as follows:

Sunday, Tuesday, and Thursday		Monday and Friday		Wednesday and Saturday	
Bread	1*d*.	Bread	1*d*.	Bread	1½*d*.
Beer	½*d*.	Beer	½*d*.	Beer	¾*d*.
Meat	2½*d*.	Pease	¾*d*.	Cheese	1*d*.
Veg.	1*d*.	Butter	1¼*d*.	Butter	1¼*d*.
		Cheese	½*d*.	Veg.	½*d*.
		Veg.	1*d*.[3]		

In addition, the Government claimed that it paid 12*d*. per
day for maintenance and medicine of men taken to hospital.[4]
As a reprisal for reported ill treatment by the French, the subsistence was ordered in March 1703 to be cut to 3*d*. per day, but
the order was rescinded on 3 April 1703.[5]

It was alleged by Nottingham that the French allowed the
English soldiers only five sous a day, but in the same letter
he admitted by implication that the French treated officer
prisoners better than the English did.[6]

Disorganization and shortage of money made some hardship
inevitable. Little of the suffering of the prisoners is overwhelm-
ingly out of proportion to the routine suffering of the country's
own soldiers, or indeed her servants in less venturesome ways
of life. There is, however, conclusive evidence of some ill-treatment and persecution, but this was never officially countenanced, and in England at least strict orders were issued against
these practices. Correspondence and recrimination between
France and England on the subject lasted, nevertheless, throughout most of the war. The first mention I have seen of official attention to the question is Nottingham's instruction on
5 October 1702 to the Commissioners for Sick and Wounded
to hold an inquiry. The Queen, he stated, wished the prisoners
properly treated 'without the ill-usage practised in France'. He
was himself informed by a Frenchman the following month:
'I hear French prisoners are dying every day in prison.'[7]

[1] Murray, i, p. 563.
[2] *Dom. Cal.*, i, p. 90.
[3] *H.M.C.H. of L.*, vii, pp. 162–3.
[4] *Dom. Cal.*, i, pp. 624–6.
[5] Ibid., pp. 628–9 and 674.
[6] Ibid. ii, p. 14, 14 June 1703.
[7] Ibid. i, pp. 266 and 286.

In their report the Commissioners dealt, among others, with a subsequent case where on 4 December 1702 a captain in charge, when spat at by a prisoner whom the others refused to identify, brought all before him two by two 'and beat many of them as they passed, breaking two or three swords, and as many muskets upon them'.[1] It was alleged that at Southampton the jailer issued bad bread, only half cooked, so that it would weigh more, which 'gives (the prisoners) pains inside'. The beer was bad, and—understandable complaint in any circumstances—insufficient. The meat was only of bullocks' or cows' heads, 'so that there is not the size of an egg . . . for every man's portion'. In reply to the complaints the jailer produced a certificate with an impressive array of signatures to say that those who appended their names were all well fed. The only objection that could be laid against it was that 'those who signed it . . . were not in prison'.[2] In disorders which broke out in the prison shortly afterwards, one French prisoner was killed.[3]

There were, too, a number of methods by which enterprising government servants might, at the expense of the prisoners, overcome the lack of provision by the Treasury. The jailers at the Gate House in the Fleet prison, for example, had to be specifically instructed not to take fees for lodging, not to demand money for allowing prisoners into the court yard, to allow the officers servants, and to give them beds 'fitting for their condition'.[4]

The inhabitants of Southampton complained in June 1703 of 'oppression from the number of prisoners, and the liberty which any of them who will pay the Marshal a small fee can have to walk abroad'.[5] Despite, or because of, all this an escaped French prisoner went out of his way in 1704 to pay tribute to his treatment; which was more than any English prisoner is recorded as having been able to do.[6]

The sufferings of our prisoners at the hands of the French, and more especially their mercenary Irish jailers, are a large item in the long catalogue of patient endurance by the soldiers and sailors of that age. Out of less than 600 at Dinan in February 1703, eight to ten were dying daily. 'If this continues', wrote one,

---

[1] *Dom. Cal.*, i, p. 342.   [2] Ibid., pp. 243–4.   [3] Ibid., p. 280.
[4] Ibid., p. 675.   [5] Ibid., p. 538.
[6] Ibid. ii, p. 525, 7 Dec. 1704.

'they need not trouble about a cartel' (for exchange). The dead were removed only once every three to four days, while in another jail men were not allowed to leave their rooms 'and do everything that nature requires in common where they lie'. It was claimed that in England fresh straw was issued every fourteen days, and that tubs and other necessaries were issued 'for keeping the prisoners clean and removing nuisances'. The sick were kept apart, 'and doubtless carried out of the prison immediately on their death'.[1] At Dunkirk in January/February 1703, there were 70–80 men to a room where half had to stand up to let the rest lie down.[2] At Dinan the food was cabbage, porridge, and black pease full of dirt. There were no medicines and the investigator reported that practically all the prisoners bore bruises from the jailers. 'He can't but observe the cunning barbarity of the French in committing them to the care of the Irish who never fail in showing such marks of their kindness.'[3] The concomitant barbarity of the Irish was presumably unremarkable.

Dinan probably compared favourably with other prisoner locations for it was under closer observation as a transit camp for prisoners on their way home. A proportion of the 1,200 who were there at once in peak periods themselves paid 4s. per night for lodgings while the remainder were lodged in chateaux. Twenty to thirty went daily to hospital, 'many bare-footed, bare-legged, and almost naked'. An equal number were carried back each day, 'the hospital having been full of sick Englishmen for several months where they daily died in inexpressible misery to the apparent concern of the French themselves'.[4]

Joseph Gyde, the investigator from whose report the above is taken, was himself later imprisoned by the French while carrying out his duties as Agent for the Care of Prisoners and their Exchange under the Commissioners for Sick and Wounded.[5] He mentions in his report that it was the custom to lend the prisoners money so that they would be in debt and thus ineligible for exchange. As a result, the only way they had, in the end, of discharging their obligations was to enter the French service. Thomas Wright, who accompanied Gyde, told of the sick men compelled to travel naked, and whipped 'in a dreadful

---

[1] Ibid. i, pp. 582 and 588.　　　　[2] Ibid., pp. 581–2.
[3] *H.M.C.H. of L.*, vii, pp. 151–2.
[4] Ibid., pp. 150–1.　　　　[5] *Anne Cal.*, p. 16, 23 Nov. 1704.

manner' with horse whips. When they complained, the Irish prison-keeper 'had broken several heads, and almost beat their eyes out'.[1] In order to secure the removal to hospital of forty-seven men ill of smallpox, the prisoners had to hang a corpse out of the window. A lieutenant gave evidence, presented to the Lords on 19 November 1707, that his servant had been taken from prison at Dunkirk by Irish soldiers and forced, along with ten to twelve others, into the French service. Another report told of living on beef which 'looked like carrion,' and of rations of $1\frac{1}{2}$ lb. of meat or cheese among seven, instead of the 5d. per day entitlement. When the men complained, 'a file of musketeers drub them all round with naked swords', after tying the prisoners hand to hand. Another prisoner who claimed to have seen several die of starvation, said that he could put half a day's allowance of food in his mouth at once. He was, he stated, beaten for asking for water. Men lay stark naked for fifteen days without straw, of which the issue was supposed to be 4 lb. per two men per fortnight. When they complained of this to the Commissary of Jailers at Calais he 'would drub them all round and put them in the dungeon'. James Helding, a pauper, who gave the servant of the Commissary of Prisons 'all he had in the world, two shillings', to be included out of turn in the exchange of prisoners, was only one of many.[2] Others, it was stated, gave six and seven guineas for their freedom.[3] Their pay, including off-reckonings, was in the neighbourhood of £11 per year.

I have not had access to the French records. The English naturally emphasize the delays, brutalities, and chicaneries of France. The English appear, however, to have at least aimed at a reasonable standard of conduct; the needless suffering inflicted by the French was, on the other hand, very largely due to the Irish jailers.[4] In general, however, it is probably true to state that treatment of prisoners, although governed by no formal conventions, was without the organized inhumanities to which we have progressed in recent times. The pragmatic pro-

---

[1] *H.M.C.H. of L.*, vii, pp. 151–2.

[2] Ibid., pp. 149–50.   [3] Ibid., pp. 151–2.

[4] It was ironic retribution that the French prisoners who suffered most were those lodged in Ireland, but their suffering was due to the climate. In 1704 a special request was made by the French that exchange of prisoners in Ireland be expedited 'as these poor people suffer very much in this weather. Many of them have no clothes.' *Dom. Cal.*, ii, p. 520, 27 Jan. 1704.

cedure produced little suffering for officers. The brutalities and callous treatment suffered by other ranks were not, for the most part, officially countenanced, and were largely attributable to the fact that consciences were content that men should endure conditions, either in peace or in war, which are not today sanctioned by most western nations.

RESETTLEMENT AND DEPENDANTS

Britain's soldiers have seldom lacked verbal solicitude for their welfare as civilians, particularly so long as their military services have been currently required. Queen Anne's concern matched that of her countrymen; in her address from the throne in 1713 she abjured Her Faithful Lords and Commons:

I recommend to your care those brave men who have served well by Sea or Land this War, and cannot be employed in time of peace.

The Commons obediently resolved nine days later:

That it be an instruction to the Committee who are to consider further of the supply granted to Her Majesty that they do consider of that part of Her Majesty's speech which recommends the care of those brave men who have served well by Sea or Land this war and cannot be employed in time of peace.[1]

It might, in the light of this, be judged captious to give too much weight to the petition presented six months earlier on behalf of 'a great number of soldiers lately disbanded and lying about the streets'. Her Majesty, on this occasion, 'seeing the prejudice it may be to her service to suffer such objects to be neglected and become a burden, as well as an offence to the town', called on Chelsea Hospital to assist. This, of course, presented the already overcrowded and overburdened hospital with a task it cannot seriously have been expected to perform. It was eventually ruled that the regiments to which 'such objects' belonged should be subsisted until there was room at the hospital, but this only touched the very fringe of the problem of resettlement.[2] Disbanded soldiers, like spent ammunition and dilapidated wartime camps, are no doubt an unsightly nuisance; their existence is an embarrassment well calculated to call forth

---

[1] *Journals Commons*, xvii, 9 and 18 Apr. 1713.
[2] *Treas. Cal.*, iv, p. 432: petition of 16 Oct. 1712.

sighs of regret like that heaved in Elizabeth's proclamation of 1590 concerning those 'not otherwise disposed of by the Almighty'. This proclamation laid down that the soldier should be given sufficient money to take him home. He was also to receive a pass allowing him just sufficient time to get there. Should he delay *en route*, he was liable to arrest as a vagrant. Soldiers without adequate discharge papers were imprisoned.[1] Charles I, on the disbandment of 1628, significantly proclaimed that the soldiers were to return to their homes and 'honest vocations' until he should have further occasion for their services.[2]

In the transitional period between the old feudal levies, which did not hold for politicians the same terrors as a 'standing army', and the new mass armies which obviously could not (even in the imaginations of Westminster) become props of military dictatorship, treatment of soldiers no longer required was ruthless. When the army was the servant of one like William who offended the Tory squires' insular pride by being a Dutchman and their saviour, then it had indeed to look out for itself. After the Peace of Ryswick 'The House of Commons saw its opportunity and turned savagely upon the Army. They actually passed a resolution to disband all regiments except the Guards and the three Tangier regiments; and that without providing for payment of their arrears . . . amounting to two millions sterling.'[3] Such profitable habits were not lightly cast off. 'The army under Marlborough . . . wrought marvels. They returned home to be received not as heroes, but as the plagues of the nation. Every man's hand was against them.'[3] Nottingham in 1703 wrote to Marlborough to suggest raising regiments of French refugees for a descent on the French coast. 'When there is no further service for them', he added, 'it will be easier to disband them than the English and they will expect less.'[4] They would have found it difficult to make the expectation match the event. The attitude persisted for at least upwards of 200 years. A later government official and historian wrote:

I have noticed the fact that our earlier European Wars after the Revolution were carried on by the hire of Soldiers upon the Continent, and that by this policy the country was relieved from finding employment for discharged Soldiers at the close of the War.[5]

---

[1] Cruickshank, p. 20.   [2] Clode, i, pp. 18–19.   [3] *Last Post*, pp. 16–17.
[4] *Dom. Cal.*, i, pp. 670–1.   [5] Clode, ii, p. 544.

Even Elizabeth's principles at least had been more charitable. In her time money was raised in every county by law to grant pensions not exceeding £10 for rank and file, £15 for ensigns, and £20 for lieutenants if disabled from active work. Similar Acts were passed after the Restoration for relief of Civil War veterans, but by William's time they had fallen into desuetude.[1]

Sometimes a few soldiers could be transferred to other units. When Montandre's regiment was disbanded in 1712, for instance, 200 of 'the best of the private soldiers' were drafted to the Coldstreamers and others were sent to Dunkirk. The officers and N.C.O.s were sent to Ireland.[2] In a large-scale disbandment such transfers could only be a very small minority. A few more could be admitted to Chelsea.

For the remainder there were two considerations—their release and their resettlement. The first aim was to get them out of uniform and dispersed as soon as possible. To achieve this, special provision was made in the Act of 1712 'to allow . . . officers to account with soldiers'. Accounts were to be made up by the Paymaster by 1 December of the following year. Colonels were to transmit accounts to captains, and to clear them within ten days of receipt of the accounts and the money; and the captains were allowed a further ten days to settle with their men.[3] The penalty for failure to comply was double the sum which 'appeared due'; this penalty was at no time visited on the Paymaster. The disbandment warrant of 13 August further provided that no deductions were to be made by the officers from the soldiers' pay for provisions supplied at sea—with the comprehensive exception of cases where 'any charge of that kind is made on the Regiment from the office of our Paymaster General'. To ensure compliance with the law and regulations, major-generals were frequently detailed to be present at disbandments as observers empowered, where necessary, to take executive action.[4]

In William's time, N.C.O.s and men had received fourteen days' subsistence to take them home, plus clothes, belts, knapsacks, and 3s. for their swords, except sergeants who kept theirs.[5]

[1] Walton, pp. 593–4.   [2] Entry Books WO 26/14: warrant of 13 Aug.
[3] Annae 12, cap. 11.   [4] Entry Books WO 26/14.
[5] Treas. 1/147, 23 Apr. 1712. Walton claims that in 1679 disbanded foot soldiers took away their clothes, swords, belts, and knapsacks, while troopers retained their horses and saddlery. In addition, both categories received 10s. to get

This was broadly the provision made for Anne's armies, with bayonets ranking equally with swords for the 3s. bounty. It appears to have been usual for a man who was without arms when discharged to have forfeited arrears as well as bounty.[1] Strict precautions were taken to see that disbanded men took no arms, and it was not infrequent for them to be prohibited to travel in parties of more than three once they had been discharged. Mounted soldiers with a year or more's service were allowed to take with them horses which had been paid for by levy money. Those with less than a year's service had their horses sold, and the money disposed of under the Queen's orders.[2] In practice, those who took horses normally received six days' pay, and those who did not, twelve days'.[3] In at least one case of dragoons demobilized in Ireland, however, men taking horses were given seven days' pay, and those who did not received fourteen days'.[4] Officers who had supplied troop horses for their men were refunded by the sale of the animals, and any balance then outstanding was made up by deduction from the discharged soldiers' arrears.[5]

them home. At the reduction after Ryswick, men had to return their swords, for which they received 3s., but took away clothing and accoutrements provided out of the off-reckonings. They were to receive 10 days' subsistence (3s. 4d. for a private, 5s. for a drummer, and 7s. 6d. for a sergeant) instead of the 10s. This aroused such discontent that the provision was altered to allow fourteen days' subsistence. If a trooper took his horse, he got seven days' full pay. Walton, pp. 492–3.

　[1] See Entry Books WO 26/14 for disbandment orders, e.g. 30 July 1712 and Hotham's of 1 Aug. 1712.

　[2] The disposal of cavalry horses was a fruitful cause of dispute, which had been particularly troublesome during the Civil Wars when many men mounted themselves, and many others who had been originally mounted by the state had subsequently remounted themselves. In 1647 the regiments which Parliament attempted to disband expected to be allowed to keep their horses. 'We find it provided,' complained a petition, 'that no trooper is capable of allowance or debenture for arrears, unless he delivers in such horse and arms with which he hath served, or a certificate that such horse and arms did not appertain to the state, or else was lost in actual service; which extends to the total taking away from them those horse and arms of the state's which they have used and preserved in the service, contrary to the favour allowed, and never . . . denied in the disbanding of any other army . . . It seems hard, that such as cannot deliver in those state's horses and arms, which at disbanding they understood to be their own, and so perhaps have sold or otherwise disposed of, should for that lose their whole arrears.' The procedure was later modified so that any soldier wishing to keep the state's horse did so at a fixed rate of 40s. or 50s., which was deducted from arrears due. *Cromwells Army*, pp. 247–8.

　[3] Entry Books WO 26/14: orders of Oct.–Dec. 1712 regarding Royal Regiment of Horse Guards.　　　　　　　　　　　　　　　[4] Ireland WO 8/1.

　[5] Entry Books WO 26/14 above regarding Horse Guards.

It was normally laid down that N.C.O.s and soldiers should be paid the off-reckonings due since their last clothing. In this connexion, Ranelagh had pointed out nine years earlier that since the men 'always receive by way of subsistence their full pay except what is received for clothing' there could be 'but a small matter due to them'. While it was an exaggeration to say that they always received 'by way of subsistence their full pay', the men nevertheless probably received in kind a considerable portion of it, and were in debt for items such as camp necessaries or medicines for the remainder. On disbandment, therefore, they could receive only the balance of their subsistence, and such bounty money as was available.[1] The insufficiency of such provision is convincingly evidenced in the complaints and prayers from the J.P.s of Kent in 1712.[2] They protested that soldiers not qualified for relief at Chelsea had been given passes by the Secretary at War,[3] as a result of which the local magistrates subsisted them on their way home 'without any charge to Her Majesty'.

Having arrived home, without sword, with or without horse, and almost certainly without money, the ex-soldier was entitled to such reliefs as the 1713 Act to Enable Officers and Soldiers to Exercise Trades provided. Broadly speaking, any non-deserter who had previously practised or been apprenticed to a trade was now to be permitted to exercise that trade 'irrespective of the rules about apprenticeship, without any let, suit, or molestation of any person or persons whatsoever'. Anyone taking action against an ex-soldier in this connexion and losing his case was to pay treble costs, while anyone giving false evidence of serving in order to reap the benefits of the Act

---

[1] *Journals Commons*, xiv, 30 Nov. 1702. Under Annae 12, cap. 13 of 1713, executors of colonels and agents who died in debt to soldiers were to pay those debts in preference to all others. The soldiers may have felt at times that it was unfortunate the Crown never died.

[2] *Treas. Cal.*, iv, p. 433.

[3] Specimen pass issued to discharged soldier:

The bearer hereof RICHARD PHENIX being discharged from the Lord North and Grey's Regiment wherein he formerly served is returning to his abode in IRELAND, in order whereunto all H.M. officers, civil and military, are desired to let him pass from place to place until he shall arrive at CHESTER, and from there to pass to IRELAND.

Dated 3 July 1706, and signed by St. John as Secretary at War. Entry Books WO 26/13.

was liable to three months' imprisonment. The two exceptions to this law were the Universities of Oxford and Cambridge where no one could set up in the trade of vintner 'or selling wine or other liquors' within the universities without licence from the vice-chancellor.[1] An ex-soldier setting up in trade was given three years' exemption from distraint of person, tools, or stock for debts owing when he enlisted—a further relief for the insolvent debtors who, it will be remembered, could get themselves out of jail (but not out of debt) by joining the army.

The craftsmen among the 'common soldiers'—and they must have been a not very large minority—had thus at least a modicum of protection and help. Most of the N.C.O.s and men did receive a little money on disbandment. They would, no doubt, have taken to plunder and loot otherwise. The officers of the army, being less given to turbulence and disorder of that sort, received correspondingly abrupter treatment. When Rane-lagh pointed out that soldiers had their subsistence money and bounty to come to them on discharge, he added that the officers received nothing until the money was ready, 'which many times there is not, till a year or two after the disbanding'. Regiments disbanded after the Peace of Ryswick were uncleared at least five years later.[2]

Normally the sole provision for disbanded officers was a not very large half pay establishment, usually reserved for British subjects, and not admissible to anyone who had sold out, nor for brevet rank.[3] There were occasional special grants like the £200 a year from 9 March 1702 given to Luke Lillingston 'in consideration of the long and faithful service . . . and of him having enjoyed half pay since disbanding in 1696'.[4] These were, however, the exceptions. The Royal Warrant of 23 February 1698 placed officers on half pay, which was also allowed for their servants, and was to be paid weekly or monthly 'until fully paid off and cleared or otherwise disposed of'. On the reduction

---

[1] There were other opportunities to practise cognate trades: Mother Ross records that she was given the exclusive right to sell beer in the Deer Park, Dublin, on a review day, and was also allowed to keep a sutler's tent in Hyde Park. She reaped more profit from these than from the Queen's promise that if her unborn child turned out to be a boy he would get a commission as soon as he was born.

[2] *Journals Commons*, xiv, 30 Nov. 1702.

[3] Entry Books WO 26/14, 30 July 1717.

[4] Ests. WO 24/26, 25 Apr. 1702, countersigned by Blathywayt.

after the Peace of Utrecht the Commons resolved in agreement with the Queen:

Whereas upon the disbanding several of Our forces, We have thought fit that half pay shall be allowed to the commission officers who shall by that means be discharged Our service until they shall be again provided for therein; which it is Our Royal intention they shall be in the first vacancies that may happen amongst Our forces that shall be kept on foot in preference to all other persons.

The payment was restricted to natural born subjects. It will be seen from the reference to vacancies (repeated in the directions issued by George I) that the half pay was as much a retainer for future as a reward for past services for which they could hope in due course to be 'fully paid off and cleared'.[1]

How regularly it was received, or how adequate half pay was, may be judged from the letter of 30 July 1713 from Ormonde, Lord Lieutenant of Ireland, to the Lord Treasurer. Apologizing for forwarding a number of petitions, he wrote that he would not trouble the Treasurer 'were it not that the greatest part of them are brought . . . out of prisons where these officers lie for want of money'. Some months later he had cause to refer again to officers 'the greatest part of whom' were in prison for debt.[2] Such instances were far from being confined to Ireland. Captain Martin Laycock petitioned from the Marshalsea in 1703 seven months after his arrest that he had been in great want and ten weeks in bed with wounds received in the nation's service. He 'raised men, fed them when no money was coming, and waited several years to establish his pension', but received 'neither small moneys, nor the pension voted . . . by Parliament, nor payment of out-of-pocket expenses'. At the time of his first petition when he was 'very poor and his family perishing' he was claimed to be due £264. 8s. 0d. half pay for the period 1699–1702. His case was referred to Ireland, but he objected that he was not an Irishman, and added that his wife, who was very ill, 'will perish if not relieved'. Some time later, after declaring in despair that he was 'tossed to and fro between England and Ireland', he asked to be posted to one of the regiments raised from Ireland. 'I am not', he declared, 'like the officers that threw down their commissions rather than go to the West Indies. I only want to get there.' Finally he asked for some

---

[1] Clode, i, pp. 370–2. [2] *Treas. Cal.*, iv, pp. 500 and 509.

decision before he was driven to serve the Emperor or the Dutch. A little later, nevertheless, he was again asking to be posted to any new foot regiment as he was penniless and unable to buy bread for his family. It is difficult to ascertain the result with certainty, but he seems to have been eventually granted half pay. The question of actual payment of money was no doubt another matter. He wrote on 3 May 1706 that if he could not get support from his country, having spent £2,500 from his private purse, he would 'offer his services to another'.[1] Entitlement, often difficult enough to establish, was no assurance of money, either for pay, pension, or anything else. Captain Peter Delaval who petitioned in April 1707 was as typical a case as any. He had been wounded and granted a pension of 3s. 6d. per day. He asked for the £244. 16s. 6d. due to him. The Treasury merely minuted his petition 'No fund for this'.[2]

Surgeons, physicians, and apothecaries were normally not allowed half pay since they were considered capable of earning a living at their own profession. Those concerned made precisely the opposite case that they, with impaired health due to service, had lost 'all opportunities of making friends to live' by their profession.[3] Their case was eventually conceded and half pay granted in Her Majesty's letter of 23 December 1713.[4] Chaplains, who were responsible for the soldiers' moral, as opposed to physical, welfare, had no doubt a more wearing task, and were considered to be too exhausted to earn their own living. They were deemed eligible for half pay from the start.[5]

Chelsea Hospital and the Invalide companies

Chelsea Hospital and the companies of Invalides were really one question during the war, but it will be convenient to deal briefly with the non-Chelsea Invalides separately. During the course of the war, in an endeavour to relieve the manpower shortage, it was decided to form eight companies of Invalides (i.e. ex-soldiers discharged either after long service or because of disability) to take over guard and garrison duties and thus release younger and fitter soldiers for the field. The officers applied themselves to the task with such a will that eventually twenty companies were formed. It was reckoned that in money

[1] *Dom. Cal.*, i, pp. 616/17; *Anne Cal.*, p. 289.   [2] *Treas Cal.*, iii, p. 11.
[3] SP Mil. 41/4: see p. 236.   [4] Ireland WO 8/1.   [5] *Treas. Cal.*, iv, p. 445.

terms alone this represented a saving of £9,705 on a basis of the following costs:[1]

> Clothes of 800 men at 30s. per annum £1,200
> Pay of eight captains at 4s. per day   £584
> Pay of eight lieutenants at 2s. per day £292
> Pay of six ensigns at 2s. per day   £219

This calculation, not unexpectedly, takes no account of men's pay—and might indeed have omitted officers' pay and most of the men's clothes as these details appear to have been overlooked in the raising.[2]

The sequel to the enthusiasm of those who raised the companies and performed a most valuable service was a confused and prolonged wrangle over availability of money, whether the regiments were really authorized, provision of clothes, and all the familiar squalors and degradations of the reign. Many companies were never paid until finally disbanded. Very many were unable to move from the spot where they were originally stationed, either because they were so heavily in debt locally that they dared not show signs of leaving, or because the men themselves would not move until paid. Colonel Goring when asking for money for ten companies of thirty-six privates in September 1713 said that he could neither disband them (for want of money) nor induce the men to embark for Ireland without payment of arrears. He asked at that time for £13,000 'upon account'—'a small part of what is due'. Should this be paid, he added, the officers would still be 4¾ years in arrears of clearings.[3]

The treatment of the Invalide Companies was one of the less brilliant of England's organizational ventures, only relieved, once again, by the patient devotion to duty of the men on the spot, who by persuasion, cajolery, and sheer grit got them to carry out the job for which they were intended.

Chelsea, owing its home to Nell Gwynne, who, feeling no doubt that she and the army, by repute at least, had much in

---

[1] Taking, according to the Journals of the House of Commons, the cost of a regiment of foot as £12,000.

[2] *Journals Commons*, xvii, 23 Jan. 1712. A memorial of 11 Feb. 1709 mentioned four companies which had received no clothing for two years, and another six which had received none since they were raised. Treas. 1/118.

[3] *Treas. Cal.*, iv, p. 511.

common, gave up the land for it, was the responsibility of a special body of Commissioners acting in the Queen's name, but answerable to the Secretary at War.[1] It is said that Nell used to be the first toast of the old pensioners, but she may have felt herself sufficiently recompensed by the house Charles II later built her in Pall Mall. He had also to compensate the Royal Society with £1,300 for a half-finished building, started by James I as a college for theological students, but abandoned for want of funds—the original 'college' of the Hospital's nickname.[2] The Institution of the Hospital for the relief of 'aged, maimed, and infirm land soldiers' is said to date from 1681,[3] but Charles II's warrant to provide money for its upkeep was signed on 7 March 1684.[4] It was completed in 1690,[5] and a Board of Management first constituted under the Great Seal on 3 March 1691. It consisted of three Commissioners, of whom the Paymaster-General, officiating as chairman, was one.[6] Under Charles's warrant each party to the sale of a commission had to pay poundage of 12d. in the £ towards the cost of the Hospital, and the Secretary of State was ordered not to issue a commission until he received a certificate from the Paymaster that the money had been paid.[7]

On 17 March a further warrant authorized a deduction of 5 per cent. from all military pay. Two-thirds of this was to go towards 'erecting, building, and maintaining . . . or towards the payment of the establishment'. In June the position was eased for members of the forces by the Warrant which authorized deduction of only one day's pay per annum, but cannily stipulated two in leap years.[8] Not a large proportion of this trickled through to the Hospital. Ranelagh in a statement for the King's information on 4 March 1689 showed expenditure on the Hospital at £7,350 as against income of £12,085. The £12,085 appears to be an understatement by over £10,000 as only a 'moiety' of the money produced by the 8d. stoppage is accounted for.[9]

---

[1] Walton, p. 598; Entry Books WO 26/11.   [2] Walton, pp. 598–600.
[3] Clode, ii, p. 540.   [4] Walton, p. 600.   [5] Ibid., p. 602.
[6] Clode, ii, p. 540. The first three were Ranelagh, Fox, and Christopher Wren (Walton, p. 604, footnote 1737).   [7] SP Mil. 44/69, 16 Mar. 1684.
[8] Walton, pp. 600–1.
[9] Ibid., p. 601, footnote 1729. Clode at ii, pp. 277–8, shows revenue of £12,084. 16s. 4d. and expenditure of £7,377. 9s. 2d., but states this left £4,734. 7s. 1¾d. 'in favour of the Hospital'. The difference is, in fact, £4,707. 7s. 2d. He quotes the Book of Instructions at Chelsea, pp. 51, 57. Walton quotes 'Home Office records, statement 4 Mar. 1689'. I have not been able to consult either.

The balance of £4,735 between Ranelagh's two figures was said to be 'to answer the charge of new buildings', but it appears, from a note in the report, to have been otherwise appropriated by a verbal royal order.[1]

When completed, the Hospital could accommodate only 472 pensioners, and by then the total revenue from officers and soldiers was put at £23,000, against an expenditure of £7,000–£8,000.[2] A muster of those 'disabled by wounds in fight or accident, or who, having served the Crown 20 years, had been judged unfit for service', showed a total of 579 who were put on the pension list.[3] To look after those admitted to the Hospital, there was a staff of 64.[4] It was regarded as a military station, although the pensioners were not subject to military law, and was originally organized in four companies of foot.[5]

Since all those eligible could not be accommodated in the Hospital, a system of 'out patients' was also adopted. These were organized in four companies of foot which made up the Companies of Invalides garrisoning Windsor, Hampton Court, Teignmouth, and Chester. Both 'in' and 'out' patients were paid according to rank. 'In patient' privates had 8d. per week plus food and clothing, and those not in the Hospital 5d. per day plus biennial clothing.[6] Later the eight companies in the Hospital were increased to twelve, but a report of 6 May 1703 stated that there were only ninety-eight 'out patients' and they had not been settled with since 1 July 1696.[7] These would seem, however, to have been exclusive of the four Invalide Companies, for in 1702 they were reduced to seventy-five men, three sergeants, two corporals, and one drummer each.[8] This establishment was increased in 1705 by two corporals, one drummer, and

[1] Clode, ii, p. 278.
[2] Ibid.; Walton, p. 601, footnote 1729.
[3] Clode, ii, p. 278.
[4] Governor, major, two chaplains, one physician, one secretary, one secretary's clerk, one steward, one comptroller, one clerk of the works, one chirurgeon, one apothecary, one deputy treasurer, one under-clerk of works, one chirurgeon's mate, one wardrobe keeper and comptroller to the coal yard, one master cook, one second cook, three under-cooks, one scullery man, one master butler, three under-butlers, one master baker, three under-bakers, one sexton, one usher of the hall, one yeoman of the coal yard, one porter, two sweepers, one barber, one canal keeper, one female housekeeper, one under-housekeeper, twenty-four nurses.
[5] Walton, pp. 602–3.   [6] Ibid., pp. 603–4.
[7] Clode, ii, p. 278.
[8] Entry Books WO 26/11, 30 June 1702.

twenty-five privates.[1] Of those discharged in 1702 to achieve the reduced figure, fifty were admitted to Chelsea Hospital, and the remainder given 20s. each.[2]

Originally the Hospital catered for men of disbanded regiments as well as the disabled and the long-service men. Shortly after the outbreak of war, however, the provision for admission of men from broken regiments was suspended in order to reserve the vacancies for disabled soldiers.[3] A codification of the rules some years later confirmed that those applying for admission must have no visible means of maintaining themselves and had to present certificates from their commanding officer and regimental surgeon within six months of leaving the service.[4]

As a result of the large number of disabled in the early campaigns, £4,000 was, in an outburst of enthusiasm, allotted for men who could not be admitted to Chelsea although qualified. In 1705, however, the Commissioners had to point out that, since the money was allocated for men from the 'last German campaign', those who had served in the Low Countries were ineligible. In the meantime, Marlborough, from across the sea, directed that men not qualified for a share of the 'Chelsea bounty' should be given a small allowance with passes to take them home. The Commissioners recommended payment of the 10s. 'usual for disbanded soldiers', and the last trace I have seen of the matter was the Lord Treasurer cannily calling for an estimate of the cost.[5]

The number of in-pensioners appears to have been resolved as 476, organized as officers, light horse, and four companies of foot. This figure seems to have remained substantially unaltered. Out-pensioners, after beginning as 185, were swiftly increased to 600 in the four companies, at Windsor, Hampton Court, Teignmouth, and Chester.[6] In the later years of the war, it is sometimes difficult to extract figures for out-pensioners as they are frequently mixed with those for the Invalide Home Defence

---

[1] Ests. WO 24/38.   [2] Entry Books WO 26/11, 30 June 1702.
[3] Ibid., 4 Sept. 1703 and 12 Jan. 1704.
[4] Treas. 1/145, 'Orders, Rules, and Instructions for Chelsea and Out-Patients.' It appears to have been possible to sell a vacancy obtained; *vide* Blackader on his resignation: 'I propose getting (my servant) into Chelsea as a sergeant. He inclines to stay in my service, and to dispose of the other which, he says, will give him £30 or £40.' *Blackader*, 29 Sept. 1711.
[5] *Treas. Cal.*, iii, p. 335.   [6] Walton, pp. 603–4.

Companies, first formed in 1708. Their numbers fell from 1,004 in sixteen companies in 1707 to 619 in 1708.[1] In 1711 they totalled 3,947, according to one estimate, and in the following year there were upwards of 3,800 expected, including seven companies drafted out during the year.[2]

In 1712/13, 1,882 men of twenty years' service were dismissed from pension as 'not being visibly disabled by wounds and infirmities', but £61,464 was nevertheless voted for out-pensioners, against a previous highest figure of £26,281.[3]

In 1713 in-patients were in twelve companies totalling 660, and the Commissioners ordered 'that such men as had served 30 years in the Army, though not disabled by wounds should be continued on out pension', and a list was signed for 4,102. In the following year, a fraudulent increase by Ormonde to 9,109 was detected by a Privy Council inquiry.[4]

Until the revised figure of £61,464 was produced, the estimated cost in 1712 of out-pensioners awaiting admission was £30,000 out of a total budget of £52,282. The next biggest item was £7,524 to the Treasurer, for 'exchequer fees and allowances', and to the Paymaster-General for himself and the expense of his office. The 'officers of the House' accounted for a further £2,643.[5] This total, plus nearly £6,000 for 'hospital and artificers', was almost £37,000 above the fees on sale of commissions, poundage, and day's pay deductions which were theoretically supposed to suffice.[6]

The money, of course, was only forthcoming in dribbles after long battles, and barely sufficed to keep loyal servants from jail by artifices such as those employed by the Rt. Hon. J. Howe, Paymaster of the Guards and Garrisons, who, at the formidable risk of severe punishment at the hands of a cantankerous Parliament, managed to keep the ship afloat by misappropriations of surpluses from various other heads.[7] Students of the period may feel that any Paymaster who succeeded in finding a surplus anywhere was a most remarkable man.

A pretty little sidelight on the consequences of financial

[1] *Journals Commons*, xvii, 10 Apr. 1712.
[2] Ibid.; Treas. 1/141.
[3] Clode, ii, pp. 278–9; *Journals Commons*, xvii, 14 Apr. 1712.
[4] Clode, ii, p. 279. [5] SP Mil. 41/4.
[6] SP Mil. 41/4; *Journals Commons*, xvii, 10 Apr. 1712.
[7] *Journals Commons*, xvii, 10 Apr. 1712.

management of the time is given in the letter of 25 October 1711 from the Governor and Lieutenant-Governor of Chelsea who wrote that their invalides and out-pensioners had been more than six months without subsistence or pension. Since they were allowed no quarters and the Hospital was already full of sick and disabled,

the out-pensioners are now lying in the streets in and about the Cities of London and Westminster, and severall other parts of the Kingdom in a starving and perishing condition, severall of them not having wherewithall to cover their nakedness, and their wounds yet uncured all which tends very much to the discouragement of Her Majesty's Service . . . these Poor Creatures . . . having lost their limbs or been otherwise disabled in Her armies abroad.[1]

That there were not many more 'lying about the streets' was no doubt due to the fact that they were so many months in arrears 'and their credit so sunk that many are in gaol'.[2]

Suffering was by no means confined to London. On 16 November 1704 'the poor inhabitants of Shields, Tynemouth, and adjacent places' had petitioned that, by the following 25 March (they obviously had experience of the speed with which government departments moved), they would have subsisted four companies of Invalides for a year. Many of those, they pleaded, were old and helpless with families, which, the authors added, 'they themselves must be unless Her Majesty knew their grievances'. They expected, they concluded, every day to be sent to jail by tax collectors—which was not, however, a sufficiently unusual fate for those who served their country in those days to be calculated to move many hearts.[3]

How much better off those who were theoretically catered for may be judged from Howe's report of 1707. Even he, who could find surpluses from moneys voted by Parliament, had to admit that the clothing of four companies of Invalides was 'as bad as was possible to imagine'. Each soldier was supposed to receive every two years one coat, one pair of breeches, one hat, one pair of shoes, one pair of stockings, two shirts, two neckcloths, sword, and belt. In fact, on their previous clothing they had received one shirt and one neckcloth. The Lord Treasurer's instructions,

[1] Treas. 1/139.   [2] *Journals Commons*, xvii, 10 Apr. 1712.
[3] *Treas. Cal.*, iii, p. 203.

while allowing for subsistence on the same scale as for guards and garrisons, ordered for clothing simply that the Paymaster 'contract . . . in the best manner that may be'.[1]

That this was not a flagrant case of money being plundered by the Hospital officials may be gauged from the plaintively casual statement in the memorial on Chelsea dated 19 November 1713: 'the officers of Her Majesty's Royal Hospital at Chelsea, both Civil and Military, not having been pay'd any Money upon Accot of their Sallarys since Christmas 1711 . . . '.[2]

One can only hope that they fared better in the next reign under the Agent and Solicitor to the Invalides especially appointed by Royal Order of 17 June 1714.[3]

Pensioners in a more rarefied atmosphere were the Knights of Windsor. Their order had been founded in 1348 for twenty-four 'milites pauperes, impotent of themselves or inclining to poverty'. In the same reign, two further members had been added 'such as through adverse fortune were brought to that extremity that they had not of their own wherewith to sustain them or live so gently as became a military condition'.

Henry VIII reduced their number to thirteen, and Queen

---

[1] Ibid., ii, p. 511: report of 28 May 1707.
[2] Pay of officers of Chelsea Hospital at 25 December 1707.

Colonel as Governor	£300	plus £200 as a special case.
Lieutenant-Governor	£200	
Major	£100	plus £50 'till he can be otherwise provided for'.
1st chaplain	£100	
Physician	£100	
Deputy Treasurer	£100	
Secretary	£80	'to cease with present incumbent.'
Surgeon	£73	
Apothecary	£50	
Steward	£50	
Clerk	£20	
Clerk of Works and Deputy	£20	
Adjutant	£20	
23 menservants	£438	including yeoman of the coal yards £20; turncock and water engine keeper £20.
A housekeeper and 24 matrons	£222	
Miscellaneous	£363	
Grand Total	£2,236	
(*Tres. Cal.*)		

[3] SP Mil. 44/173/396.

Elizabeth altered the charter so that they should be 'gentlemen brought to necessity such as have spent their time in the service of the Wars, Garrisons or other service of the Prince, having but little or nothing whereupon to live'. They were not only to be unmarried on admission, but were required to remain so. They were not to 'haunt the town, the ale-houses, or taverns, nor call any woman into their lodgings without it be upon a reasonable cause'. They were paid 12*d*. a day, issued at divine service. If they failed to attend the service, they were not paid. For every night they spent out of lodgings they lost 12*d*.[1]

Kilmainham was an Irish version of Chelsea, designated 'The Hospital of King Charles II for ancient and maimed soldiers of the Army of Ireland'. The Crown granted sixty-four acres in Phoenix Park for it, and the charter granted on 19 February 1684 remained substantially unaltered until George III's reign. To pay for it, there was a deduction of 6*d*. in the £ on all pay on the military establishment. The strength was 10 officers and 100 soldiers, maimed or of at least seven years' service, aged, infirm or 'unserviceable'.[2]

Widows

An age which had as scant regard for its soldiers, serving or discharged, as Queen Anne's could hardly be expected to be particularly solicitous about their dependants. The actuality did not belie the expectation. For the widows or orphans of other ranks there was no provision except the workhouse, an old but somewhat unpopular English institution. Provision for officers' widows was, at first, a further example of action by individuals to meet what today would be looked upon as a duty of the State. Later in the reign the State did formally accept the responsibility, although one writer of the period has claimed that this was in fact executed by reducing the perquisites of serving officers.[3]

The treatment of officers' dependants is indicative of the 'property' attitude towards the regiment. The officers were not a chance gathering. They comprised, as Tristram Shandy had it, the conscious 'getting together of quiet and harmless people

[1] Walton, pp. 606, 836–7.
[2] Ibid., pp. 596–7.	[3] Hutcheson, p. 6.

with their swords in their hands', who accepted thereby responsibilities and commitments towards one another as well as to their country. Orphans had, in many cases, been looked upon for some years as a regimental care, frequently discharged by commissioning a child in its father's vacancy. The practice was inevitably so abused that it became a scandal which called for severe measures to stop it. It was more particularly necessary to ensure that regiments ordered overseas were not rendered unserviceable by carrying a large number of 'officers' who were safe abed in their swaddling clothes in England. Even the order issued to achieve this, however, recognized that orphans had a claim on their fathers' regiments. 'Finding it very prejudicial to have commissions given to children and others unfit to do duty', it laid down that no one of age insufficient to serve was to be admitted to any regiment except the children of officers who had been slain or suffered 'extreamely in the service'. Of those then qualified there were never to be more than two in any one regiment, and, should the regiment be ordered on service, these two were to be cross-posted with officers in regiments remaining at home.[1]

Marlborough expanded this regimental provision for orphans into a theatre scheme for the succour of widows. Officers from all regiments in the Low Countries joined in a voluntary scheme by which they subscribed 'for the support of their widows . . . limited to such only whose husbands were actually killed or died of their wounds'. On at least one occasion the rule was so interpreted that a widow's pension was continued on her death for the benefit of four orphans.[2] The bulk of the money subscribed to this fund came from a levy on commission purchase fees, or, in cases where the officer was killed, from the entire fee paid by his successor.

A similar fund for the regiments in Spain was constituted on 14 April 1707, and in the following year 'widows' men' were officially sanctioned in that theatre under the Royal Warrant of 5 June.[3] This allowed, from various dates, fictitious men in eight regiments of dragoons and thirty-nine of foot 'in compassion to the distressed condition of several widows . . . and any others that might be'. It applied to regiments serving in Spain,

---

[1] Entry Books WO 26/13, 20 May 1705: see also p. 78.
[2] *Treas. Cal.*, iv, p. 217. [3] Treas. 1/132.

Portugal, or the West Indies.[1] The procedure was legalized in the Mutiny Act of 1708 which laid down that widows' men ordered by the Queen did not constitute a false muster.

It is quite conceivable that, in some regiments at least, 'widows' men' had, in fact, existed before the formal framing of the scheme, but they had been merged with the other 'hautboys' so that the widows were a regimental and not a national charge. Hutcheson claims indeed that, prior to formal provision for widows' men, the equivalent was provided from the perquisites of the officers who thus 'had so much less than they otherwise would have had towards . . . keeping their Troops and Companies full'. He is by no means an impeccable witness, but it seems probable that in at least some regiments this was the case.

The money provided under the 1708 Warrant made up a Royal Bounty for which formal Orders and Instructions were issued, but Marlborough strongly recommended that his system of generals and commanding officers subscribing should also be incorporated in the scheme. This, he said, would be not only a present relief for the widows 'who are very clamorous and in great necessity', but would entitle the recipients to a continuance from Parliament, or the Queen's Bounty, when the regimental allowance ceased, presumably on disbandment.[2] His idea probably was that the receipt of this payment would be accepted as proof of the bona fides of the case.

The 'Orders and Instructions to be observed in distribution and payment of Royal Bounty money to widows of officers killed or died in service in Spain, Portugal, or the West Indies' were published on 23 August 1708. They restricted the bounty to those whose husbands had been killed or died in service with regiments in the areas mentioned. A list of the widows was to be kept by the Secretary at War. Yearly rates laid down were: widow of a colonel £50; of a lieutenant-colonel £40; of a major £30; of a captain £26; of a lieutenant £20; and of an ensign, coronet, adjutant, quartermaster, surgeon, or chaplain £16. Allowing for the changed value of money these figures compare not at all unfavourably with the rates ruling today.

The widow had to swear an oath before a Justice of the Peace that she had no pension or allowance from the Crown, and no reasonable maintenance left by her husband. She had to pro-

[1] Registers WO 25/3180.   [2] Murray, iii, p. 326; iv, pp. 542, 558.

duce a certificate of identity, and, if she was not immediately admitted to the fund, was placed on a roll of replacements for beneficiaries dying. The bounty was to cease on remarriage or death.[1] This Warrant established the post of Receiver and Paymaster of Widows' Pensions, another office to be held in time by the versatile Samuel Lynn.[2] The framer of the rules, aware of women's gossip and jealousies, laid down that, while there should be a general payment every two months, if there should be insufficient money to pay all, then none should benefit. There was the customary deduction of 12d. in the £ for administrative expenses.[3]

In the following year the Treasury ordered that the Flanders armies should maintain from their voluntary fund widows of the previous war.[4] In self-defence, Marlborough, a resolute opponent of false musters as a rule, demanded an allowance of widows' men, which was granted to five Flanders regiments in the following year, and thereafter to every regiment going over.[5]

The statement of accounts for Spain, Portugal, and the West Indies in 1712 showed a deficit of £4,770—income £3,678, approved claims £8,448—without taking account of over £600 of outstanding applications. To meet this the Board of General Officers proposed first of all to amalgamate the Flanders fund with the Spanish, which would reduce the deficit by over £1,500. Any regiments not participating in the scheme were to be brought in (increasing income by £1,824), and future admissions were to be granted only on the signature of three general officers. Intensive 'vetting' of the rolls over the next six months disclosed a number of pensions being paid to women 'deceased, married, or not qualified'. When these had been struck off, the deficit was reduced to just under £33. Later in the year the General Officers found themselves with an additional £1,000 of income, and some time was spent studying whether it

[1] Entry Books WO 26/13.

[2] Ibid., 26/14. The office was not abolished until 1811. Clode, i, p. 379.

[3] Entry Books WO 26/13.

[4] A commentary on the relative strengths of public and private faith was implied in the cautious Blackader's letter where he wrote regarding the widow of his late Colonel, Cranstoun: 'Her friends are advising her . . . to seek a pension from the Queen (rather) than to take the widow's gratuity; but I humbly differ from them. The gratuity is a certain thing; she comes to it of course, and without any trouble. The other is uncertain, and depends upon interest and friends.'

[5] PGO WO 71/2: warrant of 30 May 1711.

should be allocated by 'seniority' of widowhood or 'according to some more speedy method'. At the same time they pointed out that, with the disbandments then in progress, it might be necessary to have more widows' men per regiment. They continued throughout the year, however, to add beneficiaries to the roll.[1] A further increase in commitments was accepted in 1713. Thirty-five widows of disbanded marine regiments 'in very necessitious conditions', many of whom 'may be exposed to starve (unless) we are graciously pleased to compassionate their misfortunes', were charged against the army fund at a total cost of £738.[2]

In June 1714 the fund was still healthy with a balance of £825. At this time it was sustained from the pay of two men in each troop and company—except the guards who carried one per squadron or company.[3] It appears, however, to have suffered the same uncertainties as the private soldier with regard to payment of subsistence and clearings. Only thus can the apparently contradictory references to the sums to be credited be reconciled. Instructions to Ormonde, for instance, ordered him to extend one man's subsistence for widows, but the fund statement of 1713 definitely allows clearings, i.e. a further 6d. a day per trooper, 4d. per dragoon, and 2d. per foot soldier.[4] Similarly, the memorial considered by the General Officers on 9 October 1712 showing a potential deficit of £4,770 quite definitely only took into account the subsistence of widows' men[5] while another two years earlier had been largely concerned with the arrears of £79 from clearings.[6]

[1] PGO WO 71/2.   [2] Entry Books WO 26/14, 5 Nov. 1713.
[3] Treas. Cal., iv, p. 541.   [4] Ireland WO 8/1.
[5] PGO WO 71/2.   [6] Treas. 1/130.

APPENDIX A

MILITARY STATUTES OF QUEEN ANNE'S REIGN

1702	Annae 1, cap. 17	Militia
	cap. 19	Insolvent Debtors
	Stat. 2, cap. 15	Militia
	Stat. 2, cap. 20	Mutiny
1703	Annae 2 and 3, cap. 10	Insolvent Debtors
	cap. 13	Recruiting
	cap. 14	Militia
	cap. 17	Mutiny
1704	Annae 3 and 4, cap. 5	Mutiny
	cap. 10	Recruiting
	cap. 15	Militia
1705	Annae 4 and 5, cap. 10	Militia
	cap. 21	Recruiting
	cap. 22	Mutiny
1706	Annae 6, cap. 17	Recruiting
	cap. 18	Mutiny
1706–7	Annae 6, cap. 28	Militia
	cap. 45	Recruiting
	cap. 63	Militia
	cap. 74	Mutiny
1708	Annae 7, cap. 2	Recruiting
	cap. 4	Mutiny
	cap. 23	Militia
1709	Annae 8, cap. 6	Mutiny
	cap. 13	Recruiting
	cap. 22	Militia
1710	Annae 9, cap. 4	Recruiting
	cap. 9	Mutiny
	cap. 31	Militia
1711	Annae 10, cap. 12	Recruiting
	cap. 13	Mutiny
	cap. 33	Militia

1712	Annae, 12, cap. 8	Militia
	cap. 10	Moss Troopers
	cap. 13	Mutiny
1713	Annae 13, cap. 4	Mutiny
	cap. 9	Militia
	cap. 10	Foreign Enlistment

SECRETARIES AT WAR

1702–20 April 1704	William Blathywayt
20 April 1704–25 February 1708	Henry St. John (later Viscount Bolingbroke)
25 February 1708–28 September 1710	Robert Walpole
28 September 1710–28 June 1712	George Grenville
28 June 1712–21 August 1713	William Wyndham
21 August 1713–1714	Francis Gwynn

SECRETARIES OF STATE

January 1702–May 1702	Vernon and Manchester
May 1702–April 1704	Hedges and Nottingham
April 1704–May 1704	Hedges alone
May 1704–December 1706	Hedges and Harley
December 1706–February 1708	Harley and Sunderland
February 1708–June 1710	Boyle and Sunderland
June 1710–September 1710	Boyle and Dartmouth
September 1710–August 1713	St. John and Dartmouth
August 1713–1714	Bromley and St. John

APPENDIX B

SUMMARY OF
INSTRUCTIONS ISSUED TO THE
COMPTROLLERS OF ARMY ACCOUNTS
BY THE LORD TREASURER ON
26 JUNE 1703

1. To keep an account of money issued by the Exchequer to Paymasters.

2. To keep account of arms, provisions, tents, and other items delivered out of store to regiments, troops, or companies, and to see that, where required, the value was duly charged to the regiment's accounts.

3. To inspect colonels' contracts for clothing, and to investigate regimental debts: to supervise reduction of debts and submit periodic reports to the General Commanding and to the Lord Treasurer: Paymasters not to comply with any assignment of off-reckonings by colonels to tailors without a certificate from the Comptrollers that contracts have been carried out as per pattern.

4. To inspect regimental accounts and to see 'that there be no error therein, either to the prejudice of Us or any of Our officers or soldiers'.

5. To keep account of deductions for poundage, day's pay for Chelsea, &c.

6. Examine account of payments made by Paymasters, and to examine vouchers: to see that money received by colonels or agents duly paid over to captains.

7. To ensure that Paymasters, Muster-Masters, and other officers perform muster duties as laid down in the Mutiny Acts: to supervise forwarding of muster parchment rolls to Paymaster-General's office.

8. 'To exhibit from time to time to Us, and to the General and Commander-in-Chief of the Forces, and the High Treasurer all defaults occurring. . . .'

(Based on Clode, ii, pp. 668–9.)

APPENDIX C

TABLE OF ESTABLISHMENTS

EXPLANATORY NOTES

1. The figures are for British nationals—'Her Majesty's Subject Troops'—on the English establishments only. The major part of the garrisons in Ireland and (until 1708) Scotland are, therefore, omitted as are the large number of foreign regiments hired from European princes—over 50 per cent. of the British contribution in Flanders. There were also regiments formed from deserters, Huguenot refugees, or Carlovingian Spaniards, and officered in part or in whole by British. Some of these may have been inadvertently included in the totals as they are not always easy to identify.

2. It is again necessary to emphasize that these figures were establishments, and not by any means men 'on the ground'. They take no account of the inadequate reinforcement system, sickness, or battle casualties. We know, for example, that in 1709 and 1710 Marlborough felt himself hampered for want of manpower, but the establishment figures give no guide to this. Even as 'establishments' they were undoubtedly in many cases guesses or pious hopes—'something', in Samuel Lynn's words, 'cooked up' to raise money from Parliament. The frequent discrepancy between the House of Commons figures and those in departmental papers is sufficient evidence of this.

3. In principle, it may be said that general officers appeared in establishments as general officers only to gain authority for their pay. There were exceptions, but, for the largest part, general officers were colonels of regiments, and are accounted for as 'bodies' in the establishments of their own units.

4. The figures are not intended to include any of the Ordnance trains, but it is not possible to be certain that this is always so.

APPENDIX C. Table of Establishments (cont.)

Theatre	1701			1702			1703		
	Horse and Dragoons	Foot	Total	Horse and Dragoons	Foot	Total	Horse and Dragoons	Foot	Total
Flanders									
English component of the '40,000'	..	10,010 (h)	10,010	3,327	9,968 (l)	13,295	3,359	15,008 (l)	18,367
English component of the 'augmentation'	..	..	..	..	..	..	..	..	..
Miscellaneous	..	..	..	..	..	..	..	..	..
United Kingdom									
England	2,981	4,835	7,816	2,649 (m)	4,351 (m)	7,000	1,950	5,145	7,095
Scotland (a)	..	..	..	..	..	..	..	..	..
Channel and Scilly Isles (b)	..	..	..	..	..	..	..	..	..
Garrisons in England (c)	..	239	239	..	239	239	..	239	239
Garrisons in Scotland (c)	..	27	27	..	28	28	..	28	28
Garrisons in Channel and Scilly Isles (c)	..	15 (i)	15	..	26 (n)	26	..	26 (n)	26
General officers, Provost-Marshal General, Staff, and Ceremonial appointments (d)	..	..	..	..	..	..	..	..	..
Peninsula and Mediterranean									
Spain (e)	..	..	..	..	..	..	..	..	..
Portugal	..	..	..	..	..	..	..	..	..
Minorca	..	..	..	..	..	..	..	..	..
Gibraltar (e)	..	..	..	..	..	..	..	..	..
Miscellaneous	..	..	..	..	..	..	..	..	..
Others									
Dunkirk	..	71 (j)	71	..	..	..	..	..	..
Jamaica and Leewards	..	390 (k)	390	..	..	..	..	..	..
Plantations (f)	..	..	..	..	599 (o)	599	..	599 (o)	599
For Sea Service (g)	..	..	..	..	10,000 (p)	10,000	..	10,000 (p)	10,000
TOTALS	2,981	15,587	18,568	5,976	25,211	31,187	5,309	31,045	36,354

APPENDIX C. Table of Establishments (cont.)

Theatre	1704 Horse and Dragoons	1704 Foot	1704 Total	1705 Horse and Dragoons	1705 Foot	1705 Total	1706 Horse and Dragoons	1706 Foot	1706 Total
Flanders									
English component of the '40,000'	3,351	15,008	18,359	3,273	14,937	18,210	3,280	14,937	18,217
English component of the 'augmentation'	..	3,504	3,504	..	3,504	3,504	..	3,504	3,504
Miscellaneous	..	..	..	..	..	..	..	..	..
United Kingdom									
England (a)	1,961 (q)	5,160 (q)	7,121	1,961 (ac)	5,160 (ac)	7,121	1,961	5,094	7,055
Scotland (a)									
Channel and Scilly Isles (b)									
Garrisons in England (c)	..	239 (r)	239	..	239	239	..	239 (r)	239
Garrisons in Scotland (c)									
Garrisons in Channel and Scilly Isles (c)	..	28 (r)	28	..	28 (r)	28	..	28 (r)	28
General officers, Provost-Marshal-General, Staff, and Ceremonial appointments (d)	..	26 (s)	26	..	26 (n)	26	..	26 (r)	26
Peninsula and Mediterranean									
Spain (e)	1,007 (xb)	..	8,015	1,450 (zb)	..	10,210	1,450 (y)	5,004 (w)	5,004 (w)
Portugal	..	7,008 (yb)	..	..	8,760	..	..	8,760	10,210
Minorca	..	..	..	..	..	..	..	..	..
Gibraltar (e)	..	..	..	..	..	..	..	..	..
Miscellaneous	..	..	..	..	..	..	..	..	..
Others									
Dunkirk									
Jamaica and Leewards	..	2,502 (t)	2,502	..	2,502 (u)	2,502	..	1,800 (v)	1,800
Plantations (f)	..	600 (o)	600	..	600 (o)	600	..	600 (o)	600
For Sea Service (g)	..	2,502 (t)	2,502	..	2,502 (u)	2,502	..	3,204 (v)	3,204
TOTALS	6,319	36,577	42,896	6,684	38,258	44,942	6,691	43,196	49,887

APPENDIX C. Table of Establishments (cont.)

Theatre	1707 Horse and Dragoons	1707 Foot	1707 Total	1708 Horse and Dragoons	1708 Foot	1708 Total	1709 Horse and Dragoons	1709 Foot	1709 Total
Flanders									
English component of the '40,000'	3,280	14,937	18,217	3,280	14,937	18,217	3,522	14,937	18,459
English component of the 'augmentation'	..	3,504	3,504	..	3,504	3,504	..	3,504	3,504
Miscellaneous	..	..	..	..	..	..	..	6,724 (ea)	6,724
United Kingdom									
England	1,961	5,094	7,055	1,961	5,094	7,055	..	4,036 (aa)	4,036
Scotland (a)	..	..	..	1,172	4,143	5,315 (aa)	3,965 (fa)	8,197 (fa)	12,162
Channel and Scilly Isles (b)	..	834 (v)	834	..	834 (v)	834	..	1,008 (ha)	1,008
Garrisons in England (c)	..	239 (r)	239	..	239 (v)	239	..	834 (v)	834
Garrisons in Scotland (c)	..	..	..	..	642 (ba)	642	..	241	241
Garrisons in Channel and Scilly Isles (c)	..	28 (r)	28	..	28	28	..	645 (ja)	645
General officers, Provost-Marshal-General, Staff, and Ceremonial appointments (d)	..	26 (r)	26	..	28 (ca)	28	..	28	28
Peninsula and Mediterranean									
Spain (e)	{ 2,628 (z,y)	{ 26,006 (z)	{ 28,634	{ 2,628 (da)	{ 23,734 (da)	{ 26,362	2,185 (ea)	5,813 (ea)	7,998
Portugal							1,178 (ea)	8,295 (ea)	9,473
Minorca	..	..	..	..	..	..	..	28 (ca)	28
Gibraltar (e)	..	..	..	..	11 (ab)	11	..	(ab) 11 (r)	11
Miscellaneous	..	..	..	..	..	..	..	..	..
Others									
Dunkirk	..	..	..	..	..	..	..	..	..
Jamaica and Leewards	..	1,800 (v)	1,800	..	1,800 (v)	1,800	..	1,785 (ia)	1,785
Plantations (f)	..	600 (o)	600	..	600 (o)	600	..	600 (o)	600
For Sea Service (g)	..	2,370 (v)	2,370	..	2,370 (v)	2,370	..	1,559 (la)	1,559
TOTALS	7,869	55,438	63,307	9,041	57,964	67,005	10,850	58,235	69,095

APPENDIX C. Table of Establishments (cont.)

Theatre	1710 Horse and Dragoons	1710 Foot	1710 Total	1711 Horse and Dragoons	1711 Foot	1711 Total	1712 Horse and Dragoons	1712 Foot	1712 Total
Flanders									
English component of the '40,000'	3,522	14,937	18,459	3,522	14,937	18,459	3,522	14,937	18,459
English component of the 'augmentation'	..	3,504	3,504	..	3,504	3,504	..	3,504	3,504
Miscellaneous	..	4,205 (ga)	4,205	..	3,734 (qa)	3,734	..	..	..
United Kingdom									
England	3,964 (fa)	8,214 (fa) / 1,721 (ga) / 1,710 (ga)	15,609	3,964 (fa)	8,239 (fa) / 1,721 (ga) / 1,710 (ga)	15,634	3,964 (fa)	4,442 (ua) / 8,204 (fa)	16,610
Scotland (a)	..	1,041 (pa)	1,041	..	207	207	..	725 (ua) / 207 (va)	932
Channel and Scilly Isles (b)	..	834 (v)	834	..	834 (v)	834	..	834 (v)	834
Garrisons in England (c)	..	243	243	..	243 (r)	243 (r)	..	340	340
Garrisons in Scotland (c)	..	708	708	..	708 (r)	708	..	351 (wa)	351
Garrisons in Channel and Scilly Isles (c)	..	28	28	..	28 (r)	28	..	28 (r)	28
General officers, Provost-Marshal-General, Staff, and Ceremonial appointments (d)	..	28	28	..	28 (r)	28	..	28 (r)	28
Peninsula and Mediterranean									
Spain (e)	2,592	8,997 (ga)	11,589	2,592	9,569 (ra)	12,161	589	10,523	11,112
Portugal (e)	589 (ya)	5,395 (ya)	5,984	589 (ya)	4,613 (ra)	5,202	877 (ya)	3,776	4,653 (xa)
Minorca (e)	..	11	11	..	11	11	..	16 (sa)	16
Gibraltar (e)	..	(ab) 11 (r) / 1,668 (ga)	1,668	..	(ab) 11 (r) / 1,668 (ga)	1,668	..	2,596 (za)	2,596
Miscellaneous	..	..	..	..	..	..	..	..	..
Others									
Dunkirk	..	..	..	..	12 (sa)	12	..	(sa) 12 (bb)	12
Jamaica and Leewards	..	1,785 (ia)	1,785	..	1,785 (ia)	1,785	..	1,785 (cb)	1,785
Plantations (f)	..	600 (o)	600	..	600 (o)	600	..	971 (db)	971
For Sea Service (g)	..	1,601 (oa)	1,601	..	2,561 (ia)	2,561	..	2,326 (eb)	2,326
TOTALS	10,667	57,230	67,897	10,667	56,712	67,379	8,952	55,605	64,557

APPENDIX C. Table of Establishments (*cont.*)

Theatre	1713 (first six months) Horse and Dragoons	Foot	Total	1713 (second six months) Horse and Dragoons	Foot	Total	1714 Horse and Dragoons	Foot	Total
Flanders									
English component of the '40,000'	3,816	12,780	16,596	..	3,678	3,678	..	3,678	3,678
English component of the 'augmentation'	..	..	..	..	..	..	..	..	..
Miscellaneous	..	..	..	..	..	..	..	..	..
United Kingdom									
England (a)	1,612	5,743 (*fb*)	7,355	3,253 (*lb*)	4,747	8,000 (*mb*)	2,222	4,830 (*rb*)	7,052
Scotland (a)	1,658	1,566 (*fb*)	3,224	..	..	..	..	294 (*rb*)	294
Channel and Scilly Isles (b)	..	725	725	..	..	..	..	..	..
Garrisons in England (c)	..	340	340	..	293	293	..	373	373
Garrisons in Scotland (c)	..	351 (*wa*)	351	..	302	302	..	222 (*sb*)	222
Garrisons in Channel and Scilly Isles (c)	..	28	28	..	20	20	..	28	28
General officers, Provost-Marshal-General, Staff, and Ceremonial appointments (d)	..	28 (*r*)	28	..	27 (*nb*)	27	..	27 (*nb*)	27
Peninsula and Mediterranean									
Spain (e)	..	..	..	..	..	..	..	..	..
Portugal	..	..	..	..	..	..	..	..	..
Minorca (e)	..	4,706 (*gb*)	4,706	..	2,500 (*gb*)	2,500	..	2,517 (*tb*)	2,517
Gibraltar (e)	..	3,061 (*hb*)	3,061	..	1,500 (*ob*)	1,500	..	1,500 (*ub*)	1,500
Miscellaneous	..	..	..	..	..	..	..	..	..
Others									
Dunkirk	..	8,282 (*jb*)	8,282	..	5,000 (*pb*)	5,000	..	8,205 (*vb*)	8,205
Jamaica and Leewards	..	1,450	1,450	..	890 (*qb*)	890	..	890 (*wb*)	890
Plantations (f)	..	1,249 (*kb*)	1,249	..	1,249 (*kb*)	1,249	..	1,249 (*kb*)	1,249
For Sea Service (g)	..	..	..	..	..	..	..	..	..
TOTALS	7,086	40,309	47,395	3,253	20,206	23,459	2,222	23,813	26,035

The Corps of Gentlemen of Arms consisted of 40 'gentlemen that be comen and extracte of noble blode'. They were given posts as: captain, 1: lieutenant, 1: standard bearer, 1: clerk of the cheque, 1: harbinger, 1: esquires, 35.

The Yeomen of the Guard comprised 100 men with 40 warders.

NOTES TO TABLE OF ESTABLISHMENTS

(*a*) It was only after 1707 that troops in Scotland were carried on the estimates. Previously they were on the Scottish establishment. From 1708 onwards, division between England and Scotland of troops voted under 'guards and garrisons' was not always specified. In such cases, a combined total is given.

(*b*) It is not always possible to give the numbers in the Channel and Scilly Isles as they and England were sometimes voted as a joint total.

(*c*) For distinction between 'guards' and 'garrisons' see Chapter III. These figures, when shown separately for England, consist mostly of gunners. They exclude, as far as possible, such posts as porters, storekeepers, or other miscellaneous appointments. In Scotland, the 'garrisons' contained foot soldiers.

(*d*) This is a particularly difficult entry. General officers in Flanders were frequently included on the 'guards and garrisons' estimate as though in the U.K. I have not shown these, but (since this is a table of authorized strengths and not of organization) have confined the total to those in the U.K. not also accounted for in regimental vacancies.

(*e*) The Spanish figures frequently contain all or a portion of the Gibraltar total, which was not given separately, save for garrison staff, until 1710.

(*f*) 'Plantations' is an arbitrary term. The Bermudas were usually included under this head, but not normally the Leewards or Jamaica. I have, in the main, followed the nomenclature of the estimates, and detailed the components, as far as possible, in the notes. The places most regularly included under this head were New York, Annapolis Royal, Bermudas, Placentia; but even Guernsey, Jersey, Minorca, Gibraltar, Dunkirk, and, supreme offence, 'North Britain' were on occasion so described.

(*g*) This is a debatable entry. In the main they are, on first entry, men earmarked for, or engaged on, seaborne invasions, but various items were included from time to time, such as Jamaica and the Leewards, or the Channel and Scilly Isles. Where the components are identifiable as other than 'task forces' the figures have been put under another heading, and the Sea Service total amended accordingly. The subject is very adequately dealt with in Atkinson's note 1060 in Issue xxx, no. 124, Winter, 1952, of the *Journal of the Society for Army Historical Research.*

(*h*) Ten battalions of foot from Ireland, plus the following of the staff: Deputy Paymaster, Provost-Master-General, and four men.

(*i*) These were: Paymaster-General; Commissary-General of the Musters; Judge-Advocate-General; Deputy Judge-Advocate-General in Guernsey; Provost-Master-General and three men; Drum-Major-General; Master Gunner; St. James's Park gunners (4 estimated); Surveyor of the Guard. The following are omitted: the Secretary to the Forces; the Adjutant-General (who would also be counted as colonel of a regiment); the Fire

Master to the Grenadiers; and the messengers (2) to the Secretary to the Forces and the Paymaster-General—all carried on the 'guards and garrisons' establishment.

(*j*) Leewards.

| (*k*) | Four companies New York | 337 |
| | One company Newfoundland | 53 |

(*l*) The estimates presented on 21 January 1702 showed 9,968 foot in Flanders, to be increased in the course of the year to 15,012. I have taken the lower figure for 1702, but for 1703 have shown the strength of 15,008 presented to Parliament on 6 November 1702.

(*m*) The establishment books show 1,234 horse and dragoons, and 5,155 foot. There was probably confusion at this time due to the extensive raisings for, and movements to, Flanders. It is significant that the figure passed by the Commons was the 'golden number' of 7,000 for guards and garrisons.

(*n*) Paymaster-General; Commissary-General of the Musters, 9 Deputy Commissaries-General of the Musters; Judge-Advocate-General; Deputy Judge-Advocate-General at Jersey and Guernsey; Physician, Surgeon, and Apothecary to the Forces; Provost-Master-General and two men; Drum-Major-General; Master Gunner; St. James's Park gunners (4); Surveyor of the Guard. The following are omitted: Secretary to the Forces; secretary, chaplain, physician, and surgeon to the Captain-General; Fire Master to the Grenadiers; clerks; and officers who would also count against regimental establishments.

(*o*)	Four companies New York	448/9
	One company Bermudas	58
	One company Newfoundland	93

The New York companies were each 112 strong, and later shared an adjutant.

(*p*) 8,208 of these were for Ormonde's expedition—total strength 8,520, including 312 of the train. The location or composition of the remaining 1,792 I have been unable to find. The warrant of 1 June 1702 shows 4,998 (six regiments) army and 4,998 marines. The general officers and staffs made the total 10,000. The discrepancy is probably merely the difference between estimates and regimental strengths.

(*q*) SP Mil. 41/3/56 gives:

	Horse and Dragoons	1,527
	Foot	4,898
	Total	6,425

(*r*) Figure for previous year repeated: no evidence of any alteration, and money voted remained the same.

(*s*) Details as in note (*n*). The House of Commons estimate does not, in fact, show the following who were normally detailed in the Secretary at War's books only: Provost-Master-General and staff; Drum-Major-General; Master Gunner; St. James's Park gunners; Surveyor of the Guard. The following who appeared in the Parliamentary estimates are not included: Secretary at War; two clerks to the Commissaries of the Musters; two Comptrollers of Accounts; secretary, chaplain, physician, and surgeon to the Captain-General.

(*t*) The House of Commons Journals for 19 November 1703 show the following:

For Sea Service:

Colonel Handasyde's	(to be	834
Colonel Levesay's	made	834
Colonel Whetham's	up	834
Colonel Rivers's		834
Lord Lucas's		834
A regiment landed in Ireland: to be replaced in the West Indies		834
Total		5,004

The warrant of 10 April 1704, however, issuing instructions for Handasyde's, Levesay's (for Jamaica), and Whetham's (Leewards) shows 833. I have retained the figure of 834 for these, and for the three remaining regiments. I have shown Handasyde's, Levesay's, and Whetham's under Jamaica and the Leewards, and the others under Sea Service.

(*u*) The Commons Estimates show:

In the West Indies for Sea Service   5,004

I have put under West Indies the three regiments there in 1704 and assumed a total of 834 each. The Warrant of 19 May 1707, effective from 1 June 1705, shows Handasyde's 951, Levesay's 697, and four others of 829 each—a total of 4,964. Levesay, Handasyde, and Whetham in the West Indies would give a total of 2,477 and leave 2,487 elsewhere.

(*v*) The House of Commons Journals of 14 November 1705 give:

For the Sea Service 5,004, detailed as:

Lieutenant-General Erle's	834
Colonel Handasyde's at Jamaica	966
Colonel Levesay's	702
Colonel Whetham's in the Leewards	834
Lord Mordaunt's	834
Lord Paston's	834

The Warrant of 30 April 1705, which withdrew Levesay's from Jamaica, laid down that Handasyde's was to be made up from Levesay's. I have taken 1,800 for the Leewards and Jamaica, and shown the balance of the 5,004 as Sea Service. The Warrant gives, in fact, the strength of Whetham's as 798, which would give a total of only 1,764 for the West Indies. From 1707 to 1710, Mordaunt's regiment, while still appearing as 'For Sea Service', is shown in the House of Commons Journals as being stationed in the Channel Isles. I have adjusted the totals accordingly, and also shown it there in 1711–12.

(*w*) With naval expedition to Catalonia. The House of Commons Journals stated '5000 additional forces to serve with the fleet', but the detail gave Charlemont's, Gorge's, Caulfield's, Breton's, Soames's, and Hotham's, each at 834, a total of 5,004. The Warrant of 20 April 1705 caters for six regiments of 826, a total of 4,956.

(*y*) Excluding 761 Dragoons of the French Regiment. There were also dispatched during 1707, five regiments of Huguenot Dragoons, total strength 4,000.

(*z*) Parliamentary estimate shows all as 'Spain'.

(*aa*) At the Union the Scottish establishment was 571 Dragoons and 1,927 Foot. This was increased to the figure shown on transfer to the English establishment.

(*ac*) The Warrant dated 30 April 1705 shows 1,960 horse and dragoons and 5,083 foot. The difference of one may be accounted for by an error in the number of officers holding two appointments in the dragoons.

(*ba*) The House of Commons Journals show 617 (raised from 336 pre-Union). The discrepancy may be due to my inclusion, from the establishments warrant, of men not strictly chargeable to garrisons, or to the establishment quoted being a retrospective authorization. Details of the 642 are:

Edinburgh	236
Stirling	231
Dunbarton	114
Blackness	57
Fort William	4

These figures do not include porters or storemen. An interesting point is that the Edinburgh and Stirling totals include troops of the line—approximately 200 in each case. I have shown these under 'garrisons', as that was the vote on which they were carried, and their role approximated to the present-day conception of a garrison.

(*ca*) As at (*n*), but with the addition of two Deputy Commissaries-General of Musters for North Britain.

(*da*) The figures given for 1708 are these from House of Commons Journals of 28 November 1707 as 'forces present'. The Journals make no distinction between Spain and Portugal. Below, I have separated them, as far as possible, according to records for other years.

Horse and Dragoons

Spain

Pearce	589
Nassau	589
Royal Regiment	589
	1,767 —1,767

Portugal

Harvey	418
Killigrew's	443
	861 —861
Total	2,628

(Also the French Regiment—761)

Foot

Spain

Portmore	876
Hill	876
Wade	876
Blosset	725
Royal Fusiliers	834
Mordaunt	876
Elliot	834
Watkins	834
Sibourg	725
Hotham	834
Macartney	876
Total	9,166

Portugal

Pearce	725
Newton	725
Barrymore	876
Sankey	725
Stanwix	725
Montandre	834
Breton	834
de Magny	725
Alnut	834
Stuart	876
Blood	876
Total	8,755

Low Countries although on Peninsula Establishment

Gorge	876
Southwell	834
Mohun	834
Bowles	834
Caulfield	834
Mark Ker	725
Mountjoy	876
Total	5,813

The 'post-mortem' on 1708—House of Commons Journals, 1 February 1709—shows, however:

Horse and Dragoons

Spain

Harvey	418
Royal Regiment	589
Pepper	443
Nassau	589
Total	2,039

(Pearce's regiment was reduced during 1708)

Foot

Spain

As for 28 November 1707, with the addition of:

Harrison	876

giving a total of 10,042

Portugal

Pearce	725
Barrymore	876
Paston	834
Sankey	725
Stanwix	725
Newton	725
Total	4,610

These had a total deficiency of 500, which gave a total of 4,110.

The following were reduced during 1708:

Alnut, Montandre, Breton, de Magny.

The following were actually in Ostend, and transferred during the year to Guards and Garrisons:

Wightman	876
Gorge	876
Mountjoy	876
Mark Ker	725
Total	3,353

The following were moved to Ostend under Erle:

Dormer	834
Macartney	876
Caulfield	834
Total	2,544

(*ea*) Walpole in his estimates for 1709 continued his endeavour to show accurately where regiments were. The following were carried on the establishment for 'Spain, Portugal, or on board the Fleet':

Miscellaneous	4,187	in Flanders but 'expected every day from Ostend'.
	2,537	at Antwerp
Total	6,724	
England	2,586	recruiting
	1,450	Guards and Garrisons
Total	4,036	

Two discontinued regiments, 1,668, not shown by me.

Detail

Spain

Horse and Dragoons		*Foot*	
Harvey	418	Harrison	834
Royal Regiment	589	Mordaunt	876
Pepper	589	Wade	876
Nassau	589	Elliot	834
		Watkins	834
Total	2,185	Hotham	834
		Sibourg	725
		Total	5,813

Portugal

Dragoons		*Foot*	
Galway	589	Pearce	725
		Paston	834
In lieu		Carle	785
Guiscard	589	Sankey	725
		Newton	725
Total	1,178	Barrymore	876
		Stanwix	725
		Four in lieu:	
		Blosset	
		Montandre	
		de Magny	
		one unspecified	2,900
		Total	8,295

At Antwerp		*At Ostend*	
Hamilton	876	Dormer	834
Macartney	876	Caulfield	834
Wynn	785	Farrington	809
		Moore	834
Total	2,537	Johnson	876
		Total	4,187

Recruiting		*In Garrison*	
Portmore	876	Gorge	725
Royal Fus.	834		
Stuart	876	Mountjoy	725
Total	2,586	Total	1,450

(*fa*) Voted in the estimates as U.K. It was customary for all Dragoons to be stationed in Scotland—see, for example, the distribution of troops for 1710 in SP Mil. 41/27 dated 19 December 1710.

(*ga*) The Peninsula vote produced its familiar crop of anomalies:

4,205 (5 regiments) on the establishment actually served in Flanders, and are shown by me as Flanders miscellaneous.

1,721 voted for Spain served in U.K., and are so shown by me.

1,710 voted for Portugal served in U.K., and are so shown by me. (They are shown as 1,668 in the House of Commons Journals.)

1,668 of the Spanish vote served in Gibraltar, and are so shown.

785 'a Spanish regiment', have not been included by me.

876 Montandre's regiment—'a discontinued regiment the officers being exchanged, to be raised again'—is not included in the 5,396 for Portugal in the House of Commons Journals, but is included in the same total in the Secretary at War's Establishment Book.

1,938 Horse and Dragoons (6 regiments) which appear for the first time on the Portugal Establishment, I have taken, from the colonels' names, to have been Portuguese, and are not shown.

(*ha*) Maitland's (Fort William) appeared in the estimates as

Sea Service	834
3 independent companies	174
Total	1,008

Voted as Sea Service and consisting of:

(*ia*)		
Handasyde (Jamaica)	951	
Jones (Leewards)	834	
Total	1,785	

(*ja*)   Edinburgh   236
                      Stirling   232
                      Blackness   57
                      Dunbarton   116
                      Fort William   4
                                                   ———
                                  Total   645

(*la*) Excluding Maitland's (834)—see note (*ha*), Handasyde's and Jones's (1,785)—see note (*ia*), and Mordaunt's (834)—see note (*v*).

(*oa*) The following were also voted as Sea Service:

    Mordaunt's   834   shown by me under Channel Isles where they
                                   were stationed—see note (*v*).
    Maitland's   834   shown by me under Scotland—see note (*pa*).
    Handasyde's   951 ⎱ shown by me under Jamaica and Leewards
    Jones's   834 ⎰   where they were stationed—see note (*ia*).

(*pa*)   Maitland's (Fort William)   834
                      3 independent companies   207
                                                   ———
                                  Total   1,041

(*qa*) The five Flanders regiments on the Spanish establishment are shown in the Establishments Book as changing during 1710–11 to this figure.

(*ra*) I can find no House of Commons vote for the Peninsula in 1711, but the Secretary's Estimates Book reference quoted for 1710 (15 November 1710) includes the following changes in 1710–11 and I have viewed their completion as the difference between 1710 and 1711.

Spain

Foot

Extra men added to regiments   360
A discontinued regiment to be re-raised   725
                                                ———
                                                1,085
Less miscellaneous reductions   513
                                                ———
                                  Total   572

Portugal

Foot

Additional men   263
Reductions   1,045
                                   ———
A net reduction of   782

In the 1,045, however, were 785 of Montandre's Regiment. I have viewed these as being previously included in the 1710 total, although it will be remembered (note (ga)) the House of Commons Estimates did not so include them.

(sa) Military members of garrison staff. A number of officers probably counted also against regimental establishments.

(ta)

	Seymour	876
	Farrington	876
	Mark Ker	809
	Total	2,561

One of these may have been in Scotland—see note (pa) reference Maitland's which must have changed hands as it does not appear under this name in any of the 1711 Establishments. Mordaunt's (834) in the Channel Isles (note (oa)), Handasyde (951) in Jamaica, and Jones (834) in the Leewards (note (ia)) were also voted for the Sea Service.

(ua) The nominal 3,734 shown in 1711 as Flanders miscellaneous (voted for the Peninsula—see note (qa)) were made up—from regiment(s) in Scotland— to 4,442 for Jack Hill's Canadian expedition. This is disclosed only in the estimates for 1712 which show the 725 (Col. Grant's) thus 'remaining' in Scotland. It is probable that this reinforcement came from the successor to Maitland's regiment, voted for Sea Service—see note (ta). The 4,442 given in the estimates as 'in Great Britain recruiting, lately returned from Canada' are shown by me separately under 'England'.

(va) Three independent companies at Fort William.

(wa)

	Edinburgh	143
	Stirling	118
	Dunbarton	57
	Fort William	5
	Blackness	28
	Total	351

(xa) Money was also voted for 2,185 Horse and Dragoons, and 5,915 Foot on the Peninsular Establishment, 'the greatest part to be applicable to the pay of prisoners taken at Brihuega and the remainder for recruiting the regiments captured as Her Majesty's Service should happen to require'.

(ya) It is difficult to determine which Dragoon Regiments were actually 'subject' troops. The following were carried on the estimate of 'Her Majesty's Forces' passed on 29 March 1709:

Galway	589
Tavora	323
de Gamia	323
de Mello	323
Prada	323
de Norbanna	323
Another	323

Total   2,527

I have shown only Galway's for 1710 and 1711.
The corresponding estimate passed on 2 February 1712 showed:

Bouchetier	554
Withers	323
Tavora	323
de Gamia	323
de Norbanna	323
d'Affa	323

Total   2,169

I have shown Bouchetier and Withers for 1712, although this would seem to imply that one of the Portuguese regiments had become 'subject troops'.

(*za*) Three regiments plus 10 military members of garrison staff, to whom note (*sa*) applies.

(*ab*) A garrison staff of Governor (*m*), Commissary (*m*), Deputy Judge-Advocate (*m*), Town Major (*m*), town adjutant (*m*), chaplain (*m*), turnkey, chirurgeon major (*m*), two mates (*m*), postmaster and secretary to the governor, signalman (*m*), and provost (*m*), of whom I have counted those marked (*m*) as military. It is probable that some (e.g. governor and town major) counted also against regimental establishments.

(*bb*) There was also established in Dunkirk from 10 October 1712 a hospital with an establishment of 14.

Voted as Sea Service and consisting of:

(*cb*)	Handasyde's (Jamaica)	951
	Alexander's (Leewards)	834

Total   1,785

(*db*)	Four companies Annapolis Royal	364
	Four companies New York	449
	One company Newfoundland	93
	One company Bermudas	58
	Annapolis Royal garrison staff	7

Total   971

(*eb*)	Seymour	876	
	Windsor	725	
	Montandre	725	
	Total	**2,326**	

also voted as Sea Service:

	Mordaunt	834	in Channel Isles— note (*v*)
	Handasyde	951 ⎫	in West Indies—
	Alexander	834 ⎭	note (*cb*)

(*fb*)	Two regiments	1,450
	Two independent companies	116
	Total	**1,566**

(*gb*) Includes 16 military members of garrison staff—see note (*sa*).

(*hb*) Includes 10 military members of garrison staff—see note (*za*).

(*jb*) Includes:

   12 military members of garrison staff—see note (*sa*)
   14 hospital staff—see note (*bb*)

(*kb*)	Four companies Annapolis Royal	364
	Four companies New York	449
	Four companies Placentia	364
	One company Bermudas	58
	Garrison staff Placentia	7
	Garrison staff Annapolis Royal	7
	Total	**1,249**

(*lb*) At the House of Commons sitting of 27 May 1713 the estimates presented were those here given for Jamaica and the Leewards, Minorca, Gibraltar, and Dunkirk. The House then voted also that the number of troops for the last six months of 1713 'for guards and garrisons in Great Britain, Guernsey and Jersey be 8000'. It was in accordance with this resolution that the further figures, given here, were produced, without detail of the location of the troops. The warrant of 15 June 1713 shows 3,252 Horse and Dragoons, but otherwise corresponds with the figures put forward in the House.

(*mb*) No sub-division of location is given in either House of Commons Journals or Establishments Warrant Book.

(*nb*) See note (*n*). The only difference was that the Provost-Master-General had three men instead of two. I have omitted, further, clerk to the courts martial in North Britain.

(*ob*) Includes garrison staff of 15.

(*pb*) The Warrant of 20 July 1713 shows, in fact, 4,009 Foot, and 12 garrison staff—governor, town major, three adjutants, captain of the ports, governor of the citadel, commandant of Fort Lewis, commandant of the Risbank, secretary to the Governor and Commander-in-Chief, Deputy Judge-Advocate and Commissary of the Musters, Provost Marshal. A number of these would count against regimental vacancies.

(*qb*)	Handasyde at Jamaica	445
	Alexander in Leewards	445
	Total	890

(*rb*) Three independent companies.

(*sb*) The Establishments Warrant Book shows garrisons in Scotland as 182.

(*tb*) Includes 17 military members of garrison staff.

(*ub*) Includes 11 military members of garrison staff.

(*vb*) The House of Commons estimate states 'six battalions of foot', but details only five:

Royal Regiment of Foot	1,343
Hull's	669
Hertford's	669
Hamilton's	669
Desney's	669
Total	4,019

It also shows, separately, a total of 4,019. The Warrant Book gives 8,192 for Ghent, Bruges, Nieuport, and Dunkirk, plus ten garrison staff at Dunkirk, and three general officers.

(*wb*)	Handasyde (Jamaica)	445
	Alexander (Leewards)	445
	Total	890

The regiment in Jamaica was reduced to 224 (two independent companies) by the Warrant dated 29 May 1714. The Establishments Book gives 25 August as the effective date.

(*xb*) I have taken the figures from the Warrant Book of 30 April 1705, purporting to show those actually present. The Warrant also shows a total of 30 general and staff officers, including hospital staff. I have not shown these, due to doubt as to how many were military and how many were already counting against regimental establishments.

(*yb*) The 1705 figure for those present was 9,523, but this includes 763 Guards and two other regiments added after 1704. The House of Commons Journals' figure (19 November 1703) is 6,132 (eight regiments). The figure here is an approximation—calculated at eight regiments of 876 each.

(*zb*) The House of Commons Journals' figure is 1,050. For general and staff officers see (*xb*).

AUTHORITIES

1701	England Garrisons General Officers in U.K. Jamaica and Leewards Plantations	Ests. WO 24/23, establishments to date from 25 April 1700.
	Flanders	Ests. WO 24/24, dated 1 June 1701.
1702	England Flanders	*Journals Commons*, xiii, 21 January 1702.
	Note (*m*) Garrisons General Officers Plantations	Ests. WO 24/26, dated 1 June 1702.
	Note (*o*)	Ests. WO 24/28, dated 28 January 1703.
	Sea Service	*Journals Commons*, xiv, 6 November 1702.
	Note (*p*)	Dalton, v, p. xiii; Ests. WO 24/26, warrant of 1 June 1702.
1703	Flanders Sea Service	*Journals Commons*, xiv, 6 November 1702.
	England Garrisons General Officers Plantations	Ests. WO 24/28, dated 28 January 1703.
1704	Flanders England Plantations Sea Service	*Journals Commons*, xiv, 19 November 1703.
	General Officers, &c.	*Journals Commons*, xiv, 19 November 1703 and 11 November 1704.
	Garrisons	Ests. WO 24/28, dated 28 January 1703.
	Portugal	*Journals Commons*, xiv, 19 November 1703; Ests. WO 24/41, dated 30 April 1705.
	Jamaica and Leewards Note (*t*)	*Journals Commons*, xiv, 19 November 1703; Ests. WO 24/37, dated 10 April 1704; Ests. WO 24/38, dated 19 May 1707.

1705 Flanders
      England   ⎫
      Plantations   ⎬ *Journals Commons*, xiv, 3 November 1704.
      Sea Service   ⎭

      General Officers in U.K. ⎫ *Journals Commons*, xiv, 3 November 1704;
      Garrisons   ⎭   Ests. WO 24/38, dated 30 April 1705.

                                  ⎫ *Journals Commons*, xiv, 19 November
      Jamaica and Leewards   ⎬ 1703; Ests. WO 24/37, dated 10 April
                                  ⎭ 1704.

      Portugal   ⎱ *Journals Commons*, xiv, 3 November 1704;
                                  ⎰ Ests. WO 24/41, dated 30 April 1705.

1706 Flanders   ⎫
      England   ⎪
      Garrisons   ⎪
      General Officers in U.K.   ⎬ *Journals Commons*, xv, 14 November
      Portugal   ⎪ 1705.
      Plantations   ⎪
      Sea Service   ⎭

                                  ⎫ *Journals Commons*, xv, 14 November
      Jamaica and Leewards   ⎬ 1705; Ests. WO 24/42, dated 30
                                  ⎭ April 1705.

                                  ⎫ *Journals Commons*, xv, 14 November
      Spain   ⎬ 1705; Ests. WO 24/38, dated 20
                                  ⎭ April 1705.

      Note (*y*)   Fort., pp. 536, 555.

1707 Flanders   ⎫
      England   ⎪
      Plantations   ⎪
      Jamaica and Leewards   ⎬ *Journals Commons*, xv, 7 December 1706.
      Sea Service   ⎪
      Channel and Scilly Isles   ⎭

      Garrisons   ⎱ *Journals Commons*, xv, 7 December 1706;
      General Officers in U.K.   ⎰ Ests. WO 24/45, dated 24 June 1708.

      Spain   ⎱ *Journals Commons*, xv, 8 January 1707.
      Portugal   ⎰

      Note (*y*)   Fort., pp. 536, 555.

1708 Flanders   *Journals Commons*, xv, 8 January 1707.

England
Scotland
Channel Isles
Sea Service
Plantations
Jamaica and Leewards
Spain and Portugal
Garrisons in England,
    Channel and Scilly
    Isles
		Journals Commons, xv, 28 November
		  1707.

	Note (*da*)	*Journals Commons*, xvi, 1 February 1709.
	Garrisons in Scotland	Ests. WO 24/24 and 24/25, dated 24 June 1708.
	General Officers in U.K.	Ests. WO 24/45, dated 24 June 1708.
	Gibraltar	Ests. WO 24/45 of 1708.
1709	Flanders	*Journals Commons*, xvi, 26 November 1708 and 4 February 1709.
	England Scotland Channel and Scilly Isles Jamaica and Leewards Sea Service	*Journals Commons*, xvi, 1 February 1709.
	Spain Portugal	*Journals Commons*, xvi, 4 February 1709.
	Garrisons in U.K.	Ests. WO 24/49, dated 13 August 1709.
	General Officers in U.K.	Ests. WO 24/49, dated 13 August 1709.
	Gibraltar	Ests. WO 24/45 of 1708.

1710	Flanders	*Journals Commons*, xvi, 19 November
		  1709; Ests. WO 24/75, dated 15
		  November 1710.

	England	*Journals Commons*, xvi, 19 and 29
		  November 1709; Ests. WO 24/75,
		  dated 15 November 1710.

	Scotland	*Journals Commons*, xvi, 19 and 29 November 1709; Ests. WO 24/75, dated 15 November 1710; SP Mil. 41/27, dated 19 December 1710.
	Jamaica and Leewards Sea Service Channel and Scilly Isles	*Journals Commons*, xvi, 19 November 1709.

1710 (*cont.*)	Spain Portugal Gibraltar	*Journals Commons*, xvi, 29 November 1709; Ests. WO 24/75, dated 15 November 1710.
	Plantations Garrisons in U.K.	Ests. WO 24/55, dated 30 September 1710.
	General Officers in U.K.	Ests. WO 24/49, dated 13 August 1709.
	Gibraltar	Ests. WO 24/45 of 1708.
1711	Flanders	*Journals Commons*, xvii, 7 December 1710.
	England Scotland Channel and Scilly Isles	WO Ests. 24/75, dated 15 November 1710. See note (*v*).
	Garrisons in U.K. General Officers in U.K.	*Journals Commons*, xvii, 7 December 1710; Ests. WO 24/55, dated 30 September 1710.
	Garrisons in Dunkirk Leewards and Jamaica	*Journals Commons*, xvii, 7 December 1710; Ests. WO 24/75, December 1711.
	Sea Service	*Journals Commons*, xvii, 7 December 1710; Ests. WO 24/75, dated 15 November 1710.
	Plantations	Ests. WO 24/75, dated 15 November 1710.
	Spain Portugal Gibraltar	Ests. WO 24/45 of 1708. See notes (*qa*) and (*ra*).
	Notes (*qa*)and (*ra*)	Ests. WO 24/75, dated 15 November 1710.
1712	Flanders	*Journals Commons*, xvii, 15 December 1711 and 2 February 1712.
	England Channel and Scilly Isles Jamaica and Leewards Sea Service	*Journals Commons*, xvii, 17 January 1712.
	Scotland	*Journals Commons*, xvii, 17 January 1712 and 2 February 1712.
	Garrisons in England, Channel and Scilly Isles	Ests. WO 24/75, dated 20 October 1713 (effective 24 June 1712).

Garrisons in Scotland } Ests. WO 26/14, dated 30 July 1712 (effective 24 August 1712).

General Officers in U.K. Ests. WO 24/49, dated 13 August 1709.

Gibraltar } *Journals Commons*, xvii, 2 February 1712; Ests. WO 24/75, dated 10 October 1712.

Minorca Ests. WO 24/75, dated 30 July 1712.

Dunkirk Ests. WO 24/75 of December 1711.

Plantations } *Journals Commons*, xvii, 2 February 1712; Ests. WO 24/75, dated 30 July 1712.

Spain
Portugal } See notes (*qa*), (*ra*), and (*ya*).

Note (*eb*) Ests. WO 24/25, dated 10 October 1712.

1713 (first six months)
Flanders
England
Scotland
Channel and Scilly Isles } *Journals Commons*, xvii, 18 April 1712; Treas. 1/160, dated 18 April 1713.

Garrisons in Scotland Ests. WO 26/14, dated 30 July 1712.

Garrisons in England, Channel and Scilly Isles } Ests. WO 24/75, dated 20 October 1713.

General Officers in U.K. *Journals Commons*, xvii, 17 January 1712.

Minorca } Ests. WO 24/75, dated 30 July 1712; Treas. 1/160, dated 18 April 1713.

Gibraltar } Ests. WO 24/75, dated 30 July 1712; Treas. 1/160, dated 18 April 1713.

Dunkirk } *Journals Commons*, xvii, 18 April 1712; Ests. WO 24/75 of December 1711; Ests. WO 24/25 of 10 October 1712; Treas. 1/160, dated 18 April 1713.

Jamaica and Leewards } *Journals Commons*, xvii, 18 April 1713; Treas. 1/160, dated 18 April 1713.

Plantations } *Journals Commons*, xvii, 18 April 1713; Ests. WO 24/75, dated 6 April 1713; Treas. 1/160, dated 18 April 1713.

1713 (second six months)
    Flanders
    Garrisons in U.K. } Ests. WO 24/68, dated 15 June 1713.
    General Officers in U.K.

    U.K. } *Journals Commons*, xvii, 1 June 1713; Ests. WO 24/68, dated 15 June 1713.

    Gibraltar } *Journals Commons*, xvii, 27 May 1713; Ests. WO 24/69, dated 20 July 1713.

    Dunkirk
    Plantations } *Journals Commons*, xvii, 27 May 1713; Ests. WO 24/69, dated 20 July 1713.

    Jamaica and Leewards   *Journals Commons*, xvii, 27 May 1713.

    Minorca } *Journals Commons*, xvii, 27 May 1713; Ests. WO 24/75, dated 30 July 1712; Treas. 1/160, dated 18 April 1713; Ests. WO 24/69, dated 20 July 1713.

1714   Flanders   *Journals Commons*, xvii, 31 March 1714.

    England
    General Officers in U.K. } Ests. WO 24/70, dated 29 April 1714.

    Scotland } Ests. WO 24/70, dated 29 April 1714; Entry Books WO 26/14, dated 16 July 1714.

    Jamaica and Leewards
      and note (*ub*) } *Journals Commons*, xvii, 31 March 1714; Entry Books 26/14, dated 29 May 1714; Ests. WO 24/75, warrant effective from 25 August 1714.

    Dunkirk
    Minorca
    Gibraltar } *Journals Commons*, xvii, 31 March 1714; Ests. WO 24/69, dated 20 July 1713; Ests. WO 24/71, dated 20 May 1714.

    Plantations } *Journals Commons*, xvii, 31 March 1714; Ests. WO 24/69, dated 20 July 1713; Ests. WO 24/72, dated 26 May 1714.

    Garrisons in Scotland } *Journals Commons*, xvii, 31 March 1714; Ests. WO 24/70, dated 29 April 1714.

    Garrisons in England,
      Channel and Scilly } Ests. WO 24/70, dated 29 April 1714.
      Isles

APPENDIX E

TABLE OF REGIMENTAL ESTABLISHMENTS

Ranks; Appointments Regimental H.Q. (a)	Troop of Horse (Life) Guards (1) (3)	Troop of Horse Gren. Guards (3)	Regt. of Royal Horse Guards 1713 (4)	Regt. of Horse 1713 (4)	Regt. of Horse 1705 (13)	Regt. of Dgns. 1713 (4)	Regt. of Dgns. 1702 (6)	1st Foot Guards 1702–8 (3)	1st Foot Guards 1713 (4)	Coldstream and 3rd Foot Guards 1707–8 (3)	Coldstream and 3rd Foot Guards 1713 (4)	Regiment of Foot — Continent 1713 (4)	Regiment of Foot — West Indies 1704–7 (9)	Independent Company of Foot — Scotland (10) (w)	Independent Company of Foot — West Indies (11) (w)
Colonel	..	..	1	1	1	1	1	1	1	1	1	1	1	..	..
Lt.-Colonel	..	..	1	1	1	1	1	1	1	1	1	1	1	..	..
Major	..	..	1	1	1	1	1	2	2	2	1	1 (t)	1	..	..
Adjutant	..	..	1	1	1	1	1	3	1	1	1	1	1	..	..
Chaplain	..	..	1	1	1	1	1	1	1	1	1	1	1	..	..
Surgeon	..	..	1	1	1	1	1	2	2	2	1	1 (t)	1	..	..
Surgeon's Mate	..	..	..	..	..	..	..	2	2	2	1	1 (t)	1	..	..
Quartermaster	..	..	..	..	..	..	..	2	2	1	1	1	1	..	..
Solicitor	..	..	..	..	..	..	..	1	1	1	1	..	..	..	..
Drum-Major	..	..	..	..	..	..	..	1	1	1	1	1	..	..	..
Deputy Marshal	..	..	..	..	..	..	..	1	1	1	1	..	..	..	..
Kettle Drummer	..	..	1	1	1	..	..	..	..	..	..	..	..	..	..
Piper	..	..	..	..	..	..	..	..	..	..	..	(t)	..	..	..
Gunsmith (and servant)	..	..	..	..	..	..	1	..	..	..	..	(s)	..	..	..

APPENDIX D

THE TOWER OF LONDON

SPECIMEN ESTIMATE WITH DAILY RATES

	£	s.	d.	
Governor	1	18	$4\frac{1}{4}$	
Deputy Governor		16	$5\frac{1}{4}$	
Chaplain		6	8	
Tower Major		4	0	
Surgeon		2	6	
Master Gunner		2	0	
Four other gunners, each		1	0	
Gentleman porter		1	4	
40 yeomen warders, each		1	2	
Physician		1	$1\frac{1}{8}$	
Apothecary		0	$6\frac{1}{2}$	
Gentleman gaoler		1	$1\frac{1}{8}$	
The Water Pumper		0	$7\frac{7}{8}$	
'The Yeoman porter for oyl and candles for the Gates'		0	$10\frac{1}{2}$	
The scavenger		0	$3\frac{3}{4}$	$\frac{7}{8}$[sic]
The clock keeper and bell ringer		0	$2\frac{5}{8}$	
'For repairs and intelligence and sweeping the chimneys'		1	$3\frac{1}{4}$	
Fuel		0	$4\frac{3}{4}$	

This may be compared with Scarborough, which had a governor at $10\frac{1}{2}d$. per day and two gunners at $1s$. each.

(Ests. WO 24/45, dated 24 June 1708, to take effect from 24 December 1707.)

Ranks: Appointments Companies/Troops (a)(o)	Troop of Horse (Life) Guards (1)(3)	Troop of Horse Gren. Guards (3)	Regt. of Royal Horse Guards 1713 (4)	Regt. of Horse 1713 (4)	Regt. of Horse 1705 (13)	Regt. of Dgns. 1713 (4)	Regt. of Dgns. 1702 (6)	1st Foot Guards 1702–8 (3)	1st Foot Guards 1713 (4)	Coldstream and 3rd Foot Guards 1707–8 (3)	Coldstream and 3rd Foot Guards 1713 (4)	Regiment of Foot — Continent 1713 (4)	Regiment of Foot — West Indies 1704–7 (9)	Independent Company of Foot — Scotland 1710 (w)	Independent Company of Foot — West Indies 1711 (w)
Captain	1 (b)	1 (e)	1	1	1	1	1	1	1	1	1	1	1	1	1
Lieutenant	2 (b)	1 (f)		1	1	1		1 (p)	1 (p)	1 (p)	1 (p)	1 (p)	1 (p)	2	3
Major		2 (g)	1	1											
Cornet	1 (b)	1 (b)	1	1	1	1	1								
Ensign								1 (p)	1 (p)	1 (p)	1 (p)	1 (p)	1 (p)		
Guidon		1 (h)				1	1								
Exempt	4 (b)														
Sub-lieutenant		2													
Brigadier	4 (c)														
Sub-Brigadier	4 (c)														
Adjutant	1	1	1	1	1	1									
Quartermaster			1	1	1		1								
Surgeon	1	1	1	1	1	1									
Chaplain	1	1	1												
Sergeant		6				1	2	3	2	3	2	2 (u)	2	2	3
Corporal		6	2	2	3	2	3	3	2	3	2	2 (t)	3	2	3
(Kettle) Drummer	1	4	1	1		1	2	2	2	2	2	1 (t)	2	1	2
Trumpeter	4			1	2										
Hautbois	4	4					2	3		3					
Troopers	156 (d)		(m) 36 (l)	36 (l)	60 (i)										
Dragoons						38 (n)	54								
Private															100 (x)
sentinels/grenadiers/fusiliers		145 (k)						70 (q)	40 (r)	70 (q)	40 (r)	(t) 36 (l)	59 (n)	40 (l)	

NOTES TO TABLE OF REGIMENTAL
ESTABLISHMENTS

(a) This division into regimental headquarters and troops does not hold in the case of the Life Guards or Horse Grenadier Guards. Although these were nominally troops, and of troop strength, their headquarters organization, because there was no unit higher than the troop, bore such appointments as adjutant. For fuller discussion of the ranks and organization of the Life and Horse Grenadier Guards, see Chapter III.

(b) These officers are so designated in the warrants quoted, but their rates of pay show fairly conclusively that they held, in fact, ranks as captain and colonel, lieutenant and lieutenant-colonel, cornet and major, exempt and captain. This is supported by Dalton's officer composition of the 1st Troop 1702–7, which shows one of each rank so designated (exempt as 'exempt and eldest captain') under supplementary commissions. (2) Because of this the officer commanding the troop was the captain and not the major, who was, in fact, junior to the lieutenant.

(c) The sub-brigadiers are not specifically shown in the warrant of 1708, but this may well have been an oversight, since the earlier warrant shows them under 'private gentlemen, of whom four to be sub-brigadiers—100'.

(d) 'Private gentlemen.'

(e) 'Captain and colonel.'

(f) 'Lieutenant and lieutenant colonel.'

(g) 'Lieutenants and captains.'

(h) 'Guidon and captain.'

(i) These presumably included servants and widows' men, but no specific distinction is made.

(k) 'Private men': but also known as grenadiers.

(l) Including two widows' men.

(m) In 1712 there were 50 troopers, including servants and one widows' man. (5) In 1705, there were 40 troopers with no mention of widows' men. (12)

(n) Including two widows' men. Some of the regiments in 1712–13 had 50 troopers: some (e.g. Echlyn's) had only one widows' man, and some had none. (5)

(o) In the First Guards, one company, designated the Queen's Company, was normally stronger than any other in the Guards Regiments.

(p) Grenadier companies had two lieutenants and no ensigns, but were otherwise the same in strength as foot companies.

(*q*) Reduced in 1712 to 60 (including servants), of whom one was a widows' man. ([5])

(*r*) Including one widows' man.

(*s*) The Royal Fusiliers were the only foot regiment with a gunsmith, and he is not shown on the establishment for every year. The companies in this regiment had two lieutenants. ([12])

(*t*) The Royal Scots had two adjutants, two quartermasters, three corporals, two drummers, and 59 privates. Their colonel's company also had the only piper in the army. They had no surgeon's mate. ([7])

(*u*) Certain establishments in the period 1704–8 show three sergeants in the grenadier company, but this was, I feel, exceptional outside the Guards or Independent Companies. ([3]) ([13])

(*v*) Including servants. Handasyde's regiment was strengthened to 70 privates per company, including servants, in 1707. ([9])

(*w*) Strengths of independent companies depended entirely on their roles, and varied from 50 to over 300. I have chosen the two here—Handasyde's in Jamaica, as reduced in 1714, and one of the three (of equal strength) in Scotland in the same year—as random examples.

(*x*) Including servants and widows' men.

AUTHORITIES

(1) Ests. WO 24/23, dated 25 April 1700.

(2) Dalton, v, pp. 18–19.

(3) Ests. WO 24/75, dated 24 June 1708.

(4) Entry Books WO 26/14, for 12 and 13 May 1713.

(5) Entry Books WO 26/14, dated 17 October 1712.

(6) Ests. WO 24/26, dated 1 June 1702.

(7) Ests. WO 24/24, dated 1 June 1701.

(8) Ests. WO 24/37, dated 10 April 1704.

(9) Ests. WO 24/42, dated 30 April 1705.

(10) Entry Books WO 26/14, dated 16 July 1714.

(11) Entry Books WO 26/14, dated 29 May 1714.

(12) Ests. WO 24/38, dated 30 April 1705, effective 30 December 1704.

'13) Ests. WO 24/41, dated 30 April 1705 (for Portugal).

APPENDIX F

REQUIREMENTS AND RECRUITS:
1708 AND 1709

1. *Men required for 1708*

For 17 battalions in Flanders	2,000
For 14 of the Almanza battalions	10,157
To reform six reduced battalions in Spain	1,200
For four battalions in Portugal	600
For two battalions in Gibraltar	300
For two battalions in the West Indies	300
For 10 battalions in Ireland	1,500
To bring up Scots battalions to English strengths consequent on the Union	2,000
Total	18,057

Volunteers

Berkshire, Lincolnshire, and Somerset	15
Leicestershire	2
Staffordshire	20
Total	37

Pressed men

The highest totals were:

Bedfordshire	109
Lancashire	86
Cheshire	74
Devonshire	70

The lowest was:

Worcestershire	3

The counties which provided volunteers provided impressed men as follows:

Lincolnshire	7
Somerset	7
Berkshire	7
Leicestershire	17
Staffordshire	28

By far the biggest proportion of pressed men was obtained in the period 18–21 March 1708.

An earlier entry shows also 500 men for the Marines.

2. *Recruits required winter 1708–9*

150 per battalion for 20 battalions in the Low Countries (this was in addition to anticipated exchanged prisoners)	3,000
200 per battalion for 11 battalions in Ostend	2,200
Two battalions in Antwerp	290
Six battalions Portugal	1,200
Seven battalions Spain	800
Reforming three broken battalions Spain	700
Five battalions England	751
Replacement of four battalions posted ex Ireland	1,400
Re-raising of four battalions discontinued to provide funds for maintenance of prisoners of war	2,488
Re-raising a broken battalion	536
Ten battalions Ireland	1,500
Total	14,865

Journals Commons, xv, 31 March 1708.
Journals Commons, xvi, 16 January 1709.

APPENDIX G

TABLE OF PAY OF REGIMENTAL OFFICERS AND MEN

	LIFE GUARDS (g) (1)					HORSE GRENADIER GUARDS (g) (1)				
	Pay of rank	Additional pay	Servants	Forage @ 2s.	Total	Pay of rank	Additional pay	Servants	Forage @ 1s.	Total
Colonel	20s.	10s.	16s.		46s. (a)	20s.	10s. (h)	10s.		40s. (i)
Lt.-Colonel	15s.	8s.	8s.		31s. (b)	15s.	8s.	7s. 6d.		30s. 6d. (j)
Major	14s.	5s.	8s.		27s. (c)		See note (j)			20s. (j)
Adjutant	7s.				7s.	7s.				7s. (k)
Captain	12s.	See note (b)	8s.		20s. (d)	12s.		5s.		17s. (k)
Lieutenant	:	See note (c)			:	:		:		:
Cornet	:				:	:		:		:
Ensign	:	See note (d)			:	11s.		5s.		16s. (l)
Guidon	12s.		:		13s. (e)	:		:		:
Exempt	:	1s.			:	10s.				10s.
Sub-Lieutenant	10s.				10s.	:				:
Brigadier	1s.	4s. (f)			5s.	:				:
Sub-Brigadier	9s.				9s.	:				:
Quartermaster	6s. 8d.				6s. 8d.	6s. 8d.				6s. 8d.
Chaplain	6s.			2s.	8s.	6s.			2s.	8s.
Surgeon	:				:	:				:
Surgeon's Mate	:				:	:				:
Solicitor (n)	:				:	:				:
Gunsmith (n)	:				:	:				:
Sergeant	:				:	4s.				4s.
Corporal	:				:	3s.				3s.
Drum-Major	:				:	:				:
Deputy Marshal (n)	5s.				5s.	:				:
(Kettle) Drummer	5s.				5s.	2s. 6d.				2s. 6d.
Trumpeter	:				:	:				:
Piper (p)	:				:	:				:
Hautbois	:				:	2s. 6d.				2s. 6d.
Pte. gentleman/Tpr./Dgn./Gren./ Pte. Sentinel/Fus.	4s.				4s.	2s. 6d.				(s)2s. 6d.

These may be compared with the rates in the New Model in 1648: colonel of foot £1; lt.-colonel of foot 15s.; major of foot 13s.; lieutenant of foot 8s.; captain of foot 15s.; ensign 3s.; private 3s.; Horse and dragoons ranged similarly from 22s. for a cavalry captain and 2s. for a trooper or 1s. 6d. for a dragoon. There was a small increase in these prior to the Restoration.

APPENDIX G (cont.)

	Horse (2)					Dragoons (2)					Foot (2)			
	Pay of rank	Additional pay as capt.	Servants @ 2s. 6d.	Forage @ 2s.	Total	Pay of rank	Additional pay as capt.	Servants @ 2s. 6d.	Forage @ 1s.	Total	Pay of rank	Additional pay as capt.	Servants @ 8d.	Total
Colonel	12s.	10s.	15s.	4s.	41s.	15s.	8s.	9s.	3s.	35s.	12s. (g)	8s.	4s.	24s.
Lt.-Colonel	8s.	10s.	7s. 6d.	4s.	29s. 6d.	9s.	8s.	4s. 6d.	3s.	24s. 6d.	7s. (g)	8s.	2s.	17s.
Major	5s. 6d.	10s.	7s. 6d.	4s.	27s.	5s.	8s.	4s. 6d.	3s. (m)	20s. 6d.	5s. (g)	8s.	2s.	15s.
Adjutant	5s.	..	..	..	..	5s.	..	..	..	..	..	..	..	..
Captain	..	10s.	7s. 6d.	4s.	21s. 6d.	8s.	..	4s. 6d.	3s.	15s. 6d.	8s. (g)	..	2s.	10s.
Lieutenant	6s.	..	5s.	4s.	15s.	4s.	..	3s. (m)	2s.	9s.	4s. (g)	..	8d. (m)	4s. 8d.
Cornet	5s.	..	5s.	4s.	14s.	3s.	..	3s.	2s.	8s.	..	..	..	..
Ensign	..	..	..	..	..	..	..	..	..	..	3s. (g)	..	8d.	3s. 8d.
Guidon	..	..	..	..	..	..	..	..	..	..	..	..	..	..
Exempt	..	..	..	..	..	..	..	..	..	..	..	..	..	..
Sub.-Lieutenant	..	..	..	..	..	..	..	..	..	..	..	..	..	..
Brigadier	..	..	..	..	..	..	..	..	..	..	..	..	..	..
Sub.-Brigadier	..	..	..	..	..	..	..	..	..	..	..	..	..	..
Quartermaster	4s.	..	2s. 6d.	2s.	8s. 6d.	3s. 8d.	..	1s. 6d.	1s.	5s. 6d.	4s.	..	..	4s. 6d.
Chaplain	6s. 8d.	..	..	..	6s. 8d.	6s. 8d.	..	..	..	6s. 8d.	6s. 8d.	..	..	6s. 6d.
Surgeon	4s.	..	..	2s.	6s.	4s.	..	..	2s.	6s.	4s.	..	(r) 2s. 6d.	2s. 6d.
Surgeon's Mate	..	..	..	..	..	..	..	..	..	..	..	..	..	..
Solicitor (n)	..	..	..	..	..	4s. 6d.	..	..	..	5s.	..	..	..	4s.
Gunsmith (o)	..	..	..	..	..	..	..	..	..	..	5s.	..	..	..
Sergeant	4s.	..	..	..	4s.	1s. 6d.	..	..	1s.	2s. 6d.	1s. 6d.	..	..	5s.
Corporal	3s.	..	..	..	3s.	1s.	..	..	1s.	2s.	1s. 6d.	..	..	1s.
Drum-Major	..	..	..	..	..	..	..	..	..	..	1s. 6d.	..	..	1s. 6d.
Deputy Marshal (n)	..	..	..	..	..	..	..	..	..	..	1s.	..	..	1s.
(Kettle) Drummer	3s. 8d.	..	..	..	3s. 8d.	..	..	..	..	..	1s. 6d.	..	..	1s.
Trumpeter	2s. 8d.	..	..	..	2s. 8d.	1s.	..	..	1s.	2s.	..	..	..	..
Piper (p)	..	..	..	..	..	..	..	..	..	..	1s.	..	..	1s.
Hautbois	..	..	..	..	..	..	..	..	..	..	1s. 6d.	..	..	1s. 6d.
Pte. gentleman/Tpr./Dgn./Gren./Pte. Sentinel/Fus.	2s. 6d.	..	..	..	2s. 6d.	1s. 6d.	..	..	1s.	1s. 6d.	8d. (g)	..	..	8d.

NOTES TO TABLE OF PAY OF REGIMENTAL OFFICERS AND MEN

(a) Colonel and captain.

(b) Lieutenant-colonel and lieutenant. I have assumed the pay of 8s. as lieutenant since this was a dual rank, but have seen no specific mention of it.

(c) Major and cornet. Cornet's pay assumed: see (b).

(d) Captain and guidon. There was almost certainly an additional element 'as guidon', but I have been unable to find any figures.

(e) Captain and exempt. The only figure I can find is 12s. as exempt.

(f) As 'private gentleman'. The sub-brigadiers were apparently roughly equivalent to lance ranks. They are mentioned merely as '160 private gentlemen of whom four are to be sub-brigadiers with an additional 1s.'.

(g) The sources for the Life Guards and Horse Grenadier Guards are conflicting. The Household Cavalry had a special status as to rank, pay, and perquisites, and the figures here represent the best reconciliation one can, in Mr. Lynn's words, 'cook up'.

(h) I have assumed this 10s. since the rank was 'colonel and captain'.

(i) One authority gives 'lieutenant colonel 15s.', and another 'lieutenant 8s.'. I have compounded the two as the rank was 'lieutenant colonel and lieutenant'.

(j) This is taken from the warrant which says 'major for himself, horse, and in lieu of servant £1'.

(k) This is probably the most unsatisfactory entry of all. The figures are from the warrant, which normally omits to mention the extra rank pay, or consolidates it. Walton says captains had 15s. (raised from 10s. between 1680 and 1688).

(l) Captain and guidon.

(m) Estimated.

(n) Foot Guards only.

(o) Only for the Royal Fusiliers among the foot regiments.

(p) The Royal Regiment only.

(q) There were the following special rates in the Foot Guards while in London: colonel £1; lt.-colonel 12s.; major 8s.; captain 14s.; lieutenant 7s.; ensign 5s.; privates 10d. There were doubtless corresponding additions to the elements for servants, but I have been unable to find any figures. These differentials dated from 1691.

(r) For a horse to carry his chest.

(s) Walton states that when in Southwark, the troopers' pay was raised by 1s. 6d. per day.

AUTHORITIES

(1) Walton, p. 647; Ests. WO 24/49, dated 13 August 1709; Ests. WO 24/45, dated 24 December 1707—see note (g).

(2) Walton, p. 646; Ests. WO 24/41, dated 30 April 1705; Ests. WO 24/46 and 24/47; and WO 24/45, dated 24 June 1708.

PAY OF GENERAL AND STAFF OFFICERS

General Officers

	£	s.	d.
Captain-General	10	0	0
General	6	0	0
Lieutenant-General	4	0	0
Major-General	2	0	0
Brigadier	1	10	0

Commanders' personal staffs

Secretary	0	10	0
Surgeon (to commander-in-chief)	1	0	0
Physician (to commander-in-chief)	0	10	0
A.D.C. (to captain-general, general, lieutenant-general, or major-general)	0	10	0
Chaplain to commander-in-chief	0	6	8

General Staff

Brigade major	0	10	0

Adjutant and Quartermaster-General's Branch

Adjutant-General	0	10	0
Quartermaster-General (Cadogan and Ormonde's expedition)	1	0	0
Quartermaster-General (England and Flanders, 1712)	0	10	0
Assistant or Deputy Quartermaster-General	0	5	0
Judge-Advocate (England)	0	15	0
Judge-Advocate (Expeditions)	0	10	0
Provost Marshal	0	5	0
Provost Marshal's men[1]	0	1	6

Governors

Pay for governors of castles and fortresses in the United Kingdom ranged from $10\frac{1}{2}d$. per day at Scarborough and $1s$. $4d$. per day at Portland Castle to £1 $18s$. $4\frac{1}{2}d$. at the Tower of London.

---

[1] In the 1712 Flanders campaign the Provost Marshal received $6s$. per day, and his men (two) $3s$. each. There was also normally an allowance for horses and shackles.

Services

Special rates for the arms/services are shown in the appropriate chapters.

PAY OF ACCOUNTS AND PAY STAFFS

	£	s.	d.
Paymaster-General	1	10	0
Deputy Paymaster (Flanders)	0	12	6
Deputy Paymaster (Ormonde's expedition)	0	5	6[1]
Comptroller of Accounts	1	0	0
Commissary-General of Musters for West Indies[2]	1	1	11
Commissary-General of the Musters	1	5	8¾
Deputy Commissary of the Musters in England (six)	0	10	0
Deputy Commissary of the Musters in London	1	3	0
Deputy Commissaries of the Musters in Jersey and Guernsey	0	2	6

[1] £100 7s. 0d. per year: 5s. 6d. was the rate for a paymaster's clerk in the estimates of 'succour to the States General' presented on 12 May 1701.

[2] £400 per year: did not proceed on the expedition

APPENDIX H

SUBSISTENCE

Subsistence rates laid down in the 1704 Mutiny Act (Annae 3 and 4, cap. 5) applied only to other ranks and were as follows per week:

Horse	s.	d.	*Dragoons*	s.	d.
Corporals	17	6	Dragoon	8	2
Trumpeters and troopers	14	0			

Foot Guards			*Foot*		
Sergeants	7	0	Sergeants	6	0
Corporals and drummers	5	0	Corporals and drummers	4	6
Privates	4	0[1]	Privates	3	0

'And also over and above the said 6s per week to each serjeant, and 4s 6d to each corporal and drummer, and 3s a week to each foot soldier, at the end of every two months' the Commanding Officer was to be accountable for the following sums per week 'being the remainder of the subsistence': sergeants 1*s.*; corporals and drummers 2*d.*; privates 6*d.*

The following rates were laid down in the Peninsula in 1705:[2]

			Horse		
Officers—per day	s.	d.	*Other ranks—per week*	s.	d.
Colonel and captain	19	6	Corporals and kettle drummers	17	6
Lieutenant-colonel and captain	16	6	Trumpeters and troopers	14	0
Major and captain	15	6			
Captain	10	6			
Lieutenant	7	6			
Cornet	7	0			
Quartermaster	4	6			
Chaplain	5	0			

[1] The 1703 Act (Annae 2 and 3, cap. 17) ordered 3*s.* 0*d.*
[2] And again in 1708.

Horse (cont.)

Officers—per day	s.	d.
Adjutant	4	6
Surgeon	4	6

Dragoons

Officers—per day			Other ranks—per week		
As for Horse except:	s.	d.	As for Horse except:	s.	d.
Major and captain	13	0	Gunsmith and servant	28	0
Captain	8	0	Sergeants	14	0
Lieutenant	4	6	Corporals, drummers,		
Cornet	3	6	and Hautbois	10	6
			Dragoons	8	2

Foot Guards

Officers—per day	s.	d.	Other ranks—per week	s.	d.
Major and captain	16	6	Sergeants	7	0
Captain	10	6	Corporals	5	0
Lieutenant	5	6	Drummers	5	0
Ensign	4	0	Privates	4	0
Surgeon	3	6			
Surgeon's mate	2	0			

Foot

Officers—per day	s.	d.	Other ranks—per week[1]	s.	d.
Colonel and captain	16	6	Sergeants	7	0
Lieutenant-colonel			Corporals	4	8
and captain	13	0	Drummers	4	8
Major and captain	10	0	Privates	3	6
Captain	6	0			
Lieutenant	3	0			
Ensign	2	6			
Chaplain	5	0			
Adjutant	3	6			
Quartermaster	3	6			
Surgeon	3	6			
Surgeon's mate	2	0			

The warrant instructed specifically that the money was to be paid weekly.

[1] These rates were also ordered by Stanhope in 1709 when he stipulated that the money should be divided into $3\frac{1}{2}$ parts cash, one part for bread, and half a part to the paymaster for carriage of money, medicines, &c.

	Sergeant			Corporal			Private			Drummer		
	£	s.	d.	£	s.	d.	£	s.	d.	£	s.	d.
Coat, waistcoat, and breeches	4	10	0	2	10	0	1	15	0	2	10	0
Hat	1	0	0	0	5	6	0	4	0	0	5	6
Two pairs stockings	0	6	0	0	3	6	0	3	0	0	3	6
Two pairs shoes	0	9	0	0	9	0	0	9	0	0	9	0
Two pairs buckles	0	2	0	0	0	8	0	0	6	0	0	8
Two shirts	0	10	0	0	9	0	0	6	0	0	9	0
Two neckcloths	0	8	0	0	3	0	0	2	2	0	3	0
One pair mittens	0	1	2	0	1	2	0	1	2	0	1	2
One pair gloves	0	2	0	0	1	6		..		0	1	6
Drum collars		..			..			..		0	4	0
Totals	£7	8	2	£4	3	4	£3	0	10	£4	7	4

The report states that the company had no clothing in the previous year except shirts, shoes, stockings, and neckcloths—i.e. this is probably a large clothing year.

The total costs for the company are given in further detail as:

	£	s.	d.
Two drums	2	0	0
Two prs drum sticks	0	6	0
One doz drum heads	1	4	0
Six prs snairs	0	6	0
Freight etc.	10	0	0
Clothing as above	286	15	10
Total	£300	11	10

The costs for the small clothing year 1702 for the Newfoundland company were:

	£	s.	d.
88 pairs strong shoes for N.C.O.s and men @ 4s. 6d. a pair	19	16	0
80 pairs stockings for men at 18d.	6	0	0
5 pairs stockings for corporals and drummers @ 20d.	0	8	4
3 pairs stockings for sergeants at 3s.	0	9	0
160 shirts for soldiers @ 3s. 6d.	28	0	0
10 shirts for corporals and drummers @ 3s. 6d.	1	15	0
6 shirts for sergeants @ 5s.	1	10	0
160 neckcloths for soldiers @ 12d.	8	0	0
10 neckcloths for corporals and drummers @ 1s. 6d.	0	15	0

In Newfoundland in 1702 the daily rates were:

	s.	d.		s.	d.
Captain	3	0	Sergeants	0	4
Lieutenant	2	6	Corporals	0	3
Second lieutenant	2	0	Privates	0	2

Other daily rates (in 1701) were:

	s.	d.		s.	d.
Drum-major	1	6	Piper	0	8

Daily rates in Jamaica and Leewards in 1704 were:

	s.	d.		s.	d.
Colonel as colonel	10	6	Sergeant	1	0
Lieutenant-colonel as lieutenant-colonel	7	0	Corporal	0	9
			Private	0	6
Major as major	4	2			
Chaplain	5	2			
Surgeon	3	6			
Surgeon's mate	2	1			
Adjutant and quartermaster	3	6			
Captain	6	8			
Lieutenant	3	4			
Ensign	2	6			

(The above are taken from the following sources in addition to the Mutiny Acts: Ests. WO 24/47, dated 16 April 1704, and for 1708; WO 34/41 for 1705; Registers WO 25/3207, dated 1 January 1701; APC Col., ii, p. 401, meeting of 26 March 1702.)

Subsistence payable to the Household Cavalry in 1714 was as follows:

	Life Guards[1]		Horse Grenadier Guards	
	s.	d.	s.	d.
Captain and colonel	27	0	22	6
Lieutenant and lieutenant-colonel	17	6	17	6
Cornet	16	0		
Major			15	0
Guidon	15	0		
Exempt	10	0		
Lieutenant and captain			13	0
Guidon and captain			12	0
Brigadier	7	6		

[1] The Etablishment Book states 'Horse Guards', but the context, rates, and ranks indicate that 'Life Guards' were intended.

	Life Guards		Horse Grenadier Guards	
	s.	*d.*	*s.*	*d.*
Sub-brigadier	4	0		
Sub-lieutenant			7	6
Chaplain	5	0	5	0
Adjutant	5	6	5	6
Surgeon	6	0	6	0
Trumpeter	4	0		
Sergeant			3	6
Corporal			2	6
(Kettle) drummer	4	0	2	0
Hautbois			2	0
Private gentlemen	2	$10\frac{2}{7}$	2	$10\frac{2}{7}$
Marshal to Horse and Horse Grenadier Guards[1]	5	6	5	6

(Ests. WO 24/75, dated 18 December 1714.)

[1] See p. 383, n. 1.

APPENDIX I

CLOTHING SCALES

The author of the *Recruiting Essay* states that the following required:

First Year

	s.
2¼ yards red cloth @ 4s. 6d. per yard	10
4 yards Bays (baize) for linings at 13d. per yard	4
½ yard Red plan @ 18d. per yard	0
4 yards plan for vest and breeches @ 18d. per yard	6
Lining for breeches and pockets	1
Brass buttons	1
Making with thread	2
Sword and belt	6
A paick (a pack?)	4
One pair shoes	3
One pair stockings	1
Hat edged and lined	2
Garters and buckles	0
Two shirts	5
Two neckcloths	1
Total	£2 10

Second Year

	s.	*d.*
One shirt, one pair of shoes, one hat, one pair of stockings, one neckcloth, and one pair of breeches @ 4s. 6d.	14	
Grand total	£3 4	
The total for Ireland was	£2 6	

The author emphasizes the fact that the prices are not underrate but this merely serves to underline that these were his estimat (whether on good or bad information we cannot be sure) and n really sample scales and costs. It was, of course, to the advantage the case he was pleading to prove the cost as low as possible.

An official report provides the following comparison. The quota tions are for a year's clothing for a company of three sergeant three corporals, two drummers, and 80 men in Newfoundland fc 1707.

In Newfoundland in 1702 the daily rates were:

	s.	d.		s.	d.
Captain	3	0	Sergeants	0	4
Lieutenant	2	6	Corporals	0	3
Second lieutenant	2	0	Privates	0	2

Other daily rates (in 1701) were:

	s.	d.		s.	d.
Drum-major	1	6	Piper	0	8

Daily rates in Jamaica and Leewards in 1704 were:

	s.	d.		s.	d.
Colonel as colonel	10	6	Sergeant	1	0
Lieutenant-colonel as			Corporal	0	9
lieutenant-colonel	7	0	Private	0	6
Major as major	4	2			
Chaplain	5	2			
Surgeon	3	6			
Surgeon's mate	2	1			
Adjutant and					
quartermaster	3	6			
Captain	6	8			
Lieutenant	3	4			
Ensign	2	6			

(The above are taken from the following sources in addition to the Mutiny Acts: Ests. WO 24/47, dated 16 April 1704, and for 1708; WO 34/41 for 1705; Registers WO 25/3207, dated 1 January 1701; *APC Col.*, ii, p. 401, meeting of 26 March 1702.)

Subsistence payable to the Household Cavalry in 1714 was as follows:

	Life Guards[1]		Horse Grenadier Guards	
	s.	d.	s.	d.
Captain and colonel	27	0	22	6
Lieutenant and lieutenant-colonel	17	6	17	6
Cornet	16	0		
Major			15	0
Guidon	15	0		
Exempt	10	0		
Lieutenant and captain			13	0
Guidon and captain			12	0
Brigadier	7	6		

[1] The Etablishment Book states 'Horse Guards', but the context, rates, and ranks indicate that 'Life Guards' were intended.

	Life Guards		Horse Grenadier Guards	
	s.	d.	s.	d.
Sub-brigadier	4	0		
Sub-lieutenant			7	6
Chaplain	5	0	5	0
Adjutant	5	6	5	6
Surgeon	6	0	6	0
Trumpeter	4	0		
Sergeant			3	6
Corporal			2	6
(Kettle) drummer	4	0	2	0
Hautbois			2	0
Private gentlemen	2	$10\frac{2}{7}$	2	$10\frac{2}{7}$
Marshal to Horse and Horse Grenadier Guards[1]	5	6	5	6

(Ests. WO 24/75, dated 18 December 1714.)

[1] See p. 383, n. 1.

APPENDIX I

CLOTHING SCALES

The author of the *Recruiting Essay* states that the following were required:

First Year	*s.*	*d.*
2¼ yards red cloth @ 4*s.* 6*d.* per yard	10	1½
4 yards Bays (baize) for linings at 13*d.* per yard	4	4
½ yard Red plan @ 18*d.* per yard	0	9
4 yards plan for vest and breeches @ 18*d.* per yard	6	0
Lining for breeches and pockets	1	9
Brass buttons	1	4½
Making with thread	2	0
Sword and belt	6	0
A paick (a pack?)	4	0
One pair shoes	3	6
One pair stockings	1	0
Hat edged and lined	2	2
Garters and buckles	0	9
Two shirts	5	0
Two neckcloths	1	4

Total £2 10 1

Second Year

	s.	*d.*
One shirt, one pair of shoes, one hat, one pair of stockings, one neckcloth, and one pair of breeches @ 4*s.* 6*d.*	14	4

Grand total £3 4 5

The total for Ireland was £2 6 2

The author emphasizes the fact that the prices are not underrated, but this merely serves to underline that these were his estimates (whether on good or bad information we cannot be sure) and not really sample scales and costs. It was, of course, to the advantage of the case he was pleading to prove the cost as low as possible.

An official report provides the following comparison. The quotations are for a year's clothing for a company of three sergeants, three corporals, two drummers, and 80 men in Newfoundland for 1707.

	Sergeant			Corporal			Private			Drummer		
	£	s.	d.	£	s.	d.	£	s.	d.	£	s.	d.
Coat, waistcoat, and breeches	4	10	0	2	10	0	1	15	0	2	10	0
Hat	1	0	0	0	5	6	0	4	0	0	5	6
Two pairs stockings	0	6	0	0	3	6	0	3	0	0	3	6
Two pairs shoes	0	9	0	0	9	0	0	9	0	0	9	0
Two pairs buckles	0	2	0	0	0	8	0	0	6	0	0	8
Two shirts	0	10	0	0	9	0	0	6	0	0	9	0
Two neckcloths	0	8	0	0	3	0	0	2	2	0	3	0
One pair mittens	0	1	2	0	1	2	0	1	2	0	1	2
One pair gloves	0	2	0	0	1	6		..		0	1	6
Drum collars		..			..			..		0	4	0
Totals	£7	8	2	£4	3	4	£3	0	10	£4	7	4

The report states that the company had no clothing in the previous year except shirts, shoes, stockings, and neckcloths—i.e. this is probably a large clothing year.

The total costs for the company are given in further detail as:

	£	s.	d.
Two drums	2	0	0
Two prs drum sticks	0	6	0
One doz drum heads	1	4	0
Six prs snairs	0	6	0
Freight etc.	10	0	0
Clothing as above	286	15	10
Total	£300	11	10

The costs for the small clothing year 1702 for the Newfoundland company were:

	£	s.	d.
88 pairs strong shoes for N.C.O.s and men @ 4s. 6d. a pair	19	16	0
80 pairs stockings for men at 18d.	6	0	0
5 pairs stockings for corporals and drummers @ 20d.	0	8	4
3 pairs stockings for sergeants at 3s.	0	9	0
160 shirts for soldiers @ 3s. 6d.	28	0	0
10 shirts for corporals and drummers @ 3s. 6d.	1	15	0
6 shirts for sergeants @ 5s.	1	10	0
160 neckcloths for soldiers @ 12d.	8	0	0
10 neckcloths for corporals and drummers @ 1s. 6d.	0	15	0

	£	s.	d.
6 neckcloths for sergeants @ 4s.	1	4	0
Freight	5	0	0
Total	£72	17	4

(*A.P.C. Col.*, ii, p. 400 (26 March 1702) and pp. 512–13 (5 February 1707).)

APPENDIX J

ARTICLES OF WAR

One of the earliest complete sets of Articles of War extant is that published at Newcastle in 1639: 'Laws and Ordinances of Warre, for the better Government of His Majesties Army Royall, in the present Expedition for the Northern Parts, and safety of the Kingdome, under the conduct of His Excellence the Right Honourable Thomas Howard, Earl of Arundel and Surrey, Earl Marsall of England &c, and General of His Majesties Forces.' The Articles fall into two parts, the first dealing with religion and breach of moral duties, and the second with the safety of the 'Army Royall of the Kingdome'.

Part One deals with blasphemy, swearing, cursing, robbing churches, and attendance at divine service. Gambling was prohibited 'for as much as gaming is oft times the provocation into swearing, quarrelling, neglect of military duties, with the dishonour of God Almightie, loss to the souldiers with danger to the whole army'. All 'Suspitious and common women' were to be turned out of camp on discovery, and, if taken a second time, to be 'soundly whipped like common strumpets'. Death was prescribed for murder, rape, burning of houses, thefts, outrages, unnatural abuses, and notorious and abominable crimes. The Section concluded: 'No enterprise shall be taken in hand, but the company that are to execute the same shall first commend themselves to God, and pray to Him to grant them good success.'

The second part opened with an Article of general application: 'Whoever in favour of the enemy or other pretence whatsoever, shall presume to say, or secretly insinuate to any, that His Majesty's forces or Army Royall is unlawful or not necessary, shall suffer as an enemy and rebel.' Also, 'whoever shall disparage the actions or directions of any chiefs commander of the army, unlesse he be able to make it good, shall die for it'. There were Articles dealing with shouting, making noise or clamour, firing without cause—for which the offender was to be bastinadoed by his officer and thereafter imprisoned. There were familiar prohibitions concerning false musters, using victuals or ammunition in less than the appropriate time, assaulting the commissary of musters, disputing with the quartermaster on quarters, and injury of 'common souldiers' by officers. Camp sanitation was made the responsibility of the Provost

Marshal to whom all were to account for the burying of 'garbage, carrion, filth, and other noysome offences'. There was to be no breaking, burning, or pillaging of church, school, hospital, or college, and no one was 'to tyrannise over any churchmen, schollers, or poore people, women, maides, or children, upon paine of death'.

Any offence not specifically dealt with was to be handled according to the 'ancient course of marshall discipline'. Collective punishment was provided for regiments deemed guilty of an offence. All officers and every tenth soldier in any such were to be punished 'with all severity' and the remainder of the soldiers to be put on servile offices 'until by some brave exploit they purge themselves'. (Clode, i, p. 429.)

The Articles laid before the House of Commons on 4 February 1717 are of special interest because they are believed to be those in force immediately prior to that time. Clode (i, p. 146, footnote) states that they were recast immediately after being laid before the House, and there is in existence a printed version dated 1718. There are 46 Articles in each version.

1717 Edition

Articles 1–5: attendance at divine service, prohibition of sutling during service, blasphemy, oaths, execrations, profaning place of worship or assaulting chaplains. Sutling during divine service or blasphemy were to be dealt with by the civil magistrates, and for profaning a place of worship or assaulting a chaplain, corporal punishment was to be ordered by Court Martial.

Articles 6–10: treacherous words, correspondence with the enemy, mutiny, disobedience, and resistance to superior officer. Courts Martial were to punish these by 'death or such other punishment' as they might think fit.

Article 11: officers to obey regulations concerning pay.

Articles 12–14: desertion, re-enlistment of deserter, persuading to desert: punishment, death or such other punishment: officers enlisting a deserter to be cashiered.

Article 15: officers leaving confinement to be cashiered: soldiers breaking out of prison, death or such other punishment.

Articles 16–17: fleeing, abandoning post, going off for plunder, inducing others to do so—death or such other punishment: captured stores to be secured for Her Majesty.

Article 18: anyone accused of a crime which is an offence against the law and not mentioned in the Articles to be handed over to a J.P.

Article 19: lays down channels for complaints.

Article 20: anyone guilty of reproachful speeches or provoking gestures to ask pardon in presence of his Commanding Officer. Officers issuing or accepting challenges to be cashiered: N.C.O.s and soldiers to receive 'the severest corporal punishment'. All to take part in quelling disorders and to realize there is no dishonour in refusing a challenge.

Article 21: Regimental Court Martial: to judge disputes between soldier and officer, and soldier and soldier; to consist of five officers and President not under rank of captain: also authorized to try N.C.O.s and soldiers and order corporal punishment if approved by the Commanding Officer.

Article 22: trials involving the death penalty to be reserved to a General Court Martial consisting of 13 officers with a President who is to be a field officer or commander-in-chief of forces in a garrison.

Articles 23–26: oath of allegiance: false musters: leave: recording of commissions.

Article 27: no cashiering without Royal permission or sentence of General Court Martial approved by a Commander authorized to convene one: N.C.O.s to be discharged as privates: Regimental Courts Martial authorized to reduce N.C.O.s to ranks.

Articles 28–29: no soldiers to sutle: hours of sutling.

Articles 30–35: damage to quarters: payment for quarters: impressment of carriages: complaints by landlords: sleeping out of quarters.

Article 36: officers drunk on duty under arms to be cashiered: N.C.O.s and privates to ride the wooden horse, to be picquetted, or to suffer such other corporal punishment as is provided for like offences.

Article 37: sentry quitting post to run the gauntlet, 'which is a sentence we think not fit to be otherwise imposed than by the Judgment of a General or Regimental Court Martial'.

Article 38: prohibition of hiring others to do duty.

Article 39: no raising false alarms.

Article 40: speedy trials.

Article 41: no making known the watchword.

Article 42: any man spoiling arms or ammunition wilfully to run the gauntlet: an officer, storekeeper, or commissary of provisions embezzling, selling, or wilfully spoiling to be cashiered.

Article 43: a soldier selling or wilfully losing or stealing comrades' property to suffer weekly stoppage not exceeding half his pay, and confinement or corporal punishment: this to be the only stoppage permitted except under Sign Manual and to be imposed only by Regimental Court Martial: no general stoppages except by Royal Warrant or Warrant of the General Officer Commanding.

Articles 44–45: acceptance of prisoners, and disposal of property of dead officers and men.

Article 46: these Articles to be read out to the troops every two months, and to be observed by the companies of artillery and artillery trains: in Ireland questions of quartering and carriages to be regulated by the Lord Lieutenant, and overseas by Governors. (From *Journals Commons*, xviii, 4 Feb. 1717.)

1718 Edition

Articles 1–5: as in 1717 edition, but punishments for profaning church or for violence to a chaplain to be such as court decides.

Articles 6–9: as 6–10 of 1717 edition, but omitting provision concerning correspondence with enemy.

Articles 10–13: desertion, associated offences, and prison breaking, which is to be treated as desertion: death penalty.

Articles 14–16: abandoning post, quitting line of march for plunder, &c., death penalty.

Article 17: composition of Regimental Court Martial to punish 'neglect of duty, disorders in quarters, or other such crimes'.

Articles 18–19: powers of Court Martial.

Articles 20–21: composition of General Court Martial; proceedings where death penalty involved restricted to 0800–1300 hours daily.

Articles 22–23: false musters and leave.

Articles 24–25: as Articles 26 and 27 in 1717 edition.

Articles 26–27: as Articles 28 and 29 of 1717 edition.

Article 28: trials to be held within eight days of confinement.

Articles 29–46: similar to 1717 edition.

(Rules and Articles for the Better Government of Horse and Foot Guards: published by His Majesty's Command (London, 1718).)

BIBLIOGRAPHY AND REFERENCE KEY

In cases where extensive quotations or references occur in the text, the abbreviated title shown in the footnotes is shown on the right.

BIBLIOGRAPHIES

Davies, Godfrey: *Bibliography of British History: Stuart Period 1603–1714* (Oxford University Press, 1928).

Giuseppi, M. S.: *A Guide to Manuscripts Preserved in the Public Record Office* (H.M.S.O., 1924).

Lists of War Office Records Preserved in the Public Record Office (H.M.S.O. 1908).

Alphabetical Guide to Certain War Office and Other Military Records Preserved in the Public Record Office (H.M.S.O., 1931).

PUBLIC RECORD OFFICE

Manuscript Calendar of State Papers (Domestic) of the Reign of Queen Anne (1702–1714)	*Anne Cal.*
State Papers (Domestic Entry Book)	SPO
State Papers (Foreign)	SP For.
State Papers (Military)	SP Mil.
Treasury Papers	Treas.

Military Records

Secretary at War: In Letters	War Letters WO 1
Secretary at War: Out Letters	War Letters WO 2–4
Secretary at War: Out Letters—Marching Orders	Marching Orders WO 5
Board of General Officers: Out Letters	BGO: Out Letters WO 7
Out Letters (Ireland)	Ireland WO 8
Secretary at War: Establishments	Ests. WO 24
Secretary at War: Registers	Registers WO 25
Secretary at War: Entry Books of Warrants and Precedents	Entry Books WO 26
Register of Court Martial Warrants	CM Warrants WO 30
Reports and Miscellaneous Papers	Misc. WO 33
Board of Ordnance: Reference Books	Ord. Books WO 44
Board of Ordnance: Out Letters	Ord. Letters WO 46
Board of Ordnance: Journals of Proceedings	Ord. Minutes WO 47
Office of Ordnance: Registers	Ord. Registers WO 54
Ordnance Entry Book of Warrants and Orders in Council	Ord. Warrants WO 55
Commissariat: In Letters	Commissariat WO 57

Commissariat: Out Letters	Commissariat WO 58
Board of Ordnance: Quarter Books	Quarter Books WO 59
Army Lists	Lists WO 64–66
Board of General Officers: Proceedings	PGO WO 71

Military Memoranda, &c., to which special reference is made

The Customary Practice of the Army Concerning Off-Reckonings (25 April 1772)	WO 30/105
General Instructions for the Ordnance	WO 55/789
Instructions for the Government of Our Office of Ordnance Under Our Master General Thereof, Committed to Five Principal Officers (25 July 1683)	WO 55/536
Proposed Re-organisation of the Transport and Commissariat Department, 1875	WO 33/27
Proposed Transfer of the Transport, Supply, and Barrack Services to the Quartermaster General	WO 33/52
Warrant for the Regulation of the Off-Reckonings of the Respective Troops and Regiments of Guards and other Regiments of Horse, Foot, and Dragoons, 1695	Off-Reckonings

OTHER OFFICIAL PUBLICATIONS

Chronological Table of All the Statutes (1945)
Record of the Statutes from 1702: Charles Bill

Journals of the House of Commons:	*Journals Commons*
Vol. xiii, 16 November 1699–25 May 1702	
Vol. xiv, 20 October 1702–14 March 1705	
Vol. xv, 25 October 1705–1 April 1708	
Vol. xvi, 16 November 1708–9 October 1711	
Vol. xvii, 7 December 1711–1 August 1714	
Journals of the House of Lords	*Journals Lords*
Calendar of State Papers (Domestic Series) of the Reign of Queen Anne, vols. i–ii (1702–4). (H.M.S.O., 1916, 1924)	*Dom. Cal.*
Calendar of State Papers (Treasury Series) of the Reign of Queen Anne (1702–14). (H.M.S.O., 1874, 1879)	*Treas. Cal.*
Calendar of Treasury Books (H.M.S.O., 1939)	**Treas. Books**
Acts of the Privy Council of England: Colonial Series, vol ii, 1680–1720 (H.M.S.O.)	*APC Col.*

Rules and Articles for the Better Government of
Our Horse and Foot Guards, and all other
Our Land Forces in Our Kingdom of Great
Britain and Ireland and Dominions Beyond
the Seas. (Published by His Majesty's Com-
mand: 1718)

Rules and Instructions to the Muster Masters of   Muster Masters'
the Army, 1645. (Issued over the signature of   Instructions
the Clerk of Parliament)

HISTORICAL MANUSCRIPTS COMMISSION

House of Lords Papers, New Series, vols. vi–viii   *H.M.C.H. of L.*
Report on Manuscripts of Marquis of Ormonde, K.P.,   *H.M.C. Ormonde*
vol. ii (1899)
Marlborough Manuscripts, 8th Report, Appendix 3   *H.M.C. Marlborough*

BRITISH MUSEUM ADDITIONAL MANUSCRIPTS

Coxe Transcripts: Add. MSS 9092   Coxe
Cardonnel to Ellis: Add. MSS. 28918   Cardonnel
Cardonnel to Wilkins: Add. MSS. 42176   Wilkins

HISTORICAL: GENERAL

Browning, Arthur (ed.): *English Historical*   Browning
Documents, vol. viii, 1660–1714 (Eyre &
Spottiswoode, London, 1953)

Bryant, Arthur: *Samuel Pepys: The Man in the
Making*, 1933
Samuel Pepys: The Years of Peril, 1935   *Years of Peril*
Samuel Pepys: The Saviour of the Navy, 1938.
(Cambridge University Press, Cambridge)

Cambridge Modern History, vol. v: *The Age of Louis*   Cambridge
XIV (Cambridge University Press, 1908)

Thomson, Mark A.: *A Constitutional History of*   Thomson
England, vol. iv, 1642–1801 (Methuen &
Co., London, 1938)

Trevelyan, G. M.: *England Under Queen Anne*,   Trevelyan
vols. i–iii (Longmans Green & Co., Lon-
don, 1934)
English Social History (Longmans Green &   *Social History*
Co., 1948), Reprint Society Edition
Select Documents for Queen Anne's Reign (Cam-   *Select Docs.*
bridge University Press, Cambridge, 1929)

Williams, Basil: *Stanhope: A Study in 18th-Century*   *Stanhope*
War and Diplomacy (Clarendon Press, Lon-
don, 1932)

Williamson, Hugh Ross: *Four Stuart Portraits*   Williamson
(Evans, London, 1949)
Wood, A. E. L.: *The Age of Queen Anne* (Thomas   Wood
Nelson & Sons, London, 1928)

HISTORICAL: MILITARY

Clode, Charles M.: *The Military Forces of the*   Clode
Crown: their administration and government (John
Murray, London, 1869)
Cruickshank, C. G.: *Elizabeth's Army* (Oxford   Cruickshank
University Press, London, 1946)
Dalton, Charles: *English Army Lists and Com-*   Dalton
mission Registers (1661–1714) (Eyre & Spottis-
woode, London, 1892–1904)
Ferguson, James: *Papers Illustrating the History*   Scots Brigade
of the Scots Brigade in the Service of the United
Netherlands 1572–1782 (Edinburgh University
Press, Edinburgh, 1899)
Ffoulkes, Charles: *Armies and Armament: An*   AA.
Historical Survey of the Weapons of the British
Army (Harrap, London, 1945)
Firth, C. H.: *Cromwell's Army: A History of*   Cromwell's Army
the English Soldier during the Civil Wars, the
Commonwealth, and the Protectorate (Methuen,
London, 1902)
Forbes, A.: *A History of the Army Ordnance Services,*   Forbes
vol. i (The Medici Society, London, 1929)
Fortescue, J. W.: *A History of the British Army,*   Fort.
vol. i (Macmillan, London, 1899).
The Royal Army Service Corps: A History of   Fort. RASC
Transport and Supply in the British Army, vol. i
(Cambridge University Press, Cambridge,
1930)
Gordon, Hampden: *The War Office* (Putnam,   Hampden Gordon
London, 1935)
Johnston, S. H. A.: *British Soldiers* (Collins,   Johnston
London, 1944)
King, C. Cooper: *The Story of the British Army*   Cooper King
(Methuen, London, 1897)
Lloyd, E. M.: *A Review of the History of Infantry*   Lloyd
(Longmans Green & Co., London, 1908)
Masse, C. H.: *The Predecessors of the Royal Army*   Masse
Service Corps 1767–1888 (Gale & Polden, Lon-
don, 1948)
Porter, Whitworth: *History of the Corps of Royal*   Porter
Engineers, vol. i (Longmans Green & Co.,
London, 1889)

Walton, Clifford: *History of the British Standing*   Walton
Army 1660–1700 (Harrison & Sons, London,
1894)

HISTORICAL: DUKE OF MARLBOROUGH

Alison, A.: *The Military Life of the Duke of*   Alison
Marlborough (Wm. Blackwood, Edinburgh,
1848)
Atkinson, C. T.: *Marlborough and the Rise of the*   Atkinson
British Army (Putnams, London, 1921)
Belloc, Hilaire: *The Tactics and Strategy of the*   Belloc
Great Duke of Marlborough (Arrowsmith,
London, 1933)
Churchill, W. S.: *Marlborough: His Life and*   Churchill
Times (Harrap, London, 1938)
Edwards, Henry John, and E. A.: *A Short Life*   Edwards
of Marlborough (G. Bell & Son, London,
1926)
Fortescue, J. W.: *Life of the Duke of Marlborough*   Fort. *Marl.*
(Peter Davies, London, 1932)
Lediard, Thomas: *The Life of John, Duke of*   Lediard
Marlborough (J. Wilcox, 1736)
Murray, Sir G.: *Marlborough's Letters and*   Murray
Despatches, vols. i–v (John Murray, London,
1845)
Taylor, F.: *The Wars of Marlborough 1702–1709*   Taylor
(Basil Blackwell, Oxford, 1921)

CONTEMPORARY TRACTS AND PAMPHLETS

The Souldier's Accompt or Tables showing the   *Souldier's Accompt*
personal allowance of pay to all officers and
soldiers belonging to an army, either foot or
horse from a day to a week, from a week to a
month, from a month to thirteen months,
also to all officers and attendants on a train
of artillerie consisting of thirty-six pieces of
ordnance together with the charge of pay to
40,000 foot and 10,000 horse from a day to a
year. By T. R. (Printed by M. F., 1647)
The Case of the Officers of the late Count   Nassau's
Nassau's Regiment of Foot Taken Prisoner
at the Battle of Almanza
An impartial inquiry into the management of   Inquiry
the war in Spain by the ministry at home,
and into the conduct of those generals to
whose care the same has been committed
abroad

Abstracts of the Numbers and Yearly Pay of the
Land Forces of Horse, Foot, and Dragoons
in Great Britain for the Year 1718, and of
the Charge Continued on the Publick by the
Wrong done to the reduced Officers on the
British Establishment of Half Pay in filling
up by others Commissions in the 13 Regiments
of Dragoons and Eight Regiments of Foot
which were raised after the Month of June
1715, and also, of the Accompt of Half Pay
for the Year 1718, delivered into Parliament,
and dated the 28 of November 1717, with
some remarks relating to the same. By a
Member of Parliament (1718). (The member
of Parliament was A. Hutcheson)
                                             Hutcheson

A View of the Danger and Folly of Being Public
Spirited and Sincerely Loving One's Coun-
try; in the deplorable case of the Londonderry
and Inniskilling Regiments, being a True and
Faithful Account of their Unparalleled Ser-
vice and Sufferings at and since the Revo-
lution to which is Added the Particular
Case of William Hamill, gentl, their Agent.
By a Member of Parliament (1721). (Also
A. Hutcheson)
                                             Inniskillings

An Essay on the most effective way to Recruit
the Army and render it more serviceable by
preventing desertion. (By a Lover of his
Country and the Army, 1707)
                                             Recruiting Essay

Several Queries Relating to an Act of Parliament made in the Second and Third years of
Her Most Sacred Majesty's Reign Entitled
An Act for the Discharge Out of Prison Such
Insolvent Debtors as shall Serve or Procure
a Person to serve in Her Majesty's Fleet or
Army. (Sent in a letter by a gentleman in the
country to his Friend a Counsellor at Law
in LONDON: with his Answer thereto, and
opinion thereon: 1704)
                                             Several Queries

Bishop, Matthew: The Life and Adventures of
Matthew Bishop of Deddington in Oxford-
shire containing an account of several actions
by sea, battles, and sieges by land in which
he was present from 1701 to 1711 interspersed
with many curious incidents, entertaining
conversations, and judicious reflections. (J.
Bridley, London, 1744)
                                             Bishop

Crichton, Andrew: The Life and Diary of
Lieutenant Colonel John Blackader, of the
Cameronian Regiment, and Deputy Gover-
nor of Stirling Castle, who served with
distinguished honour in the wars under
King William and the Duke of Marlborough
and afterwards in the rebellion of 1715 in
Scotland. (H. S. Baynes, Edinburgh 1824)   *Blackader*

Deane, Private John Marshall: A Journal of the   Deane
campaign in Flanders A.D. MDCCVIII including
the Battle of Oudenarde and Siege of Lille
by John Marshall Deane of the First Battalion
of the Foot Guards. (1846)

Fitchett, W. H.: Wellington's Men: Some   Fitchett
Soldier Autobiographies. (John Murray,
London, 1900)

Millner, John: A compendious journal of all the   Millner
marches, famous battles, sieges, and other
most noteworthy heroical and ever memor-
able actions of the triumphant armies of the
ever glorious confederate high allies in the
late and victorious war against the powerful
armies of proud and lofty France, in and
on the confines of Holland, Germany, and
Flanders, so far as our successful British
troops extended in conjunction therein.
Digested into 12 campaigns begun in
A.D. 1701 and ended in 1712. By John
Millner, Serjeant in the Royal Regiment of
Foot of Ireland. (London, 1733)

Parker, Captain Robert, Royal Regiment of   Parker
Foot: Memoirs of the Most Remarkable
Military Transactions from the year 1693
to 1718 containing a more particular account
than any ever yet published of the several
battles, sieges, etc., in Ireland and Flanders
during the reigns of King William and Queen
Anne. (1747)

ESSAYS, MAGAZINES, AND JOURNALS

Corbett, Julian S.: 'Queen Anne's Defence   *Monthly Review*
Committee' (*Monthly Review*, 1904)

Edwards, J. T.: 'The Master Gunner, St.   *Army Quarterly*
James's Park' (*Army Quarterly*, vol. liv, no. 10,
April 1947)

Fortescue, J. W.: *Historical and Military Essays*   *Fort. Hist.*
(Macmillan, London, 1928)
The Last Post (Blackwood, Edinburgh, 1934)   *Last Post*
Six British Soldiers (Williams & Norgate, London, 1928)   *Six British Soldiers*
Journal of the Society for Army Historical Research   *JSAHR*
Laws, A. E. S.: 'Army Doctors in the 18th   *RUSI*
Century' (*Royal United Services Institution Journal*, vol. xcii, no. 571, August 1948)

MISCELLANEOUS

Abbott, W. C.: *Colonel Thomas Blood, Crown Stealer.*
Bland, H.: *A Treatise on Military Discipline.*
Bradlaugh, Charles: *John Churchill, Duke of Marlborough.*
Bryant, Arthur: *The National Character* (Longmans Green & Co., London, 1934)
Defoe, Daniel: *Moll Flanders.*
     The Life and Adventures of Mrs. Christine Davies (Mother Ross). (? Defoe).
Elliott, H. F. H.: *Life of Sidney, Earl Godolphin.*
Farquhar, George: *The Recruiting Officer*   *Recruiting Officer*
Feiling, K.: *History of the Tory Party (1640–1714).*
Foot, Michael: *The Pen and the Sword* (MacGibbon & Kee, London, 1957)
Hallam, Henry: *The Constitutional History of England.*
Hill, Richard: *Diplomatic Correspondence, July 1693–May 1706.*
Kane, William: *Campaigns of William and Marlborough* (textually similar to Private Deane's Journal).
King, William: *Memoirs of the Duchess of Marlborough.*
Leadam, I. S.: *The Political History of England 1702–60*, vol. ix.
     Lives of the Two Illustrious Generals.
Lecky, W. E. H.: *History of England in the 18th Century*, vol. i.
Luttrell, Narcissus: *A Brief Historical Relation of State Affairs from 1680 to 1716* (6 vols.—Oxford University Press, 1857).
Macaulay, Lord: *History of England.*
Mahon, Lord: *History of the War of the Succession in Spain* (London, 1832).
Maitland, F. W.: *Constitutional History of England.*
Marlborough, Duchess of: *Memoirs of: Life and Conduct* (London, 1741).
     Private correspondence (2 vols.—London, 1838).
Molloy, J. F.: *The Queen's Comrade.*
Omond, J. S.: *Parliament and the Army 1642–1904* (Cambridge University Press, 1933).
Orkney, Earl of: 'Letters of the first Lord Orkney during Marlborough's campaigns' (*English Historical Review*, April 1904).
Parnell, Arthur: *The War of the Succession in Spain* (London, 1888).
Ryan, P. F. W.: *Queen Anne and Her Court.*
Smollett, Tobias: *Roderick Random.*
Stanhope, Lord: *Reign of Queen Anne.*

Sterne, Laurence: *Tristram Shandy.*
Swift, Jonathan: *The Conduct of the Allies.*
Woodruff, Phillip: *Colonel of Dragoons* (Jonathan   Woodruff
   Cape, London, 1951)

INDEX

ROYAL WARRANTS